TEACHING READING

EFFECTIVE SCHOOLS, ACCOMPLISHED TEACHERS

TEACHING READING

EFFECTIVE SCHOOLS, ACCOMPLISHED TEACHERS

Edited by

Barbara M. Taylor
P. David Pearson

2002

LAWRENCE ERLBAUM ASSOCIATES, PUBLISHERS

Mahwah, New Jersey   London

Lawrence Erlbaum Associates, Inc., Publishers
10 Industrial Avenue
Mahwah, NJ 07430

Cover design by Kathryn Houghtaling Lacey

Library of Congress Cataloging-in-Publication Data

Teaching reading : effective schools, accomplished teachers / edited by
   Barbara M. Taylor, P. David Pearson.
         p. cm.
   Includes bibliographical references and index.
ISBN 0-8058-4133-4 (cloth : alk. paper)
ISBN 0-8058-4134-2 (pbk. : alk. paper)
1. Reading (Elementary)—United States—Case studies. 2. School
   improvement programs—United States—Case studies. 3. Effective
   teaching—United States—Case studies. I. Taylor, Barbara M., 1950-
   II. Pearson, P. David.
LB1573 .T3895 2002
372.4—dc21

                                                          2001033987
                                                          CIP

Books published by Lawrence Erlbaum Associates are printed on acid-free
paper, and their bindings are chosen for strength and durability.

Printed in the United States of America
10 9 8 7 6 5 4 3 2

Contents

Foreword

Steven A. Stahl
CIERA / *The University of Georgia*

This book tells the stories of a select group of schools and teachers, those who "beat the odds." Many of these schools serve a high proportion of children in poverty, generally defined as a proportion of children in the school eligible for free or reduced cost lunch, who have average or better levels of achievement. These are not the only schools that have reached this level, but for every school that has beat the odds, there are, unfortunately, many that have succumbed to them. Although the teachers in this book do teach in a variety of settings, we worry most about children of poverty.

Many of the schools and teachers chronicled in this book are associated with the CIERA School Change project, directed by Barbara Taylor and P. David Pearson. The goals of this project are, first, to identify characteristics of schools that beat the odds, and, later, to work with other schools so that they, too, can help children of poverty reach average or above levels of reading achievement. Other chapters are associated with the studies of effective first-grade teachers by Michael Pressley, Leslie Morrow, Cathy Collins Block, and their many colleagues. This project looked at the characteristics of effective first-grade teaching, regardless of the student population. Joseph Johnson, Jr., examines high-performing inner-city schools and James Mosenthal and his colleagues examine high-performing rural schools. These four chapters present complimentary, yet slightly different, perspectives on successful schools and effective teaching. Paris and his colleagues' chapter on assessment spotlights this important component of school reform, drawing on the teachers from the School Change project.

These are not the first studies that have looked at effective schools and accomplished teachers—nor will they be the last. Studies in this line of research have appeared since the 1970s, since Weber (1983), who found four schools that succeeded over a long term in educating the children of poverty who attended them. He found a number of characteristics common to those schools—strong instructional leadership, high expectations for achievement, good atmosphere, strong emphasis on reading, additional reading personnel, use of phonics, individualization, and careful evaluation of student progress. Many of these features characterize the schools profiled in this volume as well.

In education, we tend to examine the relations between individual charac-teristics (phonological awareness, dialect, and so on) and achievement. This emphasis may be misplaced. A meta-analysis of the effects of poverty found that the mean correlation between SES and achievement was 0.68, when the school was the unit of analysis (White, 1982). The same studies found that the mean correlation between SES and achievement was considerably lower, 0.23, when the individual was the unit of analysis. Thus, the effects of schools serving large numbers of children of poverty is just about three times as great as the effects of poverty alone on achievement. This suggests that there is something about schools with a lot of poor children that inhibits children's achievement. More optimistic are the findings of Snow, Barnes, Chandler, Goodman, and Hemphill (1991) who examined children of poverty who succeeded in school. They found that, although it is best that children have a strong home literacy background and good instruction, good instruction by itself can overcome the effects of a weak home literacy background. In other words, if we want to solve problems in education, we need to look at schooling.

Weber (1983) concluded, in a radical statement that rings its challenge to the present day, "the failure in beginning reading typical of inner-city schools is not the fault of the children or their background—but of the schools" (p. 547). That is, if children of poverty can succeed in these schools, then why are they failing elsewhere, and what can we do to provide similar experiences for all chil-dren everywhere?

One commonality in approach taken by the schools in this book do not try to "fix" the child, by either "blaming the victim" or "embracing the victim." By concentrating on what schools and teachers can do to help children achieve, the responsibility is placed on the teacher, rather than on the child or his parent. I find that many schools who are failing to teach their children blame the par-ents for their lack of support. This seems to be a characteristic of schools that are not working. The schools in this book reach out to parents, but do so not to "fix" the home, but out of a shared commitment to the child's education.

Another commonality of approach is a belief that school change must grow from within, rather than be imposed from without. We have tried a number of approaches to imposing externally developed comprehensive school reform models on schools. The results of these external models are mixed. For example,

Success for All has had mixed success (Madden, Slavin, Wasik, & Dolan, 1997; Venezky, 1998). Although Success for All must be voted for by 75% of the faculty, there is minimal flexibility in implementing it. The comprehensive approach is one route to school improvement, one that might be useful for many schools. But many other schools might bristle under the structure imposed from without (see Elmore, Peterson, & McCarthey, 1996).

Another strength of the book is that it is research based on observations and data rather than on politics. The *No Excuses* project (Carter, 2000) is another attempt to look at inner city schools that have high levels of achievement. This was sponsored by the Heritage Foundation and its findings—use of continual assessment for diagnostic purposes, the failure of "progressive education" especially for inner-city children, making parents responsible for their children's learning, the need to re-educate teachers to make up for poor teacher training—reflect its sponsor's conservative agenda. In research of this type, one's perspective will color one's findings. Quality research, such as that presented in this volume, generally pushes against one's predispositions, to reflect on both one's biases and what one observes, to truly understand the setting.

Although academics will read this book, I see this book being more useful to teachers working together in a school. As Taylor and Pearson point out, it would be useful for teachers to read each chapter as a self-study group, discuss what characteristics their school has and how those characteristics reveal themselves, and what their school is missing and how it can attain those characteristics. It is a wonderful opportunity for thoughtful reflection about how each of these schools is like or not like my school. The schools in this book are urban and rural and suburban; poor and middle class, all across the country. This book does not tell teachers and schools how to be schools that "beat the odds." Instead, it is like a rack of dresses or suits in a department store. This is not a "one size fits all" rack. Some fit; others do not. Some flatter; others do not. Some may need a little alteration, letting out the hem, shortening the trousers. The only way one can choose is to try them on. But there has to be a model to fit each teacher and each school. As Ladson-Billings (1996) pointed out, successful teachers can use a number of different teaching styles and philosophies.

Schools have their own character; their own ecology. Schools are affected by the teaching staff, by the children in the schools, by the principal or instructional leader, and by district and state mandates. Reform has to respect that ecology. But at the same time there *are* general principles that should work over all different settings. In this volume, some general principles are laid out in the first section; the stories of particular schools and teachers in the second and third sections, followed by a summation. One cannot understand fully the general principles without knowing how they play themselves out in the different settings. One cannot understand cases without seeing the commonalities across different schools meeting similar goals. You need to understand both in order to use this information to make changes.

This book continues Weber's (1983) call that we cannot blame our children for their own failure, but that it is the responsibility of our schools to help them succeed. The schools and teachers in this book have done this.

REFERENCES

Carter, S. C. (2000). *No excuses: Lessons from high-performing, high poverty schools*. Washington, DC: Heritage Foundation (http://www.noexcuses.org/lessons/)

Elmore, R. F., Peterson, P. L., & McCarthey, S. J. (1996). *Restructuring in the classroom: Teaching, learning and school organization*. San Francisco: Jossey-Bass.

Ladson-Billings, G. (1996). *The Dreamkeepers*. San Francisco: Jossey-Bass.

Madden, N. A., Slavin, R. E., Wasik, B. A., & Dolan, L. J. (1997). Reading, writing, and language arts in Success for All. In S.A. Stahl & D.A. Hayes (Eds.) *Instructional models in reading*. (pp. 109–130). Mahwah, NJ: Lawrence Erlbaum Associates.

Snow, C. E., Barnes, W., Chandler, J., Goodman, I., & Hemphill, L. (1991). *Unfulfilled expectations*. Cambridge, MA: Harvard University Press.

Venezky, R. L. (1998). An alternative perspective on Success for All. In K. Wong (Ed.), *Advances in educational policy, vol. 4*. Greenwich, CT: JAI Press.

Weber, G. (1983). Inner city children can be taught to read: Four successful schools. In L. Gentile, M. Kamil, & J. Blanchard (Eds.), *Reading research revisited*. (pp. 527–547). Columbus, OH: Charles Merrill. (Originally published in 1971).

White, K. R. (1982). The relationship between socioeconomic status and academic achievement. *Psychological Bulletin, 91*, 461–481.

Preface

Bringing the current volume into being has been a labor of love for those of us involved in its creation. Both terms in that metaphor, *labor* and *love*, are important. It has been hard work for all of us—the authors, editors, and publishing staff that actually produced the book, but, more importantly, the teachers and administrators who created the programs described in the pages of this book. But it is work borne out of *love* of learning and literacy, out of a conviction that all students in all schools can learn to read if teachers, administrators, and parents persist in searching for that optimal mix of materials, instructional approaches, personnel deployment, and programmatic features that suit their particular context, school, and students.

It all began in August of 1997 when the Office of Educational Research and Innovation informed our CIERA consortium (comprised of researchers from five cooperating universities—University of Michigan, University of Virginia, Michigan State University, University of Minnesota, and University of Southern California) that we had been awarded a Cooperative Agreement to implement a research center focused on issues of early (pre-K through Grade 3) reading. Among the studies that we had agreed to implement in year 1 was what we came to call our CIERA Beat the Odds Study, which was the catalyst for the present volume. But more on the significance of the name later.

The Beat the Odds study, for us, was the first step in a 5-year study in which we wanted to study the process by which low-achieving schools built new reading programs that would, hopefully, lead to increased reading achievement. The ultimate question we wanted to answer was, *What school-wide program features* (administrative arrangements, collaborative practices, materials, professional development activities) *and classroom instructional strategies* (e.g., grouping practices, interaction strategies, curricular emphases) *lead to increased student achievement?* At the end of 5 years, we wanted to be in a position to offer districts, schools, and teachers advice about changes they might consider in their own reading programs. The logic of the Beat the Odds phase, in year 1, was simple. We reasoned that if we wanted to offer advice to low-achieving, high-poverty schools about programs and practices, we should begin by asking the experts (i.e., those teachers, administrators, and supervisors who work in high-poverty schools that are also high achieving schools). These are the schools that "beat the odds" dictated by the school's socio-economic status. These are outlier schools, schools that defy the all-too-common and powerful correlation between poverty level and achievement. These are schools, we reasoned, where we are likely to find good ideas and good models to share with other schools, with similar demographic characteristics, that only aspire to higher-than-expected achievement. And so we began this work.

Between August and October of 1997, we recontacted all the schools that had, when we submitted the proposal in May of 1997, agreed to participate with us. These were schools we had selected for one of two reasons: (a) they had already demonstrated that they were defying the correlation between poverty and achievement, or (b) they represented interesting instantiations of recently developed national models of reading reform, such as Success for All, Core Knowledge, and the like. In response to our proposal reviewers, we added more schools to the sample, namely schools that, although demographically similar to our nominated schools, were not currently "beating the odds." These were needed, our reviewers reasoned, in order to demonstrate isolate program features and practices that distinguished our beat the odds schools from comparison schools. Amazingly, we managed to get our act together in time to begin collecting data in November of 1997. And at the end of that year, we had collected and analyzed all of the data described in chapter 1 of this volume.

While we were conducting this study of effective schools, when we realized, first at a gut level and then with the sharp edge of the analytic razor of our research, we knew that a book had to be written about this whole endeavor—not just about the overall findings, but about the stories of particular schools and particular teachers. If we were going to convince others to take our work seriously, they would have to hear not only the numbers but also the voices of those who created the programs that allowed the numbers to do their work. So, in its first iteration, this was a book about the particular schools that were a part of our 1997–1998 CIERA study. And, it still is, because several of the chapters (chaps. 6, 7, and 8) focus on the programs in our most effective schools or the practices of our most accomplished teachers (chap. 12).

But as the book played itself out, it grew, both in size and scope. As we became aware of colleagues around the country who were doing similar research, we said to ourselves that our message would be more powerful if we could show that others were discovering similar findings and similar stories. These other stories came from many sources. First, from our CIERA colleagues, Charles Fisher and Martha Adler began conducting case studies of exemplary high-poverty schools to determine how they allocated internal resources to achieve programmatic reform. And

Scott Paris, another CIERA colleague, had completed an interesting analysis of the assessment practices in Title I schools that had received recognition as Blue Ribbon Schools by the national Title I office or by the International Reading Association. We learned about the very interesting work on Hope for Urban Education conducted by Joseph Johnson and his colleagues at the Charles A. Dana Center at UT-Austin. Michael Pressley, Leslie Morrow, and colleagues at the Center for English Language Arts were well into an examination of the classroom practices of highly effective primary-grade teachers. Jim Mosenthal and Marjorie Lipson, and their colleagues in Vermont were also documenting the practices in outlier rural schools. Carol Sue Englert provided us with important research on effective teachers working with diverse learners and Rosalinda Barrera and Robert Jimenez were able to share important research on effective literacy instruction of bilingual Latino students. When it came time to put together this volume, we asked those responsible for each of these efforts to submit chapters documenting cases of exemplary schools, exemplary teachers, or cross case analyses of programs and practice.

The book is divided into four sections. The first section looks at large scale studies that have recently examined characteristics of effective schools and teachers. The second section provides case studies of six schools in which children are achieving at high levels in reading. The third section deals with case studies of effective teachers of reading. The fourth section contains a summary of research on effective schools and teachers and a concluding chapter by Gerry Duffy and Jim Hoffman in which they reflect on the chapters in the book and possible directions for further research on effective schools and teachers. A brief annotation of these chapters is provided below,

Part I: Large Scale Studies

1. Effective Schools/Accomplished Teachers: Lessons About Primary Reading Instruction in Low-Income Schools by Barbara M. Taylor, P. David Pearson, Kathleen Clark, and Sharon Walpole. This article reprinted from The Elementary School Journal (November, 2000) reports on a national study of 14 schools, four of which were found to be especially effective. Both school and classroom factors contributing to the schools' success are presented.

2. Exemplary First-Grade Teaching by Michael Pressley, Ruth Wharton McDonald, Lisa M. Raphael, Kristen Bogner, and Alysia Roehrig. In this chapter Pressley and his colleagues summarize four studies that they have conducted over that past 5 years focusing on characteristics

of effective first-grade teachers. Common findings across this body of work are discussed.

3. High-Performing, High-Poverty Urban Elementary Schools by Joseph E. Johnson, Jr. This chapter is the overview chapter of a 1999 U.S. Department of Education study, "Hope for Urban Education: A Study of Nine-High-Performing, High-Poverty Urban Elementary Schools" conducted by the Charles a. Dana Center, University of Texas at Austin. This chapter briefly describes the schools and focuses on the similarities across the nine schools in terms of school-level factors contributing to the schools' success.

4. Literacy in Rural Vermont: Lessons from Schools Where Children Succeed by Jim Mosenthal, Marjorie Lipson, Susan Sortino, Barbara Russ, and Jane Mekkelsen. In this chapter the authors investigate a sample of rural schools exhibiting high student performance on statewide literacy assessments at second and fourth grade, to determine the contexts and practices that contribute to those schools' success. These rural schools in Vermont represent another type of "beat the odds" schools.

5. Effective Practices for Assessing Young Readers by Scott Paris, Alison Paris, and Robert Carpenter. In this chapter the authors describe effective assessment practices that K through third-grade teachers use in their classrooms. They begin with a report of a large national survey of the assessment practices of teachers in outstanding schools. They conclude with a discussions of a) a developmental approach to assessment for young children and b) typical assessment problems that teachers must solve.

Part II: School Case Studies

6. Sunnyside Elementary, Mounds View, MN by Barbara Taylor and Ceil Critchley. This chapter provides a case study of one of the schools that was determined to be highly effective in the Effective Schools/Accomplished Teachers study discussed previously. The school in suburban Minneapolis had 38% of its students qualify for subsidized lunch in the year the study was conducted. Additional positive changes at the school since the time of the study have been added to the case study.

7. Rocky Mountain Elementary School, Longmont, CO by Jackie Colt and Rebecca Mills. This chapter provides a case study of a second school that was determined to be highly effective in the Effective Schools/Accomplished Teachers study. This school is in a small town with 40% of its students Hispanic and 55% qualifying for subsidized lunch.

8. Stevenson Elementary School: Schoolwide Success by Sharon Walpole. This paper provides a third case study of one of the schools that

was determined to be highly effective in the Effective Schools/Accomplished Teachers study. This school is in a rural area in Virginia, with a primarily white student body and 50% of the students qualifying for subsidized lunch at the time of the study.

9. Scott Elementary School: Home Grown School Improvement in the Flesh by Glenda Breaux, Jennifer Danridge, and P. D. Pearson. Although not one of the schools included in the analysis of schools in the Effective Schools/Accomplished Teachers study, this school was identified as an effective school as a part of a larger research effort related to that project. In this inner-city school in a mid-Western city, 63% of the students qualified for subsidized lunch and a majority of the students were African American.

10. Serna Elementary School by Martha Adler. This case study describes one of the schools included in a CIERA resource allocation study of high-performing, high-poverty schools conducted by Martha Adler and Charles Fisher. The student population was diverse, in which about one third of the students were Hispanic, one third African American, and one third white, and approximately 70% of the students qualified for subsidized lunch.

11. In Pursuit of Academic Excellence: The Story of Gladys Noon Spellman Elementary by Pamela Smith, Joseph E. Johnson, Jr., and Brent Jones. In this chapter the authors describe one of the nine schools identified as highly effective in the Hope for Urban Education study (summarized in Part I.) At Spellman, located in Maryland about 5 miles from Washington, D.C., 73% of the students were African American, 17% Hispanic, and 9% white at the time of the study, with 63% of the children qualifying for subsidized lunch.

Part III: Teacher Case Studies

12. Highly Accomplished Primary Grade Teachers in Effective Schools by Barbara Taylor. This chapter focuses on four of the highest rated teachers in exceptional schools from the Effective School/Accomplished Teachers study. The chapter describes similarities across these first- and second-grade teachers' beliefs and practices in their efforts to establish independent, successful learners.

13. A Case Study of Exemplary Practice in Fourth Grade by Leslie Mandel Morrow. The practices of four exemplary fourth-grade teachers from three different schools in one state are presented. The author cleverly describes a single teacher who is actually a composite of the four exemplary teachers.

14. Scientific Literacy and Diverse Learners: Supporting the Acquisition of Disciplinary Ways of Knowing in Inclusion Classrooms by Carol Sue

Englert and KaiLonnie Dunsmore. In this chapter the authors describe the Literacy Environments for Accelerated Progress (LEAP) Project that was designed to address the need for literacy curricula that would provide *access* to the general education curriculum and enhance the *participation* of students with disabilities. The authors conclude with a summary of the best practices that typified effective instruction by the LEAP teachers.

15. Bilingual Teachers Speak About the Literacy Instruction of Bilingual Latino Students by Rosalinda Barrera and Robert Jimenez. In this chapter the authors present the results of a series of focus group interviews with 30 primary grade teachers of Latino children in schools with successful bilingual education programs in Chicago, El Paso, and Washington, D.C. In this chapter the authors describe these teachers' knowledge and understanding of school literacy practices that maximize success for this group of students.

Part IV: Syntheses Across Cases

16. Research-Supported Characteristics of Teachers and Schools That Promote Reading Achievement by Barbara Taylor, Michael Pressley, and David Pearson. In this reprint of an NEA Reading Matters Research Report the authors summarize across recent research studies of effective teachers of reading and effective schools. Not surprisingly, many common elements across studies were revealed in this review.

17. Beating the Odds in Literacy Education: Not the "Betting on" but the "Bettering of" Schools and Teachers by Gerald Duffy and James Hoffman. In this final chapter, the authors look across the research included in this volume and make suggestions for needed future research.

So there you have our story of how this volume came into being. As we consider what ties all of this work together, several metaphors come to mind. First is variations on a theme. In our mind, the theme is excellence and the variations are the particular programs and practices that account for the excellence we found in each classroom. The second metaphor is improvisation. By improvisation we mean to highlight the unique ways in which each school and each teacher achieves the magic found in these schools. The third is signature. The signature metaphor shares with improvisation the element of uniqueness but it also adds the dimension of ownership—our school, my practices! All three metaphors fit, so we ask you to hold each in mind as you read.

We hope that you find the chapters that await you interesting, provocative, and, above all, useful to you in learning how successful schools and teachers manage to pull off this amazing feat of beating the odds dictated by the demographics of poverty. We find it interesting that the turn of the century witnessed a renaissance in a tradition that was first popularized in the late 1970s and early 1980s. The logic of the earlier work was that if we could only learn how effective schools work and how effective teachers teach, we could teach all of the less effective schools and teachers to do likewise. And that was the undoing of the effective schools and effective teaching movements. It was just not that simple. We like to think that the work we report in this volume is different, that things are better the second time around. We now know that no matter how reliable the findings about effective school programs, that no matter how consistent the results on effective classroom practice, groups of teachers in schools have to use the research to improvise their own programs and practices, to create variations on a common theme, to put their signature on those variations, and make them their own. The research can serve as a guide, prevent us from getting lost in a labyrinth of cul de sacs and garden paths, and give us a head start down the road to excellence. But it is only when the teachers in a school decide to transform the findings from research into a set of practices that they own and implement that good things happen for students and families. This is a book about how these remarkable professionals make those good things happen.

—*P. David Pearson*
—*Barbara M. Taylor*

I
Large Scale Studies

Use for:
- leadership
- time well spent
- high expectations
- staff cohesion
- Staff Development

Effective Schools and Accomplished Teachers: Lessons About Primary-Grade Reading Instruction in Low-Income Schools[1]

Barbara M. Taylor
University of Minnesota/CIERA

P. David Pearson
Michigan State University/CIERA

Kathleen Clark
University of Minnesota/CIERA

Sharon Walpole
University of Virginia/CIERA

[1]This research was conducted as part of CIERA, the Center for the Improvement of Early Reading Achievement, and supported under the Educational Research and Development Centers Program, PR/Award Number R305R70004, as administered by the Office of Educational Research and Improvement, U.S. Department of Education. However, the contents of the described report do not necessarily represent the positions or policies of the National Institute on Student Achievement, Curriculum, and Assessment or the National Institute on Early Childhood development, or the U.S. Department of Education, and you should not assume endorsement by the federal government.

We all want the best schools possible for our children, schools that help them acquire the knowledge, skills, and dispositions they will need to pursue whatever dreams and paths they wish. Yet the reality is that many of our children are not reading well enough to keep up with the demands of school (Campbell, Donahue, Reese, & Phillip, 1996; Donahue, Voelkl, Campbell, & Mazzeo, 1999), let alone the demands of our society or their personal dreams. In the recent national report, *Preventing Reading Difficulties in Young Children*, a National Academy of Science Committee concluded that "quality classroom instruction in kindergarten and the primary grades is the single best weapon against reading failure" (Snow, Burns, & Griffin, 1998, p. 343). The committee recommended that our number one priority for funding research should be to improve classroom reading instruction in kindergarten and the primary grades.

In a recent report of a 3-year study of schools implementing special strategies to improve reading achievement, researchers described classroom instruction as " in one sense, distressing" (Stringfield, Millsap, & Herman, 1997, p. 2). In the elementary schools, instruction was predominantly teacher-led, focused on discrete skill instruction, and driven by management concerns. There were relatively few observations of students engaged in sustained reading or students applying what they were learning. On the other hand, Stringfield, Millsap, and Herman (1997) pointed out that even in schools nominated as exemplary, there was ample room for instructional improvement, which would, if implemented, lead to greater gains in reading achievement.

In addition to advocating improved classroom reading instruction, the Committee on the Prevention of Reading Difficulties in Young Children discussed the importance of systematic, school-wide restructuring efforts in reading. The committee (Snow et al., 1998) recommended that poor performing schools consider reading reform efforts with a dual focus on school-wide organizational issues *and* improved classroom reading instruction.

In their special strategies study, Stringfield, Millsap, and Herman, (1997) found that reform programs that focused on the primary grades had larger achievement gains in reading than schools that spread their efforts out across the elementary grades or into the secondary grades. They also found that schools that adopted externally developed programs had greater achievement gains than schools that developed their own programs.

In a report of a large national study of 400 Chapter 1 schools, researchers found that higher levels of poverty, greater application of grade-retention policies, and higher levels of student disciplinary actions were related to lower student

leadership

achievement (Puma et al., 1997). Only 5 schools in the pool of 400 were identified as exceptional. These schools tended to have a "more experienced principal, a school-wide Chapter 1 program, some tracking by ability in Grades 1 through 6, lower rates of teacher and student mobility, a balanced emphasis on remedial and higher-order thinking in classroom instruction, and higher levels of community and parent support" (p. 62). Except for first grade, in which grouping was used, whole class instruction was the dominant practice in all schools.

In a recent study of nine high-performing, high-poverty urban elementary schools, important similarities found across the schools included the following: a collective sense of responsibility for school improvement including a focus on putting the children first, a well-behaved student body, an increase in the amount of time spent on instruction, collaborative planning and learning time for teachers with a focus on instructional issues, instructional leadership and support provided to teachers to help them focus on their teaching and students' learning, and increased effort to collaborate with patterns (Charles A. Dana Center, 1999). However, this study did not focus on reading specifically, or on instruction within classrooms.

These recent national reports highlight the importance of and need for additional research on schools that serve the needs of poor children by increasing their achievement and, hence, their educational opportunities. The purpose of the present study was to examine the instructional and organizational factors that might explain how and why some schools across the country are attaining greater than expected primary-grade reading achievement with populations of students at risk for failure by virtue of poverty. We pause to emphasize the terms *instructional* and *organizational,* for it is our belief that only when we attend to both school level (organizational) and classroom level (instructional) facets of reform do we meet our aspirations.

Within this broader framework, we were, like the researchers in the special strategies study (Stringfield et al., 1997), interested in both *imported* models of reform (where they had adopted an external school reform program) and *homegrown* reform efforts. To that end, we sought schools in both categories. We were also interested in schools that had adopted early reading interventions, both tutorial and small-group interventions for at-risk youngsters. As it turned out, we had a number of schools that had adopted early reading intervention programs set within a homegrown school-wide reform effort.

EFFECTIVE SCHOOLS

Research on effective schools relevant to reading achievement, much of which was conducted in the 1970s and early 1980s, was documented in a review entitled

"Teacher and School Effects in Learning to Read" by Hoffman (1991) in the *Handbook of Reading Research, Volume II*. Hoffman described eight attributes of effective schools frequently summarized in the literature (e.g., Shavelson & Berliner, 1988), including:

- a clear school mission,
- effective instructional leadership and practices,
- high expectations,
- a safe, orderly, and positive environment,
- ongoing curriculum improvement,
- maximum use of instructional time,
- frequent monitoring of student progress, and
- positive home–school relationships.

In a study of four outlier inner-city schools, Weber (1971) found strong leadership, high expectations, positive school climate, strong emphasis on reading, and continuous evaluation of student progress related to the identified school reading success criteria of median achievement level on a normed standardized reading achievement test and having a relatively small number of children with serious reading difficulties. In a study of 5 schools found to be most effective out of a sample of 741 schools that were part of a study of compensatory reading programs, Wilder (1977) found the following factors common to all 5 schools: reading identified as an important instructional goal, leadership in the reading program provided by either the principal or reading specialist, attention given to basic skills, breadth of materials made available, and communication of ideas across teachers, a process that was typically fostered by the program leader.

In a more recent, longitudinal study on schools implementing special strategies for educating disadvantaged children, Stringfield et al. (1997) found that the schools demonstrating the greatest achievement gains worked hard at both initial implementation and long-term maintenance of an innovation. But the researchers also noted the importance of systematic self-improvement in these schools, in which the innovations continued to evolve and expand. Externally developed research-based programs and programs that focused on whole school reform were related to greater achievement gains than locally developed programs and innovations composed of various pull-out programs. The study also found support for the premise that students placed at risk of academic failure could achieve at levels that met national averages.

In a study of five effective Title I schools, Puma et al. (1997) found that high-performing, high-poverty schools had lower-than-average teacher and student mobility, principals with more years of experience, and more orderly school environments than average high-poverty schools. Better school climates and better relations with administration and the community were also reported as well as greater parent involvement and more parents with high expectations for their children's future educational attainment. All of these high-performing schools had tracking by ability in Grades 1 through 6. In three of the five schools, teachers emphasized basic skills and higher order comprehension skills in reading.

Although research on effective schools has been favorably received by school leaders and policymakers, Hoffman (1991) reminded us of the limitations of this research, due mainly to its lack of connection to classroom practice and to insufficient information on the process schools went through to become effective. Even so, the fact that the same characteristics arise time and time again has led many reformers to suggest that these findings ought to be translated into policies that can guide reform.

Caution to research

EFFECTIVE TEACHERS

In addition to research on effective schools, Hoffman (1991) summarized a considerable body of research, spanning the 1960s through the 1980s, on teachers who were exceptionally effective in helping students learn to read. Hoffman reported on a literature review of effective teaching by Rosenshine and Furst (1973) in which they found several teacher behaviors consistently related to student achievement: clarity, variability, enthusiasm, task orientation, teacher directness, student opportunity to learn criterion material, use of structuring comments, multiple levels of questions, and criticism (which was negatively related to achievement).

In a study of the achievement of students of 165 second- and third-grade teachers conducted over a 3-year period, Brophy (1973) reported on the patterns of the most effective teachers, who represented about a third of the sample. He found the most effective teachers were business-like with a strong sense of task and direction for themselves and their students, had high expectations for their students' achievement, and redoubled efforts when failure was experienced, especially in low socioeconomic status (SES) environments. The most effective teachers had strong management skills, but their classrooms were not stern or oppressive. They had high levels of student engagement and were proactive in preventing disruptions. The most effective teachers engaged in the practice of probing individuals when incorrect responses were offered instead of simply calling on someone else or giving the answer themselves. The students in low-SES classes of the most effective teachers had a success rate of about 80% correct when answering teacher-directed questions, almost all of which were literal. In a follow-up intervention study of first-grade teachers engaged in small group instruction, Anderson, Evertson, and Brophy (1979) found that greater achievement was related to more time spent in reading groups, more active instruction, shorter transitions, introduction of lessons with an overview, and follow-up by teachers to incorrect responses with attempts to improve on them.

In a study of 166 first- and third-grade teachers of children who had been in Head Start, variables positively related to gains in reading included time spent in academic activities, frequency of small-group instruction in basic skills, and frequency of supervised seatwork activities (Stallings & Kaskowitz, 1974). The lowest SES students benefitted most from intense, small-group instruction.

In a study of 25 second-grade and 21 fifth-grade classrooms, Fisher et al. (1980) found that the more effective teachers had higher amounts of time allocated to academics and higher student engagement than less effective teachers. High success rates on tasks were also found to be related to learning gains, with higher optimum success rates found for low-ability than for high-ability students.

Knapp (1995) studied 140 Grade 1 through 6 classrooms in 15 high-poverty schools in California, Maryland, and Ohio over a 2-year period. They found that students in Grades 1, 3, and 5 who were exposed to meaning-oriented reading instruction performed 5.6 national curve equivalents higher, and students in Grades 2, 4, and 6, 1.4 NCEs higher, at the end of the school year, than students in classrooms with skills-oriented approaches to reading instruction. They also studied effects in math and writing and concluded that meaning-oriented instruction was effective in high-poverty classrooms. The teachers they observed teaching for meaning wanted to give children more responsibility for learning, wanted to provide academic tasks that asked more of students, and sustained engagement in learning among children.

The work of Wharton-MacDonald, Pressley, and Hampston (1998) echoes and extends the earlier research on effective teachers of beginning reading. Because they worked out of constructivist rather than a behaviorist perspective, they were able to focus their work on a broader range of teacher actions and intentions than would have been possible 20 years earlier; even so, they were able to look very closely at those aspects of instruction that clearly distinguished the very best teachers from their colleagues. Three of the nine first-grade urban teachers in their sample were identified as most effective based on their students' end-of-year reading and writing achievement. These teachers demonstrated instructional balance, focusing on both literature and skills. They taught decoding skills explicitly and also provided their students with many opportunities to engage in authentic, integrated reading and writing activities. In contrast, the other teachers in the study either focused on skills or whole language approaches or combined the two in disjointed ways. The three most effective teachers extensively used scaffolding to help their students learn. They encouraged self-regulation by teaching their students to monitor their learning, the quality of their work, and their work time. They also encouraged self-regulation by teaching students to use strategies to be good readers and to fix problems they encountered as they were reading. The best teachers had high expectations for their students and masterful classroom management skills. They were skilled in managing time as well as behavior. They were well prepared for their lessons, and they mentioned the importance of routines in terms of activities and expectations. Finally, the most effective teachers were clear about the purposes of their activities and practices.

In the conclusion to their paper, Wharton-MacDonald et al. (1998) pointed to the need for additional research on the role of school factors and district policies on teacher practices and student performance. Hoffman (1991) also observed that there has been a paucity of research simultaneously investigating *both* school and classroom factors affecting reading achievement. Clearly, more research operating at the effective school—effective teacher nexus is needed. Such research would, in a single effort, examine school level factors (e.g., building climate, home–school relations, school-wide organization for reading collaborative efforts) while examining classroom/teacher factors (e.g., time spent in reading instruction, time on task, student engagement, approaches to word recognition and comprehension instruction, teachers' interactive styles).

In this study, we attempted to wed these important but seldom integrated lines of inquiry. We used quantitative and descriptive methods to examine the programs and practices in 11 moderate- to high-poverty schools selected because of their dual reputation for implementing recent reading reform and for promoting greater than expected primary-grade reading achievement. We also examined three schools chosen because they allegedly produced rather ordinary achievement. However, during the course of the data collection, some schools surfaced as more effective than others (see Stringfield et al., 1997, for a similar phenomenon). Therefore, rather than rely on a priori labels, we sought to pinpoint and explain school level (i.e., program) and classroom level (i.e., teachers' instructional practices) factors that distinguished the most effective schools from other schools in the study.

METHOD

Participants

Fourteen schools geographically dispersed throughout the country took part in the study, including schools in Virginia, Minnesota, Colorado, and California.

A summary of the characteristics of each school, including type of intervention and type of school-wide reform, if any, in reading appears in Table 1.1. Schools ranged from 28% to 92% poverty, and included four rural, four small town, and one suburban school, as well as five inner-city schools from three large metropolitan districts.

We started by trying to identify schools with two characteristics: (a) those that had recently implemented reform programs to improve reading achievement, and (b) those with a reputation for producing higher-than-expected results in reading with low-income populations. Because we were interested in special interventions for students most at risk for failure, we selected 8 schools that had carefully implemented one or another externally developed model of early reading intervention; our sample included one Book Buddies school (Invernizzi, Juel, & Rosemary, 1997), two Early Intervention in Reading schools (Taylor, Short, Frye, & Shearer, 1992), three schools with Right Start in Reading (Hiebert, Colt, Catto, & Gury, 1992), and two Reading Recovery schools (Pinnell, Lyons, DeFord, Bryk, & Seltzer, 1994). In 6 of these schools, the interventions were set within a broader context of homegrown program reform in reading. The other two schools in this group of eight had implemented early reading interventions without school-wide reform of their reading program. Additionally, we selected two schools that had implemented externally developed, nationally recognized school-wide reform programs—Success for All (Madden, Slavin, Karweit, Dolan, & Wasik, 1993) and Core Knowledge (Hirsch, 1987). Also included in the sample was one homegrown reform school with its own homegrown early intervention. Operating on the assumption that all 11 of these *reform* schools might demonstrate similar achievement profiles, we recruited 3 *typical* schools for comparison purposes; these were schools with similar populations but with no history of either exceptionally high achievement or reform activity. Two of the typical schools were in large urban districts and one was in a rural area. We wanted to include typical schools to provide a comparison base (both in terms of achievement and instructional practices) for the schools that had already undertaken and achieved some level of reform. All three of these schools were nominated by district administrators as meeting our criteria in terms of primary-grade students' reading achievement.

Thus we began the study with 11 experimental schools and 3 control or comparison schools. However, as Stringfield et al. (1997) found in their work, not all schools believed to be exemplary in our study were, in fact, found to be so. Rather than rely on reputation, we decided to define school exemplarily empirically. We used a combination (a) gain scores from our own classroom reading measures, and (b) scores on whatever achievement test the district normally used. Based on

TABLE 1.1

Characteristics of Schools in the Study

School and Grades	Type of community	% of stdnts. Sub. lunch	Type of early intervention	Type of school-wide reform. program	Programs for English Language Learners	School eff. rating
1. Riverside K–5	Rural	46	Nat'l, Grade 1: Tutorial	National		1
2. Stevenson K–5	Rural	49	Local K–3: Groups and tutorial Regional	Home-grown		3
3. Grant K–5	Town	66	Grades 1–2: Tutorial	Home-grown		2
4. Calvert K–5	Town	40	None	National		2
5. Richland K–5	Rural	28	Nat'l, Grade 1: Tutorial	None		1
6. Woodlawn K–5	Suburb	38	Regional K–3: Group	Home-grown		3
7. Edison K–5	City	56	None	None	ESL – Hmong	1
8. Lincoln K–6	City	77	Nat'l, Grade 1: Tutorial	None	ESL-Hmong	2
9. Rosemont K–3	City	85	Nat'l, Grade 1: Tutorial	Home-grown	Bilingual Kdgn.-Span. ESL-Hmong, Span.	2
10. Wheeler K–2	City	92	Regional grades K–2: Group	Home-grown		3
11. Hilltop K–2	Town	55	Regional grades K–2: Group	Home-grown	Bilingual & ESL, K–2 Span.	3
12. Colfax 3–5	Town	62	Regional Grade 3: Group	Home-grown	Bilingual & ESL, Grade 3 Span.	2

TABLE 1.1 (*continued*)

Characteristics of Schools in the Study

School and Grades	Type of community.	% of stdnts. Sub. lunch	Type of early intervention	Type of school-wide reform. program	Programs for English Language Learners	School eff. rating
13. Franklin K–6	Rural	47	Regional Grade K–3: Group	None	Bilingual and ESL, K–3 Span.	1
14. Whitman K–5	City	78	None	None	Bilingual and ESL, K–3 Span.	2

Note. For a more detailed version of this table the reader is referred to the technical report (Taylor, Pearson, Clark, & Walpole, 1999).

this aggregate index, four schools in the present study were determined to be most effective. These schools were doing as well as or better than others in our sample in reading growth and/or doing better than average for their district, considering their poverty level. Six additional schools were determined to be moderately effective (neither exceptionally high nor low on the two indices that made up our school effectiveness rating), and four schools were determined to be least effective—lower than other schools in our study on our composite index, but typical for their district in primary-grade reading achievement.

Within each building in each of Grades K through 3, the principal was asked to identify two good or excellent teachers who would be willing to take part in the study. We did not include *all* teachers because we wanted to focus on exemplary practice. Similar to what we discovered for schools, however, not all teachers were found to be exemplary, at least according to the judgments of our expert ratings of teacher accomplishment. They varied widely along the scale of accomplishment that we used to characterize their practices. The principals contacted the teachers they had nominated to request their participation. A total of 22 kindergarten, 23 first-grade, 25 second-grade, and 22 third-grade teachers participated in the study. All teachers were female except for 2 male second-grade and 2 male third-grade teachers. Because of the detail and complexity of the study, results in this chapter related to student performance and classroom observations are limited to Grades 1 through 3.

Each principal was also asked to participate in the study. The principal recruited the teachers, responded to a survey, completed an interview, and provided demographic information about the school, including the number of students on free and reduced lunch, the school's overall performance on district tests, and Grade 3 standardized test achievement (expressed as a percentile).

Mindful of problems with attrition and absences, we asked each teacher, in the fall, to divide their students into thirds, representing high, average, and low-performing readers, and to identify four typical average-achieving and four typical low-achieving children, based on teachers' perceptions of reading performance (or emergent literacy performance), to complete pretests. From this pool we randomly selected two low and two average students. If these children were no longer in schools as we prepared to collect posttest data, we used achievement level and gender balance to reduce the classroom pool to four (two average and two low achieving) students. We were only able to test 4 children per class in the spring due to resource limitations. However, from a sampling standpoint it was preferable to obtain fewer data points in more classrooms than more data points in fewer classrooms.

Basic Data Collection Tools

Fall and Spring Outcome Measures.   Children were pretested in November and again in May. All tests were administered by members of our research team who had been specially trained for this project and the administration of these tests.

Grade 1.   In the fall, children were individually tested on upper- and lower-case letter name identification, phonemic blending, phonemic segmentation (Pikulski, 1996), and a list of preprimer words (described later).

In the spring, children were individually assessed on a specially constructed word reading test and reading passages from the QRI-II (Leslie & Caldwell, 1995). An instructional level (highest level with 90% word recognition accuracy or better) was determined for each student. Then, irrespective of decoding ability, each student was asked to read a Grade-1 passage so we could obtain a common fluency measure for all students—the number of words a child could read correctly in one minute (wcpm, Deno, 1985).

Also, children were asked to retell each passage they read. A 4-point holistic scoring rubric (see Appendix A, Colt, 1997), was used to score the retellings on the passage that proved to be at their instructional level, 90%. All of the retellings were scored by a single member of our research team. A second member read and scored 15% of the retellings to establish interrater reliability (91% agreement).

The reading words test was developed by the research team for the project in order to ensure that our word test included an appropriate mix of decodable and basic sight words. Half of the words at each grade level were high-frequency words from the QRI-II and half were decodable words garnered from an extensive review of the decodable patterns introduced in the four most popular basal series. The decodable words were controlled to match the QRI-II words in terms of frequency (Carroll, Davies, & Richman, 1971). There were 20 words at each grade level, preprimer through Grade 3, for a total of 100 words.

Grades 2 and 3.   In the fall, Grade-2 children were individually tested by a member of our research team on the reading words test for Grade 1 and a Grade-1 passage from the QRI-II. The number of words the child read correctly in the first minute was recorded. The child's word recognition accuracy on the passage was also recorded. Each child was asked to retell the passage, and the 4-point scoring rubric was used to score the retellings.

In the spring, children were individually tested by a member of the research team, starting with the reading words test. On the QRI, each child began with a Grade 1 passage and continued until an instructional level was found, after which each child read the Grade 2 passage (to obtain the fluency measure) if it had *not* been read as a part of the procedure seeking to establish instructional level. For each passage, we asked the child for a retelling, and the retelling for the instructional level passage was scored using the 4-point rubric described earlier.

Grade-3 children followed the same procedure as Grade-2 children except for the passages read: In the fall, they read a Grade-2 passage and word list, and in the spring, they read a Grade-3 passage to obtain a fluency (wcpm) measure.

OBSERVATIONS

Members of our research team at each site were trained to conduct classroom observations. Observers practiced coding video segments of instruction until they had at least 80% agreement with the principal investigators on the coding of teacher and student behaviors. Beginning in December, a member of our team conducted a 1-hour observation of instruction during the basic reading program in every classroom once a month for 5 months. The observations were scheduled for an hour in which reading instruction was occurring. Due to resource limitations, we were not able to observe for more than 1 hour per classroom during each monthly visit. During the observations, the observers focused on the teacher and the children. Observational notes included classroom dialogue as well as comments about general classroom activity, children's involvement in the lesson, and other events that seemed noteworthy. The observer recorded what the teacher was saying and doing as well as what the children were saying and doing during the lesson. Additionally, every 5 minutes the observer recorded any of the following teacher behaviors that were observed in the previous 5-minute segment: coaching/scaffolding, modeling, engaging the children in recitation, explaining how to do something, telling, or engaging the children in a discussion. A description of each of these behaviors is provided in Table 1.2. After the observation, the observer summarized the lesson by completing a summary that required a statement about each of these characteristics: overall impression, teacher instruction and teacher–student interaction, activities and materials, student engagement, classroom management, and classroom environment.

LOGS

We asked every classroom teacher to keep a log of daily instructional activities in the classroom for 1 week in February and 1 week in April. We asked them to

TABLE 1.2

Teacher's Interaction Styles

Style	Description
Coaching / scaffolding	Teacher supports / prompts / coaches child as he or she tries to perform a task.
Modeling / demonstrating	Teacher shows how to do something by actually performing a task or thinking aloud.
Engaging students in recitation	Teacher engages children in a questioning session in which he or she is looking for short, specific answers.
Telling students information	Teacher gives facts in the abstract without directions on how to use the information or what to do with it.
Explaining how to do something	Teacher provides direct explanation of processes involved in a task.
Engaging students in discussion	Teacher leads students in a formal discussion in which the social conventions of a discussion apply.

indicate how long they spent on various activities, including reading instruction (teacher directed reading of narrative and expository text; instruction in phonics, vocabulary, and comprehension; literature circles); student independent reading; writing in response to reading; other written composition; spelling; reading aloud to students; and other academic activities. Teachers also indicated the *group setting* in which each activity occurred: students working as a whole group, working in a small group, or working independently. Teachers recorded activities in 15-minute intervals and could include more than one activity during a time period. We divided the number of minutes for an interval by the number of activities coded to get number of minutes spent on an activity during that interval. For example, if a 15-minute interval was coded as whole group reading instruction, independent reading, and writing in response to reading, we coded each activity as occurring for a child for 5 minutes.

QUESTIONNAIRES

In April or May, the principal and teachers from each school completed surveys that had been developed by a team of CIERA researchers for a broader national survey of "beat the odds" schools. The principal survey dealt with the following topics:

- attributes of effective schools and effective instruction,

- use of goals and standards,
- factors/reasons for success in improving reading/language arts instruction,
- approaches to professional development,
- ways to increase the reading achievement of struggling readers,
- consequences of assessment and assessment training,

The teacher survey embraced most of the same topics and some additional ones:

- types, frequencies, and purposes of assessments,
- types of reading/language arts helpers and their activities,
- home–school communication, and
- community activities.

Across the 14 schools, the return rate was 88%.

INTERVIEWS

We interviewed all principals and at least three teachers from each school. Principal questions focused on the community and links to parents, the principal's view of his or her leadership role, factors contributing to the school's success, challenges as well as things on which the school was still working, and advice to schools that wanted to significantly improve their reading achievement. Teacher questions were similar but also included questions about a teacher's general approach to teaching reading, behavior management systems, and her or his expectations for students. We transcribed the interviews and used them as a source of information for writing case studies for each school and for generating several school variables.

CASE STUDIES

For every school, a common outline was followed to guide our research team in crafting a case study. A model case study was also provided to create some common expectations for content, format, and depth. Major topics within each case study included

1. school demographics,
2. history of the school,
3. primary-grade reading performance data,
4. community/home/school relationships,
5. school factors (leadership, effective schools/school change factors, professional development, format of school reading program),

6. grade-level classroom practices (instruction, curriculum, student engagement, classroom management, classroom environment),
7. other factors believed to be enhancing beginning reading achievement,
8. challenges, and
9. advice to other schools.

Case studies were written by the principal investigator or by the research team member who had spent the most time in a particular school.

Creating Variables for Data Analyses

Overall Strategy

Quantitative and descriptive analyses were conducted using multiple sources of information used for both types of analyses. Analyses were conducted at the school and at the classroom level. To examine the natural variability within our sample, we developed empirically driven indices of effectiveness for both schools and teachers, grouped the schools or teachers into categories of effectiveness (most, moderately, and least), and then investigated the systematic differences among schools or teachers on other sets of variables. The procedures and criteria used to determine these variables are summarized in Tables 1.3 and 1.4. (More detail can also be found in the technical report, Taylor, Pearson, Clark, & Walpole, 1999). We used the data emerging from the observations, surveys, and interviews to create and operationalize both school level and classroom level variables.

CONSTRUCTING SCHOOL VARIABLES

School Effectiveness Rating. To categorize schools as most effective, moderately effective, or least effective, we used two school-based measures: (a) students' growth on project measures of reading, and (b) students' performance on district measures of reading. These two scores were combined to create a general rating of effectiveness. (See Table 1.5 and Appendix B).

School Efforts to Link to Parents. An initial reading of the case studies indicated that schools varied in the extent to which they reached out to parents. Schools were judged to be *high* on the linking-to-parents factor if a large percentage of teachers communicated regularly with parents, had an active site council in which parents helped to make school decisions, *and* engaged in prac-

TABLE 1.3

Descriptions of School Factors

Definition	Description	Sources of data
1. School Effectiveness Rating: Based on three project reading measures and mean Grade 3 percentile on district standardized reading test	Composite z-score from: 1. Composite z-score on three project reading measures: spring reading words residual, spring retelling at reading level residual, and spring words-correct-per-minute residual 2. Z-score from residual on third-grade standardized reading test percentile (poverty used as a covariate)	One half of rating from three project reading measures and one half from district standardized reading test.
2. Parent Links: Based on teachers' mean level of home communication and on efforts of school to reach out to parents	Rating with three levels: 3 – High – high on parent communication and high on involving parents 2 – Avg. – One or the other of the above 1 – Low – none of the above or low on parent communication (see teacher factor)	Teacher survey, interviews and case studies.
3. Systematic Internal Assessment of Student Progress: Regular monitoring of reading progress, used by all teachers, results shared, data used to make instructional changes.	Rating with two levels: 2 – Present 1 – Absent As determined from teacher perceptions (on survey), in interviews, and /or case studies.	Teacher surveys, case studies and interviews.
4. Building Communication/ Collaboration: Based on teachers' rating of "communication of ideas across teacher" (from survey) as indicative (5) down to absent (1) in school, also based on positive or negative comments in interviews, case study about communication and collaboration across teachers.	Rating with three levels: 3 – High – high on teachers' perceptions of building communication/ collaboration and positive comments in interviews/case study 2 – Avg. – Average teacher perceptions 1- Low – low teacher perceptions and negative comments in interviews / case study	Teacher surveys, case studies and interviews.

19

TABLE 1.4

Descriptions of Teacher Factors

Definition	Description	Sources of data
1. Home Communication: Based on teacher's report on survey.	Rating with five levels: 5 –Very High – exceeded rating of 4 4 –High – Called home at least once a month and sent letter, newsletter, or traveling folder at least once a week 3 –Avg. – Called home 2–3 times/year; sent letter, newsletter or folder home once a week 2 –Lower than Avg. – Called home 2–3 times a year; sent letter or folder monthly 1 –Low – less than what is required for a rating of 2	Teacher surveys.
2. Student Time on Task: Based on comments in observations about student engagement.	Rating with three levels: 3 –High – high in maintaining on-task behavior—most students on task (in most comments in observations) 2 –Avg. – Average in maintaining on-task behavior—some comments indicated high on-task behavior and others indicated a number of students off-task 1 –Low – low in maintaining on-task behavior—many comments indicated many students often off-task	Observation notes and observation summaries.
3. Time spent in reading instruction and activities.	Activities included whole group, small group, or independent grouping pattern on the following activities: • reading instruction (teacher directed reading, word recognition, comprehension, or vocabulary work; literature circle) • independent reading • writing in response to reading • reading aloud to students • written composition • spelling • other academic activities	Teacher logs.

Definition	Description	Sources of data
4. Preferred Interaction Style: Based on most frequent behavior coded in observations	Six behaviors coded: 1 – coaching/scaffolding 2 – modeling 3 – engaging students in recitation 4 – explaining how to do something 5 – telling students information 6 – engaging students in discussion	Observation notes.
5. Approaches to word recognition instruction.	1. Coaching on use of word recognition strategies during reading of stories. 2. Providing explicit phonics instruction 3. Practicing sight words	Observations notes.
6. Approaches to comprehension instruction.	1. Asking text-based questions to be answered orally after reading 2. Asking higher-level questions to be answered orally after reading 3. Writing in response to reading	Observation notes.
7. Teacher Accomplishment Rating: Based on two experts reading observations	Rating with three levels: 3 – Demonstrating many of the elements of effective instruction 2 – Demonstrating some of the elements of effective instruction 1 – Demonstrating few of the elements of effective instruction	Observation notes and summaries.

tices such as focus groups, phone surveys, or written surveys to find out parents' needs and concerns.

Schools were judged to be *average* or low on the linking to parents measure if fewer of the above factors were present in their school. Six schools were determined to be high on the linking to parents school factor, five were determined to be average on this factor, and three schools were determined to be low. The two raters evaluating schools on this factor achieved 93% agreement in their categorizations.

Systematic, Internal Assessment of Student Progress. A school was coded as systematically assessing student progress if at least two thirds of teachers on the survey perceived this to be an attribute of their school, and if com-

TABLE 1.5
Z-Scores for School Effectiveness Rating

School	Standardized composite z-score from z-scores (by grade) for residual words correct per minute, residual retelling, residual reading words	Z-score for residual mean percentile on district standardized reading test (controlling for poverty)	Sum of Z-scores (columns 2 & 3)	School effectiveness score–standardized score (from column 4)	School effectiveness rating (3-level)*
1	-.74	-.22	-.96	-.58	1
2	.74	.53	1.27	.77	3
3	-.22	-.36	-.58	-.35	2
4	-.01	-.52	-.53	-.32	2
5	.03	-.91	-.88	-.53	1
6	1.33	2.04	3.37	2.04	3
7	-1.39	-1.28	-2.67	-1.62	1
8	-.41	1.17	.76	.46	2
9	1.16	-.56	.60	.36	2
10	1.74	-.39	1.38	.82	3
11	.28	1.45	1.73	1.05	3
12	-.39	-.36	-.75	-.45	2
13	-1.91	-.75	-2.56	-1.56	1
14	-.32	.15	-.17	-.10	2

Note. *3 (most effective if > .50 SD above mean of 0), 2 (moderately effective if < .50 SD above mean but > −.50 SD below mean of 0), 1 (least effective if < −.50 SD below mean of 0)

ments in the case studies and/or interviews supported this perception. Across schools, all but four were coded as systematically assessing student progress. These were not externally imposed standardized testing systems; they were internally developed systems for monitoring individual student progress within a school-wide curriculum. The data from these systems were used frequently by individual teachers to make grouping and instructional decisions.

Building Communication and Collaboration.   In a number of the interviews and surveys, staff commented about either good or poor collaboration and/or communication among teachers. Schools judged to be *high* on the building communication/collaboration scale had a high mean score on teachers' perceived building communication rating (from the teacher survey) *and* positive comments in the case study or in interviews about good collaboration among teachers within and across grades. Schools judged to be *average* or *low* on this building communication factor had fewer positive and/or more negative comments in the case study or interviews. Two raters achieved 86% agreement on this judgment. Across the 14 schools in the project, 6 schools were judged to be high on the building communication factor, 5 were judged to be average, and 3 were judged to be low.

Use of an Externally Developed Early Reading Intervention.   Within each grade level a school was coded as either having or not having an externally developed early intervention in place. Out of the 14 schools, 10 had an externally developed intervention, 5 across two or more grades, 4 in Grade 1 only, and 1 in Grade 3 (in a Grade 3 through 6 building.) Four schools had no externally developed intervention in place.

Constructing Classroom (Teacher) Variables

Home Communication.   On the survey teachers indicated how often they communicated with parents and in what ways. The areas in which there appeared to be the most variability were the frequency with which teachers reported (a) calling home, (b) sending a letter or newsletter home, or (c) sending a traveling folder home. A 5-point scale was used to rate teachers on the extent to which they communicated with parents. Across the sample of teachers in Grades 1 through 3 in this project, 22% received a rating of 5, 21% a rating of 4, 35% a rating of 3, 14% a rating of 2, and 8% a rating of 1. The mean rating was 3.35 ($SD = 1.22$). One research team member rated all teachers, and a second rated a 25% sample; interrater agreement was 95%.

Student Time on Task.   From the observations, we searched for comments about children's on-task behavior, Most helpful in this regard were the summaries that each observer completed at the end of each observation session; one of their tasks was to summarize and point to evidence to support any conclusions about students' level of on-task behavior. Based on these summary comments a teacher received a high (3), average (2) or low (1) rating in maintaining students' on-task behavior. One member of our research team rated all teachers and another team member rated 25% of the teachers on this dimension. Across the pairs of ratings for each teacher, there was 100% agreement. Across teachers, the mean rating was 2.30 (SD = .76), with 48% of teachers receiving a rating of 3 (high), 34% a rating of 2 (average), and 18% a rating of 1 (low) in level of on-task student behavior.

Preferred Interaction Style.   As reported earlier (under observations), at the end of each 5-minute segment during the classroom observations, observers coded instances of interactions observed during that segment, using these categories: coaching/scaffolding, modeling, engaging students in recitation, engaging students in discussion, explaining how to do something, or telling students information (these activities are described in more detail in Table 1.2). The total number of times a teacher was coded as engaging in each of these behaviors (more than one was possible within each segment) was calculated, and the behavior coded most frequently across all five observations was determined to be the teacher's preferred interaction style. Across teachers in Grades 1, 2, and 3, 24% had a preferred interaction style of *coaching*, 31% had a preferred interaction style of engaging students in *recitation*, 39% had a preferred interaction style of *telling* students information, and 6% had a preferred style of *modeling*. To evaluate the trustworthiness of these ratings, three members of the research team read the observational notes and rated a sample of 25% of the teachers; they agreed with the original coder on 82% of the original codings. If and when mismatches occurred, we reverted to code most frequently marked by the classroom observer.

Approaches to Word Recognition and Comprehension Instruction.   The data from the observations were analyzed to determine how teachers provided word recognition and comprehension instruction. A number of approaches were coded on a frequency scale, and the frequencies were collapsed into three categories: frequently (observed in two or more of the five observations), occasionally (observed in at least one observation), and never. The three word-recognition approaches that occurred most frequently were selected for more elaborate analysis; these were (a) coaching children in the use of strategies to figure out unknown words as they were reading text, (b) providing explicit phonics instruction, and (c) practicing sight words.

Coaching involved prompting children to use a variety of strategies as they were engaged in reading during small-group instruction or one-on-one reading time. They fell out into several subcategories, as listed in the chart below:

Coaching in Word Recognition Strategies During Reading

Metacognitive Dialogue on Strategies

A teacher reviews independence in using word recognition strategies with his students, "The point is to be able to read on your own this summer. What if you come to a big long word? Yes, sound it out. What else can you do? Yes, you can twist it a little (e.g., try a different vowel sound in 'terrible'). Also you can ask yourself if it makes sense. And if you try these things, then what do you do? Yes, skip it, or what else? Yes, you can ask someone."

Metacognitive Review of Strategies Used to Figure Out a Word

After a child came up with "squirt" while reading, the teacher asks, " How did you figure out 'squirt' Tom?

Tom: I sounded it out.

Teacher: You could also look at the picture.

Tom: Also make sure it makes sense.

Praise for Use of Strategies

After a child has read, the teacher says to the group, "I noticed that Mara got stuck and skipped it and read around it and then came back to it. That's good thinking."

Prompts to Figure Out Words: Specific

A child is stuck on a word while reading the teacher asks, "What could give you a clue on that word?"

Prompts to Figure Out Words: Specific

The teacher is helping a group as they are reading aloud.
"Woah, back up there. Frame the work with 'i–n'. What is the
first sound? What is the second sound? What's the word?"

Explicit phonics instruction included work on a chart, whiteboard, worksheet,
or word cards dealing with word study, word families, introducing or comparing
phonic elements (i.e., *er*, *ir*, and *ur* all have the same sound), making words
(Cunningham & Cunningham, 1992), writing words, and reading words with a
particular phonic element in isolation. The following chart depicts the most
common approaches observed:

Explicit Phonics Instruction	*Working on Phonic Elements*
	"There are a lot of words that don't have the long or short vowel sound because they have a bossy letter. 'Ur' says /ur/ in 'hurt'. In 'born', 'or' says /or/. In 'her' if it was a long e it would say /here/ but 'er' says /er/. Can anyone think of an /ur/, /or/, or /er/ word?"
	Making Words
	Children get letter cards: a, I, g, k, n, p, r. "Let's start with 2 letters to make 'in'. Change 1 letter to make 'an'. Add one letter to make 'pan'. Rearrange these to make 'nap'" The children continue until they end up with a word from the story, "parking."
	Working on Word Families
	"Let's warm up with a few word families." Children read: cat, hat, fat, mat. The teacher uses a sliding device so the first letter can be changed. The children continue to read: Dan, fan, man, can, pan, ran. "Good for you! Excellent. One more family." The children read: Pig, dig, rig, big, twig.
	Word Study
	A child sorts picture cards by first letter: lamp, letter, game, gate, girl, October, otter, officer. "Let's check and see if you got them right. "G" makes the /g/ sound. Game, October, gate, girl. There is 1 that doesn't belong. Let me say them. Do you hear 1 that doesn't belong? Right, where would October go?"

Practice on sight words involved teachers using flash cards, a pocket chart, or a
word wall to review words the students were expected to recognize instantly as
sight words.

Practice on Sight Words   *Flash Cards*

> The teacher reviews sight words with his group. He gives them the word card if they say if first. "These 2 look like they rhyme," and he points to goes and does, "but do they?"

Chart

> The teacher puts a chart of No Excuses words on the board: a, an, and, for, in, will. She calls on individual children to read the words. "Yesterday we read this word in our story: will. Now use your white board and write 'will.'"

For comprehension instruction, eight different instructional practices were observed and coded: doing a picture walk; asking for a prediction; asking a text-based question; asking a higher-level question, aesthetic response question; asking children to write in response to reading (including writing answers to questions about what they had read); doing a story map; asking children to retell a story; and working on a comprehension skill or strategy. For further analysis, we focused on those categories for which 10 or more teachers were frequently observed using the strategy. The practices that met the 10 teacher criterion were asking text-based questions, asking higher-level questions, and asking children to write in response to what they had read.

One member of the research team coded all teachers and a second member coded 25% of the teachers, achieving 96% agreement on coding of the various approaches to word recognition instruction and 97% agreement on the coding of the various approaches to comprehension instruction.

Teacher Accomplishment Rating. Two experts in teacher supervision at the elementary school level read all teacher observations. One expert was a whole language advocate, and the other was a reading skills advocate. They used the checklist of elements of effective instruction from the principal survey (based on the work of Anderson et al., 1979; Barr & Dreeban, 1991; Hoffman, 1991; Pressley, Rankin, & Yokoi, 1996; Roehler & Duffy, 1991; Wharton-MacDonald et al., 1998; see Table 1.6).

Based on a thorough reading of the observations and summaries, each rater rated each teacher separately on each item on the list, providing a judgment about whether there were many, some, or only a few instances of that attribute in the data

TABLE 1.6

Criteria Used To Rate Teacher Accomplishment[*]

Elements of effective instruction	
1. awareness of purpose	12. redoubling of teaching efforts when students have difficulty
2. enthusiasm	13. effective use of praise
3. task orientation	14. extensive content coverage, instructional density
4. high student engagement	15. explicit modeling and scaffolding
5. short transitions	16. teaching skills in context
6. much time spent in reading/language arts activities	17. extra instruction for low readers
7. frequent instruction in skills and strategies	18. encouragement of self-regulation
8. high success rate	19. instructional balance
9. masterful classroom management	20. much reading of connected text
10. positive classroom climate	21. much writing of connected text
11. high student expectations	22. activities appropriate, meaningful, challenging

Note. [*]Based on the work of Anderson et al., 1979; Barr and Dreeban, 1991; Hoffman, 1991; Pressley et al., 1996; Roehler and Duffy, 1991; Wharton-MacDonald et al., 1998.

set (or if there were no data, they coded the item as *could not determine*). The two raters then arrived at an overall rating (on a 3-point scale) based on the mode (the most commonly occurring point on the scale of many, some, or only a few) of the individual items. For the overall rating, the two raters demonstrated 80% agreement. In those instances in which disagreements occurred, a third judge conducted an independent rating. In all instances, the third judge agreed with one of the other two judges, and that score point was used in the final analysis. Across teachers in Grades 1 through 3 in our sample, 42% were identified as demonstrating many of these elements (most accomplished), 34% demonstrated some of these elements (moderately accomplished), and 24% demonstrated only a few of the elements of effective instruction (least accomplished).

RESULTS AND DISCUSSION

The results are organized by level of analysis. First we report and discuss results, largely descriptive, at the school level. Second, we use both descriptive and statistical tools to examine the variations among instructional practices of teachers within the levels of school effectiveness. Third, we report and discuss the variations we found in instructional practice as a function of levels of teacher accomplishment .Throughout the results we refer to the most effective schools by pseudonym: Hilltop, Stevenson, Wheeler, and Woodlawn.

Analyses related to student performance at the school and all at the teacher level were based on classroom mean scores. Mean classroom performance measures by school effectiveness and teacher accomplishment levels are reported in Tables 1.7, 1.8, and 1.9.

SCHOOL LEVEL ANALYSES

Linking to Parents

Parent links were positively and statistically significantly related ($r = .73$) to the school effectiveness rating and to all measures of student growth, fluency ($r = .60$), retelling ($r = .37$), and reading words ($r = .41$; see Table 1.10).

The most effective schools reported more links with parents than the moderately effective and least effective schools. Three of the four most effective schools reported having an active site council in which parents served on this committee with teachers and other school staff and helped to make decisions concerning school practices. Four of six moderately successful schools also reported having an active site council, but only one of the four least successful schools reported having such a body in place.

Additionally, the most effective schools reached out to parents in other ways. Wheeler scheduled focus groups to learn how to better meet parents' and students' needs. Woodlawn had regular focus groups and conducted phone surveys to determine parents' concerns and needs. Stevenson school officials sent a written survey home to parents, and the principal attempted to communicate with all parents regularly. None of the moderately successful or least successful schools reported engaging in any of these practices.

Hilltop, another of the most effective schools, had developed an at-home reading partnership in which books were sent home in English or Spanish so that parents could read to their children. Woodlawn and Stevenson also cited successful at-home reading partnerships, all with high parent participation, in which parents listened to their children read on a regular basis.

When asked about reasons for their success, Stevenson and Hilltop mentioned the importance of strong home–school connections, reaching out to parents and making them feel like welcome partners in the school. One teacher at Stevenson conveyed the common sentiment succinctly: "One factor responsible

TABLE 1.7

Grade 1 Means (and Standard Deviations) for Pre- and Posttest Scores by School Effectiveness Rating and Teacher Accomplishment Rating

School	n*	Letter ID	Fall			Spring		
			Phonemic awareness	Preprimer words	Reading words	WCPM** on Grade 1 passage	Retelling at reading level	
School rating*								
1	8	47.95	9.38	9.90	56.28	34.68	2.52	
		(3.51)	(1.71)	(4.58)	(14.40)	(12.09)	(.64)	
2	8	44.75	6.56	7.38	55.87	41.19	2.34	
		(5.82)	(3.85)	(4.44)	(16.89)	(14.99)	(.30)	
3	7	45.80	7.48	9.94	68.29	50.75	2.51	
		(3.97)	(2.51)	(3.87)	(9.01)	(17.03)	(.35)	
Teacher rating**								
1	3	43.00	4.52	4.58	41.58	25.58	2.17	
		(1.64)	(4.68)	(2.18)	(14.63)	(11.22)	(.14)	
2	7	45.83	7.11	7.67	66.18	44.40	2.38	
		(4.42)	(1.96)	(3.80)	(17.70)	(15.96)	(.37)	
3	12	46.74	8.57	10.67	60.48	44.44	2.59	
		(5.13)	(2.87)	(4.23)	(10.32)	(15.39)	(.52)	

Note. *Number of teachers.
**Words correct per minute.
***1 = Least effective, 2 = moderately effective, 3 = most effective.
****1 = Least accomplished, 2 = moderately accomplished, 3 = most accomplished.

TABLE 1.8

Grade 2 Means (and Standard Deviations) for Pre- and Posttest Scores by School Effectiveness Rating and Teacher Accomplishment Rating

School	n*	Fall			Spring	
		Grade 1 words	WCPM** on Grade 1 text	Reading words	WCPM** on Grade 2 text	Retelling at reading level
School rating***						
1	8	13.88	50.46	79.59	66.30	2.56
		(3.59)	(18.92)	(5.88)	(19.24)	(.69)
2	10	15.88	59.77	86.98	73.35	2.99
		(2.18)	(13.07)	(6.04)	(14.65)	(.36)
3	6	14.42	47.98	84.58	70.17	3.06
		(3.46)	(17.31)	(7.99)	(13.18)	(.40)
Teacher rating****						
1	8	13.91	56.83	80.22	64.47	2.66
		(2.50)	(13.38)	(8.09)	(17.37)	(.78)
2	8	15.20	55.63	84.82	71.40	2.99
		(3.58)	(14.38)	(7.00)	(17.20)	(.39)
3	8	15.44	48.68	86.72	74.75	2.95
		(3.12)	(21.31)	(4.73)	(11.80)	(.30)

Note. *Number of teachers.
**Words correct per minute.
***1 = least effective, 2 = moderately effective, 3 = most effective.
****1 = least accomplished, 2 = moderately accomplished, 3 = most accomplished.

31

TABLE 1.9

Grade 3 Means (and Standard Deviations) for Pre- and Posttest Scores by School Effectiveness Rating and Teacher Accomplishment Rating

School	n*	Fall		Spring		
		Grade 2 words	WCPM** in Grade 2 passage	Reading words	WCPM** on Grade 3 passage	Retelling at reading level
School rating*						
1	7	16.95	73.19	90.99	85.70	2.80
		(2.15)	(14.48)	(3.76)	(18.98)	(.29)
2	2	15.27	75.58	89.89	91.13	3.06
		(3.74)	(22.79)	(8.14)	(29.13)	(.43)
3	3	16.81	72.58	96.25	105.38	3.31
		(2.03)	(8.82)	(1.17)	(16.92)	(.47)
Teacher rating**						
1	5	15.95	71.70	90.60	88.49	2.96
		(2.27)	(11.67)	(3.91)	(27.83)	(.38)
2	9	16.28	75.88	91.44	92.08	3.14
		(3.67)	(17.37)	(8.21)	(23.59)	(.50)
3	7	16.20	77.11	92.33	94.58	2.92
		(3.23)	(23.06)	(46.48)	(31.35)	(.35)

Note. *Number of teachers.
**Words correct per minute.
***1 = least effective, 2 = moderately effective, 3 = most effective.
****1 = least accomplished, 2 = moderately accomplished, 3 = most accomplished.

32

TABLE 1.10

Correlations for School Effectiveness Rating and School Factors

	School effectiveness score	Z-score resid. Words (class mean)	Z-score resid. Fluency (class mean)	Z-score resid. Retelling (class mean)
Links to parents	.73	.41	.60	.37
	$p < .01$	$p < .001$	$p < .001$	$p < .01$
	$n = 14$	$n = 70$	$n = 70$	$n = 70$
Systematic assessment of student progress	.42	.21	.53	.37
	$p > .05$	$p > .05$	$p < .01$	$p < .01$
	$n = 14$	$n = 70$	$n = 70$	$n = 70$
Building communication	.37	.07	.43	.35
	$p > .05$	$p > .05$	$p < .001$	$p < .01$
	$n = 14$	$n = 70$	$n = 70$	$n = 70$
Research-based intervention in place	.00	.14	.02	.05
	ns	ns	ns	ns
	$n = 14$	$n = 70$	$n = 70$	$n = 70$

for our success is working closely with the home. I include parents in as many ways as possible—send a letter explaining a unit, send homework tips. I try to communicate to parents the power they have in influencing their students' growth."

Although realizing that correlation does not imply causation, we conclude that part of positive home–school relations, so often cited in the literature and so prevalent in our most effective schools, is making a concerted effort to reach out to parents. As an example of this concerted effort, the principal at Stevenson, although perhaps an exception in this respect, made time herself to call all homes just to compliment parents on the academic or social achievements of their children.

Systematic Internal Assessment

Systematic assessment of student progress figured prominently in our findings. Systematic assessment was related to students' growth in reading fluency ($r = .53, p < .01$) and with their retelling performance ($r = .37, p < .01$). All four of these schools used some form of systematic assessment of student progress. In all four cases, this meant that all the teachers in the school regularly (at least three times throughout the year) administered some sort of common classroom-based assessment tool to all students *and* shared the information about class-room-level performance with the principal and fellow teachers. Wheeler imple-mented four assessments across the school year, relying on a fluency measure (wcpm), sight words, and letter identification in Grades 1 and 2, and letter iden-tification and concepts about print in kindergarten. Woodlawn used a fluency measure as a curriculum-based indicator five times a year (three times in first grade). Hilltop used an informal reading inventory three times a year. Stevenson used an informal inventory (Grade 1) or basal tests (Grade 1–2) three times a year as well as a developmental spelling test three times a year in Grades 1 through 3 and a words-in-isolation-and-in-context test in Grade 1 ev-ery 6 weeks. Four of the six moderately effective schools also reported having systematic assessment of student progress in place, while two of the four least ef-fective schools had an assessment system in place.

We would emphasize that these were curriculum-based, classroom assess-ments intended to provide information for monitoring individual student prog-ress and to shape individual and classroom (and occasionally school-wide) curricular and instructional decisions; they were not external, accountabil-ity-focused assessments. Instead of external accountability, these classroom level data provided a form of internal accountability (to one's colleagues) while providing teachers with a useful benchmark on each student's progress. The public sharing of the data was important in all four schools. The principal at Hilltop related that the teachers had learned how to confront data, to keep data in front of them, to use data to identify specific strategies to help struggling read-ers, to provide support in the implementation of strategies, and to align major school events and celebrations around the meeting of school-wide goals. In other words, the staff at this particular school had learned how to make perfor-mance data a useful ally rather than a cause of constant alarm or frustration.

Building Communication and Collaboration

The building communication and collaboration rating was positively related to the fluency measure ($r = .43, p < .01$) and retelling ($r = .35, p < .01$). Five of the 10 moderately effective or least effective schools revealed concerns about communication across teachers and program articulation across grades. The in-terviews with staff in one moderately and one least effective school revealed several instances of negative communication and collaboration, including low morale among teachers due to the existence of different factions among the staff and perceived lack of cooperation among teachers. In one of the least effective schools, all of the teachers rated communication of ideas across teachers as moderate to low in their school. In another least effective school, working as a team across the entire school was highlighted as something the school had just begun to work on; seven of nine teachers in that school rated the presence of building communication as moderate to low in their school.

In contrast, teachers in all four of the most effective schools reported collaboration within and across grades as a reason for their success. Factors such as peer coaching, teaming within and across grades, working together to help all students, and program consistency were mentioned as aspects of collaboration that teachers valued in these most effective schools. In contrast, in the moderately and least effective schools, concerns about program compatibility, instructional consistency, and common instructional terminology were more prevalent. One of the teachers at Wheeler, one of the most effective schools, summed it up this way:

> Teaming with other staff is important. You can't do it by yourself. Teaming also builds a sense of community. If the children see us working together and getting along, that means a lot to them. The children also get to see other teachers and get to know them. That builds caring and community.

This sentiment was echoed by teachers at Hilltop School, who suggested that peer coaching and collaboration, because they led to school-wide buy-in, were key factors in their success.

Building collaboration played an important role in the delivery of reading instruction in all of the most effective schools. All four of the most effective schools had reorganized their instructional delivery system within the past few years to make use of a collaborative model for reading instruction. In three schools, this meant that special personnel—a Title I, reading resource, or special education teacher—went into the classroom for 1 hour a day to help provide instruction for small, ability-based groups.

Wheeler deployed a resource teacher in the classroom with the classroom teacher during reading time for 1 hour and an aide for a second hour of reading. Children received guidance in small groups with a teacher, a resource teacher or the aide in one-on-one settings. At this school, a total of 2½ to 3 hours a day was spent on reading/language arts instruction and practice. Clearly, helping all children learn to read was a priority at this school. Woodlawn sent a reading specialist and a special education teacher into the classroom to work with small groups along with the classroom teacher for 1 hour each day. In this school, 2½ hours a day were spent on reading/language arts instruction in Grades 1 and 2. At Stevenson, using a similar push-in collaborative model, children also received about 2½ hours a day of reading/language arts instruction and practice.

A Title I teacher or aide worked in the classroom for 50 minutes each morning. The Title I teachers returned to the first- and second-grade classrooms for 30 minutes in the afternoon to provide one-on-one or one-on-two help to struggling readers. At Hilltop, teachers also used a collaborative model, but in this case the children who were struggling most in reading left the classroom during the 2½ to 3 hour literacy block to receive small-group instruction for 45 minutes. This small group instruction, delivered to two or three children at a time, was highly compatible with the instruction the children received in their regular classroom.

A common element of all four of these building-wide approaches was the focus on small group instruction. Additionally, in all four of these most effective schools, teachers spent a large amount of time, averaging 134 minutes a day, on reading instruction. In interviews, teachers in three of these schools mentioned that reading was a priority at their school; their time allocation to reading is strong evidence of this commitment.

Early Reading Interventions

The nature of the interventions implemented in the schools in our sample are presented in Table 1.1. The use of interventions was not limited to the most effective schools; in fact the proportion of schools with externally developed interventions does not vary dramatically by level of effectiveness: Most = 3/4; moderate = 4/6, least = 2/4. However, the nature of the interventions and their implementation does vary by level of effectiveness. In the three most effective schools with interventions, they tended to be small group, locally or regionally developed, and implemented across the primary grades; in the moderately or least effective schools, they tended to be one-on-one interventions, either regional or national in origin, and implemented in Grade one only.

Teachers and administrators in the most effective schools felt strongly that the early interventions in place in their buildings were key to their success. In the words of one Hilltop teacher, "Our early intervention makes all the difference in terms of taking care of kids' needs." One Woodlawn teacher puts it this way: "With our early reading intervention kids experience success and look forward to the time [in the intervention] … because of the teacher and the success." Teachers or administrators from the moderately or the least effective schools did not express such enthusiasm or regard for their interventions. Although the sample of schools in this study is limited, the data nonetheless point to reading success in the most effective schools achieved through a combination of regionally (or in the case of 1 school, locally) developed small group interventions set within a homegrown school reform model (see Table 1.1). This stands in contrast to a national push (e.g., the 17 programs listed in the Comprehensive School Reform Demonstration Program legislation; see Herman, 1999) for off-the-shelf reading intervention programs and school reform models (American Federation of Teachers, 1997; Herman & Stringfield, 1997; Slavin & Fashola, 1998; Wang, Haertel, & Walberg, 1998).

Ongoing Professional Development

During interviews, teachers and/or principals in three of the four most effective schools cited a yearlong staff development effort related to their early intervention program as responsible for their success, indicating that it helped them "stay in a learner mode," and "all be of one accord." For example, at Hilltop the teachers took two or three yearlong courses (at the beginner, experienced, or advanced level) on the philosophy of the intervention and the implementation of the strategies within the classroom. Teachers were encouraged to take at least two of the three courses, which met for 2 hours a month during the school year. There was also a time for every class participant to meet with a peer coach for 45 minutes once every 2 weeks.

In addition to the information about professional development related to the early reading interventions, teachers were asked in the survey about preferred approaches to professional development. In three of the most effective schools, a majority of teachers rated "visits to schools with innovative programs followed by sharing of observations with colleagues" as an effective approach to professional development that had been used in their school. Also, in three of the four most effective schools, a majority of teachers rated "district or school sponsored yearlong workshops" or "graduate-level courses" as an effective approach to professional development, which had been used in their school.

Summary of School Factors

Across the four most effective schools in this study, reading was clearly a priority. The teachers and principals considered reading instruction their job and they worked at it. They worked together, worked with parents, and worked with a positive attitude to reach the goal of all children reading well before they left the primary grades. They were able to reach consensus on school-wide monitoring systems, a collaborative approach for delivering reading instruction, and professional development, with the constant goal of improving an already effective reading program.

Instructional Practices Within Levels of School Effectiveness

Multivariate Analysis

To investigate the relationship between school effectiveness and classroom instruction, we initially conducted a multivariate analysis of variance (MANOVA) with the school effectiveness rating serving as the independent variable and eight teacher variables serving as outcome measures (See Table 1.11). To ensure that we were focusing on potentially powerful variables, only those classroom factors that were statistically significantly related to one or more of the measures of student or teacher accomplishment (school effectiveness rating; teacher accomplishment rating; fluency, retelling, or reading words measure) were included in the MANOVA (See Table 1.12). A statistically significant MANOVA, F (14,108) = 2.56, p < .01, led us to conduct follow-up univariate analyses of variance (ANOVAs; see Table 1.11).

Univariate Analysis

Home Communication.   The follow-up ANOVA on home communication was statistically significant, F (2, 65) = 5.25, p < .01. Tukey post hoc tests revealed that the teachers in the most effective schools communicated more with parents/caretakers than teachers in the moderately effective or least effective schools.

Teachers in the most effective schools were more likely to send a letter or newsletter home weekly and call home regularly than teachers in the other schools. Teachers in the most effective schools had a higher mean score on the home linkage scale than teachers in either the moderately or least effective schools. In three of the four most effective schools, more than half of the teachers reported calling home at least once a month. In only one of six moderately effective schools and one of four of the least effective schools did a majority of teachers indicate that they called home as frequently. In one of the most effective schools, teachers made a concerted effort to call home with positive comments, and 51% of parents who were asked said they had received such calls. Looking at both teacher and school factors, the analysis of links to families suggests that personnel in the most effective schools made a more concerted effort than in other schools to reach out to parents.

Student Time On Task.   The univariate ANOVA revealed no statistically significant school effectiveness effect for the student time-on-task rating, F (2, 67) = .82, p > .05, across levels of school effectiveness. As we see later, this re-

TABLE 1.11

ANOVAs on Teacher Factors With School Effectiveness Rating

	F	P	School rating[*]	Mean	SD	n of teachers
Home communication (mean is based on 5-level rating)	5.25	.008	1	3.09	1.22	22
			2	2.95	1.12	27
			3	3.75	1.03	19
			$3 \neq 2 = 1$			
Time on Task (mean is based on 3-level rating)	.82	ns	1	2.18	.73	22
			2	2.24	.74	29
			3	2.4	.84	19
Time in small-group instruction (mean is minutes/day)	9.63	.0002	1	37.94	27.19	20
			2	26.0	20.16	24
			3	59.82	28.46	19
			$3 \neq 2 = 1$			
Time in whole-group instruction (mean is minutes/day)	2.20	ns	1	30.20	18.42	20
			2	36.66	20.93	24
			3	24.86	14.64	19
Time in independent reading (mean is minutes/day)	4.24	.02	1	18.63	9.43	20
			2	27.04	13.30	24
			3	28.14	10.50	19
			$3 \neq 2 = 1$			
Preferred interaction style of coaching	2.32	ns	1	.23	.43	22
			2	.21	.41	29
			3	.47	.51	19
Preferred interaction style of telling	2.01	ns	1	.41	.50	22
			2	.41	.50	29
			3	.16	.37	19
Preferred interaction style of recitation	.17	ns	1	.32	.48	22
			2	.34	.48	29
			3	.26	.45	19
				.27	13.3	

Note. [*]1 = least effective, 2 = moderately effective, 3 = most effective.

TABLE 1.12

Correlations for School Rating, Teacher Rating, Reading Growth Scores, and Teacher Factors

	School rating	Teacher rating	Z-score resid. Fluency (class mean)	Z-score resid. Retelling (class mean)	Z-score resid. Words (class mean)
Teacher rating	.23		.27	.10	.18
	$p = .05$		$p < .001$	ns	ns
	$n = 71$		$n = 69$	$n = 69$	$n = 69$
Home communication	.26	.27	.06	.25	−.09
	$p = .03$	$p = .02$	ns	.04	ns
	$n = 68$	$n = 68$	$n = 66$	$n = 66$	$n = 66$
Time on task	.14	.79	.21	.17	.18
	ns	$p < .001$	ns	ns	ns
	$n = 70$	$n = 70$	$n = 68$	$n = 68$	$n = 68$
Time spent in small-group instruction	.30	.31	.41	.10	.22
	$p = .02$	$p = .02$	$p < .01$	ns	ns
	$n = 63$	$n = 63$	$n = 61$	$n = 61$	$n = 61$
Time spent in whole-group instruction	−.11	−.41	−.03	−.22	.06
	ns	$p < .01$	ns	ns	ns
	$n = 63$	$n = 63$	$n = 61$	$n = 61$	$n = 61$
Time spent in independent reading	.32	.10	.33	−.11	.20
	$p = .01$	ns	$p < .01$	ns	ns
	$n = 63$	$n = 63$	$n = 61$	$n = 61$	$n = 61$
Preferred tchg. Style – coaching/scaff.	.20	.40	.07	−.18	−.03
	ns	$p < .01$	ns	ns	ns
	$n = 70$	$n = 70$	$n = 68$	$n = 68$	$n = 68$
Preferred tchg. Style – telling information	−.20	−.53	−.27	−.14	−.01
	ns	$p < .01$	$p = .03$	ns	ns
	$n = 70$	$n = 70$	$n = 70$	$n = 70$	$n = 70$
Preferred teaching style – recitation	−.04	.04	.18	.24	.07
	ns	ns	ns	$p = .05$	ns
	$n = 70$	$n = 70$	$n = 68$	$n = 69$	$n = 68$

	School rating	Teacher rating	Z-score resid. Fluency (class mean)	Z-score resid. Retelling (class mean)	Z-score resid. Words (class mean)
Time spent wrtg. In resp. To reading	−.13	.03	−.18	.03	.01
	ns	ns	ns	ns	ns
	n = 63	n = 63	n = 61	n = 61	n = 61
Time spent reading aloud	.17	.14	.19	−.07	.14
	ns	ns	ns	ns	ns
	n = 63	n = 63	n = 61	n = 61	n = 61

sult is to be contrasted with the finding for levels of teacher accomplishment (when teachers who exhibit accomplished characteristics are considered independently of the school in which they work).

Time Spent in Small- and Whole-Group Instruction. The ANOVA on time in small-group instruction revealed a statistically significant effect for level of school effectiveness, $F(2, 60) = 9.63, p < .001$. Tukey post hoc tests revealed that students of teachers in the most effective schools spent more time daily in small-group instruction ($M = 59.02$ minutes per day) than students of teachers in the moderately effective schools ($M = 26.10$ mpd) or the least effective schools ($M = 37.94$ mpd). The one way ANOVA for school effectiveness rating on time spent in whole-group instruction was not statistically significant, $F(2, 60) = 2.20, p > .05$. However, even the students in the most effective schools, who were spending an hour a day in small groups, were in whole-class instructional activities across an average of 25 minutes per day.

In addition to differences in the amount of time spent in small-group instruction by school effectiveness, the ratio of small- to whole-group instruction is important to consider. In each of Grades 1, 2, and 3, children in the most effective schools spent more time in small-group than in whole-group instruction. In Grades 1 and 2, the small group/large group ratio was 2/1 (see Table 1.13).

When asked on the survey to select the four most important factors for improving struggling readers' achievement, 83% of the teachers in the four most effective schools selected small group instruction as an important factor. Additionally, in two of the schools, teachers mentioned the focus on small group instruction as a factor contributing to their success. "Small, flexible groups at students' instructional level are important. They need to be coached at their instructional level" contended a Hilltop teacher. Comments about the virtues of small-group instruction were commonly heard in the interviews at the most effective schools, such as those by a Woodlawn teacher—"Small groups or one-on-one every day really makes a difference"—and a Wheeler teacher—"Small groups are crucial. Children are more likely to succeed when they are in two groups of six with two teachers than when there are 12 children with one teacher."

In all of the most effective schools, the basis for forming the small groups was perceived ability, an observation that suggests that these teachers were more concerned about meeting students at their instructional level than they were about any damage to children's self-worth that might accrue from being a part of a group socially and personally sanctioned as the low group. Even so, the teachers in the most effective schools were very aware of the need to make sure that the groups were flexible, that students moved to another group when their performance (as measured by their internal school-based monitoring system) merited movement. The importance of school-wide monitoring cannot be underestimated in this regard. These data provided teachers with regular, recurring opportunities to reflect on the validity of their instructional groupings and modify membership accordingly. The principal at Stevenson talked about a mental change that occurred when her school became a school-wide Title I building. Teachers began to talk more about children's needs during the year and made changes in students' reading group placement. "A reading group was no longer a yearlong placement for children, particularly for the lowest children." At Woodlawn, teachers also voiced commitment to the idea of flexible instructional level groups. They used running records and periodic measures of words read correctly in 1 minute to move children to a higher group whenever they could. Furthermore, in three of the four most effective schools, early reading interventions were in place across the primary grades to provide high-quality, special assistance to children who were struggling to learn to read. Recall also that in these most effective schools, students also averaged 25 minutes a day of whole-group instruction in which they were interacting across ability levels.

Time Spent in Independent Reading. The ANOVA on time spent in independent reading was statistically significant, $F (2, 60) = 4.24, p < .05$. Tukey post hoc tests revealed that students in the most effective schools ($M = 28.14$ minutes per day) and moderately effective schools ($M = 27.04$ mpd) spent more time in independent reading than students in the least effective schools ($M = 18.63$ mpd).

TABLE 1.13

Mean Time in Instruction (and Standard Deviation) by Grade Level and School Rating

	School rating*	n**	1 Time in whole group rdg. instr.	2 Time in small group rdg. instr.	3 Time in indep. activity	4 Indep. reading	5 Writing in response to reading	6*** Total time in reading
Grade 1	1	7	19.27 (20.39)	47.30 (22.09)	4.69 (7.78)	15.30 (10.08)	18.07 (11.97)	104.16 (21.73)
	2	7	29.06 (17.78)	28.56 (22.20)	12.43 (20.74)	28.66 (14.92)	17.14 (13.46)	115.84 (49.20)
	3	8	23.05 (15.51)	66.96 (38.50)	11.68 (12.54)	27.79 (7.04)	17.44 (11.13)	146.91 (35.46)
	Grade Mean	23	23.76 (17.48)	48.49 (32.21)	9.69 (14.32)	24.09 (12.13)	17.55 (11.58)	123.57 (39.91)
Grade 2	1	8	29.05 (8.91)	38.23 (32.16)	13.15 (16.95)	18.11 (9.36)	19.65 (7.72)	118.19 (20.65)
	2	7	30.54 (22.86)	37.20 (22.59)	11.33 (7.82)	21.99 (11.85)	9.21 (9.91)	110.27 (34.79)
	3	7	23.93 (8.58)	58.50 (21.68)	4.17 (4.62)	29.66 (12.11)	13.19 (6.47)	139.49 (25.80)
	Grade Mean	22	27.90 (14.37)	44.35 (26.89)	9.71 (11.67)	23.02 (11.64)	14.25 (8.93)	119.25 (27.26)

TABLE 1.13 (continued)

Mean Time in Instruction (and Standard Deviation) by Grade Level and School Rating

School rating*	n**	1 Time in whole group rdg. instr.	2 Time in small group rdg. instr.	3 Time in indep. activity	4 Indep. reading	5 Writing in response to reading	6*** Total time in reading
Grade 3							
1	5	47.34	24.38	8.14	24.10	13.98	117.94
		(16.41)	(24.23)	(8.31)	(7.67)	(13.27)	(19.70)
2	10	46.27	16.61	3.37	29.44	16.40	112.09
		(19.58)	(13.02)	(4.74)	(13.47)	(11.79)	(33.88)
3	4	30.15	47.85	3.75	26.20	9.70	117.65
		(22.99)	(11.42)	(7.50)	(15.55)	(4.89)	(46.76)
Grade Mean	19	43.16	25.23	4.71	27.35	14.35	114.80
		(19.68)	(19.80)	(6.36)	(12.24)	(10.94)	(32.08)
****School rating 1 (Least)	20	30.20	37.94	8.94	18.63	17.68	113.38
		(18.42)	(27.19)	(12.40)	(9.43)	(10.47)	(20.68)
****School rating 2	24	36.66	26.10	8.33	27.04	14.52	112.66
		(20.93)	(20.16)	(12.47)	(13.30)	(11.81)	(37.44)
****School rating 3 (Most)	19	24.86	59.82	7.24	28.14	14.24	134.34
		(14.64)	(28.46)	(9.63)	(10.50)	(8.70)	(34.88)

School rating[*]	n[**]	1 Time in whole group rdg. instr.	2 Time in small group rdg. instr.	3 Time in indep. activity	4 Indep. reading	5 Writing in response to reading	6[***] Total time in reading
Mean across teachers		31.05 (18.78)	40.03 (28.40)	8.20 (11.50)	24.7 (11.94)	15.44 (10.47)	119.42 (33.19)

Note. [*]1 = least effective, 2 = moderately effective, 3 = most effective.
[**]Number of teachers
[***]Sum of columns 1–5
[****]Pooled across grades.

In three of the most effective schools, teachers mentioned providing time for students to read authentic texts as a factor contributing to their school's success. "I give my students lots of time to engage in reading/writing opportunities. Lots of opportunities to read all kinds of texts," explained a Hilltop teacher. Or, as a Woodlawn teacher put it, "You become a better reader by reading. My students read at least 20–30 minutes a day. Also, partner reading—they love it." "Everyone in the whole school is taking books home at night for reading. It's one of our school improvement goals," pointed out another Hilltop teacher. These findings complement earlier research documenting that time spent in independent reading in school does make a difference in students' reading achievement (Anderson, Wilson, & Fielding, 1988; Elley & Mangubhi, 1983; Taylor, Frye, & Maruyama, 1990).

Reading as a Priority.   When one looks across time spent in a variety of categories that fall roughly under the general rubric of reading instruction—whole-group instruction, small-group instruction, independent (seatwork) activities, independent reading, and writing in response to reading—the averages across levels of school effectiveness were: most effective— 134 minutes; moderately effective—113 minutes; and least effective—113 minutes. Across the four most effective schools, teachers were averaging 134 minutes a day on reading activities. Eighty-five minutes of this was either small-group or whole-group instruction, and almost 30 minutes of the total was independent reading. These times, based on teachers' logs from two different weeks, do not include time spent reading aloud to children, time spent in composition (in contrast to writing in response to reading), and time spent in spelling. The amount of time devoted to reading activities indicates that reading was an "operational" priority in the schools as a whole as well as in the classrooms of the teachers in the most effective schools. In the words of one teacher at Stevenson, "My advice to other schools is let kids READ, READ, READ! WRITE, WRITE, WRITE! THINK, THINK, THINK!"

Preferred Interaction Style.   While the trends were provocative, with half the teachers in the most effective schools preferring coaching compared to about a quarter of teachers in the moderately and least effective schools, the ANOVAs on preferred interaction styles by school effectiveness level were not statistically significant—coaching, $F(2, 67) = 2.32, p > .05$; telling, $F(2, 67) = 2.01, p > .05$; or recitation, $F(2, 67) = .17$ (see Table 1.11).

Supplementary Analyses of Reading Specific Teaching Strategies

In addition to the question of the use and impact of more generic teaching practices, we were able to apply nonparametric analyses to two additional reading-specific teaching domains—word recognition and comprehension instruction. In the case of word recognition, we were limited to Grades 1 and 2 because of the paucity of word recognition instruction observed in Grade 3.

Approach to Word Recognition.   Chi square tests revealed that in comparison to the moderately effective schools ($\chi^2 = 5.0$, $p < .05$) and least effective schools ($\chi^2 = 5.4$, $p < .05$), more Grade 1 and 2 teachers in the most effective schools were frequently observed coaching in the use of word recognition strategies as children were reading to teach word recognition. More teachers in the most effective ($\chi^2 = 5.5$), and least effective schools ($\chi^2 = 8.5$), were frequently observed practicing sight words than teachers in the moderately effective schools. There were no differences in the incidence of teachers in Grades 1 and 2 who provided explicit phonics instruction (e.g., focusing on letter-sound correspondences or word families on the board, on a work sheet, or with letter cards) across the three types of schools (see Table 1.14).

In third grade, very little word recognition instruction was observed anywhere. In one most effective school, third-grade teachers provided small-group instruction to struggling readers in which they coached them to decode multisyllabic words as they were reading. In another most effective school and in one moderately effective school, struggling third-grade readers received small-group instruction from resource teachers who used a combination of coaching while reading and work on word families to teach word recognition. In one most effective school and three moderately effec-

TABLE 1.14

Approaches to Word Recognition Instruction: Frequency of Teachers
in Grades 1 and 2 (by School Effectiveness Rating) Frequently Observed
Using a Particular Strategy

		Coaching in word recognition strategies during reading	*Providing explicit phonics instruction*	*Practicing sight words*
School rating*	1	2/15 (13%)	9/15 (60%)	6/15 (49%)
	2	3/18 (17%)	11/18 (61%)	0/18
	3	8/15 (53%)	9/15 (60%)	4/15 (27%)
		$3 > 2, \chi^2 = 5.0, p < .05$		$3 > 2, \chi^2 = 5.5, p < .05$
		$3 > 1, \chi^2 = 5.4, p < .05$		$1 > 2, \chi^2 = 8.5\ p < .05$

Note. *1 = least effective, 2 = moderately effective, 3 = most effective.

tive schools, third graders continued to do word study as a subject separate from reading.

Although not universal across all teachers, there was a definite trend in the most effective schools for Grade 1 and 2 teachers to combine (a) explicit phonics instruction in isolation with (b) coaching students to use a range of strategies to figure out unknown words when they encounter them in everyday reading. In contrast, the teachers in the moderately effective schools primarily provided explicit phonics instruction, with only a few adding the coaching component. In the least effective schools, teachers primarily provided explicit phonics instruction, with about half adding practice on sight words.

When asked about reasons for their success, teachers in two of the most effective schools mentioned the importance of teaching students strategies, not skills, as a factor contributing to their success. As one Hilltop teacher put it, "I focus on strategies rather than specific skills—metacognitive strategies, demonstrations, how to do think-alouds. I am process oriented so kids become independent rather than reliant on the teacher." This sentiment was echoed by a Woodside teacher, "You're not going to improve as a teacher if you don't get into teaching strategies. I teach my students strategies to become independent."

Approach to Comprehension Instruction.   Chi square tests revealed that more teachers in the most effective schools were frequently observed asking higher-level questions about stories students had read than teachers in moderately effective (2 of 29, $\chi^2 = 9.1$, $p < .01$) or least effective (0 of 22, $\chi^2 = 9.8$, $p < .01$) schools (see Table 1.15). That said, we must reiterate the overall low rate of these more cognitively challenging activities in the overall sample.

Word recognition work and reading practice were much more the focus of reading instruction in Grades 1 through 2 across all schools in this study than was comprehension. Explicit instruction in comprehension strategies was seldom witnessed across Grades 1 through 3. Discussions that stretched children's thinking were also infrequent across Grades 1 through 3.

The Relationship of Instructional Practice to Teacher Accomplishment

The analyses of instructional practices within levels of school effectiveness document the fact that, on average, teachers within effective schools operated differently than did teachers in other schools. These average differences, however, masked instructional variation among teachers within schools. Not all of the best teachers worked in the most effective schools. In fact, only 52% of the teachers in

TABLE 1.15

Approaches to Comprehension Instruction: Frequency of Teachers (by School
Effectiveness Rating) Frequently Observed Using a Particular Technique

		Asking text-based questions	Asking higher level questions	Having students write in response to reading
School rating*	1	10/22 (45%)	0/22	6/22 (27%)
	2	10/29 (34%)	2/29 (7%)	7/29 (24%)
	3	7/19 (37%)	7/19 (37%)	9/19 (47%)
			$3 > 2, \chi2 = 9.1, p < .01$	
			$3 > 1, \chi2 = 9.8, p < .01$	

Note.   *1 = least effective, 2 = moderately effective, 3 = most effective.

Grades 1 through 3 in the most effective schools were perceived from the observations to be most accomplished teachers (as compared to 36% in the least effective schools and 34% in the moderately effective schools). In order to gain additional insight into other factors that might lead to explanations of how to nurture teaching strategies that promote student learning, we undertook an analysis of instructional practices that was independent of student achievement. Instead, we used the ratings assigned to teachers on the effective instruction scale to classify teachers into three levels of accomplishment (most, moderately, and least); these levels were used as predictor variables to explain variations in the instructional practices used by teachers (see Table 1.6).

To investigate the relationships among the various indicators of teacher expertise and classroom practices, we subjected this large set of teacher variables to a MANOVA. We used three levels of the teacher accomplishment rating (most, moderately, and least accomplished) as the independent variable and eight scores from the set of generic teaching practices derived from our empirical data (time spent in small-group instruction, time spent in whole-group instruction, time spent in independent reading, student engagement rating, home communication rating, preferred style of telling, preferred style of recitation, and preferred style of coaching) as the set of dependent measures. The MANOVA was statistically significant, $F (14, 108) = 10.77, p < .001$, thus follow-up univariate ANOVAs were conducted (see Table 1.16).

Communicating to Parents.   The ANOVA on level of home communication was not statistically significant, $F (2, 65) = 2.40, p > .05$. That is, no differ-

TABLE 1.16
ANOVAs on Teacher Factors With Teacher Rating

	F	P	Teacher rating	Mean	SD	n of teachers
Home communication (mean is based on 5-level rating)	2.4	ns	1	2.88	1.22	17
			2	3.23	1.23	23
			3	3.64	1.03	28
Time on task (mean is based on 3-level rating)	85.41	<.001	1	1.29	.47	17
			2	2.21	.51	23
			3	2.93	.26	29
			(3≠2 (1)			
Time in small-group instruction (mean is minutes/day)	3.08	.05	1	25.35	26.09	13
			2	38.67	33.00	23
			3	48.25	21.51	27
			(3≠1)			
Time in whole-group instruction (mean is minutes/day)	8.66	<.01	1	47.94	18.38	13
			2	28.98	17.12	23
			3	24.69	15.78	27
			(3=2≠1)			

	F	P	Teacher rating	Mean	SD	n of teachers
Time in independent reading (mean is minutes/day)	.87	ns	1	23.97	11.77	13
			2	22.51	10.98	23
			3	26.92	12.81	27
Preferred interaction Style of coaching	5.92	<.01	1	.06	.24	17
			2	.21	.41	24
			3	.48	.51	29
			$(3 \neq 2 = 1)$			
Preferred interaction style of telling	16.60	<.001	1	.745	.440	17
			2	.375	.491	24
			3	.069	.258	29
			$(3 \neq 2 \neq 1)$			
Preferred interaction style of recitation	1.00	ns	1	.18	.39	17
			2	.38	.49	24
			3	.34	.48	29

ences were observed in the frequency with which teachers of different levels of accomplishment communicated with students' parents or guardians. Recall that this factor was statistically significant in both school-level analyses; that is, most effective schools had higher composite school ratings and teachers in the most effective schools had higher ratings on the same home communication scale. The differences between the school-level and the accomplishment analyses suggest either that the most accomplished teachers are not necessarily the best communicators or that teacher effects are moderated by a school-level ethic for this type of activity.

Student Time on Task. The ANOVA for the student time on task rating was statistically significant, F (2, 67) = 85.41, p < .001. Tukey post hoc tests revealed that the most accomplished teachers had a higher rating for maintaining student on-task behavior (M = 2.93 out of a possible 3) than the moderately accomplished teachers (M = 2.21), who, in turn, had a higher mean score than the least accomplished teachers (M = 1.31).

To shed more light on this teacher factor, in six of our sites, we were able conduct a special analysis to learn more about the impact of the student time on task variable, using a procedure first used by Pressley et al. (2001). During the last two observations, observers were asked to interrupt their normal observational protocol every 5 minutes, scan the room quickly, and record the proportion of children in the class who were perceived to be on task (i.e., productively engaged in their assigned activity). Grade 1 through 3 teachers rated as most accomplished were found to have an average of 96% of their students on task when the 5-minute counts of students on task were taken. By contrast, the time on task rates were 84% and 61%, respectively, for the moderately accomplished and least accomplished teachers. Because these numbers are based on only 30 teachers and 60 observations, they should be interpreted cautiously. Even so, they underscore the importance of student time on task as a key curricular and management concern for teachers as they implement reading programs in their classrooms. The findings suggest that, unlike a variable such as parent communication, wherein individual teacher practices appear to be moderated by school-level efforts, promoting high levels of student on-task behavior is a teaching practice not easily influenced by school-level practice. Instead of putting a school-level practice in place (e.g., calling home monthly), an individual teacher must develop the disposition as well as the curriculum, instruction, and interaction tools required to keep students on task.

Grouping Practices. The ANOVA on time spent in whole group, F (2, 60) = 8.66, p < .01, indicated that students with teachers rated as least accomplished spent more time in whole-group instruction (M = 47.94 minutes per day) than teachers rated as moderately accomplished (M = 28.98 mpd) or teachers rated as most accomplished (M = 24.69 mpd). A two-way (teacher accomplishment by grade) ANOVA showed a statistically significant effect for grade level, F (2, 54) = 7.90, p < .01, with a strong tendency for whole-group time allocations to increase with grade level, but no statistically significant grade by teacher accomplishment interaction. Means and standard deviations by grade level and teacher rating are shown in Table 1.17.

The ANOVA on time spent in small-group instruction revealed an effect for level of teacher accomplishment, F (2, 60) = 3.08, p = .05, with students in the classrooms of teachers rated as most accomplished spending more time in small-group instruction (M = 48.25 minutes per day) than students with teachers rated as moderately accomplished (M = 38.67 mpd), who, in turn, spent more time than students with teachers rated as least accomplished (M = 25.35 mpd).

The ANOVA on time spent on independent reading indicated no statistically significant differences between teachers at different levels of accomplishment. Students averaged from 23 to 27 minutes a day in independent reading across all conditions of teacher accomplishment. This finding is at variance with the parallel analysis for teachers in the most effective schools, where reliable school effectiveness differences emerged for independent reading. As with the parent outreach finding, it suggests that teacher practices for independent reading may have been moderated by school level initiatives, interactions, and/or philosophies.

Interaction Styles. The ANOVA on preferred interaction style of coaching and teacher accomplishment was statistically significant, F (2, 67) = 5.92, p < .01. Tukey post hoc tests revealed that more of the most accomplished teachers had a preferred interaction style of coaching (48%) than the moderately (21%) or least accomplished teachers (2%; see Table 1.18 for a complete presentation of the interaction preferences).

The ANOVA on preferred interaction style of telling (see Table 1.18) was statistically significant, F (2, 67) = 16.60, p < .001. Tukey post hoc tests revealed that more least accomplished teachers (75%) preferred telling than moderately accomplished teachers (38%), who, in turn exceeded the most accomplished teachers (7%). There were also more moderately accomplished teachers with a preferred interaction style of telling than teachers rated as most accomplished (the ANOVA on preferred interaction style of recitation and teacher accomplishment was not statistically significant). The data on coaching and telling may well be two sides of the same coin. Although our ob-

TABLE 1.17

Mean Time in Instruction (and Standard Deviation) by Grade Level and Teacher Rating

	Teacher rating*	n**	1 Time in whole group	2 Time in small group	3 Time in indep. Act. (Excldg. #'S 4 and 5)	4 Indep. reading	5 Writing in response to reading	6*** Total time in reading
Grade 1	1	3	50.00 (3.06)	32.83 (35.92)	15.4 (5.70)	15.97 (10.06)	25.70 (11.29)	123.70 (38.78)
	2	7	23.53 (15.71)	49.17 (47.98)	10.34 (4.23)	23.44 (13.28)	9.87 (7.61)	116.36 (48.02)
	3	12	17.33 (14.64)	52.00 (20.24)	7.88 (11.27)	26.50 (11.90)	19.98 (11.80)	139.90 (30.90)
	Grade Mean	22	23.76 (17.48)	48.49 (32.21)	9.69 (14.32)	24.09 (12.13)	17.55 (11.58)	123.57 (39.91)
Grade 2	1	6	36.45 (18.09)	28.25 (27.46)	9.05 (10.67)	20.95 (10.75)	14.25 (10.09)	108.95 (22.17)
	2	7	26.79 (13.12)	47.34 (29.00)	45.60 (16.55)	21.19 (11.42)	16.76 (7.58)	127.14 (24.67)
	3	9	23.06 (11.05)	52.78 (22.66)	5.58 (5.26)	25.82 (13.06)	12.74 (9.83)	119.98 (32.37)

	Grade[*]	n[**]	1	2	3	4	5	Sum[***]
Grade 2		22	27.90 (14.37)	44.35 (26.89)	9.71 (11.67)	23.02 (11.64)	14.25 (8.93)	119.25 (27.26)
Grade 3	1	4	63.63 (14.25)	15.38 (20.05)	10.03 (8.84)	34.50 (7.98)	16.80 (8.52)	140.33 (26.60)
	2	9	34.93 (20.53)	23.79 (19.85)	3.30 (4.86)	22.81 (9.95)	9.81 (5.08)	94.65 (23.47)
	3	6	41.85 (11.80)	33.97 (19.16)	3.27 (5.69)	25.40 (16.11)	19.53 (16.50)	128.02 (30.62)
	Grade Mean	19	43.16 (19.68)	25.23 (19.80)	4.71 (6.36)	27.35 (12.24)	14.35 (10.94)	114.80 (32.08)
Teacher rating 1[****]		13	47.94 (18.38)	25.35 (26.05)	10.82 (8.91)	23.97 (11.77)	17.68 (10.20)	125.75 (28.33)
Teacher rating 2[****]		23	28.98 (17.12)	38.67 (33.91)	9.15 (15.30)	22.51 (10.98)	11.79 (7.07)	111.14 (34.59)
Teacher rating 3[****]		27	24.65 (15.78)	48.25 (21.51)	6.09 (8.48)	26.92 (12.81)	17.47 (17.35)	123.42 (33.87)
Mean across teachers			31.05 (18.78)	40.03 (28.40)	8.20 (11.50)	24.70 (11.94)	15.44 (10.47)	119.42 (33.19)

Note. [*]1 = least accomplished, 2 = moderately accomplished, 3 = most accomplished.
[**]Number of teachers.
[***]Sum of columns 1–5
[****]Pooled across grades.

TABLE 1.18

The Relationship Between Teacher Accomplishment
and Preferred Style of Interaction

	Teacher Rating		
	Least accomplished	*Moderately accomplished*	*Most accomplished*
	Preference for coaching		
Yes	1 (6%)	5 (21%)	14 (48%)
No	16	19	15
Total	17	24	29
	Preference for telling		
Yes	13 (75%)	9 (38%)	2 (7%)
No	4	15	27
Total	17	24	29
	Preference for recitation		
Yes	3 (18%)	9 (38%)	10 (34%)
No	14	15	19
Total	17	24	29

servation system allowed for the possibility that a teacher could receive both codes within a given 5-minute observational block, we nevertheless found that for individual teachers, the one seems to be an alternative to the other. Furthermore, preferred styles of coaching and telling can be predicted by teacher accomplishment.

In contrast to statistically nonsignificant differences for teachers-within-levels of school effectiveness, these statistically significant differences among teachers across schools suggest that a teacher's preferred style of interacting with students is a teaching dimension that is less well influenced by the practice of others at the school level than other dimensions of teaching being investigated in our study such as time spent by students in independent reading or degree of home communication. As with high levels of student on-task behavior, a preferred style of coaching during reading instruction may be a teaching skill which, to develop, requires time and/or support from more accomplished teachers.

Approaches to Word Recognition Instruction.   Of the 22 teachers in Grades 1 and 2 who were rated high on the composite teacher accomplishment rating, 10 (45%) were frequently observed coaching children on how to use different word recognition strategies to figure out unknown words while they were reading connected text. By contrast, of the 15 moderately accomplished teachers in Grades 1 and 2, 3 (20%) were observed frequently coaching children as they were reading. Of the 11 teachers perceived as least accomplished, none was frequently observed using the coaching-while-reading strategy to teach word recognition. Chi square tests confirmed the fact that these differences were statistically significant.

Chi square tests revealed no systematic relationship between teacher accomplishment and explicit phonics instruction. In fact, a majority of teachers in both Grades 1 and 2 and across the three levels of accomplishment were frequently observed providing explicit phonics instruction.

A chi square test indicated that compared to teachers identified as moderately accomplished, more teachers identified as most accomplished were frequently observed engaging students in sight word practice.

What emerges is a pattern in which the most accomplished teachers demonstrate a more balanced portfolio of approaches to assist in word identification (i.e., more of them do a little of each practice) and are, by and large, the only group of teachers across levels of teacher accomplishment who demonstrate the ability to help students apply the alphabetic principle to everyday reading tasks.

Comprehension Instruction.   Across all schools, comprehension instruction was minimal in Grades 1 through 3. Primary modes of working on compre-

TABLE 1.19

Approaches to Word Recognition Instruction: Frequency of Teachers (by Teacher Accomplishment Rating) Frequently Observed Using a Particular Strategy in Grade 1 or 2

		Coaching on word recognition strategies during reading	Providing explicit phonics instruction	Practicing sight words
Teacher accomplishment rating*	1	0/11	5/11 (45%)	1/11 (9%)
	2	3/5 (20%)	11/15 (73%)	1/15 (7%)
	3	10/22 (45%)	13/22 (59%)	8/22 (36%)
		$3 > 1, \chi^2 = 7.17$, $p < .05$		$3 > 2, \chi^2 = 4.27$, $p < .05$

Note. *1 = least accomplished, 2 = moderately accomplished, 3 = most accomplished.

hension included asking questions (many of which were literal) about the story as children were reading, either in small groups or in a whole class setting, and having children write in response to stories they had read. This writing was most typically in the form of a journal entry or answers to written questions. Twenty-nine of 70 teachers were frequently observed asking text-based questions, and 27 were frequently observed having children write in response to what they had read. Only 11 of 70 teachers were seen frequently asking higher-level questions about children's feelings or about their lives in relation to a story they had read. Only 5 teachers were frequently observed providing instruction (not including worksheet completion) about a comprehension skill or strategy (see Table 1.20.)

Nonetheless, when looking at teachers across the three levels of teacher accomplishment, chi square tests revealed that these practices were not randomly distributed. Compared to least accomplished teachers (0%), more most accomplished teachers (31%) were frequently observed asking higher-level questions and having students write in response to reading, where the difference was 17% versus 48%. The most accomplished teachers also differed from the moderately accomplished teachers on the higher order scale. Chi square tests for text-based questions were not statistically significant (see Table 1.21). Another way to examine these data is to suggest that the most accomplished teachers were more

TABLE 1.20

Number of Grade 1–3 Teachers (Out of 70) Observed Using a Particular Comprehension Technique

	Frequently observed	Occasionally observed
Doing a picture walk	5	9
Asking for a prediction	6	20
Asking text-based questions	29	22
Asking higher level, aesthetic response questions	11	16
Having children write in response to reading	27	26
Doing a story map	2	16
Having children retell a story	2	20
Working on a comprehension skill or strategy	5	22

balanced in their employment of comprehension fostering activities; they tended to emphasize some of each of these three common strategies, whereas the other two levels of teachers tended to omit at least one of the categories. In the bigger picture, however, what we found in comprehension instruction is disconcerting, with only 16% of the teachers in Grades 1 through 3 in this study were frequently observed asking higher level, aesthetic response questions.

OVERALL DISCUSSION

One contribution of the current study is that it focused on classrooms as well as schools to get a richer picture of what was happening in schools that excel in promoting growth in reading among its students. Because we have already discussed the findings of this complex study as they were presented, the primary role of the overall discussion is to revisit key findings with an emphasis on connections among classroom-level and school-level factors. We also contextualize our work within the long-standing effective schools and effective teaching traditions, confess our limitations, and provide a few broad conclusions.

Revisiting Key Findings

Small-Group Instruction

Our finding that time spent in small-group instruction characterized the most accomplished teachers and the teachers in our most effective schools

TABLE 1.21

Approaches to Comprehension Instruction: Frequency of Teachers (by Teacher Accomplishment Rating) Frequently Observed Using a Particular Strategy

		Text-based oral questions	Higher-level (aesthetic response) oral questions	Students write In response to reading
Teacher accomplishment rating[*]	1	4/17 (24%)	0/17	3/17 (18%)
	2	11/24 (46%)	2/24 (8%)	10/24 (42%)
	3	14/29 (48%)	9/29 (31%)	14/29 (48%)
			$3 > 1, \chi^2 = 6.56, p < .05$	$3 > 1, \chi^2 = 4.32, p < .05$
			$3 > 2, \chi^2 = 4.11, p < .05$	

Note. [*]1 = least accomplished, 2 = moderately accomplished, 3 = most accomplished.

hearkens back to important findings in the process–product work of the 1970s (e.g., Anderson et al., 1979; Stallings & Kaskowitz, 1974). The advantage of our most effective schools in providing small-group time is a prime example of how classroom-level and school-level variables interact to produce a desirable outcome. The greater time allotted for small-group instruction did not just happen. It was made possible by the collaborative model used in all four of the most effective schools. In that collaborative model, the classroom teacher, a resource teacher, an ESL teacher, and/or a special education teacher worked together, often simultaneously in a single classroom, to enable every child, but especially those most in need of extra help, to have two blocks of small-group instruction.

Although ability-grouped instruction has been criticized in the past because it has been found to doom struggling readers to a lifetime in these low groups (Anderson, Hiebert, Scott, & Wilkinson, 1985; Barr & Dreeban, 1991; Gamoran, 1992; Hiebert, 1983; Oakes, 1985) and a persistently unambitious curriculum (Allington, 1983; Hiebert, 1983), it is important to remind ourselves of how teachers perceived and implemented grouping in these effective schools. First, teachers in interviews talked about the importance of *instructional level grouping* (a term they preferred to *ability grouping*) to meet students' needs. Second, teachers used systematic assessment to prevent the groups from being rigid and inflexible, shifting group membership on a regular basis. Besides establishing another layer of cultural barriers among students, the other major detriment of grouping is the differential nature of instruction accorded to different ability groups (see Allington, 1983). Although differential treatment of different groups was not an explicit focus in our observations and teacher logs, our data that indicate this did not occur in the four most effective schools. To the contrary, students in the lower instructional level groups spent as much time on higher-order activities as did average achievers. Also, the teachers felt that it was necessary to make sure that most students spent most of their time interacting with books that were within their grasp (i.e., at their instructional level). It is important to note that this practice is another example of the interaction of school and classroom variables. In this case, two school level factors, a common assessment system that enabled flexible movement between groups, and a collaborative model that enabled flexible deployment of teaching personnel, combined to allow teachers to maximize small group instruction, a classroom level factor.

Coaching

Although different terms have been used to describe what we have called coaching (e.g., use of structuring comments, probing of incorrect responses, scaffolded instruction), others have found this type of "on the fly" instruction to be a characteristic of effective teachers (Anderson et al., 1979; Brophy, 1973; Rosenshine & Furst, 1973; Wharton-MacDonald et al., 1998). Our most accomplished teachers exhibited a "general" preference for coaching over telling or recitation, whereas the least accomplished teachers engaged more commonly in telling. Although a coaching preference did not emerge as a general difference among teachers across school effectiveness ratings, we did find the practice of coaching during reading to provide word recognition instruction to be characteristic of both the most effective schools and the most accomplished teachers. Perhaps coaching for word recognition instruction during children's reading of text is a place for teachers to begin to develop the more general ability to coach.

Phonics, Yes, but Phonics and ...

The importance of systematic phonics instruction in learning to read has been repeatedly documented (Adams, 1990; Bond & Dykstra, 1967; Chall, 1967; Snow et al., 1998), as has the need for phonics to be developed in conjunction with real reading and writing (Adams, 1990). Wharton-MacDonald et al. (1998) found that the most effective first-grade teachers in their study taught decoding skills explicitly and provided their students with many opportunities to engage in authentic reading. However, systematic phonic instruction in isolation only, along with sheer opportunity to practice through reading connected text, may not be the optimal path toward a rich repertoire of word recognition strategies. Our data suggest that it is what teachers do to promote application of phonics knowledge during the reading of connected text that matters most. A majority of teachers in Grades 1 and 2 across all schools taught phonics explicitly, in isolation. What distinguished the most accomplished teachers and the majority of teachers in the most effective schools from their peers was their use of coaching to help students learn how to apply word recognition strategies to real reading. Although more research is needed to unpack the specifics of these coaching and application strategies, our results suggest that conversations about systematic phonics instruction and opportunity to practice need to be broadened to include on the job coaching during everyday reading.

Higher-Level Questions

In the present study, we found that more of the most accomplished teachers and teachers in the most effective schools frequently encouraged higher-level responses to text than less accomplished teachers or teachers in the moderately and least effective schools. These findings lend support to earlier research (Knapp, 1995; Puma et al, 1997; Rosenshine & Furst, 1973) documenting the benefit of combining higher-level and more basic-skill instruction. These encouraging differences notwithstanding, we must also remind ourselves that only 16% of the teachers in the entire sample could be considered to truly emphasize comprehension.

BALANCED INSTRUCTION

We did not set out to examine the degree to which the most accomplished teachers or the teachers in the most effective schools engaged in what has come to be called balanced reading instruction (McIntyre & Pressley, 1996; Gambrell, Morrow, Newman, & Pressley, 1999). Nonetheless, it is not difficult to describe our findings within a balanced instructional framework. On several dimensions—variable grouping patterns, support for reading (e.g., guided or independent), approaches to word recognition instruction, modes of interacting with students, practices to support text comprehension, the most accomplished teachers and/or the teachers in the most effective schools exhibited more balanced instructional portfolios than their peers. Although we can only speculate about the motives for greater balance, we can point to the fact that our very best teachers expressed commitment to principle that they would do whatever it took to meet the wide array of individual student needs encountered every day in their classrooms.

OTHER PROMISING FINDINGS

The findings related to small group instruction, coaching as pertains to the teaching of word recognition, and higher-level questioning were found across both the effective schools and accomplished teacher analyses. Additionally, a number of findings were characteristic of either the teachers in the most effective schools or most accomplished teachers but not both.

Reaching Out to Parents.   At the school level, the most effective schools made more of an effort to reach out to parents than the moderately and least effective schools. At the classroom level, the teachers in the most effective schools made more of an effort to regularly communicate with parents than teachers in the other schools. These results suggest that the teachers in the most effective schools realized that good communication and collaboration, found amongst the staff, must also extend to the parents of the children in their schools.

Independent Reading. In the present study, we did find that the students in Grades 1 through 3 in the most effective and moderately effective schools spent more time in independent reading than the students in the least effective schools. These results support findings from earlier research that time spent in independent reading in school does make a difference in students' reading achievement (Anderson et al., 1988; Elley & Mangubhai, 1983; Taylor et al., 1990). It is interesting to note that accomplished teachers did not allocate any more time to independent reading than their peers, suggesting, as we proposed earlier, that this is an instructional practice amenable to school-level influences.

Maintaining Student On-Task Behavior. As has been found in the research on effective teachers (Brophy, 1973; Wharton-MacDonald et al., 1998), the most accomplished teachers in this study managed, on average, to engage virtually all of their students in the work of the classroom. By contrast, the least accomplished teachers achieved decidedly lower rates of on-task activity. This finding for our most accomplished teachers did not extend to the teachers in the most effective schools, who, as a group, did not differ from the teachers in the other schools in this study in maintaining on-task activity. This lack of consistency between the two teacher analyses (teachers in different levels of school effectiveness vs. teachers of different levels of accomplishment) suggests that maintaining high levels of time-on-task behavior is a teaching practice that is less amenable to building-level influence than other teaching practices, such as encouraging all students to engage in independent reading.

Local Versus National Reform Models. Although we included both national and local reform models in our sample, our data do not permit a definitive comparison between the two. However, it is worth noting that none of the schools in our most effective category used national reform models; all were home-grown. Furthermore, we found no regional variations in this pattern; the local reform models that proved most effective came from very different regions of the country. We are not alone in finding support for local models of school reform. For example, in the Hope for Urban Education Study (Charles A. Dana Center, 1999), seven of the nine high-performing schools had not adopted an off-the-shelf reform program. The common denominator seems to be that whatever the model, national or local, it must privilege school and classroom practices that have proven effective in carefully designed and implemented research efforts. We mention the efficacy of local models in the face of increasing pressure for schools to adopt "research-proven" national models (American Federation of Teachers, 1997; Herman, 1999; Herman & Stringfield, 1997; Slavin & Fashola, 1998; Wang et al., 1998). Perhaps what needs to be done is to make sure that the "approved" lists of research-proven programs always include "Home-Grown" (with a capital H and capital G) as a researched-based option right along side of Success for All, Core Knowledge, America's Choice and other New America's Schools models, and so on.

Teacher Accomplishment and the Possibilities for Mentoring

Although the argument is admittedly speculative, we want to suggest that the consistencies between our findings for teachers in the most effective schools and those for the most accomplished teachers may provide encouraging news for those who regard professional development as the center of gravity in any reform movement. Although many of the practices of the most accomplished teachers in this study, such as coaching in word recognition during actual reading and asking higher-level, aesthetic-response questions, were mirrored in our analyses of teachers in the most effective schools, this does not mean that all of the most accomplished teachers worked in the most effective schools. As reported earlier, only 52% of the teachers in Grades 1 through 3 in the most effective schools were identified as most accomplished teachers (as compared to 36% in the least effective schools and 34% in the moderately effective schools). It is plausible, however, that these teachers were serving as models or coaches who brought particular areas of expertise to interactions with their colleagues. Our interviews certainly provided rich examples of this possibility. As the principal at Hilltop School explained, she had "worked to help people begin to appreciate the experts emerging within the building by bringing staff to the point where they acknowledged their expertise and by bringing teachers together to share their expertise and learn together."

Whatever the relationships among teachers (and we desperately need to learn more about how these relationships play themselves out and how to help skeptical teachers accept the belief that even the poorest children in their classes can learn), the fact that not every teacher in the most effective buildings is classified as a most accomplished teacher should be heartening to reformers who want to increase learning and achievement in our poorest-performing schools. What it suggests is that a critical mass of highly accomplished teachers, which by our definition means teachers who possess more of the attributes of the canonical profile of pedagogically effective teachers, may be sufficient to move a school from the aspiring into the effective camp. Large-scale staff turn-overs may not be necessary. There are exceptional teachers in all buildings who could be called on to serve as models, peer coaches, or demonstration teachers to help committed teachers gain a concrete image of what positive instruction looks like and, in the process, improve their teaching.

Limitations

Although we are encouraged by the current findings, we must remind ourselves that this work, like all of the work in the effective schools and effective teaching tradition, comes with serious limitations. When all is said and done, we are ex-amining natural correlations that exist between program and teaching factors on the one hand and student performance on the other. Although these corre-lations may be useful in planning more definitive research and in guiding the de-velopment of local programs and policies, they cannot be used to fix causes for improvements (or decrements) in student achievement. For that, we need more systematic experimentation, including control groups, randomization, and careful analyses of growth over time. It is to that agenda that we soon turn our attention.

Our work carries a number of additional, more specific limitations. We would have liked to assess more students per classroom simply to improve the preci-sion and trustworthiness of our work. Because we did not test the full range of students within classrooms, we were unable to examine aptitude by treatment interactions.

Also, our prior information about schools was unintentionally misleading. In terms of selection, schools that we had expected to rise to the top of our achievement scales (because of their reputations) did not always do so. Con-versely, some schools that were thought to be ordinary in terms of achievement and reform did better than our information would have led us to believe. What this suggests is that the static assumptions about school status that we used to select schools were inappropriate. All of these schools were, and are, on the move, in one direction or another. Curriculum leaders and teaching staffs come and go, and with them the energy to initiate or sustain school-wide and class-room level practices and reform.

Our measures were not perfect. We would have liked to use more and better measures of a wider range of skills and strategies, including writing ability. Fur-thermore, those who adopt a psychometric lens would take issue with our reli-ance on classroom-based assessments administered by multiple assessors in multiple sites. Most informal inventories, writing samples, word lists, and even the available tests of phonemic awareness do not possess the psychometric underbelly of standardized multiple-choice tests. Those who would adopt a lens of authenticity would be equally disappointed in our measures. Although they are classroom-based, they are not the stuff of constructivist-based reform. Lacking is any appreciation of response to literature and personal engagement with text. Those who adopt a cultural lens would find both our student and our teacher measures wanting. They would find that our student measures are not likely to be sensitive to the special skills or perspectives that children develop in culturally rich settings. And they would find that our observational lenses did not guarantee that observers would look directly for culturally responsive (or culturally insensitive) instruction. In defense of what we did, all we can say is that, like all school-based research efforts, we made compromises motivated by cost and credibility. Because we were personally and painfully aware of the problems of using group assessments, especially with young readers, and because we wanted assessments that would be credible with the teachers in these schools, we were committed to one-on-one assessments, oral reading samples, and retellings—all practices we knew would appeal to teachers.

Some of our data, such as from the interviews, logs, and questionnaires, were based on self-report. However, the interview data on effective school-wide practices from three teachers and one principal per school corroborated what we found from the questionnaire data based on six to eight teachers per school (depending on the number of grade levels involved in the study). Also, the log data on reading instruction minutes, events, and grouping patterns was based on a reporting of what actually happened in the classroom every day for a week as opposed to teachers' self-reporting of how they typically spent time during their reading/language arts block. Furthermore, the observations provided balance to the self-report data in the analysis of effective classroom practices.

Another limitation was that we only conducted five 1-hour observations during the reading block in each teacher's classroom over a 5-month period. However, this data was balanced with the two weekly logs that the teachers completed to account for how they spent time on what reading/language arts activities during all of their reading/language arts instruction.

CONCLUSION

Beating the odds in reading predicted by poverty takes dedication and hard work. A school needs good morale and teachers willing to work tirelessly and collaboratively. Teachers and schools also have to go the extra mile to reach out to parents. The results of this study suggest that children in the primary grades make the greatest growth when a high proportion of their reading instruction is delivered through small achievement groups, when their progress is monitored regularly, and when they have ample time to read and to learn needed skills and strategies. Teachers who are most accomplished in helping children thrive in reading are skilled in coaching and in keeping all children academically on task. The findings of this study also suggest that schools, even our most effective schools, have a long way to go in improving reading instruction in the primary grades.

It is clear from this study that a combination of sound building decisions and collaborative efforts as well as effective practices within individual classrooms are needed if schools are to succeed at beating the odds in terms of primary grade students' reading achievement. From the descriptive analyses and case studies, it is clear that the process of becoming a school that promotes the learning of all its students is complex; equally complex are the conditions that characterize an effective school. Staff in all of these effective schools talked about the work they had been doing over a number of years to improve and the work still lay ahead of them. In other words, there is no single quick answer to the question of how best to reshape a school's reading program and the repertoire of instructional practices teachers employ in of the quest of helping all children read well by the time they leave the primary grades. What is equally clear is the educators who combine a thirst for improving their classroom practice, a commitment to strong, collaboratively forged school-wide programs, and plain old-fashioned hard work can meet great expectations for the children with and for whom they work.

In all of the most effective schools and most of the other schools in this study, the building environments were positive, and the schools were friendly places for children to learn. In most schools, the teachers and principals were genuinely concerned about developing the abilities of struggling readers, and in many, were willing to take the steps necessary to improve the reading achievement of all their students. The question that lies before us, and one to which we are currently turning our attention, is how (and whether) we, as a profession, can help develop the sorts of values and practices found in the most effective schools in other schools that only aspire to these levels of accomplishment.

APPENDIX A

QRI	Retelling Sheet
Passage	Child
Retelling:	Ask, "What happened in this story?"

Record student's response as best   Score:1234
as possible:

- Student offers little or no information
  about the selection.
- Retelling is incomprehensible.
- Stated ideas do not relate to the
  selection.
- Student relates details only.
- Student is unable to recall the gist of
  the selection.
- Retelling is incomplete or ideas are
  misconstrued.
- Sequence is not logical.
- Student relates some main ideas and
  some supporting details.
- Retelling is fairly coherent.
- Sequence is not logical.
- Student relates some main ideas and
  some supporting details.
- Retelling is fairly coherent.
- Sequence is logical.
- All major points and appropriate
  supporting details are included.
- Degree of completeness and coherence.
- Student generalizes beyond the text.

APPENDIX B

First, we created residual scores for all the relevant spring reading measures, using appropriate fall scores as covariates. In grade 1, spring residual scores for
reading fluency (wcpm) and retelling were created by using fall phonemic segmentation and blending scores as covariates. In grades 1–3 spring residual
scores for reading words were created by using fall reading words scores as a
covariate. In grades 2–3, spring residual scores for reading fluency and retellings
were created by using fall reading fluency scores as a covariate. Within each
grade level, these residual scores were converted to z-scores, which were calculated from the mean and standard deviation for the entire grade level sample, so
that the data could be aggregated across grade levels. Then, the residual

z-scores for retelling (at instructional level), fluency (wcpm on a grade level passage), and reading words were aggregated and standardized to create a composite index of reading growth.

Second, we calculated what might be called a primary (as in primary grades) outcome index, using the end-of-grade-3 scores on the district-mandated test. As it turned out, these were, in each case, standardized achievement tests (six schools used the Stanford Achievement Test 9; two used the Metropolitan Achievement Test 7; two used the California Achievement Test; two used the Northwest Evaluation Association Levels Test; and two used a district-normed test.) A residual mean percentile score for each school was calculated by controlling for the school's poverty level (as indexed by the percentage of students receiving free or reduced lunch). This was done because students' achievement scores are depressed in schools with 50–75% of students living in poverty and *seriously* depressed in schools with 75–100% of students living in poverty (Puma et al., 1997). The residual scores were then converted to z-scores.

Third, the z-scores on the project measures and primary grades outcome measure were summed and standardized. When we examined these scores, we looked for natural breaks in the distribution that would divide the schools into three groups of approximately the same size. These breaks occurred at .5 standard deviations above and below the mean. Breaking at those two points yielded four most effective, six moderately effective, and four least effective schools.

Instructions for Administering Word Lists

Examiner Instructions

Directions for administering word lists are the same for all grade levels. Begin administration with the Preprimer list and have the child continue reading from one list to the next until he or she makes seven (7) consecutive errors. Count the number of correct responses for each level and record the number at the bottom of each sheet.

Continue to administer a new list in this fashion until the child misses 7 or more words. Give the child time to attempt each word. Then uncover the remaining lists, and put a check next to any additional word that the child reads. Count those words and record the totals at the bottom of the record sheets.

Instructions for the children

I have some lists of words that I want you to read one at a time. Some of the words will be easy for you and some I expect to be very hard. Don't worry. I don't expect you to know all of them. I cannot help you because I want to see what you can do on your own. Do your very best. Look right above this card. That's where you will see each word. Are you ready? (and after the child has missed 7 consecutive words on any list) Thanks for your reading. Now I'm going to let you look at the rest of my words. Are there any that you know?

REFERENCES

Adams, M. J. (1990). *Beginning to read: Thinking and learning about print*. Cambridge, MA: MIT Press.

Allington, R. L. (1983). The reading instruction provided readers of differing abilities. *Elementary School Journal, 83*, 548–559.

American Federation of Teachers. (1997). *Raising student achievement: A resource guide for redesigning low-performing schools*. (AFT Item Number 3780). Washington DC: Author.

Anderson, L., Evertson, C., & Brophy, J. (1979). An experimental study of effective teaching in first-grade reading groups. *Elementary School Journal, 79*, 193–223.

Anderson, R. C., Hiebert, E. H., Scott, J. A., & Wilkinson, I. A. (1985). *Becoming a nation of readers*. Washington, DC: National Institute of Education.

Anderson, R. C., Wilson, P. T. , & Fielding, L. (1988). Growth in reading and how children spend their time outside of school. *Reading Research Quarterly, 23*, 285–303.

Barr, R., & Dreeban, R. (1991). Grouping students for reading instruction. In R. Barr, M. Kamil, P. Mosenthal, & P. D. Pearson (Eds.), *Handbook of reading research, Vol. II* (pp. 885–910). New York: Longman.

Bond, G. J., & Dykstra, R. (1967). The cooperative research program in first-grade reading instruction. *Reading Research Quarterly, 2*, 5–142.

Brophy, J. (1973). Stability of teacher effectiveness. *American Educational Research Journal, 10*, 245–252.

Campbell, J. R., Donahue, P. L., Reese, C. M., & Phillip, G. W. (1996). *NAEP 1994 reading report card for the nation and the states*. Washington, DC: Office of Educational Research and Improvement.

Carroll, J. B., Davies, P., & Richman, B. (1971). *The American heritage word frequency book*. Boston: Houghton Mifflin.

Chall, J. S. (1967). *Learning to read: The great debate*. New York: McGraw-Hill.

Charles A. Dana Center, University of Texas at Austin. (1999) *Hope for urban education: A study of nine high-performing, high-poverty urban elementary schools*. Washington, DC: U.S. Department of Education, Planning and Evaluation Service.

Colt, J. (1997). *A scoring rubric for children's story retelling*. Longmont, CO: St. Vrain Valley School District.

Cunningham, P., & Cunningham, J. (1992). Making words: Enhancing the invented spelling-decoding connection. *Reading Teacher, 46*, 106–107.

Deno, S. L. (1985). Curriculum-based measurement: The emerging alternative. *Exceptional Children, 52*, 219–232.

Donahue, P. L., Voelkl, K. E., Campbell, J. R., & Mazzeo, J. (1999). *NAEP 1998 reading report card for the nation*. Washington, DC: U.S. Department of Education.

Elley, W., & Mangubhai, F. (1983) The impact of reading on second language learning. *Reading Research Quarterly, 19*, 53–67.

Fisher, C., Berliner, D., Filby, N., Marliave, R., Cahen, L., & Dishaw, M. (1980). Teaching behaviors, academic learning time and student achievement: An overview. In C. Denham & A. Lieverman (Eds.), *Time to learn*. Washington, DC: National Institute of Education.

Gambrell, L. B., Morrow, L. M., Newman, S. B., & Pressley, M. (1999). *Best practices in literacy instruction*. NY: Guilford Publications.

Gamoran, A. (1992). Is ability grouping equitable? *Educational Leadership, 50*(2), 11–17.

Herman, R. (1999). *An educator's guide to school-wide reform*. Washington, DC: American Institutes for Research.

Herman, R., & Stringfield, S. (1997). *Ten promising programs for educating all children: Evidence of impact*. Arlington, VA: Educational Research Service.

Hiebert, E. H. (1983). An examination of ability grouping for reading instruction. *Reading Research Quarterly, 8*, 231–255.

Hiebert, E. H., Colt, J. M., Catto, S. L., & Gury, E. C. (1992). Reading and writing of first-grade students in a restructured Chapter 1 program. *American Educational Research Journal, 29*, 545–572.

Hirsch, E. D. (1987). *Cultural literacy: What every American needs to know*. New York: Vintage.

Hoffman, J. V. (1991). Teacher and school effects in learning to read. In R. Barr, M. L. Kamil, P. B. Mosenthal, & P. D. Pearson (Eds.), *Handbook of reading research, Vol. II*, (pp. 911–950). New York: Longman.

Invernizzi, M., Juel, C., & Rosemary, C. A. (1997). A community volunteer tutorial that works. *Reading Teacher, 50*(4), 304–311.

Knapp, M. S. (Ed.). (1995). *Teaching for meaning in high-poverty classrooms*. New York: Teachers College Press.

Leslie, L., & Caldwell, J. (1995). *Qualitative reading inventory—II*. New York: Harper Collins.

Madden, N. A., Slavin, R. E., Karweit, N. L., Dolan, L. J., & Wasik, B. A. (1993). Success for All: Longitudinal effects of a restructuring program for inner-city elementary schools. *American Educational Research Journal, 30*, 123–148.

McIntyre, E., & Pressley, M. (1996). *Balanced Instruction: Strategies and skills in whole language*. Boston, MA: Christopher-Gordon.

Oakes, J. (1985). *Keeping track: How schools structure inequality*. New Haven, CT: Yale University Press.

Pikulski, J. (1996) *Emergent literacy survey*. Boston: Houghton Mifflin.

Pinnell, G. S., Lyons, C. A., DeFord, D. E., Bryk, A. S., & Seltzer, M. (1994). Comparing instructional models for the literacy education of high-risk first graders. *Reading Research Quarterly, 29*, 8–39.

Pressley, M., Rankin, J., & Yokoi, L. (1996). A survey of instructional practices of primary grade teachers nominated as effective in promoting literacy. *Elementary School Journal, 96*, 363–384.

Pressley, M., Wharton-McDonald, R., Allington, R., Block, C. C., Morrow, L., Tracey, D., Baker, K., Brooks, G., Cronin, J., Nelson, E., & Woo, D. (2000). A study of effective first-grade literacy instruction. *Scientific Studies of Reading, 5*, 35–58.

Puma, M. J., Karweit, N., Price, C., Ricciuti, A., Thompson, W., & Vaden-Kiernan, M. (1997). *Prospects: Final report on student outcomes*. Washington, DC: Planning and Evaluating Service, U.S. Department of Education.

Roehler, L., & Duffy, G. (1991). Teachers' instructional actions in learning to read. *Handbook of reading research, Vol. II* (pp. 861–884). New York: Longman.

Rosenshine, B., & Furst, N. (1973). The use of direct observation to study teaching. In R. M. W. Travers (Ed.), *Second handbook of research on teaching* (pp. 122–183). Chicago: Rand McNally.

Shavelson, R. J., & Berliner, D. C. (1988). Evasion of the education research infrastructure: A reply to Finn. *Educational Researcher, 17*, 9–11.

Slavin, R. E., & Fashola, O. S. (1998). *Show me the evidence! Proven and promising programs for America's schools*. Thousand Oaks, CA: Corwin Press.

Snow, C. E., Burns, S., & Griffin, P. (Eds.). (1998). *Preventing reading difficulties in young children: Report of the Committee on the Prevention of Reading Difficulties in Young Children*. Washington, DC: National Academy Press.

Stallings, J., & Kaskowitz, D. (1974). *Follow through classroom observation evaluation 1972–1973* (SRI Project URU-7370). Stanford, CA: Stanford Research Institute.

Stringfield, S., Millsap, M. A., & Herman, R. (1997). *Urban and suburban/rural special strategies for educating disadvantaged children: Findings and policy implications of a longitudinal study*. Washington, DC: U.S. Department of Education.

Taylor, B. M., Frye, B. J., & Maruyama, G. M. (1990). Time spent reading and reading growth. *American Educational Research Journal, 27*, 351–362.

Taylor, B. M., Pearson, P. D., Clark, K., & Walpole, S. (1999). *Beating the Odds in Teaching All Children to Read* (CIERA Report #2–006). Ann Arbor, MI: Center for the Improvement of Early Reading Achievement, University of Michigan.

Taylor, B. M., Pearson, P. D., Clark, K., & Walpole, S. (2000). Effective schools and accomplished teachers: Lessons about primary-grade reading instruction in low-income schools. *The Elementary School Journal, 101*, 121–165.

Taylor, B. M., Short, R. A., Frye, B. J., & Shearer, B. (1992). Classroom teachers prevent reading failure among low-achieving first grade students. *Reading Teacher, 45*, 592–597.

Wang, M. C., Haertel, G. D., & Walberg, H. J. (1998). *What do we know: Widely implemented school improvement programs*. Philadelphia, PA: Center for Research in Human Development and Education.

Weber, G. (1971). *Inner city children can be taught to read: Four successful schools* (CGE Occasional Papers No. 18; ERIC Document Reproduction Service No. Ed 057 125). Washington, DC: Council for Basic Education.

Wharton-MacDonald, R., Pressley, M., & Hampston, J. M. (1998). Literacy instruction in nine first-grade classrooms: Teacher characteristics and student achievement. *Elementary School Journal, 99*, 101–128.

Wilder, G. (1977). Five exemplary reading programs. In J. T. Guthrie (Ed.), *Cognition, curriculum, and comprehension* (pp. 57–68). Newark, DE: International Reading Association.

2

Exemplary First-Grade Teaching

Michael Pressley
University of Notre Dame

Ruth Wharton-McDonald
University of New Hampshire

Lisa M. Raphael
Kristen Bogner
Alysia Roehrig
University of Notre Dame

EXEMPLARY FIRST-GRADE TEACHING

Everyone interested in reading instruction knows about the great debates surrounding the teaching of beginning reading (Pressley, Allington, Wharton-McDonald, Block, & Morrow, 2001). In the middle part of the 20th Century, the debate was between those favoring systematic teaching of phonics and those advocating for the whole-word approach (Chall, 1967), which was most often operationalized with the then popular Dick-and-Jane-type readers. Students learned whole words by sight while proceeding through Dick-and-Jane lessons, only learning to analyze words into components after a substantial number of sight words had been learned. As the 20th Century proceeded, the whole-word approach faded, falling victim to analyses such as Chall's (1967) summary, which made the case that systematic phonics produced better reading achievement than whole-word methods. As whole word faded, another approach, whole language, rose to take its place. The major tenet of whole language is that literacy acquisition goes best when children are immersed in real reading and writing. The whole-language theorists felt there was no good produced by decontextualized skills lessons, with them especially emphatic that it made no sense for grade 1 to be filled with skill teaching and practice (e. g., Goodman, 1986). This latest version of the great debate, one that played out through the 1980s and into the 1990s was no less acerbic (e.g., Smith, 1994) than previous versions (e.g., Flesch, 1955).

In the early 1990s, Pressley and his colleagues, while reviewing the great debate literatures, noticed a peculiar gap in the data base. Those investigators were also aware that much progress had been made in understanding how complex tasks can be accomplished through an approach known as expert analysis. That is, cognitive psychologists had been studying various types of domain expertise (e.g., ability to read x-rays or fly a jet plane) by observing and interviewing domain experts and same-domain nonexperts (i.e., the cognitive psychologists studied how expert radiologists did their work and how very experienced commercial pilots flew jets; see Chi, Glaser, & Farr, 1988; Ericsson & Smith, 1991; Hoffmann, 1992). Thus, the gap that Pressley and his coworkers spotted was that no analyses of expert beginning reading teachers were mentioned in the great debates. None of the great debators had systematically watched excellent primary-level teachers do their work, nor had they even bothered to interview or survey them. That is, a potentially important data base that was directly relevant to the great debates surrounding beginning reading was overlooked.

The Pressley group responded to that gap in the literature with a series of studies that continue as this chapter is being written. The overarching goal of the research cited in this chapter is to understand just what effective primary-level teachers do to develop literacy skills in their students. This research has been methodologically diverse, with survey data complemented by ethnographic data. Despite the methodological differences between investigations, the main conclusions converge across the various studies. This presentation generally will follow the chronological order of the various studies, a rhetorical approach that permits much to be said about the origins of the conclusions now being offered by our group about Grade-1 instruction.

A SURVEY OF INSTRUCTIONAL PRACTICES
OF PRIMARY TEACHERS NOMINATED AS EFFECTIVE
IN PROMOTING LITERACY

Pressley, Rankin, and Yokoi (1996) set out to study effective primary-level literacy as it was carried out in the entire United States. Thus, using the data base of the International Reading Association, they identified reading-teacher supervisors across the country, asking them to nominate exceptionally effective primary teachers in their school district. The supervisors were permitted discretion in how they made their choices, with the following factors entering into their considerations as they did the nominations: (a) achievement records of students in nominated teachers' classes, (b) conversations with nominated teachers about their instructional approaches, (c) direct observations of teaching by the supervisor, (d) interactions with teachers during in-services, and (e) positive comments from other teachers, administrators, and parents.

The teachers nominated by the supervisors were then contacted through the mail by Pressley et al. (1996). The first mail contact with these nominated-outstanding teachers included a short survey. The survey asked these teachers to specify 10 instructional practices that were essential in their reading instruction, with separate lists generated for good, average, and weaker readers. Each of the instructional practices submitted by the 113 teachers who responded to the survey (out of 135 who were contacted) was developed as a question item on a second questionnaire sent to participating teachers, one that included 436 questions about beginning literacy. Although there was some variety in the formatting of questions, in general, teachers indicated which of the hundreds of instructional practices mentioned on the questionnaire were, in fact, practices that they used with their students. Eight-six teachers completed this second questionnaire, including 23 kindergarten teachers, 34 Grade-1 teachers, and 26 Grade-2 teachers.

The findings of the study were striking: These teachers reported classrooms filled with print—in-class libraries, displays of student work, chart stories and poems, posted word lists, posted signs, learning centers, and much story reading by students and the teacher. Most reading was of excellent children's literature. The teachers reported extensive modeling of literacy processes and much student practice of the reading and writing processes. The teachers reported using many types of grouping in their classrooms depending on the activity. They also indicated great sensitivity to individual differences between students, reporting that instruction was individualized according to student needs. In particular, the teachers reported being more explicit about letter-sound and word-level skills with weaker compared to more able readers. That said, the teachers also reported much more teaching of basic skills in the context of real reading and writing than in a decontextualized fashion (e.g., 95% reported the explicit teaching of phonics, with 90% reporting that such explicit teaching occurred in the context of real reading and writing). The teachers reported many types of reading experiences in their classrooms (e.g., choral reading, shared reading, student read-alouds, and book sharing). The teachers reported their students did a lot of writing, with explicit instruction of the writing process. The teachers also reported doing much to motivate the students to be literate (e.g., making the classroom a risk-free environment, providing positive feedback, conveying the importance of literacy). They also reported much accountability, including having students read aloud to them frequently and having students keep a writing portfolio.

In summary, the nominated-effective primary-level teachers in Pressley et al. (1996) reported that much was occurring in their classrooms. Moreover, in a follow-up study, Rankin-Erickson and Pressley (2000) obtained reports from elementary-level special education teachers who also were nominated as exceptional in promoting literacy in their students. Again, they reported classrooms filled with high quality literacy activities. In fact, so much activity was reported in these surveys that one journal reviewer of the Pressley et al. (1996) piece questioned whether any classroom anywhere could be so busy! Of course, the reviewer's comment reflected the suspicion that in many survey studies, those responding to the survey sometimes report more than they do. The Pressley group recognized that they needed to conduct some observations of excellent primary-level classrooms, although the Pressley et al. (1996) survey prepared them for the possibility that there might be a lot to see in an effective Grade-1 room.

OBSERVATIONAL STUDIES OF EFFECTIVE
GRADE-1 CLASSROOMS

The Pressley group has conducted two ambitious studies aimed specifically at elucidating just what distinguishes an effective Grade-1 classroom from a less effective one. The two studies were very similar, although one was carried out in just one locale in the United States and the other included data from five places spread across the country. The outcomes obtained in the two studies, however, completely converged. Moreover, the outcomes obtained in these observational studies were consistent with the outcomes obtained in the Pressley et al. (1996) survey.

Wharton-McDonald, Pressley, and Hampston (1998)

A strength of the Pressley et al. (1996) study was that the survey methodology permitted the perspectives of many teachers to be tapped. It also permitted the inclusion of teachers from across the country. With the resources available to the Pressley group in mid-1995, when their first observational study of effective reading instruction was planned, there was no hope of observing a large sample of effective Grade-1 teachers over the course of a school year or of traveling very far to do so. Thus, Wharton-McDonald et al. (1998) planned to study 10 Grade-1 teachers intensely, with all of them within an hour's drive of SUNY-Albany, where the group was working at the time. The investigators asked local school districts to nominate teachers who they believed were outstanding in promoting literacy in their Grade-1 students as well as teachers who were more typical of district standards. The researchers began the study with five teachers nominated as outstanding by district personnel and five nominated as more typical.

Rather than accepting the district's verdicts about the teachers' effectiveness, the researchers watched carefully for indicators of achievement as they did their observations. Over the course of the study, one teacher dropped out for personal reasons. By the end of the study, the investigators felt they had three groups of teachers. Three of the teachers really did seem effective, with their students consistently engaged in reading and writing. By the end of the year, the students in these classrooms were writing compositions that were several page long, with good mechanics and spelling. By the end of the school year, most students in these three effective classrooms were frequently seen reading books at or above end-of-first-grade level. In contrast was a second group of three teachers. In their classrooms, engagement was more variable. Writing was less impressive. A smaller percentage of students seemed to be reading grade-level books at the end of the year.

Then, there was a third group where engagement was consistently low in the class. Writing was even less impressive, with many student compositions only one or two sentences long and frequently containing poor capitalization and punctuation. At the end of the year, many children in these classrooms were reading more beginning-of-first-grade and mid-first-grade books than in the most effective classrooms, where students were more likely to be reading books that required end-of-first-grade skills.

One important insight emerging from this study was that there was a lot of similarity across these classrooms regardless of effectiveness. Thus, in all nine classrooms, there was a mix of skills instruction with real reading and writing.

All of the teachers did some teaching of the writing process (i.e., plan, draft, and revise), with daily writing in all the classrooms as well. In all but one classroom, spelling was taught with spelling tests. Seven of the nine teachers used worksheets, at least occasionally. All of the teachers used conventional classroom management strategies (e.g., grouping desks together to promote student cooperation, a larger table in the room for teacher-led small group activity). In all but one classroom, there was a lot of positive reinforcement across the day. All of the teachers cared about their students and seemed dedicated to helping them grow. All of the teachers also were aware of the need to involve parents in literacy instruction and made efforts to do so.

More critically, however, the teaching in the most effective classrooms did differ in some ways from the teaching in the other classrooms observed in the study, especially in the case of the three teachers who were most ineffective. In particular, the balance between skills instruction and more holistic reading and writing seemed most effective and best integrated in the highly effective classrooms.

All three of the most effective teachers taught decoding skills explicitly. All three also complemented their group teaching of skills with much individualized instruction and review of skills with students who needed additional input. All three teachers were very competent at providing mini-lessons to students who were struggling during lessons.

The three most effective classrooms were very busy compared to the other classrooms, with a high density of instruction apparent. The teachers seemed to be teaching constantly, with whole group, small group, and individual minilessons simply intermingled throughout the day. The scaffolding of students in the most effective classrooms was really apparent, with students never allowed to flounder for long in these classrooms. When the teacher did provide help, she did just enough to get the student back on track rather than do the task for the student or give the student an answer (e.g., providing hints about where the student might find a word she or he wanted to spell rather than spelling the word for the student).

The three most effective teachers also did much to encourage self-regulation in their students—they did much to encourage their students to take charge of their learning. They encouraged them to check whether they understood what they read, to read their compositions to others for suggestions, and to try to use strategies when they were stuck. Early in the year, the most effective teachers developed the expectation that when the teacher left the room, everyone was to continue working. And, in the most effective classrooms, that is exactly what happened. This expectation, of course, was just one of many high expectations in the most effective classrooms, with the most effective teachers certain their students could learn and determined they would learn. Such expectations were as important as any other part of their overall classroom management, with the students so self-regulated that disciplinary encounters were rarely seen in the most effective classrooms.

The integration of content learning into reading and writing was simply amazing in the most effective classrooms. The current science theme, for example, would be reflected in what was read during reading as well as the current writing assignment. There would be artifacts all over the room reflecting the theme, including student compositions and art work consistent with the theme. With so much reading, writing, and art connected to content themes, it was little wonder that the students seemed so charged about what came off as dull topics in the more typical classes—such as reproduction, covered around the theme of hatching chicken eggs. In a most effective classroom, there was suspense as the students did the math to figure out when the eggs would hatch, read stories about chickens, and wrote about everything they had done to make sure the eggs would hatch. In contrast, a lesson on the same topic in a more typical classroom revolved around a very dull question-and-answer session in front of a poster outlining the hatching process. The content really cooked in the more effective compared to the more typical classrooms.

In summary, the instruction in the most effective classrooms differed in many ways from the instruction in the least effective classrooms. Most interesting, however, was that Wharton-McDonald et al. (1998) were able to identify many ways that the most effective classrooms were similar to each other yet different from more typical classrooms. Although not taken up in this chapter, in addition to the striking similarities between the most effective classrooms, there was striking variability between the more typical classrooms: That is, the more typical classrooms seemed more different from one another than more similar, prompting the conclusion that although there seemed to be a set of common characteristics in effective Grade-1 classrooms, there were many ways to be more typical and ineffective. Was it just this way in effective classrooms in upstate New York, or had Wharton-McDonald et al. (1998) discovered a more general pattern?

Pressley, Wharton-McDonald, et al. (2001)

The Pressley group realized that the only way to know whether the pattern reported by Wharton-McDonald et al. (1998) was general was to study more Grade-1 classrooms, documenting both the effectiveness of instruction and the nature of instruction. In Pressley, Wharton-McDonald, et al. (2001), rather than restrict themselves to one region of the United States, they studied classrooms in upstate New York, urban New Jersey, Dallas-Fort Worth, Madison WI, and rural northern California (see also Pressley, Allington, Wharton-McDonald, Block, & Morrow, 2001). Again, they recruited classrooms purported to be effective and more typical by district administrators, although the ultimate determination of effectiveness was made in light of actual researcher observations. Again, the researchers judged effectiveness on the basis of the extent of engagement in reading and writing as well as the quality of the reading and writing observed in the classroom.

At each site, the researchers identified a teacher whom they felt was most effective and one who was least effective among the teachers observed. As in the previous work, the instruction in the most effective classrooms was striking in that there were many similar elements across the effective classrooms, despite the fact that these classrooms were in very different U. S. locales. All of the excellent classrooms had excellent classroom management; positive, reinforcing, and cooperative environments; much teaching of skills; a strong literature emphasis; much reading and writing; matching of task demands to student competencies, with demands increasing as students improved; much teacher monitoring of student efforts and scaffolding of students as needed; much encouragement of students to be self-regulated; and extensive connections across the curriculum, with reading and writing occurring during content instruction.

True, many of these same elements were observed in more typical classrooms, which prompted an analysis of the data to identify elements of instruction that were really unique to the most effective classrooms in comparison to the least effective classrooms in each locale. There was a very striking set of indicators that emerged from this analysis:

- There is a high density of skills instruction in the most effective classrooms, with as many as 10 to 20 skills taught an hour, including minilessons to address student needs.
- The most effective teachers very explicitly teach their students to self-regulate.
- The most effective teachers instruct their students to use multiple cues to read words, including phonics, word parts, looking at the whole word, picture and other semantic context cues, and syntactic cues.
- Effective teachers teach comprehension skills (i.e., making predictions, constructing mental images of story content, summarizing, looking for story grammar elements in stories).
- Effective teachers extensively scaffold writing.

- The teaching of the writing process as planning, drafting, and revision is salient in effective teachers' classrooms, with publication of students' final products also salient (e.g., there are many big books that students have written on display in the room). There are many props available to support the writing process, such as cheat sheets listing how revisions are made.
- Effective teachers make high demands on their students to use writing conventions, such as capitalization, punctuation, and correct spelling of high frequency words.
- The tasks in most effective classrooms are designed so that students spend much more time on the academically demanding parts than on less demanding parts (e.g., when assigned to write a story and draw a picture to accompany the story, much more time is spent on the writing than on the art).

In summary, Pressley, Wharton-McDonald, et al. (2001) observed effective classrooms that were very similar to the effective classrooms observed by Wharton-McDonald et al. (1998). The effective Grade-1 teacher is not married to any of the extremist philosophies that are the anchor points for many participants in the contemporary reading wars (see Smith, 1994). Thus, rather than constructing classrooms that are entirely focused on skills teaching, reading of literature, or writing, the effective teacher constructs a classroom that balances and blends the teaching of skills, reading of great literature, and student creation of new stories. Rather than constructing a classroom in which classroom management is prominently present, consistent with the prescriptions of many who feel discipline is primary in education, the excellent Grade-1 teacher manages so well that it's not apparent she or he is managing, with very few disciplinary episodes occurring in the classroom. The management that is occurring is producing a positive, cooperative environment. The most effective classrooms visited by the Pressley group were generally happy and productive places—every single day, every single hour. There were never days when the teacher was angry with the class or even individual children in the class; there were never days when there wasn't transparent excitement about learning in these classrooms. The teachers who were most effective created motivating classrooms, with examination of such motivation taken up in a study that followed up on Wharton-McDonald et al. (1998) and Pressley, Wharton-McDonald, et al. (2001).

Bogner, Raphael, and Pressley (in press)

In reviewing the field notes generated in Wharton-McDonald et al. (1998) and Pressley, Wharton-McDonald, et al. (2001), it was transparent that much was going on with respect to motivation in the effective Grade-1 classrooms. Indeed, as the group reflected on the motivating instruction observed in effective classrooms, there was a sense that the teaching in these classrooms was saturated with attempts to motivate. What was also apparent, however, was that the notes were incomplete on this issue, for to capture everything that went on with respect to motivation would have required focusing on just that element of instruction. It was time to do a study that did just that, one that moved motivation to the foreground.

During school year 1999–2000, Kristen Bogner, Lisa Raphael, and Michael Pressley intently observed seven Grade-1 classrooms in Catholic schools in the city of South Bend IN. The explicit goal of these observations was to document what the teachers did to motivate literacy engagement in their students.

Consistent with Wharton et al. (1998) and Pressley, Wharton-McDonald, et al. (2001), there were huge differences between the classrooms with respect to literacy engagement. Two classes, in particular, had consistently high engagement, with these two classrooms, in fact, resembling the most effective classrooms in the investigations reported earlier in this chapter. For example, with respect to achievement, the writing observed in both of these classrooms was more ambitious than in the other five classrooms observed in the study. There was real intellectual excitement in these classrooms, with many connections made between literacy and content learning.

Over the course of the year, the observers were able to document that a number of motivational mechanisms were used in the Grade-1 classrooms. Forty-seven of the motivational practices were very positive ones—that is, practices that would be expected to increase interest in and enthusiasm for school. These included using cooperative learning and teaching, having a gentle and caring manner, supporting appropriate risk-taking, providing appropriate challenges to students, favoring depth of coverage over breadth of coverage, and communicating that academic tasks deserve intense attention. In contrast, there were 15 other motivational practices that were negative, that is, ones with the potential to undermine literacy engagement. These included fostering classroom competition, giving students very easy and/or boring tasks, providing negative feedback, making students aware of their failures, and using punishment. In summary, there were lots of approaches to motivation blended in the classrooms that were observed.

The most important finding in the study, however, was that the classrooms varied dramatically in how many of the motivational mechanisms were used and whether positive or negative motivational mechanisms were employed. For the two teachers with highly engaged students (i.e., the two teachers with classrooms most resembling the effective classrooms studied in our previous investigations), there was a clear pattern. Both of these teachers used most of the positive motivational approaches and few of the negative approaches. That is, collapsing across all observations, one teacher used all 47 positive motivational mechanisms and only one negative motivational mechanism; the other engaging teacher used 43 of the positive motivational mechanisms and only one of the negative mechanisms.

In contrast, the other five teachers observed in the study used fewer positive motivational mechanisms (i.e., ranging from 4 to 18 positive mechanisms) and more negative motivational mechanisms (i.e., ranging from 5 to 11 negative mechanisms) than did the most engaging teachers.

Throughout the year of observation, Bogner et al. (in press) were aware that the two most engaging classrooms they were observing were simply saturated with motivating teaching. They observed these teachers being very motivating on every day they were in the classroom—in fact, during every hour of observation, and indeed, during almost every minute of teaching. It was simply impossible to get all the motivational mechanisms in the field notes, for these teachers did so much to stimulate their students. Hence, if anything, the researchers underestimated the amount of motivation in the most engaging classrooms. In contrast, they had no problem keeping up while recording the motivating instruction in the other five classrooms in the study.

Just how motivating these classrooms were can be appreciated by reflecting on what went on in Nancy Masters' classroom (i.e., Nancy was one of the two really motivating teachers). Nancy believed completely that all children can learn. This motivated her to create a classroom that was upbeat and filled with interesting books and activities. There were always artifacts of recent projects in the room, from a slab of concrete created by a local builder as part of his demonstration during careers week to a map detailing the location of other classrooms that Nancy's class interacted with over the Internet.

Nancy created a supportive environment, with her students getting lots of praise for their accomplishments. Discipline was rarely necessary, always done discreetly and constructively. Thus, when a hyperactive boy blurted out answers, Nancy gently chided, "Slow down, we'll never catch up with you." She cared about her students, and it showed. For example, when students were ill, she called and wrote the student, with Nancy keeping the class abreast of the students' healing.

Nancy emphasized effort continuously, letting her students know that achievement depends on effort. Thus, when she distributed report cards, she was emphatic that their most important grade was for "effort."

Nancy prepared her students for the challenges they faced, with much instruction directed at assuring success on upcoming tests (e.g., making certain students knew what they had to do on a standardized test tapping phonics knowledge). When students did have difficulty with tasks, Nancy retaught concepts, thinking hard about how the content might be taught so that it would be understood and learned better. There was a lot of cooperative learning, including collaborative reading and writing and working on science projects. Nancy was emphatic that students should help one another, with her frequently nudging students to provide assistance to others who were experiencing some difficulties with a task.

Nancy selected content that was really interesting to her students. Most striking was that she read long and mature books to her students, building sufficient background knowledge in the students through discussion so that everyone in the class was simply riveted by her readings of classics like, *A Christmas Carol*, *Call of the Wild*, and *Tale of Two Cities*. Sometimes this reading connected to content-area learning. Hence, during Black History Month, there was reading of stories and books about notable African-Americans, with this work also connecting to discussions about ethics (e.g., civil rights while reading *The Story of Ruby Bridges*). Although there was a great deal of literature and writing, there was also a great deal of skills instruction in Nancy's classroom. Often, this instruction took place during more holistic tasks, as when she modeled creating images while reading of *A Christmas Carol* (e.g., imagining Scrooge being escorted by one of the ghosts).

The interpersonal connections were deep in this classroom. Parents often came to school to help out in the classroom. They assisted with their student's homework every night. Nancy frequently mentioned her connections to students' family members, for example, telling students that she was going to mention to their moms how they were doing in class. Nancy also tried to connect students to their personal futures, frequently discussing how what they were learning in first grade would help them in second grade. Nancy's students knew that their first grade experience was continuous with their home experiences and with the schooling experiences to come.

In short, Nancy did much to motivate her students, with the result students who were reading and writing whenever the outside observers visited the classroom. By the end of the year, the class created a big book for the observer team to thank them for visiting the classroom. Most of the student essays in the book were at least two sides of a piece of paper (i.e., four to six sentences) with excellent mechanics and spelling. In contrast, there were other first grades in the study in which the best writer in the class would not even come close to the typical writing performance in Nancy's class. All of this was especially impressive when it was considered that Nancy's school serves a neighborhood with plenty of students that would be at risk for school difficulties in many classrooms. In Nancy's classroom, those same students simply whizzed through the state assessment, doing well on it because the test was much less demanding than the tasks Nancy presented to her students all the time, tasks that her students completed well all the time with Nancy teaching and scaffolding them.

DISCUSSION

The position most consistently espoused by the Pressley group (e.g., Pressley with McCormick, 1995) is that good thinking involves using the strategies used by capable people (i.e., with respect to literacy, capable readers and writers). Capable thinkers know when and where to use the strategies they have acquired because they possess extensive metacognition about strategies, knowledge about the contextual appropriateness of strategies which has largely developed from actual use of strategies. Good thinkers are motivated to use appropriately the strategies they know, largely based on past successes in using strategies but also because of previous instruction and feedback that strategic effort pays off. Strategies work well for good thinkers, largely because they also have well developed knowledge of the world, in part a consequence of using effective strategies in the past. Because good thinking involves strategies, metacognition, motivation, and world knowledge, then it would make sense that excellent education promotes these competencies.

In fact, the excellent Grade-1 teachers we have observed did teach strategies in ways that should increase metacognition about the strategies. Their teaching was designed to motivate their students. The rich content in their classrooms should have gone far to increase their students' world knowledge.

To elaborate, excellent Grade-1 teachers teach a variety of word recognition strategies; they also introduce their students to the comprehension and composition strategies used by good comprehenders and writers. Literacy strategies are not just in the curriculum. They are a big deal, a salient part of the Grade-1 educational experience in effective classrooms, with students getting lots of instruction about strategies, lots of support in using them, and much practice applying strategies across the school year. The teaching and practice permit many opportunities to learn when and where it makes sense to use such strategies—that is, to develop the metacognition that permits intelligent use of strategies.

The motivation to use strategies largely depends on coming to understand that learning follows effort, the effort required to use effective strategies (e.g., Borkowski, Carr, Rellinger, & Pressley, 1990). Motivation to do things literate is more complex, however, with it definitely helping if there are interesting texts available to read and what is being read links meaningfully to the young reader's world (see Pressley, 1998, chap. 8, for a review). Literacy engagement is not an automatic by-product of learning to recognize words or learning to write but depends on immersion in interesting reading and writing and learning experiences (e.g., Guthrie & Wigfield, 2000). It is not surprising that when literacy engagement is high, it is obvious that the teacher is saturating the classroom with motivation, using the many mechanisms known to increase student motivation. Effective Grade-1 teachers create exciting literacy environments every day for their students, with this apparent as their students read, read, and read every day and write with enthusiasm.

What gets read in excellent Grade-1 classrooms? The answer is simple—the good stuff! Excellent Grade-1 classrooms are filled with the best of children's literature, books that convey important scientific and social scientific concepts, as well as experiences that enrich children's minds as they inspire children to think beyond their everyday experiences (e.g., when members of different professions visited Nancy Masters' classroom to talk about what they did for a living, including demonstrations, such as making a cement slab for the class). Excellent Grade-1 teachers develop worthwhile cultural content, and world knowledge in their charges.

When we have presented this work publicly, a typical question is whether it is possible to develop more Grade-1 teachers who are like the Grade-1 teachers described in this chapter. One possibility, of course, is that such teaching skill is a natural gift, and hence, not easily developed in those who do not naturally evidence it. The alternative is that teachers can be taught to teach the literacy strategies children need to learn. They can be taught to help children practice and apply word recognition, comprehension, and composition strategies appropriately to a variety of problems, with such practice stimulating student understanding about when and where to use the strategies taught. Teachers can be taught how to motivate their students, and they can learn to fill their classrooms with content that is worth thinking about, information and experiences that expand students' understanding and appreciation of the world.

We expect in the very near future to explore whether and how much grade-1 teaching can be improved. We are very optimistic, however, that primary-grades teachers can become better teachers through instruction about excellent Grade-1 literacy instruction. This optimism is fueled in part by Roehrig,

Pressley, and Sloup's (2001) experiences in Madison, Wisconsin. They studied a group of teachers there who learned how to be Reading Recovery tutors. Most striking, when these teachers returned to regular classroom teaching, they imported many of the Reading Recovery experiences into their classrooms. These teachers taught their students to re-read books to the point of fluency, "stretch" words in order to hear the sounds in them, use word "chunks" and both letter and context cues to identify words, consult the word wall when needing to spell high frequency words, and self-correct when reading—all strategies emphasized in Reading Recovery but not observed often in many more typical Grade-1 classrooms. These Madison teachers certainly could learn new tricks, ones they could easily adapt and apply in their classrooms. Similarly, we are betting that the envisionments of good first-grade teaching developed in the work summarized in this chapter can be the beginning of the development of many better Grade-1 teachers.

REFERENCES

Bogner, K., Raphael, L. M., & Pressley, M. (in press). How grade-1 teachers motivate literate activity by their students. *Scientific Studies of Reading, 5,*

Borkowski, J. G., Carr, M., Rellinger, E. A., & Pressley, M. (1990). Self-regulated strategy use: Interdependence of metacognition, attributions, and self-esteem. In B. F. Jones (Ed.), *Dimensions of thinking: Review of research* (pp. 53–92). Hillsdale NJ: Lawrence Erlbaum Associates.

Chall, J. S. (1967). *Learning to read: The great debate.* New York: McGraw-Hill.

Chi, M. T. H., Glaser, R., & Farr, M. J. (Eds.). (1988). *The nature of expertise.* Hillsdale, NJ: Lawrence Erlbaum Associates.

Ericsson, K. A., & Smith, J. (Eds.). (1991). *Toward a general theory of expertise.* Cambridge, UK: Cambridge University Press.

Flesch, R. (1955). *Why Johnny can't read—And what you can do about it.* New York: Harper & Row.

Goodman, K. S. (1986). *What's whole in whole language?* Richmond Hill, Ontario, Canada: Scholastic.

Guthrie, J. T., & Wigfield, A. (2000). In M. L. Kamil, P. B. Mosenthal, P. D. Pearson, & R. Barr (Eds.), *Handbook of reading research* (Vol. III, pp. 403–422). Mahwah NJ: Lawrence Erlbaum Associates.

Hoffmann, R. R. (1992). *The psychology of expertise: Cognitive research and empirical AI.* New York: Springer-Verlag.

Pressley, M. (1998). *Reading instruction that works: The case for balanced teaching.* New York: Guilford.

Pressley, M., Allington, R., Wharton-McDonald, R., Block, C. C., & Morrow, L. M. (2001). *Learning to read: Lessons from exemplary first-grade classrooms.* New York: Guilford.

Pressley, M. (with Christine B. McCormick). (1995). *Advanced educational psychology for educators, researchers, and policymakers.* New York: HarperCollins.

Pressley, M., Rankin, J., & Yokoi, L. (1996). A survey of instructional practices of primary teachers nominated as effective in promoting literacy. *Elementary School Journal, 96,* 363–384.

Pressley, M., Wharton-McDonald, R., Allington, R., Block, C. C., Morrow, L., Tracey, D., Baker, K., Brooks, G., Cronin, J., Nelson, E., & Woo, D. (2001). A study of effective grade-1 literacy instruction. *Scientific Studies of Reading, 5,* 38–58.

Rankin-Erickson, J. L., & Pressley, M. (2000). A survey of instructional practices of special education teachers nominated as effective teachers of literacy. *Learning Disabilities Research and Practice, 15,* 206–225.

Roehrig, A., Pressley, M., & Sloup, M. (2001). Reading strategy instruction in regular primary-level classrooms by teachers trained in Reading Recovery. *Reading & Writing Quarterly, 17,* 323–348.

Smith, C. B. (Moderator). (1994). *Whole language: The debate.* Bloomington, IN: EDINFO Press.

Wharton-McDonald, R., Pressley, M., & Hampston, J. M. (1998). Outstanding literacy instruction in first grade: Teacher practices and student achievement. *Elementary School Journal, 99,* 101–128.

3

High-Performing, High-Poverty, Urban Elementary Schools

Joseph F. Johnson, Jr.
Charles A. Dana Center, University of Texas at Austin

There is good news for American public education based on the successes of some schools in urban districts that serve families living in poverty. Although there are far too many well-documented stories of intellectually vapid schools that perpetuate cycles of poverty and further limit the life choices of children, there are some urban schools that are giving new life to their communities and transforming the futures of the children they serve. In 1999, the Charles A. Dana Center at The University of Texas at Austin, under contract from the U. S. Department of Education, conducted a study of nine such schools. The results of that study were issued in a report entitled *Hope for Urban Education: A Study of Nine High-Performing, High-Poverty Urban Elementary Schools*. The report is about nine urban elementary schools that served children of color in poor communities and achieved impressive academic results. These schools have, in fact, attained higher levels of achievement than most schools in their states or most schools in the nation. They have achieved results in reading and mathematics beyond those achieved by students in some affluent suburban schools.

This report complements and extends the body of literature that has focused on the study of effective schools (Taylor, 1990) and more recent research on the characteristics of high-performing, high-poverty schools (Lein, Johnson, & Ragland, 1996; Reyes, Scribner, & Scribner, 1999, among others). In particular, this report not only describes the characteristics of these schools but also describes how these schools managed to transform themselves. Instead of focusing on schools that merely did better than other high-poverty schools, this study examined high-poverty schools that performed better than the average for all schools in their states. Instead of focusing on schools in one state or region or on schools serving one ethnic population, this study included schools from different parts of the country and schools that served diverse populations. In addition to reporting descriptions of the current state of these schools, this study attempted to tell the story of the change process so that others might gain a deeper understanding of how a school begins, maintains, and sustains the journey toward excellence for all students.

All nine of the schools used federal Title I dollars to create Title I schoolwide programs. This means they were allowed to pool all of their resources to improve achievement throughout the entire school, instead of targeting federal resources to only those children who met eligibility criteria based on educational need. These schools are a powerful affirmation of the power of Title I to support comprehensive school improvement efforts. In these schools, many of the most important change efforts were enhanced through the use of federal education resources. On the other hand, although Title I supported the change efforts, Title I was not the catalyst of the change effort. The true catalyst was the strong desire of educators to ensure the academic success of the children they served.

SELECTING THE SCHOOLS

In the fall of 1998, the U.S. Department of Education commissioned a set of case studies of nine high-performing urban, public elementary schools. The researchers identified nine urban elementary schools in which the majority of children met federal free or reduced-price lunch criteria and in which student performance on reading and mathematics assessments exceeded the average for schools in the state (or the average for schools in the nation, when nationally normed assessments were used). Finding such schools was not easy.

Some states did not have a common statewide assessment system in the fall of 1998. In some states, such systems were under development or were in pilot phases. Some states did not have data about the achievement levels of individual schools (only district-wide data were available). In some cases, individual school data existed but were not easily accessible given the study's short timeline. In some states where school achievement data were accessible, there were no urban schools, serving predominantly poor communities, in which the level of achievement in mathematics and reading exceeded state or national averages. In many such places, improvements in the achievement of some urban schools were noted, but the level of achievement was still substantially below the state or national average. Data collected by the Council of Chief State School Officers were valuable in identifying some schools. State department of education data made available through World Wide Web pages were particularly useful in some states. Also, staff in research and evaluation offices in state and district offices were helpful in making data available.

Fortunately, there were some states where data were available and accessible and in which several schools met all the criteria for inclusion in the study. Additional information was sought about those schools. In particular, an effort was made to remove from consideration any schools that had selective admissions criteria. For example, magnet schools that only admitted students with high academic grades or test scores were removed from the pool of schools under consideration. Also, a school was removed from consideration if it was determined that a large percentage of children had been exempted from the state assessment because of issues of language proficiency or disabilities. Similarly, a school was removed from consideration if there had been a substantial change in the demographics of the school that might explain the improvement in achievement. The researchers sought to be certain that the demographics of the schools included were typical of urban, high-poverty schools in every aspect.

Achievement test data from prior years—at least the last 3 years—were reviewed to examine trends in academic performance. In a few cases, schools were excluded from consideration because, although performance was high, the performance had decreased in recent years. Finally, a few schools were removed from consideration if they had already received substantial attention in educational literature. Although the researchers respected the substantial accomplishments of these schools, this study was perceived as an opportunity to highlight schools that had not yet received substantial national attention.

Among the schools eligible for consideration, the researchers sought a sample that would provide great diversity. As such, the nine schools selected had varying ethnic and racial compositions. Also, the researchers selected some schools that had made dramatic, rapid turnarounds in performance and some that had a longer history of improvement.

Of course, it was necessary to obtain permission to visit and study the selected schools. Both schools and district offices needed to grant permission for the research activities. In a few cities, the school or schools that best met the selection criteria did not choose to participate in the study. In other cities, the researchers were more fortunate and were able to acquire permission to include their first-choice schools. Ultimately, nine high-performing, urban elementary schools were selected. These schools were in Atlanta, Georgia; Boston, Massachusetts; Chicago, Illinois; Detroit, Michigan; East St. Louis, Illinois; Houston, Texas; Milwaukee, Wisconsin; Cheverly, Maryland (in metropolitan Washington, D.C.) and San Antonio, Texas. Table 3.1 provides a list of the nine schools.

PROCEDURES

As described above, a variety of quantitative data were used to identify schools. Once schools were identified, the research team used qualitative data to gener-

TABLE 3.1

List of Nine Schools Studied

School	District	City	State
Baldwin Elementary School	Boston Public Schools	Boston	Massachusetts
Baskin Elementary School	San Antonio Independent School District	San Antonio	Texas
Burgess Elementary School	Atlanta Public School District	Atlanta	Georgia
Centerville Elementary School	Cahokia School District #187	East St. Louis	Illinois
Goodale Elementary School	Detroit Public Schools	Detroit	Michigan
Hawley Environmental School	Milwaukee Public Schools	Milwaukee	Wisconsin
Lora B. Peck Elementary School	Houston Independent School District	Houston	Texas
Spellman Elementary School	Prince George's County Public School District	Cheverly*	Maryland
Ward Elementary School	Chicago Public Schools	Chicago	Illinois

Note.   *In the Washington, D.C. Metropolitan area.

ate case studies for each school. A team of two or three researchers visited each school. The research visits occurred over a 2-day period.

During the visits the researchers interviewed principals, at least one teacher from each grade level, other campus administrators, and parents. In some cases, principals arranged for interviews with parents who played a major role at the school. Often, however, researchers were able to conduct on-the-spot interviews with parents who were picking up their children, volunteering, or otherwise visiting the campus. Often, the researchers used focus groups to gain the perspectives of several teachers or parents. Personnel from the district office were also interviewed. Either the superintendent or the administrator who supervised the principal of the school studied was interviewed. Before the site visits, phone conversations with principals were helpful in identifying important informants and arranging interviews. As well, after the site visits, phone conversations with principals helped provide clarifying information.

The research team included 12 individuals with an array of backgrounds and skills. Six of the team members had prior experience as teachers. Three had been school administrators. All had experience as qualitative researchers. Their backgrounds included bilingual education, higher education, psychology, anthropology, policy, and special education.

In addition to interviews, the researchers observed a variety of settings, including classrooms at different grade levels, cafeterias, playgrounds, and hallways. Where possible, researchers observed staff meetings or other professional development activities. As well, a variety of documents were reviewed. Campus planning documents, program descriptions, meeting agendas, school budgets, achievement reports, and other documents were examined.

The phone calls, interviews, observations, and document reviews were structured to acquire a detailed picture of the current status of the school, as well as to acquire an understanding of how the school had improved over time. The researchers sought to understand not only the current status of each school's reform efforts, but also sought to understand how the school transformed itself over the years. Thus, for example, if the current principal of the school had been at the school for only a year or 2 and important aspects of the school's reform had been initiated 3 or 4 years prior, the researchers sought to identify and interview the previous principal. Intensive efforts were made to understand what had changed and how the changes were made. Table 3.2 summarizes the data collection efforts at each of the nine schools.

The researchers relied heavily on interviews with the various informants to construct a picture of the processes, events, and programs that were influential in bringing about improved academic performance. The researchers probed in

TABLE 3.2

Data Collection Strategies at Each of the Nine Schools

- Conduct an interview with the superintendent.
- Conduct interviews with the central office staff person who supervises the principal.
- Conduct interviews with the school principal. If the principal was new to the school (came after the current reform efforts began) conduct interviews with the former principal.
- Conduct interviews with at least one teacher at each grade level.
- Conduct an interview with a parent who has been actively involved in the school's improvement (such as a PTA/PTO officer).
- Conduct focus group sessions involving parents.
- Conduct observations of classrooms.
- Review the budget for the school.
- Review student achievement data from the school.
- Review the school's planning documents (e.g., school improvement plans).

response to the issues that emerged through the interviews and looked for confirmation of changes in observations and reviews of documents. What may have been important in the story of change at one school may have been absent or have had only minimal importance in the story of change at another.

DIFFERENCES AMONG THE NINE SCHOOLS

Although all nine schools served urban, minority, and low-income communities and all nine boasted high levels of academic achievement in reading and mathematics, there were important variations among the schools. They varied in their student enrollments, grade spans, ethnic composition, rate of improvement, and the extent to which they used school reform models. They also varied in their relationship with their district offices and in the extent to which they experienced turnover in teaching staff through the process of reform.

Student Enrollment

The schools had enrollments that ranged from 283 students (at Baldwin Elementary) to 1,171 students (at Goodale Elementary). Six of the schools (Baldwin, Baskin, Burgess, Hawley, Peck, and Ward) had less than 500 students. Three of the schools (Centerville, Goodale, and Spellman) had more than 500 students. Although most of the schools had the advantage of a small enrollment (in contrast with the stereotype of large urban schools), there were large schools that achieved impressive academic results. Although school size may have been an important factor in some of these schools, it probably should also be noted that some of the smaller schools were just as small when they were considered low-performing schools by their districts or states.

Regardless of enrollment, all of the schools managed to create an atmosphere of smallness. Principals, teachers, parents, and students knew each other, cared about each other, and worked together well. Even in the largest schools, there was generally a warm, personal atmosphere enjoyed by all members of the school community.

Grades Covered

Four of the schools (Baldwin, Baskin, Burgess, and Goodale) had kindergarten through Grade 5. Hawley and Peck were similar; however, they also had pre-kindergarten programs. Centerville and Spellman served students in kindergarten through Grade 6, whereas Ward served students from pre-kindergarten through Grade 8.

Student Demographics

In six of the nine schools (Burgess, Centerville, Goodale, Hawley, Peck, and Spellman), a majority of the students were African American. However, the size of the majority ranged from 100% of the students at Goodale in Detroit to only 56% of the students at Hawley in Milwaukee. At Baskin a majority of the students (75%) were Hispanic. At Baldwin, a majority of the students (72%) were Asian American. Although 47% of the students at Ward were Asian American, there was not any racial or ethnic group that comprised a majority of the student population.

In seven of the nine schools, at least 80% of the students were designated as low-income through the federal free or reduced-price lunch program. At Hawley, 71% of the students and at Spellman 63% of the students participated in the free or reduced-price lunch program. These demographics are shown in Table 3.3, to follow.

Several of the schools had significant populations of students who were learning English as a second language. In particular, at Baldwin, Ward, and Spellman more than one-fourth of the students were learning English as a second language.

The researchers tried to discover which schools experienced substantial student mobility. Baldwin did not report mobility data. The other schools re-

TABLE 3.3

Student Demographics

School	City	% African American	% Asian American	% Hispanic	% White	% Low-Income
Baldwin	Boston	17	72	4	7	80
Baskin	San Antonio	6	1	75	18	92
Burgess	Atlanta	99	0	1	0	81
Centerville	East St. Louis	89	0	0	11	86
Goodale	Detroit	100	0	0	0	87
Hawley	Milwaukee	56	2	12	27	71
Peck	Houston	79	0	18	2	94
Spellman	Cheverly	73	1	17	9	63
Ward	Chicago	18	47	16	19	88

ported mobility rates ranging from 15% at Hawley to 49% at Baskin. Schools were not always able to explain how their mobility rates were calculated so there may be differences in the meaning of the rates. In general, these mobility rates are low in contrast to the mobility rates of some urban, high-poverty schools. Perhaps, the low mobility rates were low, at least in part, because parents did not want to move away from schools where their children were achieving important academic gains.

Comprehensive School Reform Models

All nine of the schools had engaged in comprehensive efforts to improve academic achievement for all of their students. However, only two of the schools used popular models for comprehensive school reform. Centerville Elementary used the Accelerated Schools Program (Hopfenberg & Levin, 1993). Peck Elementary used the Success for All Program (Slavin, Madden, Dolan, & Wasik, 1992). In both cases the reform model played a role in the schools' improvement efforts; however, each was only part of the overall story of reform in the school. In each of the schools, there was considerable evidence of the nine components of comprehensive school reform, as described in the federal Comprehensive School Reform Demonstration Program (U.S. House of Representatives, 1997). The nine components included effective, research-based methods and strategies, comprehensive designs with aligned components, intensive professional development, measurable goals and benchmarks, support of faculty and staff within the school, parental and community involvement, external technical support and assistance, evaluation strategies, and the coordination of resources.

Rate of Improvement

In schools like Baskin and Peck, rapid improvement in academic achievement was shown by sharp rises in student test scores during a 3- or 4-year period. In contrast, at schools such as Goodale and Centerville, teachers and administrators believed they had been engaged in steady improvement efforts since the 1990s. Respondents had varying notions about when the most important changes began. At Burgess, Goodale, Hawley, and Peck most of the respondents connected the beginning of change efforts with the arrival of the current principal. At Centerville, Spellman, and Ward the previous principal was given substantial credit for initiating the reform efforts. At Baldwin respondents perceived the presence of a new principal, as well as a new foundation supported reform initiative, and a new superintendent as converging factors that initiated dramatic improvements in teaching and learning. Similarly, at Baskin changes were attributed to both new campus and district leadership, as well as to the power of a state accountability system.

In some cases, student achievement data did not reflect the timeline of reform efforts suggested by informants. For example, although Goodale teachers and parents reported that their reform efforts had been ongoing for several years under the leadership of their principal, they also admitted that the fruits of their efforts were not shown in achievement score gains until the last 2 years.

If the selection criteria used for this study had been applied, none of the nine schools would have been considered high-performing schools 5 years ago. In fact, in most of the schools, the evidence of academic achievement was dismal before 1994. In most of the schools (specifically, Baldwin, Baskin, Burgess, Peck, and Spellman) educators and parents tended to believe that reform efforts began after 1994. However, the staff and parents at the other schools tended to believe that important improvement efforts were in progress prior to 1994, although they may not have resulted in improved test scores until after 1994.

District Involvement

Leadership and guidance from the district office played a substantial role in the improvement at Baldwin, Baskin, and Peck. In contrast, the district office played a more modest role in the improvement at Goodale and Hawley. One might note that the schools that made the most rapid gains were the schools with the greatest district involvement.

In the schools in which district involvement was greatest, the district established clear expectations for improvement, delineated a path for improvement, and provided support and technical assistance along the way. For instance, the Houston Independent School District made clear that the new principal at Peck Elementary was expected to substantially improve academic achievement as measured by the Texas Assessment of Academic Skills, the Texas School Accountability System, and the Houston Independent School District School Accountability System. The principal was given the opportunity to adopt the area district's Project GRAD program and eagerly consented to participate. Project GRAD included the Success for All Program, the Move-It Math Program, a plan for improving consistency in classroom management and discipline, and the Communities in Schools Program, which incorporated dropout prevention and social service agency components. Staff from the area district office provided support along the way, particularly as the school encountered rough beginnings on the path to improvement. Similar direction, guidance, and support were made available to Baldwin Elementary by the Boston Public Schools and to Baskin Elementary by the San Antonio Independent School District.

Even in the places where district involvement was less extensive, the schools were able to access important services from the district. For instance, the Goodale faculty was one of the best consumers of professional development offerings from the district office. Similarly, Hawley could not have been a successful city-wide school without the provision of extensive transportation services from the district office.

Teacher Turnover

At some of the schools such as Ward and Peck, academic improvements have come with few changes in teaching staff. In contrast, at Burgess, only five teachers remained in 1998–1999 from the staff the principal inherited in 1993–1994. At Spellman, one teacher described the early years of their reform effort by saying, "We would have to look up daily to see how much the staff had changed."

None of the schools reported that many teachers had been fired. However, in several of the schools, it was clear that teachers who did not accept the school's goals and vision were encouraged to leave. In some cases, principals began processes of documenting unacceptable behavior. In some cases, principals bluntly invited teachers to seek jobs elsewhere. There were some situations where principals made clear what was expected, invited people to take part, and if staff members chose not to participate, the principal offered to help them find other employment. Still in other cases, teachers began feeling uncomfortable and chose to leave when so many of their peers were trying new approaches and expressing commitment to the school's new vision.

Two factors were important in reducing teacher turnover or in creating situations where turnover was minimal. First, principals tended to be highly selective in hiring new teachers. For instance, at Goodale, candidates were hired only if they demonstrated a passion for excellence and a love for children. The principal would leave a position vacant instead of filling it with a person who would not fit into the school's culture of continuous improvement and concern for children. Second, principals organized fiscal and human resources in a manner that provided substantial support for teachers. Teachers felt supported and perceived that they had a good chance of being successful in their roles. At some of the schools (e.g., Burgess and Spellman) such support was less apparent at the beginning of the reform but has increased substantially in recent years.

IMPROVEMENT STRATEGIES

The primary purpose of this research effort was to generate a deeper understanding of how these nine urban elementary schools changed in a way that resulted in high levels of academic achievement for their students. There were several important change strategies that were used by multiple schools. In this section of the report, these change strategies are described with examples from a few of the schools.

Targeting an Important, Visible, Attainable First Goal

In several of the schools, new principals walked into difficult environments with problems ranging from student discipline, to teacher morale, to parent dissatisfaction, to academic lethargy. In response to what must have felt like overwhelming chaos, principals identified one issue or goal on which they could focus immediate attention and give an unambiguous message that the school was changing. They sought to identify an issue where they could make progress quickly. The focus varied in response to the issues that were perceived as important at each school.

At Baldwin and Hawley, the first efforts were to improve student discipline and create a safe and orderly environment. At Spellman, efforts were made to reduce the disruptions to teaching and increase the school's focus on academic instruction. At Peck, the principal disbanded the school's two, ethnically separate parent–teacher organizations and instituted a unified Parent–Teacher Association. At several of the schools, principals tried to make the physical environment more attractive for children and more conducive to learning.

By targeting a visible, attainable goal, principals were able to give students, parents, and teachers clear indicators of change in just a few weeks or months. These early accomplishments helped reduce or eliminate excuses and created a readiness for additional (often more difficult) changes. By focusing on one issue, principals were able to direct their energies in a way that would have a high likelihood of success. This first success became the cornerstone of future successes.

Refocusing Energies on Service to Children

In prior years, teachers, principals, and parents in many of the schools spent considerable time on conflicts among the adults at school. Often these conflicts siphoned away valuable energy that should have been devoted to the improvement of teaching and learning. Principals in most of the nine schools were skillful in redirecting the energy expended on such conflicts. School leaders challenged teachers, paraprofessionals, union leaders, and parents to elevate their focus beyond self-interest to a concern for the well-being of the students. This was not done as a one-time event or an occasional sermon. Instead, principals were constantly reminding the adults about the effect of decisions on students. The principals appealed to teachers, staff, and parents to put aside small differences and unite in service to students.

At Burgess, the principal challenged the staff to move from a teacher-focused school to a child-focused school. Often in discussions about important school decisions, the principal would ask the faculty to consider what was in the best interest of students.

At Peck, the principal asked the faculty to put children first, regardless of disagreements. The staff learned, in part, from the manner in which the principal articulated child-focused rationale for her decisions. The principal encouraged teachers to talk about their reasons for entering the teaching profession. She tried to learn about their goals and what she called "the desires of their hearts." Then she appealed to those desires to serve children well as she called on every staff member to refocus their efforts on the improvement of the school.

In several cases, school leaders helped teachers refocus energies during planning processes. By engaging in such processes and discussing "what we, together, can do for children," principals were able to refocus energies in ways that coincided with improvement plans. Once plans were developed, the message was reinforced often, particularly in times of conflict. As an example, at Baldwin, some teachers resisted changes in curriculum and instruction. One teacher said, "You have to have a willingness to let them go through their resistance. Then you focus them on the fact that this is for the good of the kids."

At Baskin, when performance data were reviewed, it was done in ways that were not intended to be critical of teachers. In contrast, the review was focused on the academic needs of children. At Goodale, the principal did not allow much energy to be expended on projects, efforts, or discussions that had minimal influence on the personal or academic growth of students. In staff meetings, grade-level meetings, or in other gatherings, the principal frequently refocused the staff's energy toward issues that had a substantial influence on the personal or academic success of students.

The result of the refocusing process was not only a decrease in tensions but also an increase in the extent to which students were likely to feel respected, valued, and appreciated. Visitors to these schools quickly sensed that teachers and other staff members genuinely love and care for the students.

Building Students' Sense of Responsibility for Appropriate Behavior and Creating an Environment in Which Students Are Likely to Behave Well

In all nine schools, often in dramatic contrast with their environments in past years, discipline problems were rare. The schools used many approaches to improve student behavior, focusing on helping students assume responsibility for their behavior and on creating school environments that made it easy for students to behave appropriately.

At several of the schools, time was set aside to establish clear rules and high expectations for student behavior. Teachers, administrators, parents, and often students worked together to establish simple rules that would help create a much more pleasant environment for teaching and learning. Often, rules were established that would help prevent behavior problems before they started. For instance, at Peck students walked in the hallways with their arms folded. This pattern of behavior helped reduce the possibility of conflicts as students walked throughout the school.

In all of the schools, many efforts were made to acknowledge and even celebrate positive behavior. For instance, the Buddy Reading Program at Ward and the SPARK program (Spellman Acts of Random Kindness) at Spellman helped encourage students to interact with their peers in a supportive manner. At Peck, students earned opportunities to seek positions of responsibility in the classroom. At Spellman, a banner was flown when the school achieved a fight-free day. At Hawley, students earned the chance to participate in intramural sports.

Clear and consistent rules, consequences, and rewards helped students learn to assume responsibility for their own behavior. When consequences were regular and predictable, it was easier for students to behave appropriately. The predictability of these results seemed to be positively associated with the visibility of the principal and other school leaders. The visibility of principals on playgrounds, in hallways, and in classrooms helped underscore that the rules were important and they would be enforced.

At times, rules were eliminated or modified when they were not necessary. For instance, at Peck there were many students (and some teachers) who were frequently late arriving at school in the mornings. Instead of investing a substantial amount of energy into disciplining people for being tardy, the principal instituted "Peck time." The beginning and ending times for the school day were moved back 15 minutes. In other words, children began school 15 minutes later and ended their school day 15 minutes later. Parents, teachers, and students saw the change as an effort to help them succeed at being on time. Tardiness was dramatically reduced.

Training for teachers was an important component of efforts to implement discipline plans. At Peck, teachers received training in the district's Consistency Management Discipline Plan. At Goodale, teachers participated in efficacy training that focused on building a sense of efficacy and responsibility in students. At many of the schools, the regular collaboration among teachers included attention to strategies for helping students maintain exemplary behavior.

Student responsibility for their own behavior was also nurtured by the development of student leadership activities. For instance, at Goodale and Hawley, peer mediation programs gave students important opportunities to support each other in working out problems in a constructive manner. As well, extensive uses of cooperative learning strategies at schools such as Peck provided many opportunities for student leadership.

The improvements in student behavior were also influenced by the changes in the extent to which children came to understand that they were valued and respected. At Baldwin, as in all of the nine schools, the principal knew all of the students by name and knew many of their families. The personal relationships among students and school staff created a powerful context for good behavior. At Burgess, teachers gave students time to talk about important emotional stresses in their lives. At several of the schools, counselors or social workers helped students know that they had a safe place to talk about personal concerns. Nonetheless, teachers, counselors, social workers, principals, and other support providers emphasized high expectations for student behavior, regardless of the circumstances in children's lives. They listened and provided support that helped students continue to meet behavioral expectations, as well as academic expectations, even when students faced troubling situations.

When behavioral problems emerged, they were dealt with in a prompt, objective manner that demonstrated respect for students and helped them learn responsibility. For instance, at Goodale, students were rarely suspended. The principal believed that removing a student from school did nothing to increase the students' sense of responsibility for his or her behavior nor to increase the school's sense of responsibility for educating the student. At many of the schools, the involvement of parents was a key component of their disciplinary efforts. Parents reported that they were supportive because they perceived that school leaders were fair disciplinarians who had the best interest of their children at heart.

Ultimately, student behavior was also improved by the improvement of academic instruction in classrooms. Students were more likely to be actively engaged in learning. They were more likely to be excited about the level of challenge and rigor in their curriculum. They were more likely to be positive about their chances to succeed academically. Thus, there was less of a need for students to seek attention through negative behavior. Improved instruction led to improved discipline, which led to even better instruction.

Creating a Collective Sense of Responsibility For Improvement

An important improvement strategy at each of the nine schools centered on creating an environment in which all educators shared a sense of responsibility for school improvement and the attainment of the school's goals. At several of the schools, this joint sense of responsibility was modeled by the principal, nurtured by joint planning processes, and reinforced by efforts to involve everyone in key components of the school's work.

Principals at these schools emphasized the importance of each individual's contribution to the work of the school. Principals modeled their commitment to collective responsibility by including the input of various staff members in decisions. Often teachers were given the responsibility of making important decisions. In other cases, principals made key decisions but they gave teachers and other staff substantial opportunities to contribute their thoughts and ideas.

Planning processes provided avenues for the involvement of many staff and faculty. For instance, the Accelerated Schools Program provided opportunities for many Centerville staff members to get involved in identifying school needs and establishing a vision for the school's future. At Hawley, staff members participated on committees established in response to critical issue areas identified by the staff. These structured opportunities for involvement helped emphasize that staff members shared responsibility for school improvement. The principal refused to allow teachers to think that he would "fix" all of the school's problems. The staff learned that they all shared responsibility for getting all children to achieve at high levels.

Collective responsibility became a part of the common language of the school. At Centerville, Peck, and Ward everyone talked about teamwork and the extent to which they were working as a team. At Goodale and Burgess educators talked about themselves as part of a "family" of adults responsible for the well-being of "their" children. At Baskin, the principal said, "No one can do it alone." At Ward, the principal emphasized the importance of getting the staff to feel that they were working *with* her and not *for* her.

The sense of collective responsibility resulted in staff members taking on new and different roles. At Spellman, the institution of the Canady block-scheduling approach resulted in almost all of the school's ancillary personnel participating in the teaching of reading. Similarly, at Peck many staff members helped support the Success for All reading program. At Hawley, the school social worker sponsored the after-school math club. At many of the schools, teachers voluntarily exceeded expectations.

The involvement of staff members in a variety of activities central to the success of the school helped create a deeper sense of professional responsibility among them. As professionals, teachers, and other staff were expected to contribute to an understanding of the school's problems, the analysis of possible solutions, and the implementation of commonly agreed-on approaches to improvement.

Increasing Instructional Leadership

At all nine schools, the amount and quality of time spent on instructional leadership activities was substantially increased. First, principals spent a substantial amount of time engaged in instructional leadership activities. Second, other school faculty were positioned in ways that allowed them to provide instructional leadership at the school.

Principals tended to spend a large percentage of their time in classrooms. For instance, at Burgess, the principal reported that she spent 40% of her time in classrooms, observing teaching and helping improve instruction.

At Centerville, the principal was described as a teacher of teachers. As one teacher explained, "She gets in there with you and shows you. She teaches and shows you to make sure that you understand."

Similarly, teachers at Peck and Goodale reported that their principals were frequently in classrooms watching, reacting to and reinforcing good teaching techniques and providing helpful suggestions.

In addition to the leadership provided by principals, almost all of the schools asked other educators to provide instructional leadership to the school staff. For instance, the former principal at Baskin created an instructional guide position from another administrative position. This person coached teachers on instructional strategies and later became the school principal. At Burgess and Spellman, there were instructional specialists who provided instructional assistance and support to teachers. At Goodale, Title I resource teachers assumed instructional leadership functions as they helped teachers address instructional improvement issues. At Peck, a master teacher was hired to help teachers with writing instruction while the Success for All coordinator supported teachers in improving reading instruction. At Ward, an assistant principal was responsible for helping the principal improve instruction in classrooms and head teachers provided additional assistance to their peers in improving daily classroom instruction. By encouraging and training multiple instructional leaders, the former principal at Ward helped prepare his successor and other leaders who have become administrators in other Chicago schools.

As another example of instructional leadership among the nine schools, principals kept teachers and other school personnel focused on improving instruction. At Goodale, when school planning efforts veered to a discussion of improving the parking lot, the principal helped refocus the group on improving instruction. At Hawley, the principal supported the School Beautification Committee, but made it clear that the priority had to be on improving student achievement. Often, principals kept the faculty focused on instruction by removing distractions. At Spellman, the principal insisted that the 90-minute reading block was "sacred" and would not be interrupted. Even on days shortened because of snow, everyone would have 90 minutes for reading and language arts.

One way principals and other school leaders demonstrated instructional leadership was by getting teachers to use achievement data to improve instruction. For example, at Baldwin, the principal helped teachers use data on student literacy levels to improve reading instruction. Additionally, the principal helped teachers use disaggregated Stanford 9 test scores to identify students in need of additional academic support. At Goodale, the principal helped ensure that the school's professional development plans, as well as other important plans were based, at least in part, on student results from the Michigan Educational Assessment Program (MEAP). At Hawley, the principal helped teachers use student assessment data to identify areas of strength and weakness and use such data in planning improvement strategies. At Baskin, the instructional guide helped teachers use data to understand specific objectives in mathematics that needed extra attention. At Centerville, the principal used the Accelerated Schools Program to help teachers understand and use data to improve teaching.

Principals constantly challenged the school staff to higher levels of achievement. They highlighted and celebrated the successes of students and teachers in a way that reinforced exemplary efforts and gave a message of hope. The walls of classrooms and hallways were visual celebrations of the achievement of students. Regularly, school leaders took the time to acknowledge the successes and special efforts of students, parents, teachers, and other staff members. As goals were achieved, school leaders generously praised the efforts of all contributors, and then artfully redirected the entire school toward even higher goals for the achievement of their students.

Aligning Instruction to Standards and Assessments

At the nine schools, students performed well on assessments because they were taught what the district or the state expected them to learn. Principals and teachers did not leave student performance to chance. They meticulously ensured that children were being taught the knowledge, concepts, and skills articulated in state or district standards and measured in annual assessments.

At Burgess and Centerville, curriculum alignment processes helped teachers understand the relationship between what they taught and how students performed on standardized tests. The curriculum alignment processes were important opportunities for teachers to talk about expectations, teaching, and student work. Furthermore, the alignment processes gave teachers a chance to understand precisely what students were expected to know and the extent to which students would be expected to demonstrate mastery. At Spellman, instructional specialists and teachers worked together to create performance-based practice assessments. Teachers used the data from those assessments to improve instruction. For many of the teachers, the process gave them a much deeper understanding of what instruction was needed for students to perform well on the assessment.

Alignment processes also helped ensure that teachers would be able to teach all of the knowledge and skills expected to be learned during the school year. For instance, at Baskin, the principal and the instructional guide led teachers in curriculum alignment projects in science and mathematics that gave teachers a "road map for student improvement." Teachers no longer had to guess if they were covering all the content tested by the Texas Assessment of Academic Skills. They worked together to develop a plan that would ensure adequate coverage of all important content by testing time each spring.

Getting Teachers the Resources and Training
Perceived Necessary to Teach

At several of the schools, substantial energy was devoted to making sure that teachers felt like they had all of the resources they considered necessary in order to get students to reach the school's academic goals. In particular, principals and other school leaders made sure that teachers felt like they had adequate materials, equipment, and professional development.

At Baldwin, teachers reported that the principal "went to the nth degree" to get needed instructional materials. At Goodale, teachers who had transferred from other Detroit schools were astonished at the manner in which the principal and the Title I resource teachers were able to get teachers the materials they requested in a timely manner. At Ward, teachers reported, "If teachers need it, Wilcher [the principal] gets it."

When assessment data, principal observations, or analyses of student work suggested that students were not learning an important concept or skill, the principal or school planning teams made sure that resources were allocated to help teachers learn better strategies for teaching the skill. Teachers, principals, and instructional specialists from within the school often provided this training. However, there were times when training from outside sources was needed. In such cases, principals either arranged for experts to come to the school and provide training to the staff or arranged opportunities for staff persons to attend workshops, seminars, or conferences where they could access the appropriate training. When necessary, the school provided substitute teachers so that faculty could attend training sessions. Often such training was attended by groups of teachers and administrators. Therefore, when the group returned to school, they could support each other in carrying out the practices learned. Also, they could assist other staff in learning the new strategies, concepts, or techniques.

For instance during one semester at Ward, a group of teachers participated in weekly math and science classes held at the Illinois Institute of Technology. Teachers attended classes during the school day and substitute teachers were provided. Then, experts from the institute visited the teachers in their classrooms and provided coaching. Teachers learned new skills that they were able to apply in their classrooms and practice with the support of their school administrators and fellow teachers.

Often, teachers perceived that the support provided through access to materials, equipment, and training was critical to their success. They tended to see the school's investment as a tangible indicator of support. As a result, teachers responded with a greater willingness to support school initiatives. Perhaps teachers felt more effective as a result of this support and were more willing to exert maximum effort. Perhaps, when teachers perceived that they had been given what they deemed necessary to teach well, there were fewer excuses for poor performance. Whatever the reason, this support was extremely important to teachers and was an important part of the success at several of the schools.

Often the schools used Title I funds to provide materials, instructional equipment, and professional development. These schools used the flexibility provided by the Title I schoolwide program option to improve services to all students. In some cases, (e.g., at Goodale) Title I teachers still saw some students on a pull-out basis, yet the majority of the Title I funds were used to support the improvement of the entire school.

When Title I funds ran short, some of the schools (e.g., Centerville, Baldwin, and Goodale) acquired resources from other grants to help meet these needs or combined Title I dollars with other resources. At Baskin, money from an unused professional position was diverted to purchase additional instructional materials. At Hawley, Title I and technology resources were combined to get computers into classrooms and provide associated professional development for teachers.

Creating Opportunities for Teachers to Work, Plan, and Learn Together

At all nine schools, leaders created regular opportunities for teachers to work, plan, and learn together around instructional issues. Without time for collaboration on instruction, many improvements never would have been conceived or implemented.

Many of the schools created blocks of time during which teachers met and planned together. At Baldwin, a primary team (kindergarten through second-grade teachers) and an elementary team (third- through fifth-grade teachers) each met twice a month. At Baskin, a 90-minute block of uninterrupted planning time was created for each grade level twice a week. At Hawley, the principal arranged the schedule in a way that used "banked" time (additional minutes at the beginning or end of each day) to carve out time for professional development. At Peck, the principal rearranged the schedule to provide common planning times for the staff to engage in horizontal (same grade level) and vertical (different grade levels) planning. Twice a week the entire staff came together to share experiences and strategies that achieved positive results.

Often planning times focused on important instructional issues. For instance, at Baldwin, teachers carefully reviewed student work in comparison with academic standards and discussed opportunities for improving instruction. At Spellman, this time was used to create practice performance assessments, score the assessments, and identify common areas of academic strength and need.

Often these planning times became opportunities for teachers to share and learn from each other. For instance, at Burgess teachers gave reports on what objectives were being taught and how they were getting students to learn the objectives. Time was set aside for classroom visits and sharing. At Hawley, many of the professional development activities were organized and presented by teachers to their colleagues based on the school improvement plan. In other cases, collaboration times were sometimes used as opportunities for teachers to study and research options for instructional improvement. For instance, at Baldwin teachers researched options for literacy programs before choosing one that felt appropriate for their students.

Although these collaborations generally had an academic focus, they did not always start as such. For instance, at Baskin collaboration was established when teachers started going out to lunch together once a week. At Burgess, collaborations began with staff dinners, social gatherings, and team-building sessions. Building a comfort level was sometimes an important precursor to getting teachers to discuss their teaching practices openly.

In some cases, school leaders set aside space for teachers to plan and work together. The new kind of "teacher workroom" helped teachers collaborate. At Baskin a special workroom was established that allowed teachers the space to meet, work together, and learn from each other. Similarly, Peck Elementary is in the process of developing such a space.

Mentoring programs provided another vehicle for teachers to work and plan together. Specifically, Centerville and Ward had established mentor programs that were designed particularly to support new teachers. Team teaching at Spellman (as part of the Canady model) required teachers to work with one of the school's specialists during a 90-minute block. At Goodale, shared professional development experiences often became a starting point for collaborations among teachers. Teachers would return from such events and work together toward implementation of strategies learned.

Teachers at these nine schools were constantly learning about academic content and academic instruction. Often, they learned as much from each other as they learned from any other source. Their planning efforts were central to the improvements in instruction at the schools.

Winning the Confidence and Respect of Parents and Building Partnerships With Them

At all nine schools, educators engaged in a wide variety of efforts to win the confidence and respect of parents. Educators did not simply seek to involve parents in token activities. Instead, educators sought a meaningful partnership with parents.

Successful partnerships never would have been established if parents did not see tangible evidence of the school's concern for their children. As the school made efforts to adapt to the needs of children, parents were willing to exert greater effort to support the school. The teachers and principals of the nine schools helped parents believe that the school could provide great opportunities for their children. Parents responded positively to those efforts with an outpouring of support in various forms. Parents talked about what teachers had done for their children and the kind of place the school had become. They articulated a confidence that the school staff had their children's best interests at heart.

The conventional wisdom suggests that parental involvement leads to improved achievement. However, in these schools, there was also evidence that the reverse was true—improved school achievement led to increased parental involvement. Parents were more willing to be supportive because they saw evidence that educators cared about their children and worked hard to improve achievement. Of course, this increased parental involvement then became an important tool for generating further improvements in academic learning.

An important step in building partnerships with parents was making them feel like they were welcome as equals at school. Educators at Baldwin, Centerville, Spellman, and Ward described "open-door policies" that encouraged parents to visit the school and visit their child's classroom. At Baskin, teachers and administrators stood outside the school in the morning as parents dropped off their children. They invited parents to come in and have coffee and doughnuts and chat about their child's progress. Similarly, at Goodale, parents were invited to attend "Snack and Chat" sessions with teachers during lunch. At Centerville and Peck, parent centers were established that gave parents a place to meet, organize activities, and participate in enrichment classes. At Peck, the principal showed the school office staff how to greet and work with parents in a way that made them feel welcome.

Often educators made small but significant extra steps that helped parents feel welcome. For instance, at Baskin, child care was provided during parent–teacher conferences. At Spellman, the school's automated phone service was used to remind every parent about PTA meetings. At Peck, the principal made personal phone calls to parents to encourage them to attend planning meetings.

School personnel helped build partnerships by giving parents important ways to contribute and by acknowledging the important ways in which parents already contributed to the school's success. At Baskin, many parents were involved in planning activities. Furthermore, those parents were encouraged to express their opinions and share their ideas. At Hawley, parents were invited to attend family nights with food and fun, but also, at these events, parents were asked to share their opinions, ideas, and desires for their children. At Peck, parents were asked, "What do you think we need to do to help make Peck a better school?" At these schools, parents were treated as if they were highly valued consultants with important ideas and insights.

Parents were also given important ways to contribute to their own child's academic success. At Baskin, videotapes were used to inform parents about activities in their child's classroom and to help parents understand what children were learning and how they could help at home. At Burgess, parents participated in the Saturday school program. Parental participation was encouraged and structured so parents could learn strategies they could use with their children at home. Similarly, Burgess parents got training in how to help their children prepare for the science and social science fair. At Centerville, parents participated in family science nights and family math nights that provided many ideas that could be replicated easily at home. PTA meetings at Centerville were used to teach parents strategies for assisting their children with schoolwork.

Of course, parents were also given important opportunities to volunteer at school. However, the schools made important efforts to make sure that parents felt their time was well spent. At Burgess, teachers participated in workshops designed to help them learn how to plan for the use of volunteers in their classrooms. At Centerville, the school developed volunteer job descriptions based on needs identified by staff. Parents were given the opportunity to fill those jobs that best matched their talents and available time.

Parents became important contributors to the success of these schools. Parents contributed ideas, time, and assistance that helped make the schools more responsive to the needs and strengths of children. By helping at home, helping at school, or helping in the community, parents helped the schools improve the academic success as well as the personal success of students.

Creating Additional Time for Instruction

Each of the nine schools created additional time for academic instruction. In some cases, efforts focused on creating additional time for attention to critical instructional issues during the school day. In other cases, efforts focused on creating additional time beyond the regular school day.

At Baskin, Baldwin, Peck, and Spellman, school leaders created additional time during the school day for attention to reading. In each school, there was a 90-minute period devoted to literacy. Furthermore, at each school, almost all staff were involved in teaching reading during this period, thereby reducing adult-to-child ratios. At Baskin, teachers used assessment data to change instructional groupings that provided more intensive instructional time (three-to-one groupings twice a week) for students in need of additional assistance.

At Burgess, Baldwin, Hawley, Peck, and Ward there were after-school programs intended to create additional opportunities for students to learn important content and skills. At Centerville, teachers provided valuable tutoring for students during lunch periods.

Educators at the schools assumed that they could get their students to reach high academic standards; however, they recognized that additional time was often necessary to ensure student success.

Persisting Through Difficulties, Setbacks, and Failures

None of the principals and none of the teachers interviewed reported that the transformation of their school was easy. In fact, there were many reports of difficulties, challenges, and frustrations. Perhaps, a key difference between these schools and other less successful schools is that educators in these schools persisted. They refused to give up the dream of academic success.

Initially, at Spellman, some of the staff did not like the idea of having instructional specialists and rebelled against using them. At Baldwin, some teachers perceived that the mandate to improve learning was an affront to them. At Peck, parents circulated a petition and demanded that the school board remove the new principal. In the principal's second year at Ward, teachers had to deal with a district reorganization and a slow building rehabilitation project that hampered preparation for the beginning of the school year. These difficulties and others might have been sufficient to derail improvement efforts; however, the school leaders persisted.

At Peck, the principal kept asking herself if her actions were in the best interest of children. When she answered affirmatively, she knew she should continue. Also, at Peck, as was the case at Burgess, the support of district office administrators was sometimes crucial in helping the principals hold the course.

On the other hand, there were times when principals felt the need to fend off district office directives that threatened their reform efforts. Some principals described efforts to resist district pressure and avoid hiring teachers who had been removed from positions in other schools. Some principals told how they preserved the teachers' time for collaboration and resisted district efforts to involve their staff in district-wide professional development activities that did not address the needs of their students or teachers. Some principals described other district policies that could have diffused their school's focus on academic improvement. Often those principals either negotiated compromises or found ways to comply that were minimally disruptive to the school's improvement efforts.

Perhaps, the persistence of school leaders was influenced primarily by their deep commitment to the students and families they served. They perceived their work less as a job and more as a mission. They persisted because they believed in themselves, they believed in their school staffs, and they believed in the ability of the children to succeed.

CONCLUSIONS

These nine schools are not perfect. Each school continues to struggle to improve achievement. In some schools, they are working to deepen student learning in core subject areas. In other schools, they strive to extend academic excellence beyond reading and mathematics to other areas of the curriculum. In some of the nine, they continue to work to build a team among teachers, support staff, and parents. In others, they are trying to get students to accept a broader sense of responsibility for their learning and school success. Although teachers and administrators at the schools were quick to point out the areas where they still hope to improve, all nine schools have achieved impressive results.

Surrounded by poverty and all of the negative features associated with poverty, these schools have achieved academic goals that many people would have assumed unrealistic. Their academic results compare favorably with other schools in urban, poor communities; but also, they compare well with many suburban schools that serve much more affluent populations. In some cases, their achievement is demonstrated on norm-referenced assessments. In others, their success is visible in results from criterion-referenced or performance-based assessments. In each school there are many other evidences as well of academic success in the daily work of students as they demonstrate the ability to read with understanding, write in a manner that communicates ideas clearly, and use mathematics to solve problems.

If such success were apparent in only one school, we might applaud the administrators and teachers as heroes and wish that we were so lucky to have such miracle workers in our communities. In contrast, however, there were nine successful schools in this study and if data, resources, and time were available, we probably could have identified 90 others throughout the country. These successes came from the hard work of everyday teachers, administrators, support staff, parents, and students.

Ultimately, the question posed by these schools is "Why not?" If a school in inner-city Detroit, Houston, or Boston can achieve these results, then why not the school a mile or two down the road? If a school in a poor community in San Antonio, Chicago, or Atlanta can bring almost all of its students to high levels of academic success, they why not the school in my community? If a school in East St. Louis, metropolitan Washington, D.C., or Milwaukee can achieve such a high level of academic distinction, then why not every school in America?

The answer certainly cannot be attributable to the problems of students or parents because these nine schools have students and families with the same challenges found in any poor community. The answer cannot be attributed to the quantity of resources available. Although these schools had reasonable resources, they generally had no greater resources than low-performing schools in their districts.

Perhaps, the answer to "why not," is that many of us assumed that this level of achievement could not be attained or at least, could not be attained at "my school." Perhaps, the answer is that many of us simply did not know where to begin, what to do, or how to proceed to move from current levels of performance to a much higher level of academic expectation. Hopefully, the stories of these nine schools address both types of answers and increase our resolve to create excellent schools in every community throughout the nation.

REFERENCES

Hopfenberg, W. S., & Levin, H. M. (1993). *The accelerated schools resource guide*. San Francisco, CA: Jossey-Bass.

Lein, L., Johnson, J. F., Ragland, M. (1996). *Successful Texas schoolwide programs*. Austin, TX: Charles A. Dana Center, University of Texas at Austin.

Reyes, P., Scribner, J. D., & Scribner, A. P. (Eds.). (1999). *Lessons from high-performing Hispanic schools*. New York: Teachers College Press.

Slavin, R. E., Madden, N. A., Dolan, L. J., & Wasik, B. A. (1992). *Success for all: A relentless approach to prevention and early intervention in elementary schools*. Arlington, VA: Educational Research Service.

Taylor, B. (Ed.). (1990). *Case studies in effective schools research*. Dubuque, IA: Kendall/Hunt.

United States House of Representatives. (1997, November). *105th Congress Conference Report (No. 105–390)*. U.S. Congress. Washington, DC.

To acquire a complete copy of *Hope for Urban Education*, call the U. S. Department of Education's publication office at 1-877-4ED-PUBS (1-877-433-7827).

4

Literacy in Rural Vermont: Lessons From Schools Where Children Succeed

Jim Mosenthal
Marjorie Lipson
Susan Sortino
Barbara Russ
Jane Mekkelsen
The University of Vermont

INTRODUCTION

Children who are poor, schools that are strapped for resources, and families who struggle are facts of life everywhere. Although Vermont is among the most rural states in the country, there are cities and towns, suburbs and villages—a range of communities. In this chapter, however, we discuss the most rural schools in the state.

The stories of these schools seem to result, in part, from the very smallness of their buildings. The buildings are small and so are class sizes. But, lest there be a temptation to attribute their success to their size alone, it needs to be noted that rural schools, in Vermont, have traditionally been among the least "successful" as measured in conventional achievement terms. These schools have a high degree of poverty and the communities are isolated. They have the highest percentages of students on free- and reduced-lunch programs, serve townships as opposed to towns with an identifiable center, have the fewest number of teachers and students, and pay the lowest teacher salaries in the state. We call these schools "Country" schools. Among the schools in the state, the "Country" schools have the fewest number of "first-tier" (high-performing) schools and the highest number of very low performers. Not surprisingly, these schools have the largest number of children identified as eligible for special education services. Our purpose in this study is to investigate a sample of Country schools exhibiting high student performance on statewide literacy assessments at second and fourth grade, and to determine the contexts and practices that contribute to those schools' success. These Country schools in Vermont represent another type of "beat the odds" schools.

The data for this study comes from a larger study that examined successful schools in three demographic clusters—the Country cluster of schools, the Main Street cluster (larger schools, with greater resources), and the Uptown[1] cluster (largest schools, wealthiest communities). Data were collected during September 1999–January 2000 on schools that showed high performance scores on the Spring, 1998 administration of the second and fourth grade literacy assessments.

BACKGROUND

There are a number of studies that have demonstrated the existence of "effective" versus ineffective schools. A recent analysis of 50 years of research suggests that, "the different kinds of classroom instruction and climate had nearly as much impact on learning as the student aptitude categories" (Wang, Haertel, & Walberg, 1994). In addition, the culture of the school can inform students of the acceptable forms of achievement and motivation (Dreeben, 1968), while systems features of the school such as its size, neighborhood, and structure also influence students' motivation and achievement by affecting their expectations for success, self-esteem, and performance (Schmuck, 1980). It is clear, that a number of both school and nonschool factors influence student achievement in literacy. However, much of this research is correlational, demonstrating only that norm-referenced test scores (the most common student outcome) are positively related to another factor.

---

[1]The terms *Country, Main Street* and *Uptown* are obviously fictionalized names that are designed only to help the reader characterize the nature of these clusters in the broadest terms. Within each cluster there is considerable variability and, inevitably, at least some schools seem to be a poor fit to the primary cluster attributes. School names are also fictionalized but without any significance attached to their pseudonyms.

As evidenced in this volume, researchers across the country have begun examining "beat the odds" schools for evidence of successful practice. (Langer, 1999; Snyder, 1999; Taylor, Pearson, Clark, & Walpole, 2000). Although the convergence of findings is quite stunning (see e.g., Lipson, Mosenthal, Mekkelson, Russ, & Sortino, 1999, and Taylor et al., 2000), there are still remarkably few rich studies of the contexts for success; studies that identify "successful" schools and then examine the *range* and *interaction* of factors that might account for students' success in those schools by means of a qualitative methodology. Our study, along with the others in this volume, is different in that we studied both *teacher instructional* and *school* variables in order to characterize the complex of factors that might be needed to achieve high levels of student success, particularly in schools who do not have a well-prepared and privileged student population. In addition, we used standards-based measures, making it possible to determine to what degree students have acquired sophisticated and challenging levels of literacy.

WHAT WE DID

For several years we have been studying schools in Vermont that have achieved very high levels of literacy. We spent a great deal of time in six successful and three less-successful schools representing three distinct clusters of school/community demographics. We interviewed and observed 52 Grade K through 4 teachers in the successful schools and 25 K through 4 teachers in the less successful schools. In addition, we interviewed the school principals, curriculum coordinators, and librarians; the district superintendents; and, where appropriate, other individuals. For example, in some buildings we interviewed all the para-educators, whereas in other buildings we interviewed the special educator and reading teacher.

Before we began, we examined data from *all* of Vermont's elementary schools and, using a cluster analysis, grouped the schools according to a wide range of demographic variables. Three groups, or clusters, of schools grew out of this analysis and we labeled the groups *Country*, *Main Street*, and *Uptown* to capture some of the variability and distinctiveness of the clusters. Throughout the data collection we identified critical attributes and themes in these settings in an effort to fully describe the specific contexts for success. Ultimately, the goal of the study reported in this chapter is to understand the complex and interrelated factors contributing to the success, or lack thereof, of children in Vermont's most rural schools. For a more thorough description of the larger study and of the data from all the successful school clusters refer to the report, *Elementary*

Schools Where Children Succeed in Literacy (Mosenthal, Lipson, Mekkelsen, Russ, & Sortino, in press).

The Country Schools

Of Vermont's 219 elementary schools, 36% are Country schools (as opposed to 48% and 16% for Main Street and Uptown clusters, respectively). These schools are generally small, poor, and rural with large numbers of adults who have not completed school work beyond high school. Indeed, on average, approximately 22% of the adults in these communities do *not* have a high school diploma. This is significantly higher than the Main Street communities (9.6%), and both sets of communities are significantly higher than the Uptown communities (6.21%). In contrast, many more adults in Main Street and Uptown communities have at least some college education. Whereas more than half of the Uptown adults have at least some college education (56%), only about a third of Country adults have any education beyond the high school degree (38%).

Country schools have the largest numbers of children identified as eligible for special education services (10–11%), and the lowest numbers of children with limited English proficiency (.3%) reflecting the homogeneity of these rural communities. There are very few teachers and even fewer instructional aides or other support personnel in these schools. Teachers are paid significantly less than their counterparts in the other clusters because local taxes, with limited state funding, pay for schooling, resulting in great variability from community to community.

Defining Success Across the Grades

To select high-performing schools within each cluster we looked at data from the state reading test administered at second grade and the two reading components of the New Standards Reference Exams (NSRE) administered statewide at fourth grade. Both tests were administered in the Spring of 1998. The VT-DRA and the NSRE data were both used to insure selection of schools with strong literacy performance—and thus strong practices and programs—across the elementary grades.

Based on the spring test results, we selected schools in which at least 80% of the students at Grade 2 had performed at or above the standard in reading and also in which at least 80% of the students at Grade 4 had achieved at or above the standard on both the basic understanding and analysis/interpretation components of the NSRE. This yielded a very small number of schools, with schools from each cluster represented. Of the 79 Country schools, five schools (6%)

met the selection criteria, versus eight or 8% of the Main Street schools, and five or 14% of the Uptown schools .

For our larger study we selected two of these high performing schools from within each cluster. In addition, we identified at least one additional school at or near the bottom of student performance for each cluster. The less-successful schools were tracked for one additional year. The spring, 1999 results were added to those for spring, 1998 to ensure stability in student performance trends.

In this chapter we discuss two high-performing schools from the Country cluster (Sommers and Carlisle schools) and contrast those schools with a low performing Country school (Ellis; see Table 4.1).

SUCCESSFUL COUNTRY SCHOOLS:
THE CASES OF CARLISLE AND SOMMERS

Carlisle and Sommers Schools are both members of our "Country School" Cluster, representing approximately 36% of all the schools in Vermont. Like their counterparts, Carlisle and Sommers are very small and very rural. Both the village of Carlisle and the village of Sommers are quite remote, although they are in some proximity to more extensive services and opportunities: one is 5 miles from a ski area with resort-like services, shops, and restaurants, whereas the other is about 15 miles from a small state college and its surrounding town. Both schools were "successful" schools based on our criteria for performance on the DRA-VT and the NSRE.

In these schools, success in literacy can be attributed to several major influences: teacher autonomy, ongoing professional development, collaboration among faculty, and ongoing assessment and responsive teaching. All these attributes seem to grow from the universally strong commitment of the schools and teachers to teaching every child. In addition, the Carlisle and Sommers schools have remarkably similar histories and instructional programs. Approximately 10 years ago, the teachers in each school began to undertake real change. In both schools teachers and administrators point to two over-riding factors that account for the success of their students' performance. These are: (1) an individual, influential teacher, and (2) committed teachers who have created coherent and well-articulated literacy programs throughout the grades.

In Vermont, the professional development environment has been vibrant since the late 1980s and these are teachers and schools that took advantage of that environment. An activist state superintendent of schools, a tradition of innovation, university faculty involved in constructivist research and a series of grass-roots educational movements ("whole language," "multi-age," "Reading Recovery") all contributed to the rich and varied professional development climate. At the state

TABLE 4.1

Relevant Descriptive Data for Three "Country" Schools

Relevant Data	School		
	Sommers	Carlisle	Ellis
Building size	K–8 building with 160 students	K–6 building with 110 students	PreK–6 building with 170 students
Percent of students meeting or exceeding standard on the Grade 2 reading test (VT-DRA)	82%	82%	50%
Percent of students meeting or exceeding standard on the Grade 4 reading test (NSRE)	Basic Understanding: 93% Analysis/ Interpretation: 62%	Basic Understanding: 100% Analysis/ Interpretation: 91%	Basic Understanding: 46% Analysis/ Interpretation: 21%
Percent of adults who do NOT have high school diploma	23%	29%	31%
Percent of adults with less than ninth-grade education	13.5%	14%	17%
Percent of adults with at least some education beyond high school	18%	34%	22%
Percent of students receiving Free/ reduced lunch	59%	53%	57%
Percent of students receiving Special Education services	7.6%	12.6%	12.2%
Average number of years teaching experience	14	14	14

level, new guidelines for public school approval were enacted. For the first time, the legislature and the public began to focus on instruction and assessment. The state, working in concert with concerned educators created a portfolio system for documenting and assessing writing and mathematics. In a unique, and portentous move, they created a system of "network leaders," classroom teachers with particular expertise in these areas who worked with teachers throughout the state to refine and improve instruction in writing and mathematics. State department personnel capitalized on this growing professional competence when they promoted "consortiums" of school districts to fund the first Reading Recovery training in the state and when they designed networks for the implementation of the Grade 2 reading assessment. With very little state-level funding, but a great deal of collaborative and grass-roots effort, the state has sustained a series of ambitious initiatives in both assessment and standards. In both of our successful country schools, one energetic and inspiring colleague was trained as a Reading Recovery teacher during the 1991–1993 time frame. These teachers influenced their colleagues significantly.

Carlisle Elementary School

Carlisle school is nestled in a remote village near one of the state's larger ski areas. Many people in Carlisle are employed seasonally by the nearby resort. Approximately 53% of the children are eligible for free or reduced lunch. The families have strong links to the community and school. The community library is a part of the school's physical structure, contributing to the sense of the school as the hub of the community. Sense of community is important within the school also. Each school day begins with the entire school assembling outdoors for the flag salute, morning greetings and announcements, and singing. The principal, Gerald Humphrey, knows all the children intimately and is very aware of the daily curriculum that is taking place in each classroom.

Carlisle's student population is 110, Grades K through 6, with three collaborative K through 2 multi-age classrooms, two collaborative 3 through 4 multi-age classrooms, and two collaborative 5 through 6 multi-age classrooms. Physical space is at a premium, thus teachers work in close quarters with each other—classrooms double as music and art rooms; multi-age teams eat lunch together rotating into each other's spaces, which also affords opportunities to reflect on the physical learning environment and curriculum. One primary grade teacher is also the afternoon Reading Recovery teacher and the trainer for the many America Reads volunteers that permeate the school.

Outside the school hangs a welcoming sign—a message to all who pass by: "Children Are The Future." Throughout the year, additional informative lines are added to the sign. In recognition of Dr. Seuss's birthday, for example, the following had been added to the sign:

Cat in the Hat Party
Staff and Students Read
31,165 pages in 1 week

This outward indication of the school's commitment to children and their literacy development is echoed inside the school.

Leadership, Professional Development, and Commitment

Approximately 10 years ago, the teachers in Carlisle began to undertake real change (see Fig. 4.1). Taking advantage of a regional consortium organized by the state department of education and funded by the area school districts, Carlisle's supervisory union sent one talented teacher to be trained as a Reading Recovery teacher during 1991 through 1993. Debbie influenced her colleagues, modeled strategies, took her teammates along to conferences, and shared her enthusiasm for a methodology she believed really made a difference for individual children. Her colleagues, in turn, took "Supportive Classroom" and "Guided Reading" courses.

This leadership has been sustained over a substantial period. As the building principal notes, Debbie (the Reading Recovery/ literacy expert) is a "very, very strong advocate for the whole literacy program; she's very very committed to it, it's kind of always a focus in her mind." Her Reading Recovery training strongly influences the practice the primary teachers implement and more subtly guides the direction for teachers at Grades 3 through 4.

The faculty recognize that these approaches have allowed them to "know the knower" or to teach responsively to individual children. In addition, they argue that this approach has influenced student performance because of the consistent instruction that has resulted. They believe it's critical that the children are using the same strategies, same terms, and same language throughout their primary grade experience.

At Carlisle, the size of the school and staff has definitely influenced how decisions are made regarding practice. The staff of three primary grade teachers usually eats lunch together in one of their rooms. They discuss the morning happenings, focusing on individual children and "how things are going." In 1996, as an outcome of these ongoing, informal discussions the teachers de-

Country Schools

School	1987–1988	1988–1989	1989–1990	1990–1991	1991–1992	1992–1993	1993–1994	1994–1995	1995–1996	1996–1997	1997–1998
Carlisle	Prin:** new principal		RR: district joins state sponsored Recovery Consortium	RR: Debbie, gr. 1 teacher, trained as Reading Recovery teacher		RR: K-2 teachers take course & training in guided reading & Reading Recovery		RR: PhAw: K-2 teachers change to Reading Recovery based instruction, considered a "work in progress;" teachers take courses in phonological awareness			ST: high scores on the Vt DRA and NSRE statewide tests
Sommers	Wlang.: Wendy, primary grade teacher, attends whole language conference and is influenced by Don Holdaway		Univ.: Wendy starts M.Ed. at The University of Vermont	RR: District joins state sponsored Reading Recovery Consortium		RR: Wendy trained as Reading Recovery Teacher; K-2 teachers take courses on Reading Recovery in the classroom		RR; VtDRA; Spell: Wendy teaches early literacy to Sommers' teachers; K-2 teachers train/pilot statewide 2nd grade literacy assessment; Sommers adopts Cast-A-Spell (isolated word study)			ST: high scores on the Vt DRA and NSRE statewide tests
Ellis*	***		For budgetary reasons, management team leads school from 199-1991 to 1994-1995					Prin: RR: new principal; K & Title 1 teachers train in CHEERS, a Reading Recovery program			Spell: school adopts Cast-A-Spell, an isolated word study of spelling with white boards
Vermont	Comm Pfs	PSA RR			Pfs		ROPA	VISMT Pfs	Stds	NSRE	VtDRA

*Ellis is the less successful school.
**Abbreviations identify the nature of continuous development within the school or school district.

Abbreviation	Description
Comm	new Vermont Commissioner of Education appointed
NSRE	New Standards Reference Examination in reading, writing, and math
Pfs	Vermont focus on portfolios for the assessment of math and writing statewide
PhAw	phonological awareness focus
Prin	new principal appointed
PSA	Public School Approval rating by the state
ROPA	Results Oriented Program Approval implemented based on the portfolio assessment of preservice teachers
RR	Reading Recovery Program or related training
Spell	spelling focus or training
ST	Vermont Developmental Reading Assessment implemented statewide at 2nd grade; New Standards Reference Examination in reading implemented statewide at 4th grade
Stds	Vermont Framework of Standard published to serve as the basis for a comprehensive statewide assessment
Univ	role or influence of the University of Vermont
VISMT	Vermont Institute of Science, Math, and Technology, multimillion dollar federal/state grant to improve instruction and learning in science, math, and technology
VtDRA	Vermont Developmental Reading Assessment implemented statewide at 2nd grade
WLang	whole language focus or training

*The occurrences noted in this list are occurrences that happened for a school during an 8-10 year time frame. It is not implied that each of the occurrences contributed directly in the continuous development of a school. Rather, they indicate that something was happening that was not a false start (e.g. principal turnover) vs. anything happening for the school.

FIG. 4.1.   Long-term commitment to literacy of successful versus less successful country schools, 1988–1998.

cided on a new model of instructional practice. They mutually agreed that "they all had strengths and interests" and that perhaps the children could benefit from them. The "smallness" of the group involved and the type of ongoing communication they had with their principal allowed for this type of change to be implemented. Debbie is the reading specialist for Grades K through 2 and her classroom is devoted to ongoing and engaging literacy interactions; another teacher, Carol, teaches science/health and works with first and second graders each afternoon in guided reading groups; and the third, Patricia, is the math and writing expert.

The two teachers who comprise the Grades 3 through 4 team also work closely together and make decisions in a similar manner. These teachers continually evaluate and "tinker" with the systems and programs they have in place in their constant quest to make learning "work" for the children.

Instructional Practices

The teachers at Carlisle devote large amounts of time for literacy (approximately 90 minutes each day) and the children read a great deal. There are large quantities of books in the classrooms—accessible and inviting to children. One room in the Kindergarten through second-grade classrooms is the "reading room" where over 1000 books, neatly organized and, in most cases, leveled, are at the children's fingertips. One of the two interconnected third- through fourth-grade classrooms serves as the "library" for those grades/classrooms. There is an estimated 1200 books between two grades and 28 children. (See Table 4.2 for a comparison among Country Schools of books per classroom, time spent reading, and time spent reading to children.)

The K–1–2 Multi-age Classrooms. The primary unit is comprised of three multi-age (K–1–2) classrooms. In this unit, there is a daily Read-Aloud time and a minimum of 25 minutes each day when children are reading—either silently or out loud to an adult. In addition, children are engaged with text during their guided reading group times. Carlisle's infusion of America Reads volunteers ensures that children are getting a healthy dose of one-on-one time to read (see Table 4.2). In the morning, children rotate in and out of the various rooms. In the "reading room," Debbie supports children as they engage in self-directed, individualized reading activity. Our observations reveal that children are involved in a variety of reading and book-related activities during 30-minute periods. During one of our visits, Debbie sat with a small group of kindergarten (half-day) children. One child read aloud to her; one read silently; and another worked on an "ABC" book that provided reinforcement of let-

TABLE 4.2

Opportunity To Read and Discuss Books in Two Successful
and One Less Successful Country Schools

More & Less Successful Country Schools*	Est. # of Books/Classroom	Est. Mins. Reading per day	Est. Mins. Teacher Read Aloud per Day	Total Mins. Rdg./Listening to Text per Day
Carlisle	≈675	30	25	55
Sommers	≈200	50	20	70
Ellis	Range** 50–700	20	15	35

*The Successful schools, Carlisle and Sommers (roman), scored high on the VT DRA and New Standards Reference Examination Reading Subtests administered in the Spring of 1998 (≥80% of students scored *above* the grade-level standard); Ellis Elementary School (in italic was less successful on the two tests; ≥80% of students scored *below* the grade-level standard).

**While Carlisle's and Sommers' books per classroom remained consistent across classrooms, at Ellis School the books per classroom were dramatically inconsistent, ranging from virtually none to 700, comparable with Carlisle's average books per classroom.

ter/sound recognition the child needed. The other children were involved in one of the following activities:

- listening center, listening to a story on tape (goal is to work on fluency)
- computer (working on a phonemic awareness game)
- art center, reading with an America Reads volunteer
- various, book nooks and/or lofts reading self-selected books independently—there is a cozy antique bathtub lined with soft cushions—a perfect place to curl up with a good book.

As Debbie listens to the children read aloud, she comments on their reading ("point to each word as you read"), the nature of the story ("perhaps we can look for a story that can be turned into a play next ..."), and embeds instruction ("if you come to word you don't know ..."). At the end of the half-hour, Debbie rings the chimes and the children line up to rotate into one of the other two classrooms and a new group of K–1–2s enters hers.

After lunch and recess, with the kindergartners gone, the first and second graders spend 60 minutes in the "reading room" again for a somewhat more formal literacy time. The primary teachers have been strongly influenced by New Zealand models and have adopted a Guided Reading approach. Reading Recovery provides essential service to individual children and also defines the types of classroom practice employed by the teachers. Phonological awareness, too, has taken on a priority. Thus, the ensuing block of literacy instruction is a balance of whole group spelling/phonics instruction; flexible, small group reading discussion groups; and individualized folder/workbook work.

Children are encouraged to support each other. During one observation, for example, one kindergarten child wanted to read a book she was not yet able to read. Debbie realized this and asked if someone would "read it to Sally; she can't read this one alone yet." Of course, someone obliged. These authentic opportunities for reading practice are a feature of the multi-age classrooms we observed.

There is also a daily read-aloud each morning after the morning school assembly. On one occasion the K through 2 children clustered into one of the classrooms to listen to the teacher read in their ongoing chapter book, "*Winter Days in the Woods*" by Laura Ingalls Wilder. After one of the teachers had finished a chapter, she posed an interpretive question to the whole group concerning the reasoning behind a remark that Laura (main character) had made. After several children volunteered their responses, the group dispersed to their respective classrooms. Within 2 minutes, all 47 children were settled and ready to begin their morning focus.

The Third- Through Fourth-Grade Multi-age Classrooms.   In the third and fourth grades, the teachers promote a very independent, individualized approach where children are engaged in self-selecting trade books; writing ongoing reading journal entries and summaries; conferencing with teachers and sharing their new knowledge and interests with each other. Student engagement with quality literature is a high priority in these classrooms.

The two teachers share approximately 1,200 books (multiple copies, all types of genres) and reading occurs throughout the day. The Reader's Workshop format is used and Julie and Audrey, a pair who have teamed together for 5 years, share their strong commitment to several principles. The teachers stress the importance of teaching children to choose books at their proper level and to exposing them to all genres. In addition, they insist that children write about their reading frequently. They want their students to be reflective about what they're reading. Both teachers have explicit guidelines that govern acceptable reading responses. The guidelines address both quantity and substance

During Reader's Workshop, children are engaged in reading. Our observations suggest that students may also be: researching and summarizing independent projects using books and computers; sharing a passage from a book they're reading or a story they're writing and asking for their peers' advice/perspective; engaging in "Story Sells" (summaries or impressions); and writing story summaries and/or reading journal entries in preparation for an "exit" interview about an independent book just completed. Julie and Audrey assert that the most important thing they do is, invest a tremendous amount of time making sure the library has the appropriate amount of materials for the range of children. "We want to make sure there's plenty to keep the fourth graders challenged—reading at a sixth grade or higher level, whereas on the other end we might have this child reading a second-grade level and coming in as a third grader and we've got a nice variety there. We're really open and we talk a lot about levels, nothing's a baby book, we model how we like to read."

These teachers have also been able to engage their students in reading outside of the classroom. The children in Grades 3 and 4 are part of a "Three Hundred Hour Club" that involves reading at home contractually for a total of 10 hours. As a part of this contractual work, students commit to reading a certain number of pages. A bulletin board outside the classroom informs the school community of their contractual progress.

Julie and Audrey describe how their approach to literacy instruction changes, usually in the spring, when book discussion groups take precedent over Reader's Workshop. Groups read a book together, focusing more on "book talks" than writing. They also work on story elements and presentation skills. The children are very computer literate and resourceful. There are high expectations for focused, quality work and everyone is expected to support and learn from each other. In our observations, we noted that teachers frequently call on the students' peers to offer support, resources, perspectives and teaching as needed. The climate in all classrooms suggested a community of learners supporting and learning from each other.

Classroom Management and Student Engagement

The teachers and students spend their time in classrooms that are exceptionally well-managed. The classroom environments look informal but the students and teachers are very business-like. Hardly any time is taken with transitions or behavior management. Although there are challenging children in these classrooms, the teachers are highly skilled and have high expectations—the children understand that and, consequently, almost all of the allocated time for literacy ends up being engaged time. Field notes reflect mere minutes in what could be major transition times.

The teachers are also articulate about the focused pace to their days. They realize that different subjects are beginning to compete with each other for time and consequently they are thoughtful and efficient with the time they have. Debbie, the morning Kindergarten through second-grade teacher and afternoon Reading Recovery teacher, passionately shares her concern about

> "feeling under pressure to get our children at a certain place and I feel that sometimes we're letting some parts of a balanced literacy program go by. We're having trouble reading every day to children and I just made a big issue of that because I thought especially with our kindergarten children we need to read to them every day, so we did just recently work that out so it would happen."

Julie and Audrey emphatically talk about their very high standards.

> "We're very clear with the kids (about) what the standards are; we rarely ever give an assignment that doesn't have 'I expect you to have this, this and this, here is your scoring guide' ... We view reading and writing a lot like doing practicing like you would for multiplication facts; we just write everyday and we read every day faithfully and we never give up."

The purposefulness, commitment, and management of instruction during literacy time is evident in both the teacher interviews and our observations.

One overriding commitment is very clear. The staff and administration are dedicated to exposing children to quality literature and giving time to the act of reading. One way they've achieved this goal is through the America Reads program. In preparation of the 1998–1999 school year senior citizen volunteers from the organization RSVP teamed up with America Reads and Debbie, the Reading Recovery teacher and Kindergarten through second-grade reading teacher, for "extra" training. The school atmosphere is one of children and adults, alike, committed to and enjoying books.

School Community

The teachers in Carlisle have an unusually close relationship with each other. Although their individual classrooms and styles can look quite different, their shared vision and respect for each other as professionals is very evident. There is a lively, collegial tone to their communication.

The teachers themselves articulate the strength and supportiveness of their school community. Patty, a Kindergarten through second-grade teacher, describes it this way:

> "Our staff is very open to things that are working and very willing to share with each other; everybody pitches in. If somebody comes across something they think would be useful for us, a workshop or some sort of materials they are more than willing to pass in on."

For example, Carol, another Kindergarten through second-grade teacher recently took a course on the development of phonological awareness among young children. This course was taught from a somewhat different philosophical stance than the one typified by teachers in this school, but that did not stop her from learning, nor others from taking advantage of her newly acquired information. These teachers are focused on improving instruction for individuals and they share new information and construct new teaching strategies through informal and formal dialogues with each other. As important, the community is pervasive, including teachers and classroom assistants. Julie emphasizes the role that the classroom assistants play in the success of their program:

> "There is a big part of our program that would die without our classroom—individual aides; let's clarify that, they're individual aides, they're hired to be with one particular student, but we're really fortunate in having some incredible, incredible assistants teaching multi-task at one point ... and our special education coordinator's pretty comfortable in letting us direct her schedule with what our needs are and Valarie (the Title One teacher) is great!"

The teachers also acknowledge the principal's ongoing support "to allow us to do what we need to do". It should be noted that Gerald, the principal, has been a part of the school and its journey since 1988–1989. One of the staff, Debbie, believes that "teachers have set the initiative for what they want to learn in the building and he has been very supportive of that."

The teachers in Carlisle Elementary School operate quite autonomously while being supported by a long-time principal who is highly regarded by teachers and students alike.

Sommers Elementary School

Sommers School, the other successful Country school in our study, sits on a rise above a tiny village approximately 15 miles from a small state college and its surrounding town. The only approaches to the village of Sommers are along winding dirt roads and the white steeple of the church is the only hint of a town. There are no stores, filling stations, or other businesses. What stands out are the farms, lots of them, and small houses—some well kept, others not.

Sommers, like Carlisle, is small with a school population of 160, with a classroom for each grade level, Kindergarten through eighth. There are 2 half-day kindergarten sessions and the size of the grade-level classrooms varies dramatically from year to year in such a small school. Like their counterparts in this cluster, the town of Sommers is poor and poorly educated. Seasonal farm work and logging are the most common sources of employment. Approximately 59% of the children receive free or reduced lunch. The boundaries between school, community, and family are somewhat difficult to distinguish within this remote and very small school. The only library for miles around is the school library and it is the only building large enough to house various community functions. The last day of the school year is always scheduled to be a Saturday so that they can have a half-day of school and then a community picnic. As the principal re-marked, "The teachers see the school as an extension of themselves, their fami-lies. They have a strong sense of ownership about this school."

Although the class sizes are small (on average, 13 students per grade level in Grades 1 through 4), teachers do work very hard. There are very few, if any, breaks in the day. Teachers have lunch and playground duty and there are no re-liable "special" classes (physical education, art, etc.). In Sommers, teachers have ½ hour a week for planning time. There is little transience in this area and some teachers are teaching children who are offspring of previous students.

The exterior of Sommers School is an inelegant combination that has been cobbled from an ancient core (200-year-old church) and more recently added "wings" made from free-standing metal temporary buildings. Once inside, how-ever, it is clear that Sommers' literacy program involves interesting, engaged, and publicly celebrated work. During one visit, field notes describe the:

> beautiful artwork everywhere, much of it linked to curriculum (i.e., bird studies, paint-ings of folk art symbols, etc.). The commitment to reading is everywhere! Outside the 1st grade is a display of age-appropriate authors, with short biographies and photos. Outside the 2nd grade classroom is documentation explaining Guided Reading as the "Heart of a Balanced Literacy Program." Grade 3 displays neatly typed reports and posters related to earthquakes, volcanoes, tidal waves, etc., and finally multi-media story maps are displayed outside grade 4.

Leadership, Professional Development, and Commitment

Until recently this community (like many in Vermont) had neither a book-store nor town library. With no bookstores for 20 miles, and an under-educated community, it would be easy to "blame" the families for the limited literacy suc-cess that had been the history of this school. But, the teachers in this building approached the problem differently. The challenge is described clearly by Betty, one of the primary teachers:

> "We can't do it all, so home support is a key element and some people have more of that key element than other children do and we need to find other times—and those other children stay at school—to provide experiences that we would hope could be supported at home."

As noted above, Sommers and Carlisle followed remarkably similar paths as they began to undertake real change approximately 10 years ago (see Fig. 4.1). In Sommers, like Carlisle, an individual influential teacher and Reading Recovery were key factors in improving the school's literacy performance.

In Sommers, every teacher and administrator named Wendy Sharpe as the single most important reason children were doing so well in literacy. As she tells it, she attended a Whole Language Conference in 1988 and was influenced by Don Holdaway. That conference propelled her toward a graduate program at the University of Vermont in 1990 and in 1993 she was trained as a Reading Recovery Teacher. These experiences shaped her own instruction, but also her colleagues. Like Debbie at Carlisle, Wendy shared information, introduced new strategies, encouraged her teammates to go with her to conferences, and communicated her enthusiasm for an approach she believed could turn her school around. Her colleagues, in turn, took "Supportive Classroom" and "Guided Reading" courses, often taught by Wendy and sponsored by the school district. Carolyn, the third-grade teacher, reflects on the inspiration and enthusiasm that is infectious within Sommers in describing her return to teaching after a lengthy family hiatus: "I took a week long whole language course. I was so inspired that week. I got so excited about teaching reading and also it inspired me to start reading myself."

The faculty believe the approach has worked in their school because it focuses on assessment and using assessment information to plan instruction. In addition, they argue that this approach has created a coherent program and common instructional experiences for struggling readers. According to Barbara (Grade 1): "it's critical that the children are using the same strategies, same terms and same language throughout their primary grade experience."

The teachers recognize the importance of the past principal in supporting the move to guided reading and whole language. Although that principal is no longer at Sommers, the Curriculum Coordinator from that time is—she is now the superintendent. Thus, the continuity of support and commitment to professional development complementary to what has been implemented factors into the "success" of the Sommers' students on statewide literacy assessments. One of the teachers commented: "There has been a real [mutual] trust with the administration in the past, [their trust] that we do know what we're doing and we're doing a good job."

It is important to note, that this faculty expertise emerged and developed over time. Although supported by both the local principal and the regional superintendent, the teachers at Sommers, as at Carlisle, have ownership over the changes that have occurred. Change came from extensive professional development—of the homegrown variety—relying heavily on teacher mentoring and colleagueship. Carolyn, who teaches Grade 3, explains that a colleague:

> "inspired me a lot to continue learning and going to continuing ed things and we are all moving in the same direction and we were taking a lot of the same courses and doing a lot of the same work. We are a true team."

Instructional Practices

Teachers devote large amounts of time to literacy—approximately 90–120 minutes per day. During these periods, children read a great deal. Children in Grade K through 2 read with the teacher each day for periods up to 25 minutes and among children in Grades 3 through 4, most read for at least 30 minutes each day. There are also silent reading times each day and a daily read-aloud time.

All teachers at Sommers implement the "block" of literacy time and use it for the purpose of engaging with text. Field notes describe how all teachers mention the value and priority of read-aloud; they all seem to have a clear provision for some reading practice (whether paired or silent); they maintain individualized book lists for each child (passed along from Grades 1 through 3); and Anne, the fourth grade teacher, does book groups and self-selected reading, and talks about choice and ownership with her students.

Like Carlisle, management of these routines are exemplary with no noticeable off-task behavior recorded in field notes. The classroom environments look informal but the teachers and children are very focused on academic work. Hardly any time is taken with transitions or behavior management. The teachers are skilled at managing several activities at once.

The primary teachers have been strongly influenced by New Zealand models. In interviews, teachers describe their commitment to Reading Recovery and the guided reading approach (Fountas & Pinnell, 1996). In observations, it became clear that the teachers across all Kindergarten through third-grade classrooms implement the guided reading approach with great fidelity. They meet with small flexible groups, using individual titles and sets of books that have been leveled according to Reading Recovery standards (1–20) for younger readers and the text gradient system of Fountas and Pinnel (Guided Reading) for somewhat older readers.

The third and fourth grades use trade books at various levels. During our observations, children were engaged with titles like *Stone Fox, Marvin Redpost, Ramona, The BFG, Bridge to Terabithia, Enormous Egg*, etc. Children have access to many books within their classrooms (see Table 4.2), from the 7000 volume library collection, and from the common "book room" for all leveled texts. Explicit teaching of skills is present, along with this infusion of literature. Teachers refer to well-used word walls, conduct Cast-a-Spell lessons (Educare, 1996) that focus on the spelling patterns of English, and attend to word patterns and decoding strategies during guided reading. Although teachers take skills instruction seriously, it is embedded in literature and offered somewhat opportunistically.

Teachers take on-going assessment very seriously. They use Marie Clay's (1993) Observation Survey for all children and maintain weekly running records. As one first-grade teacher remarked: "the use of running records allows me to observe and identify behaviors each child is using. I plan instruction based on these changing observations."

Finally, Reading Recovery provides essential early intervention services to individual children and defines the types of classroom practices employed by teachers. There are also Title I and Special Education professionals to supplement the work of the half-time Reading Recovery teacher who is a half-time classroom teacher.

Underlying all of this instruction is a sense that teachers have confidence in both themselves and their students. As Carolyn, a Grade-2 teacher, reflected on what has made a difference in student achievement, she concluded: "It [successful test scores] probably had to do with 1st grade instruction, setting high expectations for learning and making sure they are praised for the good things they do. And we expect them to live up to whatever those standards are."

School Community

At Sommers the teachers' "commitment to growing professionally" influences their respect for and relationship with each other. The current principal, Susan, remarked on the success of the school by saying "(there are) high quality teachers, committed teachers, teachers who talk to each other." The teachers appear to genuinely value their teammates and the relationships that have been developed around the work they do. One teacher remarked: "We have a wonderful team here, very passionate group of teachers. People willing to work as a team. They're always working overtime."

The importance of collegial talk and hard work appear to be especially important in a small school, where the potential for interpersonal difficulties is large. In addition, the effect of this strong school community has been to focus clearly on improving student learning, while taking responsibility for all students in the school. As Anne, a fourth-grade teacher said, "I think what I find best in this school [is that] I am not the soul owner of these test scores; that's the way it's approached in our school. Here at this school it's full ownership of the children."

The camaraderie amongst the faculty is strong; the result of a faculty cultivated over the years by resourceful administrators and committed teachers.

SUMMARY OF SUCCESSFUL COUNTRY SCHOOLS

Within the individual classroom walls Carlisle and Sommers schools is a unique learning environment and culture. The factors that our study singles out as imperative for "success" exist, to some degree, in each classroom: vision and commitment to literacy learning, coherence of approach, well managed and paced instruction, communication amongst faculty and administration. It is the combination and interplay of these factors that control the ultimate outcome. The manner in which they exist and interrelate are subtle, but real, and implemented thoughtfully.

CONTRAST WITH A LESS SUCCESSFUL LITERACY ENVIRONMENT: ELLIS ELEMENTARY SCHOOL

Ellis School is a part of the Country cluster of schools. Like Carlisle and Sommers, Ellis serves a poor, rural, poorly educated community, with 57% of its students receiving free or reduced lunch. Ellis School sits alone along a rural road. The "town" of Ellis is marked by only a gas station and the nearest town of any real size is 10 miles away. There are 170 children in grades Pre-kindergarten through sixth, with one teacher per grade level. Both the kindergarten and first grade are self-contained. In Grades 2/3 and 4/5, the teachers have combined the grades.

In other respects, Ellis is not at all like Carlisle and Sommers schools. Whereas more than 80% of the students in Sommers and Carlisle are reading at or above the reading standards by the end of Grade 2, only 50% of the children in Ellis are reading that well. By the end of Grade 4, as measured by the New Standards Reference Exam, student performance in reading is even less strong (see Table 4.1).

Leadership, Professional Development, and Commitment

The Ellis School timeline of change (see Fig. 4.1) provides a stark contrast with the successful Sommers and Carlisle schools. There are extensive gaps in the building leadership at Ellis due to turnover. In addition, or as a result, no leader from the ranks of the teachers emerged with the knowledge, belief, and vision that characterized Wendy at Sommers or Debbie at Carlisle. In fact, in 1990 the Ellis school board made the decision that the school would be run by a management committee. This committee lasted until 1996. Part of the committee consisted of a selected group of teachers who were given responsibility for curriculum and implementation. But without a vision of what the curriculum should be, these teachers and the committee as a whole had no purpose nor mandate to address the learning of the school's children. The demise of the management team led to a principal who stayed 2 years. The current principal, Dale, has added a degree of stability and direction that the staff desperately wants.

Instructional Practice

Although Ellis, like the successful schools in this cluster, has consistent blocks of time set aside for literacy, the time is utilized differently across the grades. Some of the classrooms, mostly the upper elementary grades, are engaged in reading quality literature for significant periods of time. The primary grades, for the most part, are focused on word level work for significant periods of time. Observational data suggest that students are reading far less at Ellis than they are in Sommers and Carlisle (see Table 4.2). In a 90 minute Language Arts Block, for example, students read for only 18 minutes. The remainder of the time was spent on isolated skill/drill work associated with a newly purchased phonological awareness program that the second- to third-grade teachers are piloting. This observation was confirmed by a primary teacher who noted that, "The focus of the majority of my reading time is the (isolated phonics) program; we supplement that program with trade books."

While teachers in Ellis shared their knowledge and expertise in many instances, the teachers do not articulate a shared commitment to what is best for their students. A contrast of teaching approach and philosophy is evident in the building; visible most strongly in differences in practice between Kindergarten through second-grade and third grade through fourth grade. Absent a common philosophy, the faculty might create a coherence by using a commercial program or by adopting an approach such as Reading Recovery (both strategies had been used by successful schools in the larger study). But neither program nor approach unify faculty around the vision of all children learning. Perhaps as a result of this disunity, the conduct of classroom instruction lacks the rigor and "on-taskness" noted for Carlisle and Sommers. In classroom observations, teachers needed to remind students frequently to focus on their work and students were occasionally chided for "not doing better." This type of management provides a sharp contrast to the efficient, energized, and respectful relationships observed throughout Carlisle and Sommers schools.

The lack of coherent professional development since the 1990s is reflected in classroom practice. Even within the primary unit, teachers are using approaches that are not linked or coordinated with work done in the surrounding grades. For example, one teacher uses an adaptation of Guided Reading while two others use an isolated phonics program as the core of their reading program. Without the purposefulness of work across grades, communication amongst teachers—community—is not directed to children's learning but to other issues, or, often, the problems they are having with children's learning

School Community

Without coherence and coordination, and with the frustrations of trying to be effective, interactions amongst teachers at Ellis tend to be contentious around decisions about the right thing to do. For example, one teacher noted: "I think there are teams that would like to pressure the other teams into using what they feel is best, like I would love to go and pressure the 1st grade to start using this program so I don't have to start at level one ... and they'd love to pressure us."

Another colleague, Donna talks passionately about the need for background information:

> People need more background information (when choosing a program to implement). I think the (isolated phonics) Program was chosen because one person, one professional said "oh yeah, that would be good for your class," and I don't think that's the way to choose a program. I think that you need to research a lot of things that are available, you need to look at current research ... There has to be some way to base the decisions we make on sound information, not just what the current trend is. You need to rely on your own knowledge of what works with kids.

The contrast between Carlisle and Sommers, the successful schools, and Ellis, the less successful school, is stark. Revolving leadership at the principal level, antagonisms amongst teachers, and idiosyncratic programs provide some of the causes. There is no synergy.

LESSONS FROM THE COUNTRY SCHOOLS

The children and community of Sommers and Carlisle—poor, rural, remote—are very fortunate to have the committed, knowledgeable, hard working teachers that they do. Although the Country schools serve a relatively homogeneous community, the literacy strengths of the students entering the school are undeveloped. More important, these schools reside happily in their community and the teachers share community norms because they have been long-time teachers at the schools. The shared history and background of the children, teachers, and school community helps to prevent the kind of gatekeeping that occurs when teachers and students do not share cultural norms.

The journey of this staff and administration is one that exemplifies how the felicitous convergence of leadership (in this case from a teacher), vision, professional development, respect, camaraderie, and support (at multiple levels) can create a vibrant, literacy rich, learning environment—one that children, families, and teachers learn and grow from. The configuration of factors perhaps reflects one aspect of the Country Schools cluster—its isolated, rural environment. Wendy and the teachers at Sommers might have been stymied in a larger environment with more points of view and a clientele more diverse in ability and the quantity of needs. In their rural environment they could do what they felt was needed. The union of whole language and Reading Recovery practices did not disintegrate in a whole language/phonics war that many other schools in Vermont underwent during the 1980s and early 1990s.

It is important to note that the strengths of the Sommers and Carlisle environments develop from a foundation of a 'homegrown' approach to the needs of the children at these schools. The teachers made it happen and could do so because of their cohesiveness, itself related to the small number of teachers and students at the schools. As the successful schools made choices in the context of their situations, so the Country schools made choices that capitalized on the characteristics of their situation, in particular, their smallness.

However, as the example of Ellis Elementary School shows, smallness in a rural context is not a sufficient reason for success. The attributes of opportunity, expertise, community, and commitment interact as a complex of forces to determine success. At Ellis, conflicting approaches, expertise undeveloped over the years, tension between faculty and community, and turnover in administrative leadership led to a school environment that did not foster children's learning.

Like Sommers and Carlisle, all the successful schools in our study represent schools that made changes in response to a time of struggle and low performance—some 8 to 10 years prior to the new 1998 reading tests in Vermont administered at second and fourth grade. In a situation where individuals are concerned about student performance, these schools engaged in activities and made decisions that have had felicitous effects—not just on student performance, but also on the professional confidence and satisfaction of individuals working in these schools.

More important, the larger context for these changes involved far more than state-wide testing. Vermont has been involved in an unusually active and productive period of educational engagement. An examination of the statewide timeline for the 10-year period that was so important to these schools reveals a wide range of professional activity at the state level. For example, the state has conducted a public school approval process that brought libraries, gyms, and support faculty to many schools. It has sponsored or launched Reading Recovery consortia around the state that proved key to the success of Carlisle and Sommers. Vermont has used portfolio assessments to create networks of teacher leaders knowledgeable about both content and professional development. The state has also conducted hundreds of teaching and assessment workshops. In addition, grass-roots efforts around whole language and multi-age classrooms produced additional examination of instructional practice. Thus, the impetus for change was certainly not test results alone, but rather a complex array of opportunities and choices that encouraged change.

Sommers and Carlisle schools reveal very similar literacy programs based on Reading Recovery practices. Reading Recovery is a research-based program of instruction tailored to the needs of the at-risk primary grade student. Its practices and their adaptations by the Sommers and Carlisle teachers is well matched to the student clientele and the low SES, rural, remote environment, and the diminished literacy skills these children bring to school. Given the very small size of the staff and students, and the low class size, these teachers were able to tailor these practices in the most effective way for the students involved. Unlike the larger schools in our study, Sommers and Carlisle did reach agreement on a focused, responsive approach to literacy instruction through the principles of Reading Recovery. Their choice—and the way it was made and cultivated—is one that could be made in the situation of a Country school.

Among schools in our larger study, however, no one approach to literacy instruction was linked strongly to literacy success. The instructional programs used at Sommers and Carlisle were *not* the hallmark of any of the other successful schools in our study. Their approaches set their literacy programs apart from other clusters and schools in our larger study. Intriguingly, a great diversity of practices were employed within and across clusters and classrooms studies. There was no consistent picture of a high performing school or classroom—regardless of the community served by the school. A variety of successful instructional approaches exist, ranging from Reading Recovery-based and literature-based programs to school-wide basal programs.

Certainly within the classrooms of Sommers and Carlisle and across the clusters and classrooms of our larger study, teachers' choices and administrators' leadership led to a great diversity of practices. Despite the diversity of practices, all the schools in our study share some common attributes: opportunity for students to read, a tangible school community, high level of teacher knowledge and expertise, and a long-term commitment to improvement in the literacy growth of the school's children.

What seems clear is that across and within clusters, high performing schools manifest a significant degree of autonomy for teachers within schools to make decisions about how to shape their literacy programs—whether as a coherent literacy program across grades or selective by teacher. This autonomy, especially in small, country schools, was directed toward creating instructional programs focused on common philosophies and goals. It relies heavily on teacher expertise and an administrative system that supports teacher initiative.

As we have seen, however, it is possible for autonomy to slide into inaction or lack of coherence. As represented in the description of Ellis school, in our less successful schools, lack of direction and a failure to re-examine practice often resulted in more limited student performance and a more divided faculty. As Fullan (1997) has noted, "Productive educational change roams somewhere between overcontrol and chaos.... You cannot mandate what matters, because what really matters for complex goals of change are skills, creative thinking, and committed action" (pp. 33–35). Sophisticated and articulate professional knowledge and committed action are clearly hallmarks of the educators in these successful schools.

REFERENCES

Clay, M. M. (1993). *An observation survey of early literacy achievement*. Portsmouth, NH: Heinemann.

Dreeben, R. (1968). *The contribution of schooling to learning of norms*. In Socialization and schools (Harvard Educational Review Reprint Series No.1). Cambridge, MA: Harvard University Press.

Educare. (1996). *Cast-a-spell*. Mansfield Center, CT: Author.

Fountas, I. C., & Pinnell, G. S. (1996). *Guided reading: Good first teaching for all children*. Portsmouth, NH: Heinemann.

Fullan, M. (1997). The complexity of the change process. In M. Fullan (Ed.), *The challenge of school change* (pp. 33–56). Arlington Heights, IL: Skylight.

Langer, J. (1999). Excellence in middle and high school: *How teachers' professional lives support achievement*. CELA Report #12002. Albany, NY: CELA/SUNY-Albany.

Lipson, M. Y., Mosenthal, J. H., Mekkelsen, J., Russ, B., & Sortino, S. (1999, December). *Schools Where Students Succeed*. Paper presented at the annual meeting of the National Reading Conference. Orlando, FL.

Mosenthal, J. H., Lipson, M. Y., Mekkelsen, J., Russ, B., & Sortino, S. (in press). *Elementary schools where children succeed in literacy*. Providence, RI: The Northeast and Islands Regional Laboratory.

Schmuck, R. A. (1980). The school organization. In J. H. McMillan (Ed.), *The social psychology of school learning* (pp. 169–214). NY: Academic Press.

Snyder, S. (1999). *Beating the odds over time: One district's perspective.* CELA Report #12004. Albany, NY: CELA/SUNY-Albany.

Taylor, B. M., Pearson, P. D., Clark, K. F., & Walpole, S. (2000). Effective schools and accomplished teachers: Lessons about primary-grade reading instruction in low-income schools. *The Elementary School Journal, 101*(2) 121–165.

Wang, M. C., Haertel, G. D., & Walberg, H. J. (1994). What helps students learn? *Educational Leadership, 51,* 74–79.

5

Effective Practices for Assessing Young Readers[1]

Scott G. Paris
Alison H. Paris
Robert D. Carpenter
University of Michigan/CIERA

Assessment is a vital part of successful teaching because instruction needs to be calibrated according to students' knowledge, skills, and interests. Tests, quizzes, and performance evaluations help teachers identify developmentally appropriate instruction. Effective instruction challenges children because it is on the edge of their independent abilities, the zone of proximal development in Vygotsky's terms. Effective instruction may also be fun, inspirational, and motivating. Most importantly, effective instruction is shaped by assessment because teachers use their knowledge about students to select materials based on interest and difficulty, and to group children based on collaborative work habits. Some of these decisions may not be regarded as "assessment" in a traditional

[1]The report described herein was supported under the Educational Research and Development Centers Program, PR/Award Number R305R70004, as administered by the Office of Educational Research and Improvement, U.S. Department of Education. However, the contents of the described report do not necessarily represent the positions or policies of the National Institute on Student Achievement, Curriculum, and Assessment, or the National Institute on Early Childhood Development, or the U.S. Department of Education, and you should not assume endorsement by the Federal government.

141

sense but they illustrate how teachers use their informal knowledge about children to guide their classroom instruction.

Successful teachers use reading assessments for many purposes. They may use informal assessments at the start of the school year to become familiar with students' fluent reading. They may use skill tests to diagnose strengths and weaknesses. They might observe decoding and comprehension strategies during daily reading. They might design self-assessments so students can monitor their own progress. They might use journals to monitor changes in children's handwriting, reading interests, and phonetic approximations to words. Of course, they prepare their students for high-stakes tests too. With many different kinds of assessments used for many different purposes, today's teachers need to be knowledgeable about when and why to use the various tools available to them (Resnick & Resnick, 1990; Shepard, 2000).

INTERNAL AND EXTERNAL ASSESSMENTS

Some reading assessments are informal, frequent, and tied to the curriculum and daily instructional routines in the classroom. For example, assessments of children's daily oral language, listening, and question answering during group reading may be made by teachers' observations. Other assessments may be more structured, such as spelling tests, weekly quizzes, journal writing, reports, and projects, but they are all under the control of the teacher and embedded in the curriculum. We refer to these assessments as *internal* because they are designed, selected, and used by teachers according to the needs of their children. Internal assessments are used to make decisions about instruction and used to report progress to parents. In contrast, *external* assessments are designed, selected, and controlled by someone other than the teacher, perhaps commercial publishers, district administrators, or state policymakers. Typical examples of external assessments include standardized and commercial reading tests. They occur less frequently than internal assessments but usually have greater importance, authority, and stakes attached to them. External assessments have been used as indicators of both educational achievement of students and the quality of instruction in schools. Although external assessments are used most often in Grade 4 and beyond, there has been an increasing tendency to use external reading assessments in Kindergarten through third-grade classrooms. Thus, we discuss briefly the impact of high-stakes tests before we examine the variety of internal assessments that successful teachers use.

HIGH-STAKES TESTING

Although we believe that the primary function of assessment is to promote teaching and learning in the classroom, assessment has increasingly become a means of educational accountability that reaches beyond the classroom. Commercial tests are used to measure mastery of the curriculum, norm-referenced tests are used to compare students to national expectations, and criterion-referenced tests are used to evaluate the attainment of state-endorsed standards of achievement (National Commission on Testing and Public Policy, 1990). Since the 1980s, there has been a steady increase in the use of standardized tests as accountability measures (Linn, 2000; Madaus & Tan, 1993). There has also been a parallel increase in concerns expressed about the liabilities of increased testing (Shepard, 2000). Some worry that the curriculum has been narrowed (Haertel, 1989); some worry that teachers are being judged inappropriately on the bases of standardized tests (Smith, 1991); and some worry that increased testing has negative effects on students' learning and motivation (Paris, Turner, Lawton, & Roth, 1991; Paris, 2000). Teachers and administrators are worried about being judged inappropriately on the bases of standardized tests (Paris & Urdan, 2000; Smith, 1991). The issue has such profound political and educational implications for reading that the International Reading Association (1999) and the American Educational Research Association (2000) published position papers pointing out the potential problems with high-stakes testing.

Several researchers have examined the impact of high-stakes testing on teachers. For example, Haladyna, Nolen, and Haas (1991) studied Arizona teachers' views of the state-mandated high-stakes test and found that many teachers thought the test was unfair to minority students and ESL students. Nolen, Haladyna, and Haas (1992) reported that many teachers engaged in inappropriate or unethical testing procedures because of the pressure they were under to produce high test scores with their students. In a survey of teachers regarding the state-required test in Michigan, Urdan and Paris (1994) found that many Michigan teachers were frustrated by external pressures to "teach to the test" and angry that the tests were used to evaluate teachers' effectiveness. Hoffman, Assaf, and Paris (2001) found that teachers in Texas felt coerced to teach skills relevant to the TAAS (Texas Assessment of Academic Skills) to the exclusion of other subjects. Many Texas teachers, like the Michigan and Arizona teachers, believed that the standardized tests were unfair to minority students and ESL students. Shepard (1991) pointed out that teachers have little control over the policies proscribing accountability through "high-stakes" tests. A growing number of educators regard high-stakes tests of reading as "fragile evidence" of children's reading accomplishments (Murphy, Shannon, Johnston, & Hansen, 1998). The pressure for accountability through testing, coupled with the lack of involvement of teachers in setting policies, has made many teachers frustrated with the growing influence of externally imposed testing on their professional practices.

Assessment and accountability have become centerpieces of many educational reforms with direct implications on teachers' daily practices. In addition to high-stakes tests, teachers are increasingly required to use new assessment tools in their classrooms. For example, since the 1990s, teachers have been encouraged or required to collect work samples, student portfolios, and informal assessments that are aligned with the curriculum. They often design new district-level tests and new report cards. It seems paradoxical that teachers are more involved with "low stakes" assessments but still judged publicly by the results of high-stakes tests. It is evident that teachers are being asked to become more proficient in designing, administering, and interpreting a variety of educational assessment tools in their classrooms. Thus, it is important to provide teachers with knowledge and training to use assessments prudently and effectively in classrooms.

In the remaining parts of this chapter we describe effective assessment practices that Kindergarten through third-grade teachers use in their classrooms. We begin with a report of a large national survey of teachers in outstanding schools to learn about the kinds of reading assessment tools they used and the purposes of the assessments. We also report teachers' opinions about the impact of various kinds of assessments on children, parents, and administrators. Next, we go beyond the survey to outline a developmental approach to assessment for young children. We conclude with a discussion of typical assessment problems that teachers must solve and a list of recommendations for effective assessment.

WHAT TEACHERS SAY ABOUT READING ASSESSMENT

The survey was designed to collect teachers' perceptions of assessment, specifically reading assessment in early elementary grades. We wanted to ask successful teachers what kinds of reading assessments they use for what purposes so that a collection of "best practices" might be available as models for other teachers. We also wanted to know if teachers felt adequately trained to administer these assessments and what they believe to be the impact of various assessments on students, parents, teachers, and administrators. Thus, we decided to survey elementary teachers who taught in "beat the odds" schools to determine their practices and views.

"Beat-the-odds" schools across the nation were defined as schools with a majority of students who qualified for Title I programs and had a mean school test score on some standardized measure of reading achievement that was higher than the average score of other Title I schools in the state. In most cases, the selected schools also scored above the state average for all schools. Candidate schools were selected from a network of CIERA partner schools as well as from annual reports of outstanding schools in 1996, 1997, and 1998 as reported by the National Association of Title I Directors. In April of 1998, survey packets were sent to more than 400 nominated schools across the nation. Each packet contained a principal survey and seven teacher surveys in addition to directions to the principal to select seven "key" teachers across Kindergarten through third-grades to complete the teacher surveys. Approximately 700 Kindergarten through third-grade staff from 140 schools responded to the surveys and, specifically, to the questions on assessment practices. The final sample of 504 teachers was established by omitting reading specialists, teachers who taught multiple grades, and other respondents who were not classroom teachers. Almost 96% of the teachers were female who were distributed across Kindergarten through third-grade levels. Almost half of the sample reported that they had advanced degrees and that they had taken an average of 6.6 reading/language arts courses. Nearly one quarter of the teachers attended a reading/language arts course within the last year. Teachers reported a wide range of teaching experience in their current grade level (M = 8.6 years) and in total experience (M = 14.8 years). Additional characteristics of the sample are reported in Table 5.1.

The data were derived from the "The CIERA Survey of Early Literacy Programs in High Performing Schools", an instrument created by researchers at CIERA (The Center for Improvement of Early Reading Achievement) in April, 1998. The assessment section of the survey included items arranged in four matrices to maximize the amount of information obtained from teachers. Each matrix listed a variety of methods to assess children's reading along the left-hand margin and required teachers to make judgments about each one according to different criteria specified in questions in the margin across the top. The topics of the four matrices were: (1) types of assessments and their frequency of use, (2) purposes of assessment, (3) consequences of different assessments, and (4) perceptions of assessment training. For the first item, teachers were provided with six categories of reading assessments (performance assessments, standardized tests, teacher-designed assessments, commercial tests, assessments of fluency and understanding, and assessments of word attack/word meaning) and

TABLE 5.1

Teacher Background Characteristics

Variable	N	Percent
Gender		
Female	477	96.2
Male	19	3.8
Grade Teach		
Kindergarten	91	18.1
First Grade	105	20.8
Second Grade	92	18.3
Third Grade	103	20.4
Education Level		
BA	114	22.6
BA + 15	139	27.6
MA	128	25.4
MA + 15	98	19.4
Ed Specialist	8	1.6
Doctorate	2	.4
Last Course Taken		
Within Last Year	121	24.0
1–3 Years ago	146	29.0
3–7 Years ago	114	22.6
7+ Years ago	104	20.6

they were asked to record the specific assessments used in their classroom within the framework provided. Our intent was to provide some structure to the responses but still allow teachers to report the variety of reading assessments that they used. Three blank lines were provided to list the types of assessment for each of the six categories. For example, after "performance assessments", teachers might fill in "running records" and "journal writing" if those were the ways they used these assessments in their classrooms. After designating the types of assessments they used in their classrooms, teachers were asked to indicate the frequency with which they used each assessment.

WHAT KINDS OF EARLY READING ASSESSMENTS DO TEACHERS USE?

High percentages of teachers reported that they used each of the various assessment types; 86% used performance assessments, 82% used teacher-designed assessments, 78% used word attack/word meaning, 74% used measures of fluency and understanding, 67% used commercial assessments, and 59% used standardized reading tests (see Table 5.2).

Among teachers who reported using performance assessments, more than 60% reported that they used observations and writing assessments. Of the performance assessments, 22% were observations, 19% were writing assessments, 15% were tests, and 9% were portfolios. For teacher-designed assessments, 34% of assessments used were observations, 23% informal reading inventories, 19% anecdotal records, 13% work samples, and 10% teacher designed tests. Note that there is some overlap among categories (e.g., observations and tests). This is due to the open-ended nature of the items, where teachers determined the categories in which to place each of the assessments. Some teachers reported "observations" as performance assessments and others reported them as measures of fluency/understanding, but it is clear that they were used very frequently.

TABLE 5.2

Examples of Different Types of Assessments

Internal Assessments		External Assessments	
Type	*Examples*	*Type*	*Examples*
Performance Assessments	Portfolios Work samples	Standardized Reading Tests	ITBS Woodcock-Johnson DRP
Teacher Designed Assessments	Daily worksheets Observations Anecdotal records	Commercial Assessments	Curriculum-based unit tests Workbooks
Fluency and Understanding	Assessments of oral reading and comprehension		
Word Attack and Word Meaning	Phonemic awareness Vocabulary Sight word assessments		

For the category of word attack and word meaning, seven different types were reported and they included phonics (29%), vocabulary (22%), sight words (19%), tests (12%), oral reading (9%), spelling (5%), and work samples (5%). Teachers reported using the following five types of fluency and understanding assessments: oral reading (43%), comprehension (25%), observations (21%), tests (8%) and work samples (4%).

Commercial and standardized tests, external assessments controlled least by teachers, were used least often. Teachers indicated that on average they used all categories of assessments, except standardized tests, approximately once per week. Teachers reported that they used standardized tests less frequently, only about two to three times a year. Teachers reported using the following five types of standardized assessments of reading; norm-referenced (69%), state level (10%), skills (4%), district (2%), curriculum (2%). The remaining 13% of standardized assessments that teachers reported using were idiosyncratic and could not be placed in any specific categories. Most of the commercial assessments were workbooks (43%) and basal readers (34%). The remaining types of commercial assessments included curriculum-based (6%), specific program (6%), specific skills (5%), and other types of commercial assessments (6%). In addition to these categories, teachers completed an "other" category where they could list assessments that did not fit within the framework. Although the "other" responses were less than 5% of the total responses, most of them were external assessments.

The survey showed that Kindergarten through third-grade teachers use a tremendous variety of assessments in their classrooms on a daily basis. Assessments designed by teachers were the most frequent type and standardized tests were the least. This contrast was most evident for Kindergarten through first-grade teachers. It may be reasonable to speculate that this trend changes in higher grades where students usually have more standardized and commercially produced tests. A main finding that emerges from the survey is that Kindergarten through third-grade teachers use observations, anecdotal evidence, informal inventories, and work samples as their main sources of evidence about children's reading achievement and progress. A second main finding is the huge variety of tools available to teachers and the large variation among teachers in what they use. This requires a highly skilled teacher to select and use appropriate assessment tools.

WHAT ARE THE PURPOSES FOR ASSESSMENT?

Another matrix in the survey provided teachers with seven different purposes for assessment and asked them to indicate whether they used assessments in each of the six categories for each purpose. Teachers were asked to indicate whether they used assessments for the following purposes: placement, referral, diagnosis, report cards, conferences, summary, and future tests. Because teachers were asked to provide dichotomous responses where checkmarks represented the use of the assessment type for each specific purpose, percentages were tabulated that represented the percentage of teachers who responded affirmatively to using each assessment category for each specific purpose.

The results showed that teachers used assessments for a variety of purposes and that they used some assessment types for more purposes than other assessments. Teachers used internal assessments of performance, fluency and understanding, and word attack/word meaning very often for diagnosis, for filling out report cards, and for discussion at parent–teacher conferences. Conversely, few teachers reported using commercial assessments and standardized reading tests for these purposes. Fewer than half of teachers said that they use commercial assessments for conferences, report cards, and diagnosis. Even fewer teachers said that they used commercial assessments and standardized tests for referral, conferences, report cards, and placement. Thus, teachers reported using internal assessments more often for more purposes than external assessments.

WHAT IS THE IMPACT OF ASSESSMENTS ON VARIOUS STAKEHOLDERS?

The next item in the survey regarding the consequences of assessments posed seven specific questions about the effects of assessments on various stakeholders. The questions were:

1. How does the assessment affect students' learning to read?
2. How does the assessment affect students' motivation to read?
3. How does the assessment affect the teacher's decisions about what skills and information to teach?
4. How does the assessment affect parents' knowledge about their child's reading performance?
5. How does the assessment affect parents' active involvement in helping their child learn to read?
6. How does the assessment affect administrators' knowledge about students' reading/language arts performance?
7. How does the assessment affect administrators' use of results in public reports?

Teachers answered these questions for each of the six assessment categories (performance, standardized, teacher-designed, commercial, fluency and understanding, word attack/word meaning) using a five-point scale ranging from "1" (strong negative impact) to "5" (strong positive impact). The actual data are shown in Table 5.3. With the exception of standardized tests, teachers reported that each of the assessment types had very positive effects on teachers' daily practices in classrooms. The highest impact of standardized assessments was on administrators' knowledge and their use of test results. Teachers reported that assessments designed by teachers, assessments of fluency/understanding, and assessments of word attack/word meaning had the least positive impact on administrators' use of results. Standardized and commercial assessments had the least positive impact on student motivation, and performance assessments had the least positive impact on parent involvement. In general, teachers reported that internal as compared to external assessments had more positive effects on students, teachers, and parents. Conversely, teachers believed external assessments had a higher positive impact on administrators. These patterns suggest that teachers differentiate between assessments over which they have control and assessments generated externally in terms of their impact on stakeholders. It is ironic that teachers believed that the most useful assessments for students, teachers, and parents were valued less by administrators than external assessments. The study suggests that high-stakes tests do not necessarily mean high benefits for classroom practices and student learning.

DO TEACHERS FEEL PREPARED TO ASSESS STUDENTS?

Teachers were asked to indicate how well they believed that they were trained to use each of the six assessment types. Teachers made judgments based on a scale ranging from "1" (No training) to "5" (Excellent training). On average, teachers reported positive perceptions of training for each of the various assessments. The means in order of least to most training were commercial assessments ($M = 3.3$), standardized tests ($M = 3.4$), performance assessments ($M = 3.8$), fluency and understanding ($M = 3.9$), word attack/word meaning ($M = 3.9$), and teacher-designed assessments ($M = 4.0$). Across all assessment types, teachers reported an overall mean of 3.7 for their perceived level of training on these reading assessments. They rated their training lower or only "Fair" on external assessments and "Good" on the internal assessments. Teacher's perceptions of training adequacy varied as a function of their backgrounds. Teachers' with a bachelors degree plus 15 credits reported significantly less training than teachers who either had a masters degree plus 15 credits, a doctoral degree, or an educational specialist degree. Also, teachers who had taken more reading/language arts courses reported that they had better training. The study shows that teachers feel most

TABLE 5.3

Mean Impact of Assessment Types on Stakeholders

Types of Assessment	Student Learning	Student Motivation	Teacher Decisions	Parent Knowledge	Parent Involvement	Administrator Knowledge	Administrator Use of Results
Performance Assessment	3.8	3.7	4.5	4.0	3.5	4.0	3.7
Standardized Reading Tests	2.8	2.6	3.7	3.4	3.0	4.1	4.1
Teacher-Designed Assessments	4.1	3.8	4.7	4.1	3.7	3.6	3.3
Commercial Assessments	3.1	3.0	3.7	3.5	3.2	3.6	3.5
Fluency and Understanding	4.1	4.0	4.5	3.9	3.6	3.7	3.4
Word Attack and Word Meaning	4.1	3.9	4.5	3.9	3.6	3.7	3.4

prepared to use the assessment tools that they create or select and less prepared to use external assessments that are given to them.

POINTS TO PONDER ABOUT THE SURVEY

Teachers in the effective schools participating in this study reported using a variety of assessments daily to assess reading. They used many specific reading tests, commercial products, and teacher-designed activities. Indeed, their responses included hundreds of assessments that we grouped according to six types of assessments. The types and frequency of assessments varied most for kindergarten teachers, as might be expected, but in general, all teachers in Grades 1 through 3 reported using many kinds of assessments on a weekly basis. Observations and writing were the most frequently mentioned informal and teacher-controlled types of assessments, perhaps because they can be done quickly as part of many curricular activities. Other surveys of teachers' assessment practices and the commercial marketplace of Kindergarten through third-grade reading assessments have confirmed the huge variety of tools available to teachers (Meisels, Paris, & Pearson, 1999). Teachers face a formidable task of finding these tools, learning about them, ordering/obtaining them, and then adapting the tools to their own purposes and students.

We noted a contrast between teachers' views of internal and external assessments. Standardized tests and commercial tests that allow little teacher control and adaptation were regarded as less useful and were used less often by teachers. Teachers also regarded external tests as the least beneficial for students, parents, and teachers. Paradoxically, the external tests were regarded as having the most impact on administrators' knowledge and reporting practices. We think that teachers' frustration with assessments is partly tied to this paradox. Few teachers reported that they had excellent training on any type of assessment but they rated their training as "Good" for performance assessments and similar teacher-designed assessments whereas they rated their training on commercial and standardized tests lower. It seems clear that when districts place a premium on the results of external assessments, they need to provide more information and training for teachers on the appropriate use and interpretation of those assessments.

There were few differences among teachers according to teaching experience and educational background characteristics. The most frequent effect was for kindergarten teachers. They used assessments less frequently than teachers in higher grades and they had more positive perceptions of the impact of assessment on parent involvement and administrators' knowledge and use. Perhaps kindergarten teachers use assessments primarily for screening, placement, and designing developmentally appropriate activities and less for comparative or accountability purposes. The similarity among other teachers in Grades 1 through 3 suggests that they use a variety of internal assessments for similar purposes.

It may not be surprising that successful teachers use assessments that they can design and control more often than "off the shelf" tests. They feel better trained to use these assessments and believe that those assessments have positive benefits for students' learning and motivation, as well as for parental information and involvement. One ironic finding is that the most frequent and beneficial evidence of children's reading may be the least visible and enduring in public reports. Observations, anecdotes, and daily work samples are certainly low-stakes evidence of achievement for accountability purposes but they may be the most useful for teachers and students. A second ironic finding is that the assessments on which teachers feel least trained and regard as least useful are used most often for evaluations and public reports. Together these findings suggest that teachers need support in establishing the value of "internal" assessments in their classrooms for administrators and parents while also demarcating the limits and interpretations of external tests. The current slogan about the benefits of a "balanced" approach to reading instruction might also be applied to a "balanced" approach to reading assessment. The skills that are assessed need to be balanced among various components of reading and the purposes/benefits of assessment need to be balanced among the stakeholders.

The critical question that many policymakers ask is, "Which reading assessments provide the best evidence about children's accomplishments and progress?" The answer may not be one test or even one type of assessment. We know that a single test or assessment cannot represent the complexity of reading. Likewise, the same assessments may not represent the curriculum and instructional diversity among teachers nor will the same assessments capture the different skills and developmental levels of children. That is why teachers use multiple assessments and choose those that fit their purposes. These assessments are the ones that can reveal the most information about their students. We believe that the most robust evidence about children's reading reveals developing skills that can be compared to individual standards of progress as well as normative standards of achievement. A developmental approach balances the types of assessments across a range of reading factors and allows all stakeholders to understand the strengths and weaknesses of the child's reading profile. Many teachers use this approach implicitly and we think it is a useful model for early reading assessment.

A DEVELOPMENTAL APPROACH TO ASSESSMENT

Not many parents or teachers expect assessments to be given to kindergarten children but they can be very useful. Five- and six-year-olds have emerging knowledge about literacy that varies widely among children depending on their home background and experiences. Early assessments can identify children who know the alphabet, who can write their own name, and who have participated in joint storybook reading—all indicators of rich literacy environments during early childhood. Kindergarten teachers may assess these skills through observation or with brief structured tasks. For example, sharing a book with a child can be an occasion to assess a child's recognition of letters, understanding of print concepts, and ability to retell a sentence or part of the story. For children who cannot identify letters and words, teachers may choose to use wordless picture books to assess a child's knowledge about narratives in connected pictures, a prereading skill and a good index of comprehension (Paris & Paris, 2000). Young children's emerging knowledge about letter–sound relations is revealed in their "invented spelling" and can be assessed by teachers who ask children to listen to a dictated sentence and then write it. Each phoneme that a child hears and represents with a letter is an indication that the child is decoding sounds that correspond to distinct letters. Kindergarten teachers can also listen to children "read" familiar books that have been memorized to assess comprehension, accuracy, and word recognition. This is a natural precursor to assessing how children read unfamiliar words and books.

Some children may begin oral reading in kindergarten but most begin in first grade. Teachers use informal reading inventories (IRIs) to assess oral reading accuracy with running records or miscue analyses. There are commercial IRIs that provide graded word lists, graded passages or leveled books, and directions for administering and scoring them. Whether teacher-designed or commercial, the IRI is a useful task for assessing children's oral reading rate, accuracy, fluency, comprehension, and retelling in a 10 to 15 minute session. First- and second-grade teachers weave reading and writing together for both instruction and assessment. For example, they might use a Writers' Workshop activity for children to draw and write about a recent event. They may use process writing in small groups as a means of assessing children's revising skills while simultaneously encouraging children to read and edit each others' work. Reports, projects, and journals are used frequently in Grades 1 through 3 because children are motivated to write about their own experiences. These work samples, whether assembled in folders, portfolios, or journals, provide excellent assessments of literacy accomplishments that can be shared with children and parents

(Paris & Ayres, 1994). Many teachers like to assess children's attitudes about reading and how often they read on their own so they may ask children to fill out brief surveys, answer open-ended questions, or keep records of when they read and what they read. Research has shown that young children often read less than 10 minutes per day outside school and we know that positive attitudes and literacy habits are the foundation for early reading success (Snow, Burns, & Griffin, 1998). Some of the most frequent Kindergarten through third-grade literacy assessments are shown in Table 5.4.

The battery of assessments shown here is similar to the Kindergarten through third-grade assessments included in the Michigan Literacy Progress Profile (MLPP, 2000) designed by the Department of Education and Michigan educators. The MLPP is intended to be a resource for teachers to be used selectively with some of their students some of the time rather than administered entirely to all students. The state legislature has recommended that the MLPP can be used to assess annual student progress as well as achievement in summer school programs. Thus, it is a hybrid assessment that has features of both internal assessments (e.g., teacher control) and external assessments (e.g., uniformity and external credibility). Other states are developing similar early assessment tools. For example, Texas has created the Texas Primary Reading Inventory (TPRI) for teachers to use as an assessment tool with Kindergarten through second-grade children.

TABLE 5.4

Assessment Tasks at Usually Assessed Grade Levels

	K	1	2	3
Letter identification; letter-sound correspondence	X	X		
Phonological awareness (e.g., rhyming, blending)	X	X		
Concepts about print	X	X		
Oral language and listening	X	X		
Decoding and word identification	X	X	X	X
Oral reading rate and fluency		X	X	X
Journals, portfolios, work samples		X	X	X
Comprehension and retelling		X	X	X
Attitudes about reading		X	X	X
Book logs, reading habits, interests			X	X

One key to a developmental approach to assessment is matching the battery of assessments to the child's emerging abilities so that teachers and parents understand the child's strengths and weaknesses. Teachers need to be aware of the many potential assessment tasks in order to choose them appropriately but the number and variety of assessments is daunting. A second key to assessment is keeping records of progress with multiple assessments throughout the year so that each child's development can be recorded and interpreted. A third point is that assessment occurs daily and is integrated with instruction in order for teachers to provide instruction that is challenging and appropriate for each child. These and other practices were noted by the National Association for the Education of Young Children (NAEYC) in a position statement in 1990. Their guidelines are summarized in Table 5.5.

SO MANY CHILDREN, SO LITTLE TIME

Using effective reading assessment is not easy. Teachers often complain that it takes too much time to assess children individually on a regular basis. They also say that the wide range of reading abilities in their classrooms make assessment difficult. Even when they can administer reading assessments, teachers report that it is difficult for them to interpret the results in a straightforward way for children and parents. Because internal assessments are regarded as having low stakes by administrators, teachers may feel frustrated that no one cares how well they use informal assessments. Our survey revealed these problems but anyone who works in schools knows them firsthand. There is no simple solution to these typical problems but we have seen how effective teachers deal with them. Here are some tips from effective assessment practices that we have observed skilled teachers using in many schools.

First, using assessment effectively must involve the entire school or district. The system of assessment gains visibility and credibility among parents when it is endorsed by the entire school. Teachers cannot create assessment systems alone; they need the emotional support, collaborative teamwork, and shared motivation to build a system of assessment tools that serves their students and community. Effective schools have principals and administrators who provide leadership in integrating assessment with the curriculum and instruction.

Second, literacy assessments cannot be built from piecemeal bits of this and that, one of the old tests, something borrowed, and something new. Effective assessment in reading is a woven fabric, not individual threads. It starts with a shared, conceptual view of the goals of reading assessment and the variety of

TABLE 5.5

Guidelines for Assessment with Children 3 to 8 Years of Age (NAEYC, 1990)

1. Curriculum and assessment are integrated throughout the program.

2. Assessment results in benefits to the child.

3. Children's development in all domains is assessed informally and routinely by teachers' observations.

4. Assessment provides teachers with useful information to successfully fulfill their responsibilities.

5. Assessment involves regular and periodic observations of children in a wide variety of circumstances.

6. Assessment relies on procedures that reflect typical activities in the classroom.

7. Assessment relies on demonstrated performance during real, not contrived, activities.

8. Assessment utilizes an array of tools and a variety of processes.

9. Assessment recognizes individual diversity of learners and allows for differences in styles and rates of learning.

10. Assessment supports children's development; it does not threaten their safety or self-esteem.

11. Assessment supports parents' relationships with their children; it does not undermine parents' confidence in their children nor devalue the language and culture of the family.

12. Assessment demonstrates children's overall strengths and progress.

13. Assessment is an essential component of the teacher's role.

14. Assessment is a collaborative process involving children and teachers, teachers and parents, and school and community.

15. Assessment encourages children to participate in self-evaluation.

16. Assessment demonstrates what children can do independently and what they can do with assistance.

17. Information about each child's development is systematically collected and recorded at regular intervals.

18. A regular process exists for periodic information sharing between teachers and parents.

tools that are available. Then it proceeds to sharing practices that work. Teachers need to make choices that provide a coherent set of assessment tools that can be used on a regular basis. State-level assessment batteries or standards, district outcomes or portfolios, or school-based report cards are all options that can be used to create a systematic approach to reading assessment.

The system of assessment indicates to students, parents, and the public what is important to master in the curriculum.

Third, there are sustained professional development activities supported by outside experts and internal teams of teachers who design and revise their assessment system. It may take several years for all teachers to understand assessment practices and to use them in similar ways. Consensus is built on regular reflection and discussion among teachers about what assessments are working well, how the assessments support parent conferences and report cards, and how assessments help individual children.

Fourth, effective reading assessment means using assessments selectively. Too many districts add new assessments on top of old ones and burden both teachers and students with too many redundant assessments. Choices must be made about which assessments are used with which students. Teachers may choose to assess their lowest achieving readers more often or more thoroughly than children reading at or above grade level. They may choose to use different types of assessment with children who are reading poorly or well so that every child can demonstrate his or her best accomplishments. Not all children need to be given the same assessments.

Fifth, teachers use assessments to reinforce their professional evaluations of children for report cards and parent conferences. Because assessment is an ongoing part of teaching in the classroom, it should have multiple sources of evidence and multiple sources of reports that are mutually supporting. Assessments of students are important public reports that support teachers' professional judgments about students. Parents need to understand the kinds of evidence used to evaluate student achievement and they need to trust teachers' interpretations of the evidence. As the public becomes better informed about literacy assessment and the evidence it provides about children, they may gain more confidence in internal assessments and less confidence in external assessments, a perspective that many teachers already value.

CONCLUSIONS

Assessment is becoming increasingly important for teachers in primary grades because administrators and parents want more detailed information about children's early literacy achievement and progress. Yet, teachers believe that their primary mission is instruction and support for the child's whole development. Many teachers resist spending time assessing children, especially if the assessments are for external purposes. Many teachers are frustrated by the pressure to assess and report results of tests that they feel provide only partial or fragile evidence of the child's accomplishments. The public needs to understand the difficulties and limitations of early assessments and the need for multiple sources of evidence. Teacher judgments, supported by prudent use of various literacy assessments, are what teachers feel trained to do and what teachers feel is beneficial for children and parents.

Effective assessment does not mean simply training teachers to use new tests wisely, although professional development of assessment expertise is important. Assessment reform in schools must involve communication and negotiation among stakeholders about the kinds of information that supports students' educational growth. The CIERA survey revealed that teachers perceive large differences between administrators' value and use of assessment information compared to other stakeholders. Administrators (and parents) need to learn how teachers use reading assessments just as much as teachers need to learn new kinds of assessments. The CIERA survey confirms and extends our understanding of effective assessment practices with young children. At the simplest level, assessment should be a way to communicate information about children's accomplishments to others. If children's welfare is the highest educational priority, then teachers, parents, and administrators should work together to design assessment systems that bring the greatest benefits to children. We believe that a developmental approach to assessment is part of the solution. It is not a one-size-fits-all approach nor an approach that gives the same test to all children on the same day. Instead, assessment is embedded in daily classroom activities in which teachers use formal and informal assessment tools to ascertain if children are improving their literacy skills and knowledge, mastering the curriculum, and meeting community standards of literacy development. These practices are effective because they empower teachers and students alike.

REFERENCES

American Educational Research Association. (2000). Position statement of the American Educational Research Association concerning high-stakes testing in pre-K–12 education. *Educational Researcher,* 29(8), 24–25.

Haertel, E. (1989). Student achievement tests as tools of educational policy: Practices and consequences. In B. R. Gifford (Ed.), *Test policy and test performance: Education, language, and culture* (pp. 25–50). Boston: Kluwer Academic Publishers.

Haladyna, T., Nolen, S. B., & Haas, N. S. (1991). Raising standardized achievement test scores and the origins of test score pollution. *Educational Researcher,* 20, 2–7.

Hoffman, J. V., Assaf, L., & Paris, S. G. (2001). High stakes testing in reading: Today in Texas, tomorrow? *The Reading Teacher,* 54(5), 482–492.

International Reading Association. (1999). *High-stakes testing in reading. A position paper.* Newark, DEL: International Reading Association.

Linn, R. L. (2000). Assessments and accountability. *Educational Researcher,* 29(2), 4–16.

Madaus, G. F., & Tan, A. G. A. (1993). The growth of assessment. In G. Cawelti (Ed.), *Challenges and achievements of American education* (pp. 53–79). Alexandria, VA: Association for Supervision and Curriculum Development.

Meisels, S., Paris, S. G., & Pearson, P. D. (1999). *Three perspectives on early reading assessment: What do we use? What do we sell? What are their consequences?* Symposium presented at the National Conference on Large-Scale Assessment, Snowbird, UT.

Michigan Literacy Progress Profile. (2000). Lansing, MI: Department of Education.

Murphy, S., Shannon, P., Johnston, P., & Hansen, J. (1998). *Fragile evidence: A critique of reading assessment.* Mahwah, NJ: Lawrence Erlbaum Associates.

National Association for the Education of Young Children. (1990). *Guidelines for appropriate curriculum content and assessment in programs serving children ages 3 through 8.* Washington, DC: NAEYC.

National Commission on Testing and Public Policy. (1990). *From gatekeeper to gateway: Transforming testing in America.* Chestnut Hill, MA: National Commission on Testing and Public Policy.

Nolen, S. B., Haladyna, T. M., & Haas, N. S. (1992). Uses and abuses of achievement test scores. *Educational Measurement: Issues and Practices, 11,* 9–15.

Paris, S. G. (2000). Trojan horse in the schoolyard: The hidden threats in high-stakes testing. *Issues in Education, 6,*(1, 2), 1–16.

Paris, S. G., & Ayres, L. J. (1994). *Becoming reflective students and teachers with portfolios and authentic assessment.* Washington, DC: American Psychological Association.

Paris, A. H., & Paris, S. G. (2000, April). Innovative comprehension assessments for nonreaders. Paper presented at the annual meeting of the American Educational Research Association, New Orleans, LA.

Paris, S. G., Roth, J. L., & Turner, J. C. (2000). Developing disillusionment: Students' perceptions of academic achievement tests. *Issues in Education, 6*(1, 2), 17–45.

Paris, S. G., Turner, J. C., Lawton, T. A., & Roth, J. L. (1991). A developmental perspective on standardized achievement testing. *Educational Researcher, 20,* 12–20.

Paris, S. G., & Urdan, T. (2000). Policies and practices of high-stakes testing that influence teachers and schools. *Issues in Education, 6*(1, 2), 83–107.

Resnick, L. B., & Resnick, D. P. (1990). Tests as standards of achievement in schools. In *The uses of standardized tests in American education* (pp. 63–78). Princeton, NJ: Educational Testing Service.

Roth, J., Paris, S. G., & Turner, J. C. (2000). Students' perceived utility and reported use of test-taking strategies. *Issues in Education, 6*(1, 2), 67–82.

Shepard, L. (1991). Interview on assessment issues with Lorrie Shepard. *Educational Researcher, 20,* 21–23.

Shepard, L. (2000). The role of assessment in a learning culture. *Educational Researcher, 29*(7), 4–14.

Smith, M. L. (1991). Put to the test: The effects of external testing on teachers. *Educational Researcher, 20,* 8–11.

Snow, C. E., Burns, M. S., & Griffin, P. (Eds.). (1998). *Preventing reading difficulties in children.* Washington, DC: National Academy Press.

Urdan, T. C., & Paris, S. G. (1994). Teachers' perceptions of standardized achievement tests. *Educational Policy, 8,* 137–156.

II
School Case Studies

6

Sunnyside Elementary School, Mounds View, Minnesota

Barbara M. Taylor
University of Minnesota/CIERA

Ceil Critchley
Mounds View School District, Mounds View, Minnesota

INTRODUCTION

Sunnyside Elementary School was one of the four schools identified as highly effective in the CIERA Study, Effective Schools and Accomplished Teachers (Taylor, Pearson, Clark, & Walpole, 2000). In carrying out that study, we created a case study for each of our highly effective schools. In this chapter, we present the case study of one of those schools, Sunnyside. This case study described Sunnyside during the 1997–1998 school year.

Background on School and Community

Sunnyside Elementary is a school with a moderate number of children on subsidized lunch (38%) in a moderately affluent suburb 10 miles north of Minneapolis.

It is regarded by teachers and administrators in the district as a challenging school with a sizable at-risk population. At the same time it was described by Michelle Brouse, the principal at Sunnyside during the time we conducted this study, as an old school (45 years old) in an area with a "small town" feel to it, an area with contrasting demographics. Some families have lived in the community for many generations, while others, residing mainly in a trailer park and an apartment complex, are much more transient. The principal reported that the central administration in the district of 11,693 students and eight elementary schools is very supportive of schools like Sunnyside at the west (low income) end of the district, which stand in sharp contrast to the east (affluent) end of the district.

There were 506 students in the Kindergarten through Grade 5 school in 1997–1998; 89% of the students were White, 4% African American, 2% Hispanic, 2% Asian American, and 3% Native American. Nine percent of the students were classified as English language learners.

There were 22 classroom teachers, 4 special education teachers, 1 Title 1 teacher, and a total licensed staff of 35. Most of the teachers at Sunnyside were very experienced and had been at the building for many years. Of the seven teachers in the CIERA study (Taylor, Pearson, Clark, & Walpole, 2000), five had 19+ years of teaching experience, and two had taught for 3 and 5 years, respectively. The median number of years teachers had been at Sunnyside was 17, ranging from 1 to 31. The principal said most teachers at Sunnyside could work elsewhere in the district because of their seniority but had a passion for working with at-risk children and, consequently, chose to stay at Sunnyside.

The principal reported that Sunnyside has traditionally had good parent involvement but this had been dropping off in recent years, something she attributed to increased employment outside the home. Parents would show up for school events if their children performed. Also, the school had been successful in recruiting parent volunteers to assist with reading coaching as part of the Early Intervention in Reading (EIR) program (Taylor, Hanson, Justice-Swanson, & Watts, 1997; Taylor, Short, Frye, & Shearer, 1992). Parents were paid a small stipend to come to school every day for a few hours to listen to children read to them.

Because of traditionally low reading scores at Sunnyside compared to other schools in the district, the primary grade teachers at Sunnyside decided in the 1995–1996 school year that they needed to revamp their reading program to help more of their students achieve success. Ceil Critchley, a Grade 1 teacher returning to Sunnyside after a 5-year term as Assistant Commissioner of Education for the State of Minnesota, knew the student population at Sunnyside had become more varied in her absence and that things had to change for her to be successful in teaching many of her first graders to read. Taking the lead, she reviewed the research, presented it to the primary grade regular education, special education, and Title I teachers, and helped the group come up with a plan for changing their reading program. The principal described the change as a team decision and team approach. "They were willing to give up some things, work together." The teachers in Grades 1 and 2 decided on a daily 2.5 to 3 hour time commitment to literacy instruction including 50 minutes of small group instruction at students' instructional level, plus 20 minutes a day of supplemental EIR instruction for struggling readers.

BEAT THE ODDS DATA

The restructured primary grade reading program unfolded in 1996–1997, the year before the CIERA project came into the school. In spring 1996–1997, 80% of the first-grade children identified as at risk of having trouble learning to read were reading independently by the end of the year. In Grade 2, 86% of the children who began the year reading primer level or lower were reading on a second grade level by May, with 53% of them reading on an end-of-Grade-2 level. By winter 1997/98, the Grade 2 students at Sunnyside met the district average of 92 words correct per minute on the district-wide fluency measure (Deno, 1985). On the district-wide norm-referenced test, Northwest Educational Assessment, the mean Grade 3 reading score at Sunnyside was at the 66th percentile. The principal called this "a tremendous change for Sunnyside," given that it is a moderately high-poverty school in an affluent area. Based on these results, the superintendent identified Sunnyside as a school "beating the odds."

School Factors Contributing to Sunnyside's Success

Like most schools that beat the odds, Sunnyside's success is a multilayered, multifaceted phenomenon. Leadership, program factors (especially the reading intervention for students at-risk for failure), and instructional practices all contributed to this success.

Instructional Leadership. The primary grade teachers at Sunnyside took the lead in the building in coming together to improve the reading program in the primary grades. Also, a core of teachers (1 Kindergarten, 3 Grade 3, and 2 Grade 4 teachers) at Sunnyside were willing to pilot the Kindergarten, Grade 3, and Grade 4 version of the EIR program because they had seen the success and enthusiasm of the Grade 1 and 2 teachers for the EIR program and their restructured reading program. Additionally, the parent coaching program, a component of the EIR program, was expanded to all grades at Sunnyside.

Michelle Brouse, the principal at Sunnyside, described herself as a facilitator and a grant-getter. The teachers in the project described her as supportive, good at finding resources, providing time for the staff to meet and plan, being complimentary to teachers, and providing emotional support. Michelle also mentioned that she had tried to keep the building focused on reading intervention, that she had tried to keep teachers from trying too many innovations too quickly so they wouldn't get overloaded, and that she has told teachers it was okay to let some things go when they were trying to implement a new program. For example, she dispensed with formal performance review for tenured teachers for 2 years when they began to make major changes to their reading program.

Other Effective Schools/School Change Factors.   When asked on a questionnaire to identify important attributes of effective schools that were present at Sunnyside, five of six teachers in the CIERA study indicated that they felt that a strong emphasis on reading/language arts was very important and very indicative of Sunnyside. Four of six teachers also expressed a personal commitment to the students and to teaching, systematic evaluation of student progress, and a breadth of materials as very important attributes that were very indicative of Sunnyside.

In an interview, three teachers in the CIERA study explicitly stated that they had high expectations for their students. "I believe all kids can learn to read and it's my responsibility as a teacher to ensure this." "I set high expectations—too high perhaps … I constantly get them to stretch and explain why I am doing this." "I demand quite a bit. They have homework, and I expect them to do it." In contrast, four teachers did not explicitly mention having high expectations for students' achievement in the interview. Their comments focused on considering children's ability and home life, helping each child make as much progress as possible, and taking children from where they were to as far as they could go.

Based on the CIERA survey, teachers were in less agreement as to which factors were very important in improving reading instruction at Sunnyside. Three of six teachers rated the following factors as very important: (a) results of school, district, or state assessments; (b) district mandates; (c) survey of student performance levels; (d) peer coaching and other forms of staff support; (e) capable leadership, and (f) continued study of progress achieved.

When asked in the interview what factors were responsible for the students' success in literacy at Sunnyside, four of seven teachers mentioned the EIR supplemental reading program and three of seven mentioned the strong emphasis on reading overall at the school. The principal cited the primary teachers working together to develop a team approach to reading instruction as a success factor. Primary grade teachers had decided that they needed to change and that they would teach reading/language arts for 2.5 to 3.0 hours per day. Teachers agreed with the principal that these were both factors contributing to students' success in literacy.

Professional Development. When asked to identify effective approaches to professional development in their school, four of six teachers in the study rated the following as effective or very effective: (a) speakers and topics chosen by teachers, (b) visits to schools with innovative programs followed by sharing of observations with colleagues, (c) district or school sponsored year-long workshops, and (d) forming committees around interests or grade levels to address instructional concerns. Conversely a similar proportion of teachers regarded alternate practices as ineffective: (a) in-service sessions during regularly scheduled faculty meetings, (b) speakers and topics chosen by the district administration, (c) in-service provided by publishing companies with the adoption of a new textbook series.

Community-Home-School Links. Teachers and support staff at Sunnyside work hard to connect parents and the community. Each year several community focus groups are scheduled to ask parents and community members how to improve the school and how to improve communications. Staff at Sunnyside also conduct a phone survey each year to find out what is important to parents. The school has an active Parent Community Involvement Committee, which established 10 areas of action to deal with over several years. One recommended activity was to get parents to supervise children at the bus stops. Another was to get teachers to call home with positive comments, and in fact, 51% of parents surveyed said they had received such a call in the 1997–1998 school year.

When asked about communication with parents, five of six teachers in the CIERA study said they sent home a weekly newsletter, and two of six called parents monthly. When asked about literacy materials sent home two of six teachers said they sent books home twice a week and three of six said they sent books home once a week.

Parents also served with teachers on a School Improvement Committee. For the 1997–1998 school year the committee chose 3 building goals: (a) maintaining or establishing reading interventions in Grades K through 5, (b) developing a gifted program in math for Grades 1 and 2, and (c) establishing a fee-based, full-day kindergarten with a sliding fee scale. As part of its early reading intervention effort, the school provided training to parents so they could help with the EIR coaching strategies at home. Parents were paid small stipends to coach EIR children at school.

Instructional Factors Contributing to Sunnyside's Success

Reading instruction has become a priority at Sunnyside. Across the primary grades, the teachers reported spending a lot of time on literacy instruction, ranging from 2½ to 3½ hours per day in Grades 1 through 3, with a median of 3 hours. A number of teachers described the reading program at Sunnyside as a balanced reading program. They used both the basal and trade books consistently; taught phonics and word recognition strategies; and regularly engaged the children in story discussions, writing in response to their reading, and independent reading. These findings will be elaborated below.

Kindergarten Reading Instruction.   At the time of our study, kindergarten was a half-day program. The one kindergarten teacher in the project reported that she relied heavily on the kindergarten EIR program to teach literacy in her classroom. In this intervention program the teacher and children had fun with literature, the children talked about stories in relation to their lives, and they acted the stories out for oral language development. Emergent literacy skills were presented for exposure, not mastery. In addition to focusing on rhyme, concepts of print, and letter-sound recognition, there was a scope and sequence of phonemic awareness activities based on words in the stories the teacher and children had shared. Extra attention was given to the children lowest in oral language and emergent literacy activities in the classroom.

Grade 1 and 2 Reading Instruction.   The entire Grade 1 and 2 staff, including regular, special and Title I teachers, met 3 times a year for a half day (subs were obtained) to talk about their reading program, what was working, and what needed to change. In addition, the teachers in each pod (two Grade 1 teachers, two Grade 2 teachers, four special education teachers, one Title I teacher, and three Title I paraprofessionals) met once every 6 weeks for 1½ hours (again subs were obtained) to plan and to talk about what to do for individual children who were struggling in reading or language arts.

As indicated earlier, the teachers spent from 2½ to 3½ hours a day on literacy. In one 50-minute block, the classroom teacher, special education teacher and Title I teacher each worked with an "achievement level" group within the same classroom. The major purpose of this small group instruction was to be sure that children were being supported as they read material at their instructional level. The classroom teachers rotated among all the small groups so they could work with all of their students over time. Along with this small group instruction, children received daily whole group instruction that varied from work in the basal to morning message to minilessons for writing workshop, and they engaged in independent reading for about 30 to 45 minutes a day.

In addition, struggling readers in Grades 1 and 2 received an additional 20 minutes of day of supplemental small group instruction from their classroom teacher through the Early Intervention in Reading (EIR) program. In the EIR program the children worked in a group of six or seven with their teacher, spending 3 days on a story. Each day they reread familiar stories, read the new story, and engaged in one of three related skill activities—the Sound Box activity, Making Words, or a guided sentence writing activity (Taylor, Short, Frye, & Shearer, 1992; Taylor, Hanson, Justice-Swanson, & Watts, 1997). The children also left the classroom for about 15 minutes a day to receive one-on-one reading coaching on the EIR story from a parent volunteer and to practice reading new and old EIR stories independently. Finally, the Grade 1 students who received EIR instruction met once a week with a Grade 3 tutor (who was also an EIR student) and the Grade 2 EIR students met with a Grade 4 EIR tutor to listen to a story and to read to the older child.

Grade 3 Reading Instruction.   The third-grade teachers also spent from 2½ to 3½ hours a day on literacy instruction and activities. As in Grades 1 and 2 both a basal and trade books were used. During this time children received small group and whole group instruction from their classroom teacher. They spent about 20 minutes a day in independent reading. A group of six or seven readers who needed to work on fluency and comprehension also received 20 minutes of daily EIR instruction from their classroom teacher. Some children left the classroom to work with a Title I or special education teacher or to receive EIR coaching from a parent volunteer.

For the EIR supplemental instruction in Grade 3 the (Taylor, Hanson, Justice-Swanson, & Watts, 1997) children practiced reading and talking about the picture book they would read on Friday to a first-grade EIR child in their story reading exchange. During the actual 20-minute tutoring session, they read the story aloud, talked about the meanings of several words, and asked the younger child a few questions about the story. Additionally, they coached the younger child as he read his own EIR story.

Curriculum: Activities and Materials.   The district required teachers to use Houghton Mifflin's *Invitations to Literacy*, a basal series adopted in the 1997–1998 school year. Sunnyside also used $20,000 in grants in 1997–1998 to purchase trade books that had been leveled for reading difficulty. In the questionnaire that was administered, four out of six teachers indicated that they used the basal for instruction and four of six also reported using trade books for instruction.

Teachers in Grades 1 through 3 reported spending a median of 42 minutes a day in teacher directed reading or literature discussion. With one exception, teachers reported spending as much teacher directed time on expository text as on narrative text.

Grouping Practices.   Teachers differed in the amount of time they spent in whole group or small group teacher directed reading. Three of five Grade 1 through 3 teachers spent more time with their students in small group than whole group instruction, and two teachers spent more time in whole group than small group instruction.

Teacher Instructional Practices.   The teachers described themselves as fairly eclectic when asked on the questionnaire to select teaching approaches they used often. Five of six said they often watched their kids read and work and provided minilessons as needed; four of five said they often directly explained and modeled new skills and strategies followed by guided practice and independent application; three of five said they often assessed students on skills and strategies, taught those not yet mastered, and then assessed for mastery.

In 17 observations focusing on reading in four Grade 1 and 2 classrooms, only 2 lessons were seen in which phonics was taught in isolation. Coaching children to use strategies as they were reading was the primary technique observed to develop children's word recognition abilities in one first-grade classroom and two second-grade classrooms. Three teachers regularly prompted children to use a variety of strategies such as:

- "Does that makes sense?" ("tease" for "teach" in *The Cow That Went Oink*).
- "What do the letters 'ch' say?" "How do you know it can't be 'dripped' (for 'dressed' in *Just Like Daddy*)."
- "Look for a chunk." (In "morning" from *Just Like Daddy*).
- "Do you see 'car'?" (in "card" from *Charlie Needs Cloak*). "Now let's reread like good readers do."

The predominant mode of comprehension instruction was asking children questions about the stories they had read. This was observed in all 7 classrooms in Grades K through 3. In 28 observations in which children were reading a story or informational text, questioning about the reading was observed in 71%

of sessions. Teachers asked both text-based questions and questions related to students' lives or feelings. Questions like the following were used to engage the children in higher-level thinking:

- "What is something you do that you father likes to do?" (After reading *Just Like Daddy*).
- "Why do you think children like Mercer Mayer books?"

Writing in response to reading was observed in 61% of the sessions. Children were asked to write in ways such as the following: (a) write about your own nickname (after reading a story about a boy and his nickname); (b) write a descriptive paragraph about a character, (c) summarize the story just read; (d) take notes from informational books for your research project.

In the larger CIERA project in which this school participated, coaching children to perform a skill or strategy or to expand on an idea was the preferred interaction style of the most accomplished teachers in the study (Taylor et al., 2000). Based on the classroom observational notes, three of seven teachers in the project at Sunnyside were seen frequently coaching their students to use a process or strategy or to expand on an answer to a question or a comment. This coaching was observed especially in the area of word recognition strategies, which is not surprising given the fact that the teachers had been trained to use the coaching strategies of EIR. Another common coaching technique used by these teachers was prompting for elaboration or clarification as children were answering comprehension questions.

- "What do you mean she lived somewhere else?" (in response to an answer to the questions about why a character had a harder time in first grade that other children.) "Why does that make it harder for her?"
- "Why don't you think of all those ideas on otters, write one that you think could be a main idea, and get back to me."

In contrast to coaching, telling children information and using the recitation format were coded much less often in these three classrooms. Examples of telling included:

- "Mercer Mayer has done over 200 books for kids. His favorite part is the pictures."
- "Always double the 'p' before adding the 'ed' ending (in 'skipped')."
- "The boom swung around and hit the boy's head. He was lucky to be knocked out (when explaining a scene from the *Wreck of the Zephyr*)."

Examples of using recitation include:

- "What do 'laughed' and 'laughing' have alike? What's the difference between them?"
- "Where does water vapor come from? Where does it go when it rises?"
- "What does 'procrastination' mean?"

Student Engagement and Classroom Management.   As classroom activities were coded every 5 minutes during reading, a count of the number of children on task was also taken. In the seven Grade K through 3 classes at Sunnyside that were in the study, the mean percent of children on task ranged from 65% to 99% with a median of 95%. Five teachers had a mean of 93% or more of their children on task. These teachers had quick transitions between activities and well-established classroom routines. Behavior problems were not seen in any of the observations in these five classrooms.

When asked about their behavior management systems, the five teachers with high levels of pupil engagement offered some interesting perspectives:

- "I set up a few rules. I expect them to use self-control a lot (kindergarten)."
- "I am positive but with clear, firm expectations. I work hard in the fall; I model, we role play, we talk about working hard, respecting others."
- "I try to reward the positive in individuals and as a class (my first choice). I don't reward with tangibles but with privileges. I have a communication sheet that goes home every day. If a child has had a bad day, I let the parents know. But I'm usually able to counter this with a positive comment. I try to send home a positive comment from one to two times a week." (Sometimes the weekly sheet went home with no comments for a particular day.)
- "My children need to know they're accountable to do their work, stay on task, and be respectful, or they'll do their work at free time."
- "If a child is making it difficult for another child, I point this out to him or her. I also include humor or some of my own experiences when talking about behavior."

Continuous Progress Monitoring.   District-wide, teachers in the Mounds View Schools used a fluency measure (words correct per minute on grade-level passages) as a continuous progress monitoring (CPM) measure (Deno, 1985). The Title I teachers conducted the assessment for all of the classroom teachers at regular intervals throughout the year, ranging from three times a year in Grade 1 to at least five times a year in Grades 2 through 5, and some teachers requested CPMs up to seven times a year. Teachers at the CPMs were useful in helping them gauge students' progress and in alerting them to particular children who were in need of extra help, or at least additional diagnosis.

Challenges and Things the School Is Still Working On

When asked in the interview about challenges in their classroom or school, four teachers mentioned insufficient parent support as a source of concern: "not having follow through at home," "kids who don't care and parents who don't care," "parent cooperation." Two teachers focused on time: not having enough time to teach, classroom interruptions, and the distraction of many other scheduled activities. Two teachers mentioned scheduling difficulties across the classroom teacher, Title I teacher, and special education teacher for the small group instruction as well as difficulties with the scheduling of reading coaches. Two teachers mentioned the need for more materials to meet students needs, and two teachers mentioned the wide range of reading abilities as challenges. The principal mentioned space shortages and the need for more books to send home.

When asked about things they were still working on in the school, four teachers mentioned the need to continue with the EIR intervention program and to move it into all grade levels: "If you can give children who are struggling a good start, maybe they'll keep going." Two teachers mentioned the need to find more resources to buy more books at children's reading level. The principal mentioned the new basal series, graduation standards, the district CPM system, and the reciprocal teaching intervention in Grade 5 as aspects of the school-wide reading program still in need of attention.

Advice to Other Schools Wishing to Beat the Odds

In our interviews, we asked, "What advice would you give to other schools seeking to significantly improve their reading achievement?" Five of six teachers and the principal mentioned intervention in general and the EIR program in various ways. The principal said that schools need a primary school improvement goal and that EIR had been theirs. One teacher said, "You need to be more cohesive across the school, and we got that when we decided to go with EIR. It's also nice that we have consistency with EIR across the district." Other recommendations included the need for small group instruction, daily one-on-one help for students at their instructional reading level, and professional development to help teachers learn how to use the coaching strategies.

One teacher leader at the school said, "You need to let go of everything you thought was gospel, be willing to look at a different way of doing things." She mentioned the importance of continuous learning, of teachers having an "I can learn so kids can be more successful" attitude. Another teacher perhaps best summed up the approach used at Sunnyside: "You need to address reading from two points of view. Use best methods in class with all children and interventions as well for those who are struggling."

SUMMARY AND CONCLUSIONS

With 38% of its students qualifying for subsidized lunch, Sunnyside is not a high-poverty school. But like many schools in first-ring suburbs around older cities, Sunnyside has seen a large increase in the number of poor children attending the school as well as a small but steady increase in the cultural and linguistic diversity of the student population. In a sense, the fact that Sunnyside was in a relatively affluent suburb only heightened the school's performance concerns. Constantly being compared to other schools in the district with very different demographics and worrying about their struggling readers, the primary grade teaching staff at Sunnyside decided they needed to change their reading program.

The pressure to change came from the teachers themselves. One teacher took the lead in reviewing the research literature, but as a group the regular, special education, and Title I teachers reached consensus on their framework for teaching reading in Grades 1 and 2. These teachers decided on a large block of time for literacy instruction. This time factor alone has probably been a major contributor to the reading gains seen at Sunnyside over the past few years. The teachers also felt that the 50 minutes a day of small group reading instruction at students' instructional level was a major contributing factor.

For the most part, the classroom reading instruction at Sunnyside was observed to be eclectic, or balanced. Teachers used the basal and literature, student discussions, and writing in response to reading with great regularity. Little drill on reading skills in isolation was seen. Most teachers in the CIERA study relied heavily on coaching children as they were reading or responding while a few relied heavily on recitation or telling, or both, to teach reading to their students.

The teachers were split were in their expectations for student learning and their perceptions of lack of parent support as a persistent problems at Sunnyside. Four teachers explicitly mentioned that they had high expectations for their students learning and five agreed that all students, regardless of background, could learn to read at grade level with strong classroom instruction and well-designed special programs. However, four teachers mentioned insufficient parental support as a challenge for them at Sunnyside. Three of six who responded to the survey felt that without parent involvement, struggling readers were unlikely to make substantial gains in reading achievement. It appears that some teachers at Sunnyside had some conflict over parental involvement and their expectations for students' reading achievement and others did not.

The teachers at Sunnyside are a dedicated group of professionals who work hard, teach well, and care about their children, factors that help to ensure reading success. The teachers have worked as a team over a number of years to improve their reading program in the primary grades. Their efforts have paid off because most children at Sunnyside are now reading on grade level in the primary grades

POSTSCRIPT: WHAT HAS HAPPENED AT SUNNYSIDE SINCE THE 1997–1998 STUDY?

Contacts with the staff indicate that achievement scores at Sunnyside continue to rise, and the reforms implemented are still in place. The results at Sunnyside have led to district-wide implementation of some of the programs and practices that they pioneered.

Changes at Sunnyside. Like all schools, things are in constant flux. At Sunnyside, seven classroom teachers in Grades 1 through 4 and three special education teachers have retired or left the building to teach elsewhere. Prospective teachers are informed in the interview process about Sunnyside's high expectations for students, the instructional practices used, and the staff development they will be required to take in order to meet these expectations. All new staff must be trained in the Early Intervention in Reading Process and Guided Reading (Fountas & Pinnell, 1996). In addition, they have a "mentor" teacher in the building to provide them with help and support.

Sunnyside's principal, Michelle Brouse, is committed to providing staff with resources and time to plan, discuss results, and maintain their programs. State provided compensatory education funds are used to support coaches hired for the EIR Program and to hire additional part-time, certified teachers to work with the classroom teachers during guided reading so all children are able to meet in small, flexible groups at their instructional level daily. Teacher teams consisting of classroom teachers, reading resource teachers, and special education teachers continue to meet monthly to talk about struggling students and to plan for instruction. Results are still monitored school-wide, and teachers continue their semi-annual grade-level planning/trouble shooting meetings with the principal and support staff.

The teachers now host parent sessions in the fall and winter to help parents learn how to "coach" their children to use word recognition strategies when they listen to them read. At these sessions, there is also time spent on comprehension in which the emphasis is on helping parents learn how to "converse" with their children about the books they are reading as well as how to stretch their child's thinking through higher level questioning. Day care is provided for the children while the parents learn these coaching strategies. Afterward, the children join the parents so they can practice what they have learned.

Some of the intermediate teachers at Sunnyside partner with a primary class as "reading buddies." All of the older students are taught the word recognition strategies used in EIR so they can assist younger students as they read. Intermediate students have been taught how to converse with the younger children about the books, also. They have been given open-ended questions to use so they do not simply rely on facts and recall. The cross-grade partner reading program specifically for struggling readers continues, and has even been expanded to Grade 5 students. During the year in which we conducted our study, Deluxe Check and Medtronics, two major corporations in the Twin Cities, began to send volunteers to Sunnyside weekly to work with at risk children in Grades 1 through 5 on reading and self esteem. This program started 3 years ago and continues to grow each year. If children remain at Sunnyside, the "friendship" continues in succeeding years with the same volunteer, permitting the two to establish a sustained mentoring relationship. The volunteers receive training in word recognition and question/discussion strategies.

District Changes.   As indicated previously, changes at Sunnyside have served as a catalyst for reform in the seven other elementary schools in the Mounds View District. In 1998–1999 and 1999–2000, the superintendent required all kindergarten through Grade-3 teachers to implement some form of research-based reading intervention in their classrooms. Most teachers chose and were trained in EIR.

Experience with leveled books in EIR led teachers across the district to ask for leveled books to use with all children (not just the EIR students) in small, flexible groups. The books have been purchased, and guided reading training has been offered to all interested teachers, first in Grades 1 and 2 and then in Grades K and 3. Although voluntary, virtually all teachers in the district have decided to participate.

In 1999–2000, the district piloted kindergarten-level guided reading in three schools. Results were so positive that all remaining kindergarten teachers decided to participate in guided reading training in the 2000–2001 school year.

Conclusions.   A goal of the Mounds View district leadership is to continue to provide opportunities for teachers to improve teacher learning and student learning. The district realizes that their teachers need both knowledge and time—knowledge of effective reading practices and time to work with their colleagues to learn how to implement these practices. They also realize that this process of professional learning must be continuous if high standards are to be met by all students.

REFERENCES

Deno, S. (1985). Curriculum-based measurement: The emerging alternative. *Exceptional Children, 52,* 219–232.

Fountas, I. C., & Pinnell, G. S. (1996). *Guided reading: Good first teaching for all children.* Portsmouth, NH: Heinemann.

Taylor, B. M., Hanson, B., Justice-Swanson, K., & Watts, S. (1997). Helping struggling readers: Linking small group intervention with cross-age tutoring. *The Reading Teacher, 51,* 196–208.

Taylor, B., Pearson, P. D., Clark, K., & Walpole, S. (2000). Effective schools and accomplished teachers: Lessons about primary grade reading instruction in low-income schools. *The Elementary School Journal, 101,* 121–166.

Taylor, B., Short, R., Frye, B., & Shearer, B. (1992). Classroom teachers prevent reading failure among low achieving first grade students. *The Reading Teacher, 45,* 592–597.

7

Rocky Mountain Elementary School, Longmont, Colorado

Jacalyn Colt
St. Vrain Valley School District, Longmont, Colorado

Rebecca Mills
Consultant, St. Vrain Valley School District, Longmont, Colorado

BACKGROUND

During the 1997–1998 school year, Rocky Mountain participated, along with 13 other schools, in the CIERA Beat the Odds Study (see Taylor, Pearson, Clark, & Walpole, chap. 1, this volume). During the course of that study, Rocky Mountain emerged as one of the very most effective schools. This chapter is the story of Rocky Mountain's journey in becoming a school that beat the odds.

Rocky Mountain Elementary School is located in the mid-size city of Longmont, Colorado, approximately 35 miles northwest of Denver. It is a Kindergarten through second-grade school serving 434 students, with approximately 140 children in each grade level. It is one of four Bilingual Center Schools in the St. Vrain Valley School District, providing literacy instruction in students' primary language of English or Spanish. In the year of our study, the student body was 66% Hispanic, 31% White, 1% Asian, 1% Native American, and less than 1% African American. Of these students, 55% qualified for free or reduced lunch and 42% had limited English proficiency.

Rocky Mountain has three kindergarten teachers who each teach two sessions, six first-grade teachers, six second-grade teachers, five Title I teachers, and three Special Education teachers, and a total licensed staff of 30. Five classroom teachers and two Title I teachers are bilingual teachers. Rocky Mountain teachers have taught an average of 10 years in the district and 50% have Masters degrees or higher.

History of the School

Rocky Mountain, named for the clear view it offers of the Colorado Rockies, sits on a hill above a city park. Several economically diverse neighborhoods comprise Rocky Mountain's attendance area. In an attempt to make the ethnic and socioeconomic populations of two neighborhood schools more balanced, Rocky Mountain was designated as a primary school when it opened in 1977. Nearby Columbine Elementary became the intermediate school. In the late 1980s, Rocky Mountain transitioned from a Kindergarten through third-grade to a Kindergarten through second-grade school.

This school has experienced a high turnover of leaders. Before Kathy Horning, the school's seventh principal, the tenure of principals averaged only 2½ years. When Horning arrived in 1992, she found the school in serious turmoil. It was low-performing and the staff was angry and hostile, partly as the result of a high turnover rate of principals. The majority of staff had been at Rocky Mountain for most of their careers. Under Horning's leadership, increased teacher attrition made it possible to select new staff members who aligned with the priorities of literacy and higher expectations of students. In addition, there was the continual need for more bilingual teachers as the percentage of Hispanic students increased from the mid-40s to the high 60s, and the percentage of Spanish-speaking children has increased from 20% to 40%.

Horning envisions school as a place where people can learn and feel joyful about learning—"not just the kids, but the adults, too." Her hope is that "this is evident ... people can sense it, can see it in the classroom, can hear it in conversations." She remarked that Rocky Mountain is closer to this vision in that she rarely hears comments such as "kids can't do this." Horning acknowledges, however, that this vision is a journey. She believes that parents bring their children to school with high hopes. It is up the school to do whatever is feasible to make sure that each child reaches his or her potential.

Given that the most critical skill sets for students are reading and writing, Horning acknowledged that this vision can only be realized when the entire staff believes that they are teachers of reading and writing, and are willing to work together, blending their expertise through team-teaching and collaboration.

Five years ago, Kathleen Horning and her staff examined data showing that only 67% of Rocky Mountain's students were reading at or above grade level by the end of second grade. First, the school examined the data in the context of increasing numbers of students qualifying for free/reduced meals and speaking a language other than English. Next, they sought answers to these questions:

1. How can we provide more students with reading instruction that will address their intense needs?
2. What strategies should we use to increase our effectiveness with students who have had limited experiences or whose language is other than English?

According to Horning, by addressing these questions, 79% of second graders were reading at or above grade level by spring of that year. The principal and staff refined the delivery structures in the school, enabling them to teach reading more effectively, and at the same time, enhanced the bilingual program. These efforts also contributed to the selection of Rocky Mountain Elementary as a 1998 National Blue Ribbon School.

Evidence of Progress. Since 1994, Rocky Mountain has administered a literacy assessment to all students each fall and spring. Once identified, the school's lowest-performing students receive intensive instruction in both the classroom and in the Literacy Lab using the Right Start Reading Program as the instructional model. Of the 37 first-grade students served in English in the Literacy Lab during the 1996–1997 school year, 76% were able to read primer text at the end of the year and 51% were able to read level-1 text. An average of 66% of second graders served in the Literacy Lab were able to read and comprehend grade-level text at the end of the year. These data describing the achievement of the school's lowest performing students have been consistent for the past 3 years. Data for the Spanish readers has consistently been less compelling and an ongoing focus for school-wide and district-level study.

Explaining Rocky Mountain's Progress

The fundamental questions about Rocky Mountain are: How do we explain its success? And, what can others learn from a close examination of its practices? A great deal, we think. The real genius in Rocky Mountain's story is that the staff did not look to any single strategy or program as a quick fix; instead, they paid attention to all aspects of developing a solid reading program. They worried about connecting the school to the community and to the homes of their students, they worked hard to develop a collaborative focus as a staff, and they attended to all of the complex details of classroom instruction. To understand why Rocky Mountain succeeded, one must attend to each of these programmatic features.

As you examine the data explaining its success, recall that Rocky Mountain participated in the CIERA Beat the Odds Study. Hence, much of the data reported in describing programs and classroom practices comes from that larger study (for a complete description of the methodology, including the instruments used, see chap. 1, this volume)

COMMUNITY/HOME/SCHOOL FACTORS

Rocky Mountain welcomes and encourages parents and community members to participate in their children's education. All school information and parent meetings are conducted in both languages. The faculty is particularly proud of the strides it has made through its Home Reading Partnership with parents. This program, in its 10th year, provides home reading books in English and Spanish so that families can read to children in their primary language. The principal explained, "Once Rocky Mountain redefined how parents could be involved, they took this on readily." Horning noted that parents have participated eagerly regardless of socioeconomic status or ethnicity and that there is strong attendance at family sessions focusing on reading and writing with children.

Several initiatives illustrate the depth and variety of the home–school connections as reported by teachers who participated in the study:

- send books home several times a week
- attend parent–teacher conferences two times a year
- send home letters weekly or monthly
- call parents monthly or quarterly
- send home traveling notebooks weekly

SCHOOL FACTORS

Linking Classroom Programs and Supplemental Programs

Because Rocky Mountain's primary focus is literacy acquisition, the school has devoted all major resources and aligned all major events and celebrations around these literacy achievement goals. Classroom teachers at Rocky Mountain use words such as *blended, eclectic, balanced*, and *varied* to describe their general approach to teaching reading. These teachers also believe in coordinating resources and programs; all of the surveyed teachers said that they strongly believe supplemental reading programs should be closely coordinated with the classroom-reading program.

Right Start, the district's early intervention program, and its Spanish counterpart, Buen Comienzo, have served as a critical component in the school's efforts toward increased literacy achievement. Right Start, implemented in partnership with the University of Colorado at Boulder, is a small-group model emphasizing guided reading of leveled text, explicit attention to word-level strategies, and coaching during brief writing segments. Early Start, the kindergarten version of Right Start, emphasizes shared reading of big books, awareness of print conventions using matching little books, phonemic awareness activities, and matching of letters and sounds.

The Literacy Lab, implemented in 1994, is an integrated services model, integrating the previously discrete Special Education, Title I, Speech and Language, and Bilingual Literacy Programs. The intention of the Literacy Lab is to provide focused, explicit instruction in a small group to an increased number of students. Another intention is to share the expertise of teachers across the various disciplines through planned collaboration.

Instructional Leadership

When interviewed, all of the teachers emphasized the pivotal role of the principal in supporting their efforts to increase literacy achievement. Teachers described Kathleen Horning, the principal, as supportive and involved. One bilingual teacher described the principal's emotional and financial support as crucial to the success of the Literacy Lab and bilingual programs. One classroom teacher described the principal as "the driving force behind the literacy movement." She earned this reputation through ongoing practices such as encouraging first-year teachers to enroll in the Right Start Program, demonstrating strong observational skills, being aware of children's needs and achievement, and working with teachers to improve the delivery of reading and writing instruction. The teachers are aware of Horning's strong knowledge of literacy instruction, and that has earned her considerable credibility among the staff. Literacy Lab teachers noted that the principal ensures that everyone is working toward a common goal. As one Literacy Lab teacher explained, "school-wide support is critical to the success of our program and without the principal's support, it would be a rough road to hoe."

In our interviews, Kathy Horning described her role as an instructional leader, cheerleader, procurer of resources, protector of time, communicator, and learner. She acknowledged her role in helping the staff examine data and identify specific strategies to help struggling readers. She continually supports teachers in the implementation of these strategies, aligning efforts among classrooms, Literacy Lab, grade levels, and schools. Horning, however, also attributed the school's success to the instructional leadership provided by the district and within the building. She described the district coaching program as "extremely powerful" and an "outstanding resource." Horning has encouraged her staff to appreciate the experts emerging within the building. The Literacy Lab teachers, for example, serve as instructional leaders as they coach other teachers in reading instruction and assessment. Some classroom teachers serve as instructional leaders by sharing their instructional expertise with other teachers.

Characteristics of the School and its Teachers

When asked to identify important attributes of effective schools, all of the participating teachers indicated that a strong emphasis on reading/language arts is very important and very indicative of their school. Nearly all of these teachers agreed on other important attributes, such as:

- personal commitment to students and teaching
- high expectations for students' learning
- systematic evaluation of students' progress
- breadth of materials
- attention to basic skills
- a clear school mission
- program stability

While positive home–school relations were recognized as a very important attribute of effective schools by nearly all of the teachers, only a few felt that this attribute is significantly indicative of Rocky Mountain. Given the home–school communication efforts reported earlier and Kathy Horning's positive vision for a strong relationship with parents and community, this is a likely goal for this school to consider in the future.

Classroom teachers identified the Literacy Lab as a significant factor in students' success. They highlighted the benefits of small-group instruction and early intervention, the program's ability to serve students with academic needs, and its role in helping all teachers and staff support students in a collaborative manner. The Literacy Lab teachers mentioned specific characteristics of the Right Start Programs as responsible for student success.

A school-wide focus on literacy and the home–school connection were mentioned as critical factors by half of the teachers interviewed. Staff development, advanced training, and peer coaching contributed to student success according to three of the five classroom teachers.

When asked to what she attributes the success of her school, the principal identified the following factors: bringing higher clarity to common goals; identifying available resources (e.g., money, time, people); sharing expertise, selecting new staff who embrace school goals; and believing in students' potential. Horning explained that when staff started to see increases in students' reading data, they became excited and had incentive to continue the initiatives. The school was then able to share these results and celebrate successes.

The most interesting feature of these attributions of success by the principal and the teachers is that they map very directly onto the research on effective schools and effective classroom teachers. Somehow, in their efforts to reform their school and their classroom instruction, these teachers found a set of answers that are consistent with our national research base.

Professional Development

In this school, collaboration is valued as a means for exploring alternative ways of working together and generating solutions to problems. Instructors in the Literacy Lab have designated one half-day per week for collaborative planning. Due to this effective planning and intervention for meeting students' needs, the numbers of students referred for special education services has been significantly reduced. Other collaborative efforts include monthly grade-level team meetings to discuss curriculum, grade-level standards, and teaching strategies. Regular bilingual meetings are held to review issues and guidelines for ensuring quality instruction and meeting programmatic regulations.

Staff development efforts include 2 hours per month for extensive training in reading strategies, peer coaching, collaboration, and other topics identified by the staff. In addition, the school has approximately 5 early-release days each year to supplement this training, and staff-development funding for attendance at relevant workshops. Literacy coaches routinely support teachers in the implementation of Right Start and Buen Comienzo strategies and two expert teachers offer the staff ESL training.

Rocky Mountain typically has one or two PIE (Partners in Education) teachers on staff each year. The PIE Program is a collaborative effort with the University of Colorado at Boulder that allows new teachers to work on a Master's Degree while teaching. A significant part of their study involves classroom practice under the direction of a mentor. The teachers also participate in monthly seminars with educators from other districts as part of their coursework.

Kathy Horning highlighted the staff development initiatives in her school: enrolling more teachers in the Right Start/Buen Comienzo Programs; helping staff become more astute about achievement data; and engaging staff in "book talks."

Teachers identified the following staff development practices to be beneficial to their learning:

- Professional conferences and workshops outside the district
- In-service sessions during regularly scheduled faculty meetings
- Visiting innovative schools followed by sharing sessions with colleagues
- District or school-sponsored yearlong courses
- Mentorship programs between experienced and new teachers

Classroom Practices/Philosophy

The reading program at Rocky Mountain is best described as a balanced program blending holistic learning with direct instruction. Observations revealed the following practices: independent reading of student-selected texts, activation and extension of background knowledge, teacher read-alouds of fictional and informational trade books, and use of nonfiction texts to gather new information. In all observed classrooms, small-group guided instruction was a significant component of the reading program. In the kindergarten classroom, the teacher employed the previously described Early Start strategies on a regular basis. The four first- and second-grade teachers used Right Start and Buen Comienzo strategies as a central component of reading instruction. This guided instruction in all five classrooms was consistent with, and complementary to, the explicit instruction provided in the Literacy Lab. The widespread use of this instructional model in classrooms and in the Literacy Lab reflects Rocky Mountain's belief that early intervention yields success and positive attitudes toward reading.

Students were also engaged in daily writing activities on both teacher-directed and student-selected topics. Often the focus was on a particular element such as description or audience.

Teacher Instruction

The classroom teachers used words such as *balanced, varied,* and *eclectic* to describe their general approaches to teaching reading, whereas most of the Literacy Lab teachers relied on the Right Start/Buen Comienzo instructional model.

Teachers reported instructional strategies that were part of their instructional repertoire, noting such practices as: directly explaining and modeling new skills and strategies, followed by guided practice and independent application (87%); observing students reading and providing guidance in the form of short minilessons (47%); and assessing students on skills and strategies, teaching those not yet mastered, and then reassessing for mastery (33%).

Coaching. Based on observational notes, we found that all five classroom teachers frequently explained a process or strategy or coached their students in the use of a process or strategy. This coaching technique was observed 50% of the time in the kindergarten classroom and an average of 62% of the time in the first- and second-grade classrooms. This technique is especially prevalent in the area of word-recognition strategies, where teachers coach students to use a variety of strategies to figure out unknown words. Examples of explicit instruction include teacher explanations of the processes or strategies, such as:

1. "Sometimes you come to a word and you see part of it that you know, a little word inside a big word … so ask yourself … 'Do I know a small word in it?'"
2. T: "What are you going to think about when you're reading?" Ch: "Does it look right? Does it sound right? Does it make sense?"

Or guiding students to look at the whole word:

3. T: "Slide your eyes all the way to the end because you have to look at the beginning, middle, and end of the word."

Also notable in one first-grade classroom was amount of coaching in the selection of independent reading material and the fostering student ownership of this process. These coaching strategies are in contrast to telling students information and recitation. Telling children information was observed 26% of the time as in example (4).

4. "If I say your friendship is 'valuable,' it means it's really worth a lot." Recitation by teachers occurred an average of 26% of the time. For example, the teacher might seek short, specific answers to a direct question such as in this example:
5. "What is a topic sentence? What is it going to tell?"

Modeling/Demonstration/Think-Aloud. Our observations revealed frequent modeling or demonstration techniques in all classrooms, but more prevalent in kindergarten. To illustrate, one kindergarten teacher frequently

modeled reading aloud and tracking and demonstrated how to make let-
ter-sounds:

6. T: To make the /v/ sound, "You almost bite your lip."

Others frequently use a "think-aloud" strategy to model the processes involved
in writing:

7. T: "There's a letter missing but I don't know what it is. I'm going to
    leave it blank for now and go back later."

The other first-grade teacher modeled the application of reading strategies:

8. T: I read, "Yo tengo un pato" and this makes sense but I looked at the
    words and realized that there weren't the right number of sounds.

Teachers modeled reading aloud from prose and poetry, writing letters, and
looking up words in the dictionary. They also demonstrated new activities as
they modeled constructing story diagrams to create stories and fairy tales.

Positive Feedback.   A third common instructional link among all five observed classroom teachers was their use of positive feedback, which was noted
an average of 54% of the time. Notably, negative feedback was observed in only
one of these five classrooms.

Often teachers validated partially correct answers or attempts such as:

9.   "Very good, it starts with a /c/ sound but what other letter makes this
     sound?"
10. "That's a good word (to fit the word pattern list), but we've got it al-
     ready."
11. "Both ideas were good but this second idea tells me more about the
     biggest idea of the story."

Student Self-Sufficiency.   A final trend among teachers at Rocky Mountain was their emphasis on guiding students toward self-sufficiency through reli-
ance on themselves, known strategies, and a variety of resources such as peers.
Teachers identified student independence, confidence, and/or self-sufficiency
as key components of their classroom vision. The kindergarten teacher explained that she aims to prepare her students so that when they finish kindergarten they will say, "I can do that." She guides her students to use their
knowledge to help their peers and encourages students to think for themselves:

A first-grade classroom teacher described a very ambitious set of "independence" goals for her children: "That all children can become independent, confident learners ... that they can leave here believing that they can and will learn ... that they can read and can write ... that they all know they can be teachers of other children, and know that they're all experts."

Observations revealed evidence that this teacher's beliefs were clearly interwoven into every aspect of her classroom, including behavior, problem solving, time management, student ownership and responsibility over classroom practices, and reliance on resources other than the teacher as noted in this interaction:

> T: "You know what? If you get your writing book, then you can go over to Ashley, because I gave her the spelling and you can get it from her."

Another first-grade teacher emphasized the importance of having her students in charge of themselves and helping each other as learners. In this classroom, she uses learning-center contracts with students. A second-grade teacher emphasized the importance of creating life-long learners in her classroom by giving students literacy skills with emphasis on thinking skills. Observations showed this teacher frequently calling for student helpers to help introduce learning-center tasks or to participate in an activity.

Curriculum: Activities and Materials

Classroom teachers indicated that they used little predictable, leveled books for instruction. Otherwise, their responses revealed a wide array of materials—reading anthologies, fictional trade books, and workbooks (although most expressed modest reliance on them). The responses to our questions about materials left us with the impression that materials were not at the core of their reading program, at least not to the degree that instructional routines leading to student independence were.

The spring teachers' logs revealed that the kindergarten teacher spent over 1 hour per half-day session on literacy instruction, distributed as follows:

Phonics/phonemic awareness	39 minutes
Reading narrative text	24 minutes
Listening/speaking	21 minutes
Teacher read alouds	12 minutes
Writing in response to reading	12 minutes

The first- and second-grade teachers' logs revealed that they spend from 3 to 4 hours a day on literacy instruction and activities. Their average times for various activities revealed this distribution:

Independent reading	53 minutes
Teacher directed text discussions	83 minutes
Writing in response to reading	33 minutes
Writing (original compositions)	56 minutes

Three teachers reported spending more time with teacher-directed reading of narrative text than with expository text, but one teacher reports exactly the reverse. All four teachers preferred small group instruction to large group configurations by about a 4 to 1 ratio. This preference extended to the upper grades; observations of a fourth teacher showed that small-group instruction was her most frequently used instructional grouping.

Teacher–Student Interaction

Consistent with the instructional focus of guiding students toward ownership of processes and strategies and toward self-sufficiency, all five classroom teachers were observed routinely explaining, reviewing, questioning, listening, coaching, and providing specific positive feedback in their interactions with children. While teachers engaged in these interactions during whole-class and small-group instruction, the majority of interactive coaching and scaffolding occurred during the small-group reading instruction.

Another notable aspect in observations is the frequency with which students initiated questions or comments about the material presented. In all five classrooms, students commented about text or illustrations or asked questions about an activity or the meaning of a story. In all of the instances, the classroom teachers responded positively to these comments, expanding on the students' ideas, answering their questions, or considering their requests. The students' comments and their teachers' responses demonstrated that students feel comfortable in classrooms that value and support their active participation as learners.

Observations of the first and second grades also showed teachers promoting peer interaction. In one first-grade class, the teacher asked students to turn to a partner to "share their ideas" before beginning an independent task. The other first-grade teacher encouraged students to practice reading a familiar text or piece of writing with an assigned or self-selected partner. Students in a second-grade classroom turned to peers for help or supplies. In the other second-grade class, the teacher frequently designed activities requiring active student participation, cooperation, and interaction.

Student Engagement

Among the other things we examined during the observations was the percentage of students who were engaged in on-task behavior during each 5-minute interval. The teachers at Rocky Mountain were masterful in their ability to engage children in their reading program. In the five Kindergarten through second-grade classrooms, the mean percent of students on-task ranged from 90% to 100% with a median of 98%. Three teachers had a mean of 98% or more of their children on-task and descriptive observations showed students consistently engaged in, and successfully completing, assigned tasks. To what can we attribute these extraordinary levels of student engagement? All five teachers had well-established classroom routines, tasks well designed for the designated time periods, clear expectations for students who finished their tasks early, and quick transitions between activities. Observations showed students particularly engaged in small-group instruction. In the kindergarten classroom, a low student-to-teacher ratio (6:1) enabled teachers to closely monitor student understanding and progress. In the first and second grades, well-established classroom routines enabled teachers to lead small-group instruction, while the remaining students completed independent reading or writing tasks or worked in small groups at clearly explained learning centers. This organization allowed teachers to closely monitor the progress of the individual students in reading groups.

Classroom Management

When asked about their behavior management systems, several teachers described their system as one involving "logical consequences." They commented on the importance of involving students in the creation of classroom rules and procedures. One teacher explained that when students "make the rules and set the boundaries, they are much more likely to stay within them." Others specifically mention the importance of involving parents in classroom management issues.

A teacher, speaking extensively on the subject of classroom management, emphasized how mistakes (academic and social) are seen as opportunities to learn. She believes in demonstrating and helping students practice problem-solving methods in order for them become self-directed, and she believes in teaching students to be independent and to work together rather than compete. The same teacher also explained how, in her classroom, she "won't solve any problem a kid has a high chance of solving for him or herself." She consistently responds to student concerns by first asking how the child plans to address his or her problem and, next, by suggesting what some kids might do. Other classroom observations revealed teachers frequently reinforcing good behavior with positive feedback, reminding students to stay on task, and reminding students to prevent problems by making good choices.

Classroom Environment

The observed teachers provided a safe, structured environment for their students and students responded with respect and cooperation. Interactions between teachers and students were consistently positive, enthusiastic, and encouraging. As teachers were respectful of their students and valued their students as learners, so too were students respectful of each other. All of the students seemed comfortable in their classrooms and their teachers exhibited high expectations of students' abilities to work independently and make informed choices. There was a particular emphasis in the first- and second-grade classrooms on fostering student ownership and responsibility in the classroom. Students in these classes demonstrated increasing ownership of literacy tasks (e.g., learning centers), resources (e.g., identifying easy, just-right and challenge books), learning strategies, and behavior.

CHALLENGES AND FUTURE GOALS

In our interview, Kathy Horning, the principal at Rocky Mountain, talked about the ongoing nature of the challenge in working toward its school-wide goal of raising reading and writing achievement. She also noted the subsidiary emphases on comprehension, genre, and reading/writing relationships. As Horning explained, the school needs to continue to view challenges such as the high number of special education students and the increasing number of Spanish speakers as opportunities for positive change. She conceded that this is hard work and described the challenge of keeping her staff in a learning mode when the tendency is to want to find a single answer or cure-all. She emphasized the need to approach issues with the attitude: "Here's how we did it this time—next time with these changing conditions we need to do it this way." Horning emphasized the need to continually change in response to needs by questioning, "What will that look like?" and "How can we shape services to address particular needs?"

When asked about challenges in their classroom and school regarding reading achievement, teachers overwhelmingly mentioned home support and/or background knowledge as the factors presenting the greatest challenges. Although some teachers suggested that progress has been made with regard to home support, all agreed that challenges still exist in terms of parental involvement in their children's education.

Several teachers indicated the challenge of an increasing number of students arriving at school with limited background experience and limited vocabulary. The kindergarten teacher described how many students begin school "not knowing colors, shapes—things we take for granted." A bilingual Literacy Lab teacher described the challenge of teaching bilingual children with limited language development in both languages, explaining that they "don't understand what books are about," and that as a teacher you "can't assume they know … what you're talking about." Also, as a second-grade bilingual teacher explained,

> It's harder to be a good reader and be interested in things when you lack experiences … Many students have never been read to, have no books in their home. You need so many resources for these kids and need to follow them all the way through. It's a challenge to serve all of these kids, giving them the experiences, and getting them on grade level.

Several other teachers mentioned the demands of time, explaining that a highly-impacted population of students requires constant immersion and that this level of need challenges teachers to find ample time to teach reading and writing. It requires them to consider: "What can I leave out to ensure literacy as the first priority?" The principal also cited the challenge of getting parents to have their children attend school consistently, noting "we can't teach kids what we're capable of teaching when they're not here."

In order to better serve this increasing population of high-needs students, and in order to close the gap between English and Spanish achievement levels, the school has identified the need for more bilingual staff, particularly in the Literacy Lab. Several teachers also mentioned class size and lack of paraprofessionals as adding to the challenge of meeting the needs of the increasing number of high-needs Special Education students in their classrooms.

Finally, although most teachers praised the collaboration efforts at their school, many suggested that continued progress in this area would benefit students. Teachers cited examples such as smoother transitions and greater consistency in teaching practices between classrooms and the Literacy Lab as important factors. One first-grade teacher explained how the school continues to seek creative ways to meet together, watch each other teach, engage in dialogue about children, and improve dialogue between grade levels and instructional settings.

Advice From the Staff at the School for Other Schools Wishing to "Beat the Odds"

Although the staff recognized the challenges still faced by their school, they also recognized the growth they have made and the importance of celebrating these successes. When asked what advice they would give to other schools wishing to significantly improve reading achievement, the principal and teachers high-lighted the importance of:

- using data to create goals
- staying in a responsive, learning mode
- establishing a well-structured intervention program
- providing a literacy-rich environment
- becoming good observers of children
- supporting staff through meaningful staff development
- collaborating and peer coaching
- establishing a strong home-school connection

In discussing the development of school goals, Horning advises: "Look at your data with open eyes and build your goals around that data. Align every major school effort around achievement of these goals—every resource, time, celebra-tion, major event, the way you hire new staff—all your efforts."

When asked for their advice to other schools, almost all teachers specifically mentioned the importance of an early literacy intervention program, such as Right Start, in order to serve as many students as possible in a small-group set-ting. Teachers suggested that schools need a well-structured and supported pro-gram along with specialists and classroom teachers dedicated to "doing it right and together." Many teachers also highlighted the importance of consistency, peer coaching, collaboration, and teaming together.

These teachers discussed the importance of carefully structuring pro-grams to ensure that services are aligned rather than duplicated. They noted that the Literacy Lab model serves more children and results in greater long-term benefits, resulting in fewer students requiring Special Education services. The principal addressed this issue in detail when speaking of rede-fining and aligning the roles of Title I and Special Education teachers. It is critical to provide training to ensure higher consistency between the pro-grams so that teachers develop a larger repertoire of instructional strategies. Schools tend to "put kids into categories although their needs aren't easy to categorize," and she emphasized that "the needs of kids ought to drive in-struction—not labels."

Advice from teachers also focused on the importance of providing a literacy-rich environment for children. The teachers emphasized the importance of components such as:

- sustained silent reading (DEAR)
- teachers as models of reading behaviors
- rich read-alouds
- writing with daily drafting
- daily small-group reading instruction
- large blocks of time for authentic reading
- reading instruction in students' primary language

Teachers also articulated a need for balance in terms of:

- balance between reading and writing strategies and skills
- balance between independent and guided reading
- a focus on reading strategies rather than skills
- specific literacy objectives for teachers and children

CONCLUSIONS

What Have We Learned From Rocky Mountain's Experience?

As the principal suggested, increasing reading achievement for all students amid the challenges faced by increasing numbers of students with special education needs and limited English proficiency, is best described as a journey. This journey requires continual change in response to the ever-changing needs of an ever-changing student population. Observations, interviews, surveys, and activity logs completed over a 7-month period demonstrate Rocky Mountain's commitment to this journey. Once the principal guided the staff to identify literacy acquisition as the school's primary goal, she used her leadership role to ensure that all major resources (materials, staff, time) were directed toward the achievement of this goal. The principal has encouraged staff to assume leadership roles; to recognize, value, and share the expertise within their school; and to learn together in a collaborative fashion.

Perhaps the most telling evidence of Rocky Mountain's commitment to literacy is its establishment and implementation of the Literacy Lab. District coaches provide ongoing training for Literacy Lab teachers in the use of the Right Start and Buen Comienzo programs, and the Literacy Lab teachers serve as instructional leaders within their school. At Rocky Mountain, the Literacy Lab has a strong presence in the school. Literacy Lab instructors and trained classroom teachers are able to provide struggling readers with consistent use and reinforcement of the same reading strategies, increased time immersed in appropriately leveled materials, and increased time in a small-group format, which allows teachers to closely monitor individual students' needs.

At Rocky Mountain, the principal and teachers recognize the critical role parents play as partners in their children's education. Recognizing that most parents wish for their children to succeed but that many parents are unsure how to help, the school has begun to take the initiative to helping parents learn how they can best help to educate their children. Although the school acknowledges that progress still needs to be made with home–school connections, the Literacy Lab and classroom teachers have worked to establish this connection and have made progress through programs such as the At-Home Reading partnership.

Observations at Rocky Mountain have shown the clear commitment of teachers to their students and to teaching. The teachers consistently demonstrate their commitment to a "balanced" instructional approach and their high expectations for student learning. It is clear that the principal and teachers have made great strides toward the vision that their school be "a place where people can learn and feel joyful about learning" and that this joy of learning be evident. The school has learned the importance of celebrating present successes while focusing on future goals that will lead it further on its journey toward greater early literacy achievement for all students.

EPILOGUE: CHANGING DEMOGRAPHICS AND RESTRUCTURING

Several significant changes in leadership, teachers, and students have taken place at Rocky Mountain since the completion of the CIERA Beat the Odds study.

Leadership.   When Kathy Horning left Rocky Mountain in 1998–1999 to become principal of a K through 5 school, her two successors stayed in the leadership role for only 1 year each. Teachers again felt abandoned, left with substantial challenges without the strong, clear guidance needed to meet these challenges. The frequent change in leadership, communication styles, and differing emphases clearly impedes the school's progress. The current principal, the fourth since 1997, is an experienced principal who has committed to staying at this school until his retirement.

Teachers.   Six of the 15 classroom teachers left Rocky Mountain that same year as Horning, some transferring to a new school, others to other schools or other districts. At the same time, the district and state is providing additional teaching positions to support classroom instruction. As a result, there were 21 classroom positions as well as two additional literacy ESL positions for the 2000–2001 school year. Most of these positions were filled with novice teachers, all of whom have mentors either at the district-level or through the Partners in Education Program. In fact, of the 32 instructional positions, 17 were filled with teachers new to the school and most new to the teaching profession.

Students. Rocky Mountain's enrollment has increased by over 100 students during the past 3 years, with portable classrooms handling the student overflow. The free and reduced lunch count has increased from 55% to over 60%. In order to strengthen communication across grades K through 5 and impact student achievement, Rocky Mountain will become a K through 5 elementary school in fall of 2001. This consolidation of Rocky Mountain Elementary and Columbine Elementary will require much planning and countless changes in personnel, curriculum, and materials. Boundary changes will result in a 47% poverty rating, keeping Rocky Mountain a Title I/ bilingual school, although with a reduced Literacy Lab staff.

Increased Accountability. Although the Literacy Lab model has remained intact and a stable component of this school, the increase of state-level accountability has created new expectations for low-performing students. Students who are not yet proficient at grade level are placed on literacy plans, defining additional instruction such as inclusion in the Literacy Lab or enrollment in a summer program. For example, over 60 Rocky Mountain students registered for last year's half-day summer program and over 30 students remained on the waiting list. Given this demand for increased instructional time, the increase of the school year for schools such as Rocky Mountain will be closely examined by the school and the district. In fact, Columbine Elementary will have a 208-day calendar for the 2001–2002 school year.

Bilingual Program. Another significant factor is the increased need for bilingual teachers at a time when there are few qualified applicants as exemplified by a Spanish Literacy position left unfilled for an entire school year. Principals and administrators from the district bilingual schools have worked with bilingual experts to address the lack of progress in Spanish literacy. As a result of their study and efforts, all assessment data demonstrate an upward trend.

These changes in leadership, personnel, student population, and grade-level configurations mandate that the staff and community reexamine goals and recreate a common, cohesive culture if this school's success is to continue. The very factors that made the initial difference will need to be readdressed and redesigned. While the journey must begin anew, there are teachers on staff who have made the trek before. They understand the value of collaboration, goal setting, use of data, and increased teacher efficacy. Although the paths taken will not be the same ones, these teachers know that the time and energy invested will yield positive results and allow the school community to reach its desired destination—that is, high literacy achievement for all students.

8

Stevenson Elementary: Schoolwide Success[1]

Sharon Walpole
University of Virginia

The CIERA Beat the Odds Study (Taylor, Pearson, Clark, & Walpole, 2000) gave me an amazing opportunity to see effective schools up close, but Stevenson Elementary is the school that really stood out to me. I was not surprised when the data were in and it was one of the most effective schools in the study. Teachers at Stevenson were helping children to beat the odds in literacy achievement. Rich and overlapping data collected there during the 1997–1998 school year (student assessments, classroom observations, time logs, interviews, and surveys) were augmented by many other informal sources of data the following summer and fall to give me an inspiring picture of one school's answer to meeting children's needs. In a time when reading and reading instruction are called rocket science (Moats, 1999) Stevenson's simple success story is especially important to tell.

After briefly sharing some characteristics of the children, families, and teachers who worked together at Stevenson, I will help you to see how the

[1]The work reported herein is supported under the Educational Research and Development Centers Program, PR/Award Number R305R70004, as administered by the Office of Educational Research and Improvement, U.S. Department of Education.

school-level characteristics that we found in our most effective schools (Taylor et al., 2000) played out at Stevenson. There were accomplished teachers at Stevenson, surely, but it was organization at the school level that was the key to accomplishment at the classroom level and achievement for the children.

EFFECTIVE SCHOOLS

The school story at Stevenson connects it not only to the other most effective schools that we studied but also to the broader literature of effective schools (see chap. 16 by Taylor, Pressley, & Pearson, this volume). The research on effective schools is rich and overlapping. In most studies (like our study) effectiveness is defined by achievement variables and then described by correlation of other variables to those achievement variables. As in our study, comparisons are often made between schools with high achievement and schools with low achievement (e.g., Teddlie, Kirby, & Stringfield, 1989).

Critical review of the research on effective schools is outside of the scope of this chapter (see, however, Davis & Thomas, 1989). However, I connect my focus on Stevenson's school story to the work of others. For example, Levine (1991) provided a thoughtful summary of the collective wisdom of many studies. Effective schools are noted for their substantial and substantive staff development. They focus their attention on real instructional change rather than just on improving their academic climate. They look first at the big picture, on issues of grouping, curriculum alignment, instruction, and testing rather than on implementing specific instructional procedures. They take on one large challenge (literacy achievement, for example) at a time. They provide meaningful technical assistance, often through on-site staff development personnel. They use data to drive and evaluate their reform efforts. Their reforms are flexible and unbureaucratic. They involve adoption of specific tried and true ideas from other similar schools. Finally, they allow for a synthesis of bottom-up and top-down change efforts.

Similar more recent efforts to define and describe the characteristics of effective schools in the United Kingdom have identified many of these same attributes. In the United Kingdom, the National Commission on Education funded a study of 11 outlier schools. Madden and Hillman's (1996) cross-case examination of those schools describes a sense of hope and a vision of improvement that came from a building leader who then involved a team and then a staff. The results of that vision were a common philosophy. Teachers and staff members worked within that philosophy to adopt a "can do better" attitude, working as a team and engaging in a continuous change process. As far as the nuts and bolts, they used space effectively, established clear policies and expectations for student behavior, and had high expectations. Also in the United Kingdom, Reynolds (1998) found productive school climates and cultures, a focus on student achievement, monitoring of student progress, site-based staff development, outstanding leadership, parent involvement, and effective instructional strategies to be common among schools with especially good literacy achievement.

Would Stevenson Elementary School's story fit within these rubrics of effectiveness? Yes, it would. The unique contribution of this case study, however, is its focus on literacy. Effectiveness at Stevenson Elementary means teaching children to read and write independently and well.

THE SCHOOL COMMUNITY

Stevenson Elementary School is a pre-kindergarten through fifth-grade school that serves over 700 children in a rural county in Virginia. The school building and the classrooms are large but not especially well equipped; the school was originally the high school for Black children in the area. In 1997–1998, 49% of the children qualified for the federal free or reduced lunch program. Forty percent of the children were African American and 60% were Caucasian. Beginning the previous year, Stevenson had schoolwide Title 1 status. For the state of Virginia, schoolwide Title 1 status is fairly unusual. In 1997–1998, for example, only 156 of the state's 1,158 elementary schools (13.5%) had that status.

Stevenson, at the time of the study, had a licensed staff of 53, with 35 classroom teachers, seven special education teachers, and four Title 1 reading teachers. Among the staff, 38% had Master's degrees. Six were endorsed as reading specialists. The eight teachers who participated in this study ranged in amount of experience from 8 years to 27 years, with a mean of 15 years experience.

CLASSROOM ENVIRONMENTS

Across the grade levels, classrooms at Stevenson were busy places. They looked busy, with children's work displayed prominently on walls and in halls. There were thematic and seasonal decorations, some commercial and some laminated teacher creations. The classroom environments were real and changing, not very neat, and not at all fancy.

Children had access to books for self-selected reading and materials for writing, but there was little unstructured time. The morning business of children at Stevenson was reading and writing, and it was routinized and well structured.

One morning I heard a child ask a Title 1 teacher for a hug, and she received a stock Stevenson answer: "OK, we'll compromise. I'll hug. You read."

Our observers at Stevenson were surprised at the length of time children remained engaged in academic literacy activities. The sheer number of activities, one after another, may have helped them to stay engaged; neither children nor teachers wasted even a second. The high level of engagement also seemed related to the high level of success that children experienced in the activities; because they *could* do the academic tasks that the teachers expected them to complete, they *would* do them.

Across the board, teachers at Stevenson maintained classrooms with high expectations for student behavior. They explained that they respected children, and they expected respect from them in return. Teachers believed that students wanted to behave respectfully and to have an orderly environment for learning. They also believed that student misbehavior was born of frustration with work that was either too hard or not hard enough. Teachers set rules and consequences. Teachers posted these rules and made sure that children knew them. Interruptions during our visits were very rare.

EFFECTIVE LEADERSHIP

Our research design was not especially sensitive to isolating the role of the administration in the effectiveness of the school, but it was surely a factor at Stevenson. The principal, Judy Dickerson, in her 7th year at the building, stood out immediately. She was a no-nonsense principal, and language arts instruction was the center of her mission. She defined herself as principal teacher, and more specifically, as principal reading teacher. She said,

> I know how children learn to read and I have to work very closely with the staff to make sure that each teacher knows how children learn to read and is actually doing the things in the classroom that will bring about success in the children. I have to make sure that the teachers know what they're doing, and have the materials with which to do it, and have the support throughout the day to go on and teach.

Teachers were loyal to Dickerson and immediately identified her as an instructional leader. According to them, she was a "listener," "encourager," someone who "backed them up" as they implemented ideas. Teachers told us that they respected her knowledge of reading and instruction, and her basic belief that literacy learning should start at home, and that direct instruction in reading and writing must start in kindergarten, and that it must continue at every grade level.

LINKING TO PARENTS

Dickerson made an effort to reach out to parents and to involve them in their children's reading instruction. Parent support with homework was a part of the picture, and it was most successful in the early grades. The reason for this, according to Dickerson, was the level of training necessary. She told us, "Most parents are comfortable working with their children as they learn letters and sounds. It becomes more difficult to help at home when children shift their focus to developing higher level comprehension."

During the year of the study, Dickerson sent a survey to parents; 306 parents responded. Ninety one percent of those parents reported that they read with their child at home and 98% reported that they helped with homework. Ninety eight percent of those parents reported that they felt that their children were really learning. She also made time to call homes herself to compliment parents and their children, sharing academic and social achievements with parents.

Teachers also reached out to parents. They documented contacts, from conference meetings to phone calls to notes home to home visits. In the 1997–1998 parent survey, 53% of parents reported having spoken with teachers on the phone, and 75% reported having met with them for conferences. Teachers sent home class and grade-level newsletters weekly, and brief homework assignments nightly.

Parental involvement in whole-school and classroom activities was very important at Stevenson. The PTA was large and active. In the 1997–1998 survey, 43% of parents reported attending PTA meetings. Dickerson reported that a small PTA meeting had 150 people, and a large one, especially one with kindergarten or first-grade children performing, had as many as 750. Each grade level also hosted free spaghetti dinners for families. These dinners were wildly successful forums for sharing information about school programs and state mandates and for building community.

Parents provided support in other ways as well. Approximately 60 parents volunteered in classrooms on a regular basis, lending assistance and establishing relationships with teachers and students. We observed parents in classrooms listening to first graders read, helping them select books, and running word study games. We also saw them helping kindergartners build and read sentences in pocket charts. We did not observe direct parent support in second and third grade during language arts time, but teachers reported that it did occur.

SYSTEMATIC ASSESSMENT
OF STUDENT ACHIEVEMENT

Data collected at Stevenson was actually used to evaluate and improve the instructional program. In 1995–1996, 2 years before this project, Stevenson undertook a large-scale look at student achievement as teachers and administrators prepared a proposal for shifting resources and creating new support programs in their schoolwide Title 1 application. During that year, 23% of Stevenson's third and fourth graders scored in the lowest quartile on the state-mandated Iowa Test of Basic Skills, a proportion that teachers and administrators found unacceptable.

The next year was the first year of state-mandated administration of the Stanford Test of Academic Skills, Ninth Edition. Taken together, Stevenson's third graders scored at the 51st percentile nationally for Total Reading. That same year, 1996–1997, Stevenson adopted a basal series, and began to monitor student progress through the end of unit and end of book tests. Table 8.1 summarizes data on students' instructional reading levels collected in March of 1997.

These measures of instructional reading level documented student achievement before the schoolwide plan was actually implemented and Stevenson had a chance to restructure and provide more intervention services. Already it was a school helping many children to beat the odds, and the instructional team had the resources to do even better. The school staff reaffirmed their commitment to the 20% of first graders, 14% of second graders, and 6% of third graders whose instructional reading level was at least 1 year below grade level.

Key to that commitment was organized collection and use of data for individual children. Classroom teachers assessed achievement on a regular schedule using classroom-based measures. Table 8.2 lists the domains assessed at each

TABLE 8.1

Instructional Reading Levels for Regular Education Children by Grade Level

	First Grade	Second Grade	Third Grade
Beginning 1st Grade	80%		
Beginning 2nd Grade		47%	
End of 2nd Grade		39%	
Beginning 3rd Grade			19%
End of 3rd Grade			75%

TABLE 8.2

Areas of assessment by grade level

Kindergarten	Letter names
	Letter sounds
	Phonological awareness
	Spelling
	Reading of high frequency words in isolation
First Grade	Letter names
	Letter sounds
	Phonological awareness
	Spelling
	Reading of high frequency words in isolation
	Oral reading fluency
	Comprehension
	Writing
Second and Third Grades	Spelling
	Oral reading fluency
	Comprehension
	Writing

grade level. These data were collected by teachers, summarized by class, and reported to the building reading specialist. She helped teachers to use the data for instructional groupings and planning, and then she shared the data with the principal. The data were collected consistently and on schedule across classrooms and became public within the school. The data helped teachers and administrators know instructional levels and plan suitable classroom and intervention programs.

We collected achievement data of our own. As part of the Beat the Odds study, teachers helped us to identify target children for their class. We assessed these children in November and in May. From those assessments I share the one most meaningful to the school—the target students' instructional reading levels. These data are presented in Table 8.3.

TABLE 8.3

Instructional reading levels in November, 1997, and May, 1998 for target children

	First Grade		Second Grade		Third Grade	
	Nov	May	Nov	May	Nov	May
Nonreaders	5	0				
Instructional at Preprimer	3	3				
Instructional at Primer		1	2	1		
Instructional at First Grade		4	6	1	2	
Instructional Second Grade				0	6	1
Instructional Third Grade				6		3
Instructional Fourth Grade						4

Note.   Data in Table 8.3 came from individually administered passages from the QRI-II (Leslie & Caldwell, 1995). Students were counted as instructional if they read with at least 90% accuracy and frustrated if they read with 89% or less. Our pre- and post-test data showed growth for all students and grade-level achievement for 17 of the 24 target children, reaffirming the story that Stevenson was writing about its successes.

BUILDING COMMUNICATION

Instructional leadership at Stevenson was a team effort, guided by the principal. Assessment information at Stevenson was shared in a systematic and elegant way: It went from the classroom teacher to the reading specialist to the principal to the parents every grading period. Because she had data on student achievement, the principal was able to identify areas of need. She took advantage of the expertise within her building, often forming committees to address issues. Together they consulted with people outside the school and read the research. When they made a plan, they communicated it clearly to teachers and then to families.

Stevenson's response to recent state-mandated curriculum in Virginia was a vivid illustration of this kind of communication within the school. As of 1997, children in the state were tested in the third and fifth grades on mastery of specific new curriculum standards in math, reading and writing, science, and history. The Stevenson team compared their existing curriculum to the new state curriculum. They found that they needed to change relatively little in their reading and math programs, but that science and history needed to be revamped.

Once they identified the mismatch, the principal was proactive in organizing her staff's response. Communication within and across grades was the key. Teachers met in their grade-level teams to make sense of their standards and to design pacing guides. Because the curriculum did not match the scope and sequence of information presented in content area textbooks owned by the school, teachers needed new texts, especially content area trade books. Individual teachers, working with the reading specialist, gathered materials for one of the units to share with other teachers at the grade level. Because the state tests in the areas of science and history were cumulative, the teachers then worked together to assemble materials at each grade level to pass on to the next year's teachers so that they could systematically review content material from previous years. At Stevenson there was a sense of shared curricular mission, and teachers regularly communicated within their grade levels and then across the grade levels.

EARLY READING INTERVENTIONS

Like the other schools that we found to be most effective, Stevenson provided intervention for struggling readers across the elementary grades. Unlike the other schools, however, Stevenson's interventions were not externally developed. They served as an internal safety net, providing both more time and smaller groups to struggling readers.

Kindergarten intervention occurred both inside and outside the classroom. Because full-time instructional assistants supported kindergarten teachers, the teachers could work one on one with struggling children first thing in the morning and during nap time. Struggling kindergarteners also received small-group phonemic awareness training outside the classroom with an instructional assistant.

First and second graders received small group Title 1 services in addition to their regular reading instruction. This instruction occurred in the afternoons. Title 1 teachers pulled children out of content instruction to provide additional small-group reading instruction. They used both basals and tradebooks for this additional work.

Third graders who were struggling participated in a volunteer tutorial program twice each week. Adapting the Book Buddies model (Invernizzi, Juel, &

Rosemary, 1997) to the needs of older struggling readers, the building reading specialist prepared lesson plans for tutors. These lesson plans ensured that third graders got additional work with word study and with text at their instructional level.

ONGOING PROFESSIONAL DEVELOPMENT

Both instructional leadership and school change at Stevenson hinged on integrated and ongoing professional development. The principal believed that the biggest issue in improving reading programs was training for the staff. She knew she could not provide that herself. She thought that large schools needed to find ways to provide intensive and consistent staff development in the area of language arts so that the staff would be instructionally strong and speaking a common language. Because of the size of the staff, that professional development could not be provided in-house. In the building, however, the professional development could be augmented through coordination of the school's program with the philosophy of the professional development and by consistent monitoring of the progress of individual students and groups of students. At Stevenson the reading specialist coordinated the language arts program, monitored student progress, and acted as a resource to the teachers.

Teachers at Stevenson took advantage of professional development opportunities. The school was within commuting distance of a large university, and the county had ongoing contracts for Master's courses in Reading Education to be taught on site. Core courses in the Master's curriculum were taught for credit at county schools. Teachers paid only for textbooks. Teachers who had taken all of those courses could then commute to the university to finish their Master's.

The Stevenson principal collected data on professional development, and 92% of her teachers had taken at least one of these graduate classes. She said "the teachers in this county have been heavily, heavily, heavily trained" in the methods of reading development through this coursework. The philosophy of literacy development in that coursework was fairly simple: phonological awareness training in a game-like atmosphere, spelling and decoding instruction based on comparing and contrasting word patterns, assessment of instructional levels with informal reading inventories, individual and small-group instruction at instructional reading level, and attention to reading fluency. When new teachers came into the district, she said they were "outsiders" (unable to speak the common language of literacy instruction) until they got involved with the professional development program.

All professional development at Stevenson was coordinated. The principal told us that she started each new school year the same way. She addressed her faculty, new and old, and told them "how we teach reading here." Although the message might change only slightly from year to year, all heard it at the same time. This helped new teachers integrate into the instructional community and it reminded returning teachers to honor the core of Stevenson's program.

BUILDING COLLABORATION

We found systematic collaboration among the staff members at Stevenson. Like in the other effective schools and for the accomplished teachers at all schools, small-group instruction at instructional level was the hallmark of the Stevenson reading program. In order to provide that type of instruction to heterogeneous classroom groups, teachers worked together in planful ways.

When we asked teachers in the study to keep track of their time and activities during two different weeks in the study, they provided data on the size of the instructional groups they were working with. Table 8.4 shows that teacher report data, simply summed across the two teachers at each grade level and converted to percentages of total time reported.

Teachers at Stevenson had both freedom and responsibility in setting up small-group time. First, they had to reserve 2 hours in the morning and 40 minutes in the afternoon for language arts instruction. Table 8.5 gives an outline of the creative use of staffing that allowed for effective small groups during that time.

For first and second grade, classroom groupings were slightly manipulated to direct resources. Each grade level had six sections. Four of those sections included struggling readers and two did not. Two Title 1 reading teachers were assigned to each grade level, pushing in to one classroom for 1 hour and to another classroom for another hour. During that hour, then, two reading groups could be run simultaneously. For some classrooms, only two groups were needed. For

TABLE 8.4

Teacher reported percentages of time spent in whole class, small group, and one on one instruction.

Grouping	Kindergarten	First Grade	Second Grade	Third Grade
Whole Class	50%	15%	52%	59%
Small Group	20%	62%	28%	41%
Individual	30%	23%	20%	0

others, more were needed and children spent part of the small group hour reading silently in independent-level texts.

For the first- and second-grade classrooms without struggling readers, an instructional assistant pushed in for one hour, helping the children to work effectively and protecting the classroom teacher to work with small groups. Because the groupings were within the classroom, children could easily switch groups as their achievement warranted and classroom teachers and reading teachers knew what texts and methods were being used with all children.

For the third grade, children were regrouped within the grade level into homogeneous achievement-based groups for the 2 morning hours. The lowest achieving children got their reading instruction from a reading specialist. Other children worked with classroom teachers, usually in two smaller groups.

Along with these grade-specific models for collaboration, there was building-level collaboration to encourage independent, silent reading. Across the grade levels, Stevenson used incentive programs to increase motivation to read and to keep track of student self-selected reading. Book It (supported by Pizza Hut) rewarded children who read widely with free pizzas each month, and hallways were decorated with reading goals for each classroom. The library also used the Accelerated Reader program to track reading in the school library, a practice that the principal believed motivated children to simply read more. These incentive programs were monitored by the building reading specialist.

TABLE 8.5

The Structure of Classroom Instruction and Intervention At Each Grade Level

Kindergarten	First and Second Grade	Third Grade
	Whole class time Teacher	Whole Class Time Teacher
Small Group Time	Small Group Time	Small Group Time
Classroom Teacher And Paraprofessional	Classroom Teacher And Reading Specialist Or Classroom Teacher and Paraprofessional	Classroom Teacher and Reading Specialist Or Classroom Teacher and Paraprofessional
Intervention	Intervention	Intervention
Classroom Teacher And Paraprofessional	Reading Specialist Or Paraprofessional	Community Volunteer

Substantive collaboration occurred at two levels. It began in the administration, as schedules were designed to link classroom teachers, reading specialists, and instructional assistants to children in an equitable way. It continued in the classrooms, as teachers and their partners taught different groups of children in the same room, creating an environment where reading instruction was organized, extended, and efficient. That collaboration allowed children access to small-group instruction at their instructional levels. It extended into the hallways, as incentive programs linked all children at the school in the goal of reading widely.

AND A CRACKERJACK KINDERGARTEN

Stevenson's story cannot be told honestly without a caveat about the kindergartens. They were truly impressive. They are part of the school-level story of Stevenson Elementary because they provided the firm foundation that would make every child a reader. Here's how the two morning hours of language arts were used in Stevenson's kindergartens.

At 9:00, children were called to circle time. During that time, which normally lasted about 30 minutes, teachers managed review and introduction of a host of information about words and their parts. Some of the work was drill and repetition, some was assessment, some was response and connection. Calendar and morning message were opportunities to develop phonemic awareness. Every child in the kindergarten classes was expected to learn letter names, letter sounds, and segmenting skills, and these things were practiced daily.

The second 30 minutes of language arts was small group time. Each day, one group worked individually, choosing among activities at a listening center, simple letter-sound activities, or phonemic awareness activities on the classroom computer. Another group worked with the instructional assistant, reviewing and applying their current word study work either with games or in a workbook. The third group met with the teacher, reading either predictable or phonics controlled books and learning to write new letter sounds and patterns.

Teachers emphasized direct instruction with children beginning in these kindergarten groups. They started with clear directions such as, "When you see a letter, you say a sound," and, "When you start reading, always go to the top of the page." During choral reading of a familiar text one day, a teacher asked the children what helped them to read, and they reported that looking at the picture could help. When they were tracking print in text-only versions of simple stories, their teacher reminded them that they could "use [their] eyes and find the holes" that mark word boundaries. Kindergarten teachers continually

stretched words for children who were reading or spelling, using a synthetic approach with phonetically regular words. By the second half of the kindergarten
year, we noticed that children were reading and representing both consonants
and short vowels in words with a high level of accuracy.

After this small-group time was finished, children gathered for a read-aloud.
Usually the teacher read an information book connected to the science or social
studies curriculum. Sometimes she read both an information book and a narrative. The read-aloud was interactive, including vocabulary and concept development and many connections to the children's lives. When the read aloud was
finished, the teacher modeled some type of simple written response to the text.
Some days, it was just a sentence or two. For example, after sharing a book about
the weather, the teacher might write, "Today it is very sunny. It is spring time.
We can go outside and play. Tomorrow it may rain." While she wrote, she
stretched sounds, and she referred to areas in the classroom where she could
find the spellings of high frequency words. When she finished, the children read
with her, fingerpointing. Then children went back to their tables to write their
own responses. When they wrote, they were responsible for correctly representing the sounds and patterns that they had learned and for using invented spellings for other sounds and patterns. The teacher and the assistant checked their
work when they were done, holding each child accountable for his or her own
letter-sound instruction, and then children illustrated their messages.

This simple schedule of whole class letter–sound work, small group instruction in text, and individual application in writing for sounds, allowed for efficient use of literacy time in these two kindergarten classrooms. This efficient
use of instructional time led to wonderful literacy achievement. All children in
these two classrooms were confident in independently writing to express themselves, all the while applying and firming their letter–sound knowledge.

CHALLENGES REMAINING

The instructional team at Stevenson was still working on many things, but that
is the nature of a school committed to student achievement. Stevenson Elementary School was a work in progress. We asked the Stevenson team about
their weaknesses and their concerns, and they were quick to identify them. As I
look back on that exercise, I see it as a sign of institutional strength. This group
of teachers could publicly acknowledge problems because it had successfully
solved problems.

The team reported concerns in meeting individual needs. Stevenson teachers were frustrated sometimes because they knew so much about how to teach

individual children and they knew that they were not always doing the right thing for each child when they were teaching groups, even groups based on achievement.

Articulation among the many, many programs that operated at the same time at Stevenson was also a continuing challenge. As the Title 1 teachers and reading specialist were working in so many different ways across grade levels, they needed to work harder to craft coordinated instructional programs for individual children and to communicate among themselves and with the classroom teachers.

Throwing out the restrictive mind-set of the old Title 1 rules and procedures was an unexpected challenge. With the new schoolwide Title 1 status and the freedom to allocate time and teachers more flexibly, teachers needed to be reminded that they could make more decisions more quickly, with less paperwork, and that they could respond flexibly to students' needs and progress. This "mental change" caused a lot more teacher talk about children during the course of the year. It allowed movement, so that a reading group was no longer a year-long placement for a child, particularly for the lowest children.

As far as the curriculum was concerned, Dickerson wanted to work harder on the writing program. She felt that it was sagging a bit, and she took some personal responsibility for that. "You get it all pumped up and in place and as an administrator you make a mistake of assuming that it continues at the same level that it did when you pumped it up." She planned to emphasize writing the following year during faculty meetings and professional development sessions.

LESSONS LEARNED

We asked Dickerson and the teachers to share advice that they had for other schools starting a journey toward more effective literacy achievement. They said that it starts with the involvement and support of all of the regular classroom teachers. Even in a large school, the program has to be integrated and consistent. Teachers have to work hard within and between grade levels to maintain balance and consistency throughout the elementary years.

Stevenson's teachers had very specific visions for their classrooms. Kindergarten teachers expected children to be prepared for first grade knowing all of their letters and sounds, forming letters correctly, spelling simple words, and recognizing sight words. They wanted students to understand the alphabetic principle and to be able to apply it in both reading and writing, with a highly automatic knowledge of letter names and sounds.

First-grade teachers wanted all of their children to be on grade level or above in terms of accuracy of oral reading. They wanted them to be independent and strategic decoders.

Second-grade teachers wanted children to be able to use decoding skills as a tool to access meaning in both fiction and nonfiction; they also wanted students to use spelling and composing as tools to express their voice. They wanted them to be self-motivated.

In the third grade, teachers wanted children to be asking questions that could drive instruction, to choose their own texts and read them successfully, to be able to incorporate skills and strategies as tools for academic achievement, and to operate independently in a variety of genres. In short, they wanted them to be readers and writers.

POST SCRIPT

Stevenson Elementary was a place where children who might fail to learn to read well did not fail. It did not have an externally designed reading program or the support of researchers. What Stevenson did have was a staff working together. They were working together to examine their options. They were working together to craft a curriculum that made sense over time. They were working together to respond sensibly to state mandates. They were working together to explore options for instruction and intervention that worked for particular children and groups of children at particular grades, because, as one teacher told us, "Children are children, whether they're mine or someone else's."

After the Beat the Odds study, I spent an additional year at Stevenson. My question that year was about comprehension instruction in this effective environment. Although we had not observed much comprehension instruction during reading instruction in this or any of our most effective schools, I wondered whether it might be integrated into other areas of the academic day besides reading instruction (Walpole, 2000). In fact, it was. Stevenson's teachers and principal taught me many additional lessons that year, and for that I am very grateful.

REFERENCES

Davis, G. A., & Thomas, M. A. (1989). *Effective Schools and Effective Teachers*. Boston: Allyn and Bacon.
Invernizzi, M., Juel, C., & Rosemary, C. A. (1997). Book Buddies: A community volunteer tutorial that works. *The Reading Teacher, 50,* 304–311.
Leslie, L., & Caldwell, J. (1995). *Qualitative Reading Inventory - II.* New York: Harper Collins.
Levine, D. U. (1991). Creating effective schools: Findings and implications. *Phi Delta Kappan, 72,* 389–93.
Madden, M., & Hillman, J. (1996). Lessons in success. In National Commission on Education, *Success against the odds: Effective schools in disadvantaged areas.* London: Routledge.

Moats, L. (1999). *Teaching reading IS rocket science: What expert teachers of reading should know and be able to do.* American Federation of Teachers.

Reynolds, D. (1998). School for literacy: A review of research on teacher effectiveness and school effectiveness and its implications for contemporary educational policies. *Educational Review, 50,* 147–162.

Taylor, B. M., Pearson, P. D., Clark, K. F., & Walpole, S. (2000). Effective schools and accomplished teachers: Lessons about primary-grade reading instruction in low-income schools. *Elementary School Journal, 101,* 121–165.

Teddlie, C., Kirby, P. C., & Stringfield, S. (1989, May). Effective versus ineffective schools: Observable differences in the classroom. *American Journal of Education,* 221–236.

Walpole, S. (2000) Instructional moves to support skilled reading. Unpublished doctoral dissertation, University of Virginia, Charlottesville.

Use for:
- *Culturally relevant materials*
- *Cooperative learning*
- *Staff development*
- *Staff Cohesion*

9 Leadership = All of same page driven by same goal

Scott Elementary School: Home Grown School Improvement in the Flesh

Glenda Breaux
Jennifer Danridge
P. David Pearson
Michigan State University

INTRODUCTION

Most research on effective urban schools approaches the issue by documenting the characteristics that seem to distinguish them from their low-achieving counterparts. Many of these studies note that the special challenges of urban schools are student poverty, hunger, health problems, large enrollment, limited resources, inadequate equipment and facilities, high faculty turnover, low teacher expectations, low morale, less experienced teachers than in suburban schools, and low parent involvement (Anyon, 1997; Barth, 1990; Kozol, 1991; Lareau, 1989; Levine & Lezotte, 1990; Stevenson & Stigler, 1992). Within urban schools literature we also find characterizations of teaching that are believed to contribute to poor student learning and low achievement. Listed among characteristics of this "pedagogy of poverty" are frequent interruptions, giving information (rather then engaging students in acquiring it), reviewing assignments and tests in class (rather than focusing on new material to be learned), and settling disputes and punishing noncompliance during instruc-

217

tional time (Haberman, 1991). According to Haberman, these teaching acts constitute the core functions of urban teaching and contribute greatly to the low student achievement demonstrated in these schools.

Most studies of effective schools look closely at schools that have already demonstrated themselves as successful, and suggest that following the same practices will increase the effectiveness of struggling schools. Many reports offer generalized advice on how to institute effective practices. Included in this advice to teachers and administrators (DuFour, 1997; Griswold, Cotton, & Hansen, 1986; Gursky, 1990; Knapp & Shields, 1990; Knapp, Turnbull, & Shields, 1990; Levine & Lezotte 1990; McPartland & Slavin, 1990; School Improvement Program, 1990; Taylor, Pearson, & Clark, 2000; also chap. 1, this volume; Waxman & Huang, 1997) are suggestions that they:

- develop strong administrative leadership;
- increase planning;
- develop safe, orderly and well-disciplined environments;
- develop effective teacher development programs;
- increase teacher self-efficacy and responsibility;
- develop adaptive teaching skills;
- increase parent involvement;
- develop high expectations; and
- develop students' test taking skills/reduce test taking anxiety.

Studies on effective urban schools provide an abundance of information on what is being done and what researchers think should be done. What they do not provide in great quantity are specific suggestions on how schools might overcome obstacles to instituting effective practices. The purpose of our chapter is to describe the school improvement process at one urban school with great specificity and in detail. To that end, we have conducted a case study of a single elementary school that has made substantial progress on external indicators of student progress to determine the programmatic and instructional processes that lie behind that increase. Over the course of 4 years (1994–1998), the fourth-grade students at Scott Community School have demonstrated remarkable achievement gains (over 60% increase in the number of students achieving satisfactory scores) as measured by the literacy section of the Michigan MEAP assessment (with similar progress in mathematics, by the way). Since that time, they have maintained those gains. Results such as these, which are derived entirely from homegrown reform efforts, highlight the importance of examining the success of such schools with greater attention to the intricacies of the reform process, both schoolwide and inside the classrooms.

METHOD

The Context

Site Description.   Scott Community School is located Flint, Michigan. It was chosen for inclusion in our research at CIERA because it has that all too rare combination of a high-poverty population of students and a tradition of high performance on external indicators of school achievement. In Michigan, this means doing well on the dreaded MEAP (Michigan Educational Assessment Program) test in reading.

Flint was once a prosperous city built to provide residence for the many workers in its factories (mostly automobile and mostly GM), but it faced the fate of many American urban centers. Industrial downsizing and relocation combined with middle-class flight to the suburbs to produce a city in decline. When the factories left the city, unemployment rates soared and economic devastation took hold. The city, while on the rebound in the economic recovery of the 1990s, is still suffering the negative effects of losing a large portion of its industrial base.

In Table 9.1 we can see that Scott has a high rate of student poverty as measured by the percentage of students eligible for free or reduced lunch. According to the principal, the student to teacher ratio has recently declined in response to the district's maximum allowance of 17:1, but the number of students has been increasing ever since the school became a school of choice.[1]

TABLE 9.1

Demographic Information about Scott School

Year	Free and Reduced Lunch (%)	Enrollment	Pupils/ Teacher	Per Pupil Expense	Average Teacher Salary	District F and R Lunch (%)
1996–1997	55	438	31.3			63
1995–1996	61.3	433	31.6	4,375	38,308	63
1994–1995	60.2				49,324	65

Note.   Source: Michigan Department of Education, www.state.mi.us/mde/cfdata/msr99/ msr_bldg.cfm, 1999 Michigan School Report

---

[1]The school of choice status means that students from other schools in Flint (and technically other communities) can choose to send their children to Scott if there are spaces. According to the principal, Sally Creech, Scott has developed a reputation as a school that serves the needs of students who do not fare well in other schools. (Principal Interview, 2/3/98)

As is common in situations such as this, where the declining tax-base leads to an eroding urban infrastructure, the school began to struggle, and student achievement on the state standardized assessment (i.e., the MEAP) plummeted between 1989 and 1994 (Ray, 1997). Our team became interested in the changes being made at the school because we noticed a large increase in the number of fourth-grade students receiving passing scores on the MEAP reading section between 1994 and 1998 (see Table 9.2).

An interview with the principal early in the Spring of 1997 revealed that this school had recently undergone some administrative changes, and a reform effort had begun. Because the reform was largely motivated by pressure from the district to improve MEAP scores, we expected that the reform effort would be geared toward the MEAP. For this reason, we decided not to focus on the increase in the scores per se, but instead to investigate the process of coming to consensus about the content of the reform document (i.e., the School Improvement Plan [SIP]) as well as the instructional philosophy and tools at the center of the reform effort.

Even so, the profile of MEAP scores over the past several years are informative because they underscore the commitment of the school to improving the performance of the students who attend Scott, and because they are taken so seriously by the staff and community of Scott School. It is noteworthy that the good results obtained in reading were not, until recently, paralleled in mathematics.[2]

Each year Scott Community School serves approximately 430 students from preschool to Grade 6. Each grade level has at least two classrooms, with some grades having three classrooms. The school has a predominately African American population (70.3%) with the remaining students being of European American (22.9%) and Asian American (4.7%) descent. Native Americans and Hispanic Americans comprise less than 3% of the student population. Thus, Scott's ESL population or those with Limited English Proficiency is almost nonexistent, with less than 1% qualifying for ESL services. Title I services are available at Scott, with over half of the students (62.29%) qualifying for these services. There are 29 licensed staff at Scott, including a school social worker, a speech therapist, and the administrative personnel (principal and assistant principal).

METHODS OF DATA COLLECTION

As suggested earlier, we began our involvement at Scott School with observations and interviews in the Spring of 1997. In the 1997–1998 school year we fol-

[2]Eighty eight and a half percent of students scored at the satisfactory level on the most recent (2000) fourth grade MEAP mathematics assessment, and 11.5% if students scored at the moderate level. No students scored at the low level.

TABLE 9.2

Trends in MEAP Scores at Scott School

Year	% Satisfactory	% Moderate	% Low	Number of Students in Grade 4
2000	88.5	11.5	0	
1999	64.5	18.6	16.9	59
1998	61.9	19.0	19	42
1997	74.5	4.3	21.3	47
1996	42.5	20.0	37.5	40
1995	43.9	29.8	26.3	57
1994	11.3	41.9	46.8	43
1989	22.2	40.0	37.8	45

Note. Source: Michigan School Report (February, 2000). www.state.mi.us/mde

lowed the methodology, for observations and interviews, used by CIERA researchers for the national study of effective schools and accomplished teachers (Taylor, Pearson, Clark, & Walpole, 2000; see also chap. 1, this volume).

PARTICIPANTS

We selected two teachers at each grade, Kindergarten through third grade, for participation in the study. At most grade levels, Scott School had only two classrooms. In Grade 1, only two of the three teachers were chosen for participation.[3] In Grades 2 and 3, one of the two classrooms at each grade level was a shared classroom consisting of two teachers with 34 students.

Classroom Observations

Between December 1997 and May 1998, each teacher was observed a minimum of five times for at least 1 hour during the reading/language arts instructional period. Our actual number of observations exceeded five in many classrooms. Because of variations in scheduling, we also managed to observe other subjects, such as math, science, and social studies. We imposed a standardized inquiry structure on the observational data collected in Scott. The structure consisted of a com-

---

[3]These two were selected because they were employed at Scott during the reform process. The remaining teacher was new to the school and to teaching. She had been working there for less than two months when the study began.

mon set of questions that each of us answered after each observation as a way of providing a common set of "summarizing" lenses for the data. These were the same as used in the larger study (Taylor et al., 2000; chap. 1, this volume).

Interviews

Each of the focus teachers was interviewed by a member of our research team for approximately 30 to 60 minutes. The interview protocol included questions about the overall school improvement process, the leadership in the school, staff development, and classroom programs, materials, and practices. The principal was interviewed on two occasions, as were support personnel.

Surveys

Teachers participated in two surveys. As a part of our CIERA work, the survey used in the larger study was completed by the teachers in the eight classrooms in which observations were conducted. Additionally, we administered a second written survey to the entire teaching staff during the early Spring of 1998. The data from this survey were collected in order to corroborate our emerging hypotheses about the nature of the school improvement process that had been derived from our analyses up to that point in time. Another purpose of this survey was to test the representativeness of the focus teacher's perceptions against the larger body of teachers. This survey served to triangulate the findings emerging from the analysis of the interviews and observations.

Data Analysis Techniques

Data were analyzed using the usual set of ethnographic tools for characterizing qualitative data. This set of tools included the development of emergent categories using a constant comparative analysis plan, the iterative refinement of questions, categories, and explanations, and triangulation across data sources (observations, interviews, and surveys). Additionally, simple descriptive statistics were used for many of the survey items.

RESULTS

Several factors account for the dramatic increase in the reading achievement of Scott students. As a group, these factors reflect the tremendous amount of energy and hard work that the administration, staff, students, and parents have committed to academic success. The School Improvement Plan is one cornerstone in the reform effort, complemented by a rich approach to promoting class-room instruction, a strong professional development program, and exemplary school leadership. We shall unpack each of these four factors in some detail.

The School Improvement Plan

We have chosen to report first on the school improvement process at Scott School because of the central role that it played in the Scott story. Although the initiation of the process was imposed from the outside by the state and the district, it is clear that the professional staff at the school decided to use the school improvement plan as a lever to propel them toward increased concern for and awareness of student achievement. According to the principal, Sally Creech, "The School Improvement Plan is a document required by the state that outlines the short and long term goals of the school. Every school in the state has to have one. It is supposed to be like an operating manual or focusing device for instruction," (Principal Interview, 2/3/98). The state and district require a new plan each year. Between 1992 (her first year at the school) and 1995, Creech created this document with the advice of a small group of teachers. In 1995 she turned the task over to the teachers, who still control the process.

The Process

The regular education teachers were required to join one of five curriculum-focused committees. The committees available were Reading, Writing, Technology, Math, and Science. The special education teachers had the option of joining a sixth committee—the Inclusion committee. Teachers signed up for the committees on a first-come-first-served basis. The committee members then decided among themselves upon a committee chair. These committees met, decided on goals, and presented their suggestions to the rest of the staff. The suggestions were then discussed and revised until consensus was achieved. The selected goals and strategies were included in the School Improvement Plan. This document was submitted to the district by September 1st of the school year to which it applied.

Sources of Information Used to Generate the School Improvement Plan

The details of Scott's School Improvement Plan are tightly linked to several other important documents that drive curriculum and teaching within the district. The four school improvement goals and strategies adopted by Scott School the for the 1997–1998 school year were:

- All students will demonstrate the ability to communicate in written form.
- All students will demonstrate the ability to construct and reflect using increased scientific knowledge.
- All students will demonstrate a basic understanding of how to accurately select and apply appropriate math skills to solve problems.
- All students will be able to distinguish structures of expository text and apply various reading strategies to construct meaning for effective reading.

These school improvement goals were adapted from and connected to the District Mission, the Board of Education Goals, and the District Literacy Model. The relationship between the SIP goals and these documents is depicted in Table 9.3.

The SIP goals and strategies are also linked to the goals in the Goals 2000 document, and the District Student Exit Outcomes for adults educated in the district. Because the Board of Education's goals emphasize curriculum and instructional alignment with assessment (that currently consists of the MEAP and the MAT), it is not surprising that the outcome goals listed in the SIP relate to performance on these tests.

An absolutely essential school-wide goal, but ironically one that did not appear in the SIP, was to achieve summary accreditation by the state of Michigan. To achieve this rating, over 66% of the students must receive satisfactory (vs. moderate or low) scores in both areas (narrative and expository text) of the MEAP reading test. Declines in performance on the state assessment can result in loss of accreditation and takeover by the state. As of 1997–1998, eight schools in the state had been taken over. According to the principal, this threat caused the teachers an enormous amount of stress, but she believed that the pressure increased their motivation to set unified goals and attain them. When we began the study, Scott had achieved interim accreditation, which means that it was close to the 66% mark. It achieved summary accreditation during the course of our inquiry, in February of 1998, and has maintained that status until the time this paper was put to press.

After the improvement goals were adopted, the committees further defined them in terms of objectives and specific strategies. These objectives are more closely linked to specific concerns within the school. For example, the objectives for the Goal #4 are:

TABLE 9.3

Influences on the Scott School Improvement Plan

School Improvement Plan Goal Statement	District Mission/Literary Model	Board of Education Goals
All students will demonstrate the ability to communicate in written form.	Develop a community of learners who, through written communication are prepared to live, work, and contribute in a changing society.	Demonstrate improvement in written communication as a result of strategies provided by the teachers.
All students will demonstrate the ability to construct and reflect using increased scientific knowledge.	Develop a community of learners who are prepared to live, work, and contribute in an ever changing society.	Demonstrate improvement in their knowledge, understanding, and applications of mathematical and scientific processes through delivery of improved teaching methods.
All students will demonstrate a basic understanding of how to accurately select and apply appropriate math skills to solve problems.	Develop a community of learners who are prepared to live, work, and contribute in an ever changing society.	Demonstrate improvement in the application of thinking (process) strategies in all areas as a result of designing and aligning the core academic curriculum, instruction, and assessment.
All students will be able to distinguish structures of expository text and apply various reading strategies to construct meaning for effective reading.	The ability to read will prepare and equip learners with the necessary tools to live and work as a productive contributor in an ever changing society.	Demonstrate improvement in communication skills as a result of effective reading and language arts strategies used by classroom teachers.

Objective 1.   All students will read from expository text in various
                  student interest areas.
Objective 2.   All students will have the opportunity to work with vol-
                  unteers on expository reading.
Objective 3.   Students will be exposed to and have a better under-
                  standing of expository reading.

The school has adopted five strategies for achieving these goals and objectives.
The five strategies, which are applied across the four goals, include:

1. *Academic Strategy*: All students will use graphic organizers (story
   maps, concept maps, etc.) when working with expository reading.
2. *Gender Equity Strategy*: Staff awareness of the significant differences in
   scores and selection of expository readings that reflect a more generic
   interest.
3. *Technology Strategy*: All students will have access to software on the
   computer that will allow them to read from various types of expository
   texts.
4. *Community Resources Strategy*: All students will attend programs that
   focus on various careers and the importance of reading expository
   texts in their particular field.

The staff also selected strategies for evaluating whether the goals had been met.
In the 1997–1998 plan, the evaluation strategies included (a) formative assessment, (b) student interest surveys to select readings, (c) teacher feedback in
staff meetings to inform the planning of thematic units, and (d) collection of
mini session surveys.

The SIP also contained sections specifying who is responsible for helping the
school reach the goals, the resources needed to reach them, the timeline for ac-
complishing them, and the strategy for documenting improvements efforts and
the level of success. Similar documentation was developed for each goal and
subject addressed by the committees.

From the generality of the goals outlined by the district and the board, it is
not difficult to see that the interpretation of appropriate courses of action could
vary widely across schools as well as within. Arriving at school-wide agreement
on specific courses of action can be a harrowing experience for educators and often, in urban schools, is not accomplished with a great degree of success. We believe we have found an explanation as to how the educators in this building
reached agreement and built a program that they could deliver to their students. In a sense, the rest of this paper documents that process. To understand
that process, we must begin at the beginning, however, which is inside the classrooms in Scott School.

Effective Instructional Practices: A Closer Look Inside Classrooms

Overall, we concluded that there was no one particular "effective" pedagogical or instructional strategy that teachers at Scott used to teach beginning readers. On the contrary, the kindergarten through third-grade teachers employed a wide variety of materials, activities, and instructional methods, with instructional variances occurring within as well as between grade levels. However, several broad characteristics, which spanned across classrooms and teachers, seemed to contribute to success of Scott School and its students. These include:

- A common set of instructional tools
- Flexible teaching approach within and across classrooms and grades
- A tight link between instruction and assessment
- Generous use of school resources to promote instruction
- Culturally relevant pedagogy

A Common Set of Instructional Tools

In the SIP, teachers generated a list of 20 instructional tools that would be used in all classrooms to promote comprehension, higher-order thinking, and metacognition. These strategies were derived from recent research that was shared during staff development meetings as well as from teachers' own experiences in the classroom. The instructional strategies to be emphasized during literacy instruction included the use of graphic organizers, whole-class reading activities, reading aloud, and higher-order questioning. The use of all of these tools was frequently observed in various settings and for multiple purposes. For example, sometimes students used Venn Diagrams to compare and contrast the presentation of a story in novel and film forms, whereas at other times they used the same visual display tool to compare and contrast various versions of a fictional story such as Cinderella. To promote comprehension and critical reasoning skills, students were often encouraged to write personal responses to factual and fictional accounts of a topic.

Teachers also reported using this common set of tools to achieve a balanced approach to literacy instruction. Although they used basals in compliance with their district mandate, especially for phonics-intensive instruction and silent reading, teachers worked extremely hard to emphasize reading–writing connections and to develop students' responses to literature via storybook reading and literature discussions. Although some teachers emphasized spelling and grammar, whereas others emphasized meaning and relating to the text, all teachers participated in activities designed to improve students' proficiency on both the mechanical and meaningful sides of reading and writing. Both mechanical and meaning-based activities were especially pronounced in the third grade where students were expected to complete longer and more so-phisticated (and more conventional) writing assignments of the sort that would lead eventually to good scores on the MEAP fifth-grade writing test.

Flexible Teaching Approaches Within and Across Classrooms and Grades

The teachers at Scott recognized the importance of instilling in their students an understanding of the social purposes and usages of literacy. They emphasized the roles that reading and writing play in the communication process, and guided students in thinking about issues of audience. In an attempt to help stu-dents understand the value of literacy for expressing themselves and under-standing others, teachers used flexible approaches for teaching reading and writing. This flexibility was observed within classrooms as well as across class-rooms, and examples of instructional approaches included:

- Using a variety of materials, including basals, trade books, novels, and films to represent a variety of topics, and a variety of modes of presen-tation.
- Embedding literacy instruction in social studies and science lessons in order to help students grasp the differences between fictional and fac-tual texts.
- Writing assignments that varied from summarizing factual informa-tion from texts, to comparing texts across media, to linking texts to personal experiences.

Wide Array of Instructional Resources

The flexibility in teaching approaches seen at Scott school was directly related to the availability of resources to support diversity in students' literacy experi-ences. Many of the teachers commented on how willing and effective the prin-cipal was in securing resources to support their efforts to enrich instruction. Teachers regularly commented on the ease of acquiring new and varied texts for their students. One teacher in a third-grade classroom was especially excited about how the allocation of resources allowed her to provide her students with integrated (across subjects) lessons. She felt that the traditional fragmentation in subject area instruction contributed to students' reading and comprehension difficulties in literacy-dependent subjects such as social studies and science. For her, the materials that promoted skill development across subjects allowed her to supplement the short discussions of science topics available in the textbook with trade books that allowed students to further pursue their interest in particular topics. Teachers at Scott wanted to use these additional resources for their literacy instruction, and felt they were limited when they could not do so. For example, the second-grade teachers were particularly upset by a district mandate that they test a new basal. They felt that this negatively affected their ability to expose their students to the variety of materials that other teachers had available to them and relied on.

Tight Link Between Instruction and Assessment

Teachers at Scott School generally used whole-group and individualized assessment procedures that aligned with their instructional philosophies. In classes where teachers assessed students individually, students were expected to correct their work on the fly and to learn from their mistakes in the process of completing their work. During this individualized assessment process, teachers typically provided immediate feedback for students during student conferences about reading and writing. In classes where students were assessed within a whole-group setting, students who produced exemplary responses served as models for a range of cognitive behaviors, including high quality thinking and problem solving. During these whole-group experiences, teachers generally walked around the classroom to check students' work and monitor their progress, but peers were also welcomed to provide assistance and feedback to those around them.

Generally, teachers viewed assessment as integrally connected to learning, with writing playing a central role. For example, teachers often used writing activities as tools to assess comprehension directly after reading from trade books or basals. They also used what they considered to be authentic activities, such as letter writing, short story writing, and other personal writing tasks to assess spelling, grammar, and other conventional aspects of literacy. This suggests that assessment was used to provide teachers with information to guide further instruction, rather than primarily as a tool for generating comparisons between students or assigning grades.

Culturally Relevant Pedagogy

Although it was not an explicitly stated goal, teachers at Scott School used effective pedagogical approaches to educating culturally diverse students. Over 70% of Scott's students were from culturally diverse backgrounds, thus understanding diversity was central to their ability to "beat the odds." To effectively teach culturally diverse students, many teachers used instructional policies and practices, which are consistent with what Gloria Ladson-Billings (1994) called *culturally relevant pedagogy*. Culturally relevant pedagogy empowers students by respecting and affirming their cultural and linguistic knowledge, and by building on their diverse home and community experiences. Although Scott staff did not explicitly characterize their pedagogy using this term, three principles of culturally relevant pedagogy were evident in their approaches to literacy instruction. Of particular interest in understanding Scott Community School are these three:

- Schools and classrooms are inviting for culturally diverse students
- Teachers foster communities of learners within their classrooms
- Teachers draw on community "funds of knowledge"

Schools and classrooms are inviting for culturally-diverse students

The principal, Sally Creech, expressed this invitational spirit: "My vision for our students at Scott is that they are eager to learn, feel comfortable and safe at school, and they know that we care ... We want students to choose to come here because they know it's a place where they can learn and grow."

Purkey and Novak (1984) contended that schools must welcome students into school by making them feel as if they are contributing members. This sense of "invitation" is particularly important for culturally diverse students because they could potentially have isolating, alienating, and disaffirming experiences at school (Nieto, 1996; Shade, Kelly, & Oberg, 1997).

The administration and staff at Scott worked extremely hard to convey a warm "invitation" to their students. For example, every morning two students were invited to lead the entire school in the Pledge of Allegiance, to make student announcements, and to recite the school motto, "We're Here Because We Want to Be," over the public announcement system. This kind of involvement seemed to give students a sense of ownership and pride in their school and its activities. Furthermore, the physical environment itself was designed to invite students to actively participate in the learning process. Creative exhibits of students' artwork and academic papers were located in classrooms and in hallways as a way to openly display and affirm students' talents and hard work. Classroom environments were also well organized and attractive. By hanging colorful bulletin boards, arranging learning centers that promoted collaboration, and collecting interesting books for their classroom libraries, teachers "welcomed" students into classroom literacy environments that were engaging, nonthreatening, and supportive.

Teachers Foster Communities of Learners Within Their Classrooms

Ladson-Billings (1994) asserted that establishing and supporting communities of learners is an effective instructional practice for culturally diverse students. The concept of community is particularly important for students from diverse backgrounds because it invites them into the classroom, and it resonates strongly with their own cultural values of family-orientedness and group-centeredness (Nieto, 1996). Also, teachers who establish communities of learners in their classrooms typically understand that students have heterogeneous abilities, learning styles, and cognitive styles, and they use flexible and varied pedagogical approaches to accommodate these differences (Brophy, 1998; Shade, Kelly, & Oberg, 1997).

Scott teachers used several instructional strategies to promote learning communities within their classrooms. One of the most important was their emphasis on collaborative learning. Although teachers at all grade levels used some individual literacy instruction (i.e., individual reading or writing conferences), they highly valued collaborative work; both in small group and whole group settings. Survey results indicated that 75% of teachers used cooperative learning formats in their classrooms. During interviews, teachers commented that using a variety of collaborative instructional strategies kept students engaged and "on task," and actually reduced teacher-initiated classroom management because students felt more responsible for their own and their peers' learning and behavior.

Furthermore, the wide variety of instructional materials and approaches we found in the school helped to promote community by enabling teachers to meet the needs of all their students in a way that made them feel comfortable in the community. Seventy-five percent of teachers surveyed reported a belief that they could successfully teach all of their students. The vast majority of teachers reported that they felt personally responsible for students' learning. At Scott, these high rates of teacher self-efficacy were demonstrated by their expertise in using multiple types of instruction and materials to teach literacy, as documented in the earlier sections on instructional tools, flexible teaching strategies, and resource usage.

Administration and Teachers Draw on Community "Funds of Knowledge"

The administrative staff and faculty wanted to establish positive partnerships with the neighboring community. As a result, they used several strategies to reach out to the community including forming partnerships with local businesses, and attending the neighborhood church and inviting community members to become involved with the students and participate in school activities. By doing so, Scott School staff hoped to draw on the local "funds of knowledge" within the community (Moll, Amanti, Neff, & Gonzalez, 1992) in ways that could make their classroom instruction more culturally centered and sensitive.

The administration welcomed community volunteers into the school to help with daily activities, such as lunch and recess, and special events. One of the most faithful and loved community volunteers was Mrs. Carlisle, an older African American woman who was the grandmother of a Scott student. For several years, she volunteered her time helping to answer phones in the office, assisting teachers in classrooms, and chatting with students as they lined up for the bus at the end of the school day. Mrs. Creech and the other teachers seemed to greatly value Mrs. Carlisle and other community volunteers because they had good rapport with the children, and their presence supported the warm, caring atmosphere that was vital to the vision of Scott School. Indeed, survey data indicated the high value that staff placed on these community members. Seventy-three percent of teachers reported that community members were highly instrumental to their reform efforts.

The administration and teachers facilitated "real-world learning" via community-centered programs and local organizations that worked directly with classroom teachers and students. The overall goal for these community programs was twofold: (1) to provide students with the unique opportunity to develop workplace skills and life skills within real-world community contexts, and (2) to serve as a professional resource for teachers and as a community liaison between the school and local businesses. For example, the *Analyze and Apply* program used workplace-based exercises and activities to promote acquisition of problem solving, team building, and technological skills. Ms. Newman, the *Analyze and Apply* program coordinator, visited each classroom and taught these skills with the assistance of the classroom teacher. The *MicroSociety* program used a more "hands-on" approach to teaching basic career and life skills. One example that the Scott students were particularly engaged in was the banking unit. Local bankers visited the students to teach them basic banking skills, such as opening and closing an account, and students were encouraged to open their own "real" savings accounts at these banks. Later that year, Scott students actually organized and ran their own small bank.

Finally, some of the teachers and administrators became actively involved in the community. For example, several teachers attended the Baptist church located across the street from the school, and Mrs. Creech reported that this church became an invaluable source of community support because it gave the school a more "direct connection" with students, their families, and their neighborhoods. Also, teachers and administrators attended local community events as a way to establish and reinforce supportive ties between Scott School and the community. In addition, one first-grade teacher adopted a strategy of making a home visit to meet each and every parent in the first month of the school year.

Professional Development

The staff at Scott strongly valued professional development, particularly workshops and sessions that emphasized teacher-centered topics. Results from the CIERA survey indicated that 67% of the staff members rated teacher-selected topics as highly valuable. By contrast, 5 out of 9 staff members rated district-initiated topics on the lower end of the scale. The individual interviews also indicated deep commitment to professional development. During her interview, Ms. Smith, a third-grade teacher, said, "Staff development plays a part because it helps teachers address their own weaknesses, and give and get suggestions from other teachers. The teachers here are very supportive of each other." Mrs. Creech was proud of the fact that the majority of staff development activities at Scott were selected, planned, and delivered by Scott teachers. This notion of building local capacity is very consistent with the overall findings from the larger beat the odds study (Taylor et al., 2000).

Strong Administrative Leadership

The district gets some credit for the strong leadership of Scott School. Mrs. Creech was placed at Scott specifically because district officials believed her leadership style would benefit the school. The strong praise of the staff attests to the wisdom of the decision. At the time of the study Mrs. Creech had been at the school for 5 years. In that period, she had made believers out of her teachers. Mrs. Offrink, a third-grade teacher explained, "Mrs. Creech is a big part of [the consistent upward trajectory and stability in test scores]. Her management style is affirming. She is positive with students and parents. She draws parents in and sponsors classes for parents so that they can help their students. The school is happy. The whole atmosphere is positive."

Mrs. Creech concurred with this assessment in her own way, describing her role as that of a cheerleader: "I don't think of myself as a boss. We all have jobs. We just do different ones. My way of thinking about the role of any leader is a cheerleader. I look for what they're doing right and praise that. I don't just tell them what's wrong."

She attributed her popularity to the importance she placed on how people feel at work. She said, "They spend so much time at work, so we do a lot of things to *effect* the *affective*. We have fun together and get to know each other. I have tried to create a sense of family."

Based on interviews and survey results, the principal was commonly, if not universally, viewed as responsible for influencing several important features of the successful program at Scott School. Between 75% and 100% of the staff suggested that Mrs. Creech was responsible for promoting:

1. *Increased staff collegiality.* To achieve this, the principal arranged retreats and nonwork outings so that the teachers could interact with each other during leisurely activities for the purposes of stress-relief and bonding.

2. *Increased interaction with community members.* This was accomplished by the principal attending community events, visiting churches, and inviting community members and parents to join councils/groups where they could discuss their concerns/suggestions, and learn about opportunities for involvement.

3. *Increased teacher–student identification.* For starters, the principal arranged for all teachers to take the MEAP assessment for the grade they teach so that they could better understand what was being asked of students and remind them of the feelings associated with test-taking.

4. *Teacher participation in the reform effort.* This was achieved by turning the SIP creation effort over to teachers so that they could feel ownership over the goals and strategies selected, and devise goals and strategies that they could reasonably be expected to carry out under the constraints they face as classroom teachers.

5. *Flexibility.* One of the major factors that allowed teachers to reach consensus so quickly and easily was the realization that the SIP was not written in stone. The understanding that the SIP was a living document that would be rewritten each year, and revised to reflect strategies that worked well and those that did not, reduced or even eliminated heated quarrels about specific strategies for teaching (and evaluating) activities and students.

DISCUSSION AND CONCLUSIONS

In many ways, especially in the surface features of their program, Scott School is unexceptional. It has not adopted any of the highly recommended national models of literacy reform. It has no special supplementary safety net in place for students most at risk. The teachers have not undergone any special intensive professional development program. They use the tools of the profession, and they use them well. But they are the same tools that we might find in many schools, including schools that do not well serve the needs of poor children. How then are we to account for the tremendous upsurge and maintenance in state test scores, teacher esprit, community involvement, and school spirit? We think that the findings we have reported really do tell the story. The staff had a plan and a planning process, and although initiation of the process was forced on them from the outside, it was a process that they truly made their own. They focused their energies on classroom instruction by selecting their own set of preferred practices and applying them in culturally sensitive ways. They crafted and implemented their own professional development program, one that enabled them to implement the instructional tools they had selected. They developed assessment tools that supported their instructional goals and tools. And the whole process was guided by a firm, sensitive leader who knew as much about leading from the sidelines as she did about leading the parade.

Most important, Scott administrators and teachers enacted their motto "We're Here Because We Want to be." They were dedicated to helping students reach their academic potential, and they took responsibility for their role in that process. Scott's teachers were on a continual quest for self-improvement. Their efforts to be the best teachers they could be were reflected not only by their attempts to improve instruction, but also by their attempts to form connections between the school and the surrounding community. These aspects of the Scott story are encouraging because they suggest that good intentions, persistence, commitment to a plan and a set of tools, and—most of all—lots of professional and intellectual muscle can form the core of a reform movement.

Finally, we must not forget the human factor in their equation. By respecting students and their families, and by demonstrating a willingness to implement curriculum and instructional strategies that respected the cultural experiences and activities of their students, the administrative and teaching staff at Scott Community School created an environment where the students, along with the parents and the teachers, were truly there because they wanted to be.

REFERENCES

Anyon, J. (1997). *Ghetto schooling. A political economy of urban educational reform.* New York: Teachers College Press.

Barth, R. (1990). *Improving schools from within: Teachers, parents, and principals can make the difference.* San Francisco, CA: Jossey-Bass.

Brophy, J. (1998). *Motivating students to learn.* New York: McGraw Hill.

DuFour, R. (1997).The school as a learning organization: Recommendations for school improvement. *NASSP Bulletin, 81*(588), 81–87.

Griswold. P., Cotton, K., & Hansen, J. (1986). *Effective compensatory education sourcebook. Volume I: A Review of Effective Instructional Practices.* Washington, DC: US Department of Education.

Gursky, D. (1990). A plan that works. *Teacher, 1*(9), 46–54.

Haberman, M. (1991). The pedagogy of poverty versus good teaching. *Phi Delta Kappan, 73*(4), 290–294.

Knapp, M., & Shields, P. (1990). Reconceiving academic instruction for the children of poverty. *Phi Delta Kappan, 71*(10), 753–758.

Knapp, M., Turnbull, B., & Shields, P. (1990). New directions for educating the children of poverty. *Educational Leadership, 48*(1), 4–8.

Kozol, J. (1991). *Savage inequalities.* New York: Crown Publishers.

Ladson-Billings, G. (1994). *The dreamkeepers: Successful teachers of African American children.* San Francisco: Jossey-Bass.

Lareau, A. (1989). *Home advantage.* Philadelphia, PA: The Falmer Press.

Levine, D., & Lezotte, L. (1990). *Unusually effective schools: A review and analysis of research and practice.* Madison, WI: The National Center for Effective Schools Research and Development.

McPartland, J., & Slavin, R. (1990, July). Increasing achievement of at-risk students at each grade level. *Policy Prospective Series.* Washington, DC: US Department of Education.

Michigan Department of Education. www.state.mi.us/mde

Moll, L. C., Amanti, C., Neff, D., & Gonzalez, N. (1992). Funds of knowledge for teaching: Using a qualitative approach to connect homes and classrooms. *Theory into Practice, 31*(2), 132–141.

Nieto, S. (1996). *Affirming diversity: The sociopolitical context of multicultural education* (2nd ed.). New York: Longman.

Purkey, W. W., & Novak, J. M. (1984). *Inviting school success: A self-concept approach to teaching and learning.* Belmont, CA: Wadsworth Publishing Company.

Ray, J. (1997, April). *From The Year 2002.* Flint, MI: Flint District Vision Statement.

School Improvement Program. (1990). *Effective schooling practices A research synthesis.* Portland, OR: Northwest Regional Educational Laboratory.

Shade, B. J., Kelly, C., & Oberg, M. (1997). *Creating culturally responsive classrooms.* Washington, DC: American Psychological Association.

Stevenson, H., & Stigler, J. (1992). *The learning gap: Why our schools are failing and what we can learn from Japanese and Chinese education.* New York: Simon & Schuster.

Taylor, B. M., Pearson, P. D., Clark, K., & Walpole, S. (2000). Effective schools and accomplished teachers: Lessons about primary grade reading instruction in low-income schools. *The Elementary School Journal, 101,* 121–165.

Taylor, B. M., Pressley, M., & Pearson, P. D. (2001). Research-supported characteristics of teachers and schools that promote reading achievement. *NEA Reading Matters Research Report.* Washington, DC: National Education Association.

Waxman, H., & Huang, S. (1997). Classroom instruction and learning environment differences between effective and ineffective urban elementary schools for African American students. *Urban Education, 32*(1), 7–44.

10

Serna Elementary School[1]

Martha A. Adler
CIERA/University of Michigan

INTRODUCTION

Serna Elementary School is one of six case-study schools investigated during the 1998–1999 school year (Adler & Fisher, 2000; Fisher & Adler, 1999) as part of a resource allocation study of high performing, high poverty schools. Schools with a minimum of 3 years of consistent enrollments of 50% or more of their students eligible for free and reduced lunch and 50% or more satisfactory achievement on a standardized reading assessment were included in the study. This case study describes Serna Elementary School, which in 1999 was named as a "Recognized School"[2] by the Texas Education Agency.

[1]This research was supported under the Educational Research and Development Centers Program, PR/Award Number R305R70004, as administered by the Office of Educational Research and Improvement, U.S. Department of Education. However, the comments do not necessarily represent the positions or policies of the National Institute of Student Achievement, Curriculum, and Assessment or the National Institute on Early Childhood Development, or the U.S. Department of Education, and you should not assume endorsement by the Federal Government.

[2]Texas awards schools in the state with ratings of Exemplary, Recognized, or Acceptable dependent on at least 45.0% of all students and each student group passed each section of the TAAS, dropout rates of 6.0% or lower and attendance rates of at least 94.0%. In addition, schools must be ranked in the top 25% quartile of its unique comparison group in both reading and math.

SERNA ELEMENTARY SCHOOL: THE SETTING

Serna Elementary School opened in 1992 in response to the district's growing student population, adding to the other 33 elementary schools in San Antonio NEISD, Texas, (46,000 students, pre-kindergarten to Grade 12). The school fronts on a service road of a city expressway loop. Single family houses of post WWII vintage—now primarily rental property—stretch for several blocks beyond Serna on the other three sides. An extensive low-rent apartment complex where a substantial contingent of Serna's students lives lies several blocks behind the school. Transience in these apartments and other rental properties nearby contributes to the school's higher than average student mobility rate. During the 1998–1999 school year, Serna's mobility rate was 41.2% (typical of previous years) compared to 22.5% for its district, 22.0% for the state, and 26.2% for its comparative group.[3] In spite of its higher than average number of students eligible for free and reduced lunch (Table 10.1) and its higher than average mobility rate, Serna students have consistently outperformed or approximated their state, district, and group averages on the Texas Assessment of Academic Skills (TAAS) for third-grade reading (Table 10.2).

The Students.   Serna students are ethnically diverse. For the past 5 years, the African American and Hispanic population has been gradually increasing, as the number of White students goes down; there is also a continued small presence of Asian/Pacific Islander and Native American students. During the

TABLE 10.1

Poverty Rates* for SES Group, District, and State Comparisons

	1993–1994	1994–1995	1995–1996	1996–1997	1997–1998	1998–1999
State	45.1%	46.3%	46.9%	48.1%	48.5%	48.5%
District	29.6%	33.5%	33.4%	35.2%	36.4%	36.6%
Group	66.3%	67.1%	72.3%	70.8%	68.9%	70.3%
Serna	63.5%	65%	72.2%	70.9%	68.8%	70.1%

Note.   *Determined by number of students eligible for Free and Reduced Lunch

[3]The Texas Education Agency provides data on schools within comparison groups. These are schools that closely match the target school's demographic characteristics (i.e., percentage of students by race—African American, Hispanic, and White, economically disadvantaged, limited English proficient, and mobility.)

TABLE 10.2

Third Grade TAAS for SES, Group, District, and State Comparisons

	1993–1994	1994–1995	1995–1999	1996–1997	1997–1998	1998–1999
State	77.9%	79.5%	80.5%	81.5%	86.2%	88.0%
District	85.1%	84.8%	88.2%	87.4%	89.7%	93.7%
Group	73.6%	76.1%	71.1%	75.8%	83.6%	84.3%
Serna	87.1%	84.1%	88.4%	94.3%	91.9%	91.1%

1998–1999 school year, approximately 37% of the students were Hispanic, 27% African American, 31% White and approximately 5% Asian/Pacific Islander and Native American. The percentage of limited English proficient (LEP) students is relatively small at Serna, because K through fifth-grade LEP students in this district attend one elementary school designated specifically for LEP support. Serna has had a school-wide Title I program since 1994.

The Teachers. In a typical recent year, Serna reported a total staff of 58: 37 teachers (including 3.3 Title I teachers), six professional support staff, two administrators, and 13 educational aides.[4] Included in this count are teachers who handle weekly "specials"[5] (music, computers, and physical education) for the entire school as well as one and one half counselors and one school nurse. Serna teachers average 10 years of experience and are predominantly White (10 % are Hispanic). There is a core of Serna teachers who have been together since the school's opening and longer. These are the teachers who came with the principal from her previous assignment when the school was opened.

DESCRIPTION OF THE EARLY
READING PROGRAM (K–2)

Allocation of Students to Classes. The average class size in Grades K through 5 is about 20 students.[6] At Serna, students receive their primary literacy instruction within their self-contained classrooms.[7] At the time of the

---

[4]The aides work primarily in special education and in the pre-kindergarten programs but not in regular K through 5 classrooms.

[5]Typically each classroom has three periods each week, referred to as "specials" when students go to another part of the school for music, computer laboratory, or physical education. On these occasions, classroom teachers have time for planning and other responsibilities.

[6]State law limits class size in early elementary school to 22 students.

[7]A handful of students at each grade level receive additional instruction from special education staff and/or from a laboratory in the school that provides activities to improve visual coordination. Special education students have averaged 14 % of enrollment, slightly higher than the state average of 11%, but lower than the 16% district average.

study, there were four classrooms serving each of the primary grades (K through 2). Assignments to specific classrooms result from a class assignment process takes place in the spring. A team comprised of the grade-level teachers, the principal, assistant principal, and some "specials" teachers work with existing class lists to assign children to classrooms for the subsequent school year. The team considers data from a school readiness inventory for children entering kindergarten and data from the *Texas Primary Reading Inventory* for students entering Grades 1 and 2. The team considers measures of ability/achievement, along with gender and race/ethnicity to create roughly comparable heterogeneous groups for each classroom. This data-driven process represents a shift from previous practice when class assignments were primarily dependent on teacher judgements of academic progress and student behavior.

Children who transfer into Serna from other schools are distributed evenly across classes as they arrive. Because Serna has a yearly mobility rate of approximately 40%, this latter group is relatively large and has a substantial impact on the school.

Reading Instruction: Grouping, Materials and Programs. At Serna, reading instruction begins in the all-day Kindergarten classes. Teachers engage their students with a variety of activities and materials that focus on vocabulary development, alphabet knowledge, and phonemic awareness. Commercial workbooks and other materials are used in a mixture of structured whole group lessons and small group work. Because kindergarten is an all day program, teachers are able to integrate literacy activities throughout the day. Kindergarten children are introduced to pencil-and-paper tasks with their workbooks as well as with tasks from the *Guided Reading* (Fountas & Pinnell, 1996) and *Structure of the Intellect* (SOI) (Meeker, 1969) programs (both described later). At Serna, there is a shared expectation that children who enter first grade from a Serna kindergarten will be prepared to start off first grade ready to read.

Essentially, first- and second-grade teachers use an eclectic array of instructional materials and programs. Although the early reading program was in transition at the time of the study, the introduction of the new components did not appear to be a dramatic shift at a philosophical level. It was clear that the primary level teachers had been approaching reading instruction from a balanced perspective for some time, incorporating aspects of whole language and phonics approaches in both the outgoing and incoming programs.

Table 10.3[8] provides a general view of the types of activities teachers engage their students in through whole group, small group, and individual instruction. These two classrooms reflect the dynamic nature of Serna's early reading program. During the 1998–1999 school year, several changes were being implemented in early reading instruction at Serna. Until that year, teachers had used the district mandated basal series[9] supplemented with the *Slingerland* phonics[10] program as their primary curriculum materials for reading instruction. In the 1998–1999 school year, all of the primary teachers began implementing *Guided Reading* as the core of their program—a program that had been introduced at the district level a few years previously. However, this was Serna's first official year with the program, having participated in training sessions over the last two summers. At the same time Serna began implementation of *Guided Reading* (Fountas & Pinnell, 1996), they also introduced two other programs as supplementary to their early reading program: *Making Words* (Cunningham, Hall, & Sigmon, 1999) with a focus on phonics, spelling and sight word development; and, *Structure of Intellect* (SOI) (Meeker, 1969) with an emphasis on visual coordination and discrimination. Although some teachers had tried all or portions of these programs prior to the 1998–1999 school year, everyone was in the process of integrating both programs into their classrooms at the time of the study with the adoption of these programs schoolwide.

At the time of our visit to Serna, three "new" programs were in their third month of implementation in classrooms: *Making Words*, *Guided Reading*, and *Structure of Intellect (SOI)*. Consequently, teachers were at varying stages of implementation, depending on their comfort levels. A brief description of each of these three programs follows.

Guided Reading, a well-developed multi-faceted program provides the centerpiece of Serna's early reading instruction. In this program, children work for approximately 1 hour per day with leveled books in small flexible groups. The program is assessment driven, with children moving from group to group as reading levels improve. The classroom teacher works with one group at a time and usually cycles through each group several times in the course of a week. The program also includes a substantial writing component.

---

[8]These schedules were constructed from interviews with teachers in November 1998. Although these schedules are incomplete and would be expected to change somewhat depending on the school and month within the school year, they do show the kinds and approximate amounts of reading and writing activities that students experienced.

[9]The adopted basal program was published by Harcourt, Brace, and Jovanovich.

[10]The Slingerland program is a classroom adaptation of the Orton-Gillingham multisensory tutorial approach.

TABLE 10.3.

Literacy Instruction in Daily Schedule for Sample Classrooms (11/98)

	First Grade	*Second Grade*
Morning (7:45 a.m.)	Skill work (phonics, word study, spelling) (*Making Words & Slingerland*) (whole group)	Journal writing (independent) (can be in any curriculum area)
	Guided Reading (small groups)	
	Accelerated Reader program (individual)	Reading with basal (3 days—skills/ spelling/ phonics) (2 days—integrate math and/or language with story of week) (3 days, literature, e.g., poetry unit) (1st semester—whole group; 2nd semester—small groups based on skills not reading levels)
		SOI whole group activities (supplements literacy activities)
Lunch		
Afternoon	Writing (whole group and/or individual)	Continued Emphasis on Literacy throughout afternoon session
	SOI whole group activities (supplements literacy activities)	Science and Social Studies include reading and writing activities.
		Accelerated Reader (individual)
Dismissal (2:45 p.m.)	Approximately 3 Hours of Literacy Activities	Approximately 2.25 Hours of Literacy Activities

While *Guided Reading* includes word level skills, it is supplemented with the *Making Words* program. *Making Words* engages students in multilevel, hands-on activities in spelling and phonics. The program was introduced to replace the *Slingerland* program and as such is in various stages of implementation as teachers move from one program to the other. With the *Making Words* program children are guided in using their phonic skills through the use of pocket charts to literally "make words."

Structure of the Intellect was the third program introduced as support for the early reading program. This program is used by all Kindergarten through fifth-grade teachers as part of their regular instruction and as a pullout program for students with special needs. At the classroom level, students typically spent about 15 minutes each day with worksheets that provide practice in skills such as directionality and fine visual discrimination.[11]

In addition to these "new" components, several ongoing programs directly, or indirectly, support the early reading program. Serna has implemented the *Accelerated Reader* program schoolwide. A large number of children's trade books have been leveled and made available in individual classrooms and in the school library for independent reading. As soon as children are able to read independently, they are enrolled in the program and continue throughout Grades 1 through 5. Once familiar with the program, students are able to self-pace their independent reading using the *Accelerated Reader* software that assesses their responses to questions on each book completed and keeps track of individual student progress. The school librarian supervises the overall program at Serna.

The school library is a well-used resource at Serna for all content areas and grade levels. In the context of the early reading program, there is a special program for first graders. In addition to managing the *Accelerated Reader* program, the school librarian pulls out children from each of the four first-grade classrooms every 6 weeks for 1-hour sessions. Each session lasts for 1 hour and covers topics such as library procedures, book selection for independent reading, and different genres in children's literature.

First and second graders have cross-grade, shared readings with fourth graders. Fourth-grade "book buddies" come about twice a month to read to, and be read to by, the younger children. The book buddy program partners an older student with a younger student for the purpose of reading for enjoyment. These cross-grade classes are sometimes extended to include other activities like art and plays.

---

[11]In addition to this classroom component, SOI also includes a laboratory for more intense work with a very limited number of children. More information about SOI is presented in a later section of this paper.

Finally, although not directly related to the early reading program, it is important to note that Serna has been a *Core Knowledge* school since 1993. As a content-based program, it contributes to the integration of reading throughout the school day in subjects like social studies, mathematics and science.

Parental Involvement. The involvement of parents in the school day as support for classroom teachers and as support for their children's learning outside school is very much the mainstay of middle-class, suburban schools. Recognizing the contributions that parents can play in the support of their children's learning to read is also a critical aspect of early reading achievement. However, for poor children and their families, parental involvement in school or support at home with storybook reading is not always possible. Consequently, high poverty schools seek the involvement and support of the significant adults in the lives of their students.

Similar to other high-performing, high-poverty schools (Adler & Fisher, 2000), Serna makes varied attempts at involving parents and/or significant adults in the literacy learning of its students. Teachers report handfuls of parents who do respond to invitations to participate in classroom activities such as storybook readings, but they do not rely on this involvement because it has proven to be sporadic and limited.

Teachers employ a variety of strategies aimed at engaging families with their children, such as encouraging 15 minutes of daily reading at home where either a parent and/or significant adult reads to the child, the child reads, or they take turns. Serna has been able to engage more families through their homework monitoring system. Children and families sign contracts at the start of the school year and weekly checklists are turned back in to teachers.

Assessment of Student Reading Performance. Teachers receive information about student reading performance from a variety of sources. The state mandated third-grade reading test, Texas Assessment of Academic Skills (TAAS), has been a key resource for Serna teachers for overall planning of the literacy program at a schoolwide level. In addition to the student, classroom and school-level scores, the school receives item analyses following each test administration. During the summer, Serna staff examine the item analyses and modify instructional emphases in light of local student performance.

However, for day-to-day instructional decisions including student grouping within classes, teachers at Serna use several assessment procedures. Some Kindergarten through second-grade teachers use a recently implemented informal diagnostic *Texas Primary Reading Inventory* (1998) that is available throughout the state. In previous years some teachers have relied on the placement tests out of their basal readers to determine instructional needs. Some first-grade teachers use running records of selected leveled books every 3 to 6 weeks to reassign students to reading groups as part of the *Guided Reading* program. Two second-grade teachers reported using oral readings and running records as their primary diagnostic tools. One second-grade teacher reported using a battery of instruments, including the *Accelerated Reader STAR Reading Assessment* (2001), as a long-time favorite reading inventory, and oral readings to place students in developmentally appropriate instructional groups. In this case, the *STAR* and reading inventory results are combined to help select independent reading materials for her students, whereas oral readings are used to assess students' strengths and weaknesses. Another second-grade teacher collects running records on readings of familiar text each week to keep track of student progress. Although individual choices for assessment may vary, teachers at Serna make regular use of data for many of their instructional decisions.

Safety Nets for Struggling Readers

Serna Elementary School offers a number of both formal and informal mechanisms to support struggling readers.[12] Typically, teachers identify struggling readers in the course of daily instruction. The state-developed *Reading Inventory* as well as the *Guided Reading* program provide formal mechanisms for determining a student's reading level and informal assessments include activities such as running records. For struggling readers who have been at Serna for 1 or 2 years, there will be a record of the student's performance from earlier classes. However, most struggling readers are transfer students who need extra help to perform at the level of their Serna classmates. Teachers have some flexibility within classes to help struggling readers and there are several schoolwide mechanisms that can be engaged as well. Each is described briefly later in this chapter.

Tutoring.   Some Serna teachers provide one-on-one tutoring as needed to their own students as well as others who need additional support. All tutoring is done on a volunteer basis and occurs during a teacher's planning period or before/after school. For before/after school hours, transportation does not present

---

[12]During the 1998–1999 school year, there were approximately eight K through second graders receiving special education services at Sapphire. These students had been identified standard district processes and were pulled out on a daily basis for portions of their reading, language arts, and math instruction.

a problem, because many children arrive early for the breakfast program or stay late for after school day care. At the time of the study, one first-grade teacher reported working with two of her students after school (one for an hour a week and the other for 2 hours). A second-grade teacher reported that none of her current students needed tutoring, but that she was working with some third graders after school. Some students from a nearby college also provided tutoring on a volunteer basis.

Structures of Intellect (SOI) Program.   One role of the SOI program is as a pullout laboratory for students with special needs, which also includes struggling readers. Although SOI is not a reading program and no one at Serna intends it to be such, Serna teachers regard the exercises that students engage in during lab sessions as effective with their struggling readers. About 20 children per grade level are referred to the SOI lab for structured activities; however, not all of these children may be struggling readers. Although there is a formal assessment process for older children to be placed in the SOI lab, Kindergarten through second-grade placements are dependent on teacher referrals only. In the SOI lab, children are provided with physical (nonpaper-and-pencil) activities designed to work on focusing skills and sensory integration. Children attend the lab twice a week for 50 minutes while their classmates are attending physical education and/or music classes.

Extended Year Programs.   *Jump Start* is a free summer school program specifically designed for Serna students. Teachers recommend students for placement in the program, and most children who are referred do participate. Teachers describe *Jump Start* as providing that "extra oomph" for some students before they start the new school year. Four-hour daily sessions, staffed by Serna teachers, are held for 3 weeks. The curriculum is designed to help children "catch up" before entering the next grade level.[13]

Serna students receive their primary reading instruction in their individual classrooms. When individual teachers identify struggling readers in their classes, they typically use one or more of the programs/strategies described above to provide extra support. If these resources do not have the desired effect, the teacher has the option of presenting the student's case to the Student/Teacher Assessment Team (STAT). This high-level, school-wide standing

---

[13]There is a separate summer school for the local school district. This program gathers students from several elementary schools on one campus and offers a variety of remedial courses. District teachers staff the district summer school and students must pay to attend.

committee considers the case and usually suggests additional strategies for help-ing the student. If these efforts are not successful, then the student may be re-ferred for additional assessment and possible entry into special education. The Admission, Review, and Dismissal (ARD) team administer this latter proce-dure, governed by the state education code. However, this referral process is only tapped after all other resources for helping struggling readers is exhausted.

Retentions.   It is through this same STAT process that a child would be recommended for retention. Serna retains children who are not achieving at grade level. Retention is based on a lengthy referral process and is only done with parental consent. At the time of the study, one second-grade teacher re-ported that she was likely to recommend one student for retention.

Other Programs/Arrangements

After School Care Program.   A local agency has been operating an af-ter-school day-care program in the school cafeteria for several years. This drop-in program includes supervised opportunities for students to play games, read, and participate in story telling activities.

Volunteers/Mentors Program.   Employees of a large local bank volunteer on a regular basis to mentor individual children. Teachers decide which of their children need mentoring and provide the activities for child and mentor to work on. Mentors come to the school once per week for about an hour. At the time of our visit to Serna there were 36 different mentor-pupil pairs in the Kin-dergarten through fifth-grade program. The content of the mentoring activities was often, but not always, concerned with literacy. Mentors also serve as pen pals and thereby helped students with both writing and reading.

Cross-Class Arrangements.   A few children attend a lower grade level for instruction in reading or other subjects. For example, one second-grade teacher has one student who goes back to first grade for reading instruction on a regular basis.

Planning for the Early Reading Program

At Serna, teachers have specific periods in the school schedule designated for individual and/or group planning. Teachers have considerable discretion over how this time is used. Planning for reading instruction occurs at three levels at

Serna: individual, within grades, and across grades. First, teachers individually plan instructional activities for their own classrooms. This kind of planning is the most frequent and often takes place outside scheduled planning periods.

The second level of planning is more formal and takes place in grade-level groups. These regularly scheduled weekly meetings are held during a common period for specials. Although these meetings deal with the breadth of the curriculum, planning for literacy instruction appears to be a frequently visited topic. With student achievement as a shared goal, these meetings are collegial and informational. Instructional successes and failures are often shared and suggestions and/or strategies for improvement offered.

Some of the group planning time is devoted to the *Core Knowledge* curriculum. Although this program specifically targets social studies, it has important implications for the types of text that children encounter and the language arts skills children practice. Serna teachers have been active in developing instructional units aligned with the *Core Knowledge* program, and some of the joint planning time has been allocated to this activity. Other teachers team teach the content areas and plan together for these shared units.

A third type of planning occurs across grade levels. These meetings are scheduled by the school administration twice a year. During these meetings teachers examine alignment issues across grades and identify strengths and weaknesses in the grade progression. This allows first-grade teachers, for example, to meet with colleagues in kindergarten and second grade "to touch base with each other."

This overall planning structure is quite flexible and the level of communication among Serna's staff is relatively high—with teachers frequently meeting over lunch or talking on the run about instructional aspects of the literacy program. Teachers reported using these opportunities to share ideas with one another and their school as "a very wonderful campus. Everyone has wonderful ideas, so they will let us go in [to classrooms] any time and we can talk to them, get ideas from anybody."

Professional Development and the Early Reading Program

Serna teachers in the early reading program represent a range of professional backgrounds that vary in educational levels attained, years of teaching, and grade levels taught. There are teachers who have just begun their careers teaching side by side with those who are nearing retirement with 29 years in the classroom. Some teachers hold degrees beyond a bachelor's in fields such as English and English as a second language. These differences notwithstanding, all the teachers at Serna reported extensive and varied experiences in professional development.

Grade-Level and School-wide Professional Development at Serna. Weekly staff meetings serve three main functions: handling of schoolwide issues, dealing with instructional/student issues, and conducting short training sessions. This mechanism provides the primary structure for coordinating high-priority programs within the school. For example, during one typical week, the issue of improving discipline on campus was taken up with a presentation of information on a specific program. As a result, an upcoming site visit was planned for staff to observe the program in action. If the program were eventually adopted by Serna,[14] then initial training would be coordinated through the staff meetings.

Programs that are adopted by the school go through a series of stages. There is a preview stage during which new programs are examined for appropriateness (like the discipline program previously mentioned). For programs that are adopted there is an intensive training stage when many staff members receive training in a relatively short time. When a program has been in the school for a year or more, a maintenance stage occurs during which fewer training sessions typically take place. This latter stage introduces new hires to the program and provides updates for the school staff as necessary. Different programs that have an impact on the early reading program are at different stages in this process.

For example, the *Structure of the Intellect (SOI)* program was introduced during the 1996–1997 school year. During this initial stage general information was provided to the staff and subsequently the decision was made to train one teacher in the program. This teacher then began the lab, which was attended by students from across the grades on a regular basis. Based on the improvement students in the program made, the program was expanded. Thus, for the following school year, the *SOI* teacher worked with others at the classroom level on program implementation. Finally, in 1998, the program was fully implemented, with both classroom modules in all grades and modules the *SOI* laboratory pull-out program for selected students. By the year of full implementation, the school's *SOI* teacher had trained the entire staff for implementation at the classroom level. However, this stage of schoolwide implementation should not be interpreted as the final word on the program; administration and staff continue to monitor its effectiveness.

---

[14]This would require an informed decision by the Campus Improvement Committee.

The *Core Knowledge* program, adopted in 1993, serves as another source for professional development. Although this program is not explicitly an early reading program, it has played an important role in the development of the overall curriculum. Teachers frequently attend training sessions sponsored by a local university with whom they are linked through the program. As part of the program, Serna teachers have been actively engaged in developing instructional units for their classrooms that often have implications for literacy. In addition, the program has allowed staff to share their knowledge at the professional level. In 1999, 19 Serna teachers made presentations at the annual national *Core Knowledge* conference in Florida.

The *Guided Reading* program has probably been the most recent intensive training effort in early reading for the staff. During the 1998–1999, the program was in its initial year of full implementation. The district reading coordinator provided the primary training with onsite bimonthly sessions. Teachers, ready to implement the program, volunteered in advance for these sessions at which they became active and engaged participants.

In addition to specific training programs such as those previously mentioned, the Campus Improvement Committee (CIC) provides an important vehicle for staff training to occur. This state-mandated committee provides the structure for Serna staff to discuss and set staff development priorities on a yearly basis. During this annual meeting, planned staff development days are placed on the calendar for the subsequent school year. This schedule is then submitted to the district for approval of district-sanctioned "waiver days."

In addition to the two in-service days at the start of the calendar year Serna teachers participate in other local opportunities for professional development. For example, in January 1999, teachers attended an international educational conference held locally. The local district also offers workshops throughout the year in what it calls "Super Saturdays." These sessions provide training in a wide range of topics. Teachers choose among many options and all sessions are voluntary.

However, Serna's district includes professional development as a category on teacher evaluations. In this way, the district (and school) can stipulate which training counts for evaluation purposes. Teachers cannot accumulate many credits for workshops that are outside those required by the school. Although it may appear that Serna teachers participate because it is required, the principal sees her teachers as professionals who "always looking for something that they're interested in or something that they feel will build their skills" whether it was required or not.

Other Developmental Activities.   Serna teachers also engage in a variety of voluntary professional development activities both during the school year and their summer vacations. For example, an informal study group meets on a regular basis to discuss professional readings. This group is flexible in terms of both membership and topics. The sessions are optional, and members suggest readings/topics. Meetings are held at school during after-school hours on a day and time agreed on by all participants. This voluntary program was initiated by the school librarian approximately 2 years ago has been encouraged by the district reading coordinator as a means to build on the district workshops and to stay abreast of reading research. Topics have ranged from curriculum areas such as reading and math to brain research.

Although few teachers had access to the Internet through their computers at school, the Internet does provide another vehicle for those who have access at home. Teachers use web sites for a variety of purposes, such as sharing instructional activities electronically with other teachers, looking for new ideas "to keep fresh" and communicating with *Core Knowledge* teachers in other states.

Finally, many Serna teachers also participate in annual state meetings of professional organizations such as the Texas Educational Association, National Education Association, and the Texas Association of Professional Educators.

Program Development at Serna Elementary School

Serna Elementary School, like most schools, is a complex, dynamic organization. Each succeeding year brings changes to the program as the staff implements new elements arising from state and district, as well as local school decisions. Although there had been a school at this site for several decades, Serna's history began in 1992. Overcrowding in other district schools led to its reopening under the leadership of the current principal, Mrs. Shirley Hasting. Since that time, Serna has been intensely engaged first in a variety of start-up activities and subsequently in several strands of program development. Table 10.4 provides an overview of key development activities from 1992 until 1998, the year of the study.

Table 10.4 contains four categories of structures and events. The first category presents selected state-mandated structures and events. The primary school planning and decision making body (CIC), two important student support mechanisms (STAT and ARD), and the state student assessment mechanism are examples of state structures that were in effect when Serna opened in 1992. These structures represented part of the start up activities for the school. In 1998, note that two additional state-mandated structures were being implemented.

TABLE 10.4

Chronology of selected events and projects at Serna School for the period 1992–1999

	1992–1993	1993–1994	1994–1995	1995–1996	1996–1997	1997–1998	1998–1999
School Reopening	x						
State Mandated:							
CIC		x	x	x	x	x	x
STAT		x	x	x	x	x	x
ARD		x	x	x	x	x	x
Texas Primary Reading Inventory							x
TAAS		x	x	x	x	x	x
Standards Alignment Committee							x
Instructional:							
Core Knowledge		x	x	x	x	x	x
HJB Basals		x	x	x	x	x	x
Slingerland Phonics				?	x	x	dropped
Accelerated Reader					x	x	x

	1992–1993	1993–1994	1994–1995	1995–1996	1996–1997	1997–1998	1998–1999
Guided Reading							x
Making Words							x
Grant writing for leveled books						x (District)	
Safety Nets:							
Tutoring					x	x	x
Structure of the Intellect (SOI)					Introduced	x	x
Jump Start					?	x	x
Summer School					?	x	x
H.O.T.S. (Upper grades)		x	x	x	x	x	x
Professional Development:							
SOI training					training	Lab only	Lab; class
Guided Reading							x
Study Groups						x	x
Super Saturdays						x	x
Core Knowledge					x	x	x

(continued on next page)

TABLE 10.4 (continued)

Chronology of selected events and projects at Serna School for the period 1992–1999

	1992–1993	1993–1994	1994–1995	1995–1996	1996–1997	1997–1998	1998–1999
Other:							
Title I (schoolwide)			x	x	x	x	x
State Commendation							Recognized
CIERA Study Participation						Survey	Visit

254

The three remaining categories present structures and activities that have a direct or indirect effect on the early reading program. Soon after reopening, Serna adopted *Core Knowledge* as a school-wide curriculum component. In its third year, Serna became a school-wide Title I site. Some curricular elements have been adopted and eventually dropped. Changes in curricular elements are sometimes accompanied by changes in professional development activities. Serna has identified and implemented a variety of safety nets for its struggling readers.

Key Elements of School Operation

A Standards-Driven Early Reading Program. To the extent that the state-mandated reading assessment reflects the state's literacy standards, the early reading program at Serna can be described as standards-driven. The state reading assessment is first administered at Grade 3 but preparation for this test has considerable impact on how students spend their class time long before third grade. At Serna, teachers acknowledged the influence of the Grade 3 state reading assessment on some instructional activities as early as pre-kindergarten and suggested that its influence increased in Grades 1 and 2.

As evidence of its importance, Serna students are given ample opportunities to work on tasks and formats similar to those on the state reading assessment. For example, 1 day per month the whole school has a "writing day" during which all students respond to a writing prompt. On some of these occasions student writing products are scored using the same procedures and rubrics as are used on the statewriting assessment. This task alone would give students more than a score of practice trials for an important test task by the time they take the initial state writing assessment at the end of third grade.

Practice standardized tests (Iowa Test of Basic Skills or tests similar to it) are administered in first and second grade, at the same time that the TAAS is being given in third grade. Staff members suggest that this procedure helps to assess student progress and, at the same time, gives students valuable test-taking experience. Some classes use specially prepared exercise materials, modeled on the state reading assessment tasks and formats, to give students additional practice.

Serna also makes regular use of item analyses provided to the school by the state education agency. These data give direct feedback on how their students performed on individual items of the most recent administration of the TAAS. Using these data, teachers fine tune instruction to help their students on subsequent state reading assessments. The state education agency provides a variety of sophisticated data on student performance by school, district, and larger units of analysis. As for many other schools in Texas, Serna faculty pay attention to student performance on the state reading measures and hence to state literacy standards. This focus on student literacy performance as a key element of the school operation has been increasing in intensity for several years. Although test performance and the literacy standards are highly emphasized at Serna, this central focus is a broader interest in and support for reading and literacy. Individual classrooms and the school library have large collections of print materials, and students can be seen reading throughout the school at all times of the day.

A Classroom-By-Classroom Instructional Strategy. As previously mentioned, Serna relies on individual classroom teachers for the students' primary instruction. Thus, individual teachers are responsible for practically all instruction in literacy, mathematics, social studies, and science. From the point of view of the early literacy program, any provisions for struggling readers are implemented by the classroom teacher. Pull-out or push-in programs are not a substantial part of this classroom-by-classroom strategy.[15]

This organizational pattern is undoubtedly influenced by various regulations set down by the state education agency. For example, the state limits enrolment in early elementary classes to 22 thereby allowing schools to hire more teachers than would be the case if the enrollment ceiling were higher. This policy choice usually implies very limited resources for either aides in classrooms or nonclassroom teaching specialists who might work with particular target groups (for example, struggling readers). At Serna, there are no classroom aides in Kindergarten through second-grade classes, and, with the exception[16] of the children who go to the SOI lab or to the primary special education classroom, there are no other teachers working with the children on a regular basis.

An Eclectic Early Reading Program. The early reading program at Serna has a variety of components drawn from a broad range of approaches to beginning reading. Like many programs, Serna's has changed over the years in its attempt to improve student performance and respond to various policy recommendations from local and state authorities. The resulting program is rel-

---

[15]One exception to this pattern is the Structure of Intellect (SOI) program. The SOI has two distinct parts. One part of the SOI is administered to every student by the classroom teacher. A second part of the SOI is a pull-out program for a small number of students—typically one or two per class in the primary grades—who go to an SOI laboratory staffed by a specially-trained teacher. A given student spends about two 30 minute sessions in the lab each week while other students in their classes are attending "specials" (for example, PE, music, or computers).

[16]Sapphire has at least one other nonclassroom based teacher who implements a Higher Order Thinking Skills (HOTS) program for Grade 4 and 5 students who have not done well on the Grade 3 state reading assessment.

atively balanced in that it includes both elements that teach phonics explicitly and elements that provide students with direct experiences with literature. During the course of a week, students in the early reading program engage a range of activities, including phonics and spelling tasks through the *Making Words* program, strategic reading and comprehension tasks through the *Guided Reading* program, and the reading of leveled books through the *Accelerated Reader* program. Basal readers and associated materials are also a component of the overall program, as well as a variety of writing and other literacy activities.

Although the implementation of an eclectic early reading program may be common in many parts of the United States, Mrs. Hasting reported that while attending a recent elementary principals association academy, she was the only one of the 10 principals in her group who did not represent a school with one commercial reading program.

It is important to keep in mind that the early reading program at Serna is dynamic. Hardly a year goes by when there is not a substantial change in one or more components of the program. A brief glance at Table 10.4 shows how specific elements have been added to the overall program during the last few years. For example, in 1998–1999 Serna introduced the *Guided Reading* as a central plank in its reading platform. As a key element of school operation, Serna has, and is likely to continue to have, an eclectic and dynamic early reading program.

Capable Active School Leadership.   Mrs. Hasting opened the school in 1992 and since then has led the school with a steady and thoughtful hand. She energetically pursues clearly stated school goals in a business-like manner. She is also very deliberate in relinquishing control and sharing responsibilities. During the first 2 years following the opening of the school, she chaired the Campus Improvement Council (CIC), a general planning and management structure required in all schools in the state. From the third year onward, the chair has been elected. This is but one indication of her tendency to encourage school-level participation from faculty.

In terms of program development, several programs have been brought to the school by Mrs. Hasting, some introduced by the district and some championed by individual teachers. In all cases, innovations have been presented for consideration to teachers and not implemented until most are in agreement. Mrs. Hasting delegates a fair amount of responsibility, keeps her staff in the picture through frequent communication, and takes staff views into account in most decisions. At the same time, she takes responsibility for velocity in the school and keeps abreast of the important issues as they arise.

Although Serna is a relatively small school, it, like most elementary schools in the state, has an assistant principal. For the last 2 years, this role has been ably filled by a veteran administrator, giving Serna stable and highly competent leadership at the school level. The distribution of responsibilities between the two administrators is based on their individual areas of expertise and interests.

Strong Relationship With the District. Serna also works collaboratively with its district administration. Unlike some other high performing, high poverty schools (Adler & Fisher, 2000; Fisher & Adler, 1999), Serna does not appear to be "out in front" of its district office either in the sense of vying with the district for programmatic leadership or ignoring the district's attempts to reform practice.

Both Serna administrators and staff consider district initiatives and district personnel as being a positive influence on literacy programming. Staff look to the district reading coordinator (assigned to the cluster of schools of which Serna is a part) as one source of leadership in their early reading program. In fact, it was the district reading coordinator who was instrumental in supporting the implementation of the *Guided Reading* program at Serna.

Although not all classrooms were electronically networked at the time of the study, there is regular communication with the district at the administrative level through email and other channels.

Dynamic School Environment. As noted earlier, the early reading program at Serna has added new elements each year in an attempt to improve reading achievement for all its children. However, this action orientation appears to be pervasive in the school as a whole. There is ample evidence of ongoing development in several areas of school operation. At Serna, the rates of change and the processes used to determine which changes to implement appear to be particularly appropriate for the setting. On the one hand, the school is neither waiting exclusively for stimulation from the outside nor is it responsive only to innovations championed from within. On the other hand, the rate of development appears to be within a range that can be accommodated by the faculty. This rate of development appears to give Serna's faculty a sense of possibility without making the task overwhelming. As a school, Serna appears to be an active growing entity.

The positive environment is supported by a number of activities and programs that provide a sense of community at Serna. For example, each day begins with an assembly presented by teachers and students on a rotating basis; the school has a strong music program that produces several substantial productions each year involving large numbers of students, and there is a school-wide policy of 20 minutes of homework each night.

CONCLUSION

Not unlike previous research (Hoffman & Rutherford, 1984; Taylor, Pearson, Clark, & Walpole, 1999; USDOE, 1998), Serna Elementary School shows evidence of able and stable leadership at the school level along with a core of experienced, knowledgeable, and hardworking teachers in the early grades. In addition, Serna has a high level of program awareness with well-developed procedures for the introduction and implementation of programs designed to improve reading achievement. It is also very evident that Serna does not remain static; since their inception in 1992, they have constantly strived to seek out solutions to the instructional challenges that they face. Although Serna faculty rely on sound classroom instruction as the foundation to its literacy program, they also depend on schoolwide mechanisms to support and facilitate what goes on at the classroom level.

REFERENCES

Adler, M. A., & Fisher, C. W. (2000). *An Initial Cross-Case Analysis of Early Reading Programs in High-Performing, High-Poverty Schools: How School-Wide Structures Make a Difference.* Paper Presented at AERA New Orleans, LA.

CIERA *Survey of Early Literacy Programs in High Performing Schools: Principal Survey.* (1998). Ann Arbor: CIERA/University of Michigan.

Cunningham, P., Hall, D., & Sigmon, C. (1999). *The teacher's guide to the four blocks.* Greensboro, NC.

Fisher, C. W., & Adler, M. A. (1999). *Early reading programs in high-poverty schools: Emerald Elementary beats the odds.* Ann Arbor, MI: CIERA Technical Report #3-009.

Fountas, I., & Pinnell, G. S. (1996). *Guiding reading—good first teaching for all children.* Portsmouth, NH: Heinemann

Hoffman, J. W., & Rutherford, W. L. (1984). Effective reading programs: A critical review of outlier studies. *Reading Research Quarterly, 20*(1) 79–92.

Meeker, M. N. (1969). *The structure of intellect: Its interpretation and uses.* Columbus, OH: Merrill.

STAR Early Literacy. (2001). Advantage Learning Systems, Inc. Renaissance Learning and School Renaissance Institute. http://www.renlearn.com/

Taylor, B. M., Pearson, P. D., Clark, K. F., & Walpole, S. (1999). *Beating the odds in teaching all children to read.* Ann Arbor, MI: CIERA Technical Report #2-006.

Texas Primary Reading Inventory, Texas Education Agency, 1998, Austin TX. http://www.tea.state.tx.us/

United States Department of Education. (1998). *Implementing schoolwide programs: An idea book on planning.* Washington, DC: Author.

11

In Pursuit of Academic Excellence: The Story of Gladys Noon Spellman Elementary

Pamela A. Smith
Joseph F. Johnson, Jr.
Brent C. Jones
Charles A. Dana Center, University of Texas at Austin

The Spellman school day officially opens at 8:55 a.m. with quiet time followed by the student-produced and hosted morning broadcast of WGNS. In the minutes before, children with backpacks and book-bags walk purposefully through the halls to their classrooms. Student safety patrols stand at regular intervals in the middle of the well-lit yellow brick corridors. Their presence silently establishes two lanes in the hallway. Older students flow by, while the patrols and adults gently guide younger ones, still unsure of their steps and the school.

Observing the children's well-choreographed arrival, one would never guess that Spellman is extremely overcrowded, serving 200 students more than the building's stated capacity, or that just last year discipline was the primary concern of teachers. Now administrators, staff, and parents describe Spellman as an organized, calm, and academically focused environment. An innovative scheduling system, small group teaching, authentic task instruction, and authentic assessment practices have all become hallmarks of the academic program at Spellman and defining elements of the culture of the school. A commitment to teaching all children is demonstrated through inclusive approaches to special education and the teaching of students who are English language learners. At Spellman every minute and every bit of space are dedicated to instruction. For instance, storage rooms have been converted to a Spanish classroom and science lab. Even part of the teachers' lounge is used on a daily basis for student instruction.

THE CONTEXT

Population Served

Gladys Noon Spellman Elementary School is located about 5 miles from Washington, D.C., in the socio-economically and racially diverse community of Cheverly in Prince George's County, Maryland. The recently renovated split-level stucco and brick building is nestled into the crest of a hill. Single-family homes and high-rise, low-income apartments surround the sparsely wooded campus. Spellman served a multicultural student body of more than 750 students in kindergarten through Grade 6. The school reflects the diversity of the neighborhood and includes many immigrant children who are bussed from all parts of the county to the school's ESOL (English for Speakers of Other Languages) Center. Three out of four of the students are Black (African American and African immigrants) and one in seven is Hispanic. The remaining population includes children who are White (European-American and Russian immigrants) and a small number of Asian American and Native American students. More than 60% of the students qualify for free or reduced-price lunches.

Academic Improvement

The performance of Spellman students on the Maryland State Performance Assessment Program (MSPAP) has improved considerably since 1994. The improvement is apparent in all six of the areas included in the assessment program (see Table 11.1.) As well, the performance of Spellman students on the MSPAP exceeds the performance of students throughout the state in all areas at the third-grade level and in most areas at the fifth-grade level (see Table 11.2).

STARTING POINTS

Spellman's story began with a single-minded focus on instruction. This approach resulted in many important improvements; however, it also had its costs.

TABLE 11.1

Percent Spellman Elementary Students at or Above Satisfactory Level

	1994	1995	1996	1997	1998
Gr. 3 Reading	17.0	26.0	49.3	41.1	69.0
Gr. 3 Writing	21.3	36.0	49.3	42.5	69.2
Gr. 3 Lang. Usage	25.5	44.6	60.5	58.4	65.2
Gr. 3 Mathematics	18.1	37.3	69.0	64.9	75.0
Gr. 3 Science	10.6	40.0	57.7	62.5	80.2
Gr. 3 Soc. Studies	17.0	37.3	40.8	48.8	74.4
Gr. 5 Reading	15.3	21.4	19.4	18.4	35.3
Gr. 5 Writing	21.2	21.4	46.2	36.6	47.6
Gr. 5 Lang. Usage	21.2	25.7	29.0	44.6	39.2
Gr. 5 Mathematics	27.1	44.3	73.1	78.5	72.0
Gr. 5 Science	22.4	27.1	48.4	63.4	74.4
Gr. 5 Soc. Studies	9.4	20.0	54.8	46.2	62.2

Many teachers believed that greater gains could be achieved with a broader focus on issues that influenced the school climate. During the 1998–1999 school year, with the direction of a new principal, Spellman increased its efforts to fill these gaps.

But change is not new to Spellman. The school has been going through a change process for more than 5 years. There is wide consensus in the school and district that the instructional reforms that began in 1994, under the administration of former principal, Sherry Liebes, have led to the constantly increasing performance of Spellman students. Liebes, who came with a background in special education, was previously the principal of a national Blue Ribbon school. She came to Spellman in 1994 1 year after the new and rigorous Maryland state

TABLE 11.2

State Versus Percent Spellman Elementary Students
at or Above Satisfactory Level

	Spellman Elementary 1998	Maryland Statewide 1998
Gr. 3 Reading	69.0	41.6
Gr. 3 Writing	69.2	47.6
Gr. 3 Lang. Usage	65.2	49.4
Gr. 3 Mathematics	75.0	41.6
Gr. 3 Science	80.2	39.4
Gr. 3 Soc. Studies	74.4	41.0
Gr. 5 Reading	35.3	40.5
Gr. 5 Writing	47.6	42.0
Gr. 5 Lang. Usage	39.2	51.4
Gr. 5 Mathematics	72.0	47.9
Gr. 5 Science	74.4	51.6
Gr. 5 Soc. Studies	62.2	43.8

assessment (the Maryland School Performance Assessment Program or MSPAP) had first been piloted.

When Liebes arrived, Spellman was a relatively large, multicultural elementary school. Teachers recalled that discipline was an issue; "There were kids running in the halls. Kids that were sent to the office got candy before they came back." Staff felt a lack of leadership. As one teacher explained, "We weren't getting too much focus from the helm."

Instruction at Spellman was delivered in a traditional style in self-contained classrooms at all times. The chief educational administrator responsible for overseeing the group of elementary, middle, and high schools, of which Spellman is a part recalled, "It was just operating as a traditional elementary school, using traditional methods with low expectations for teaching children."

There were, and still are, a large number of staff and specialists at Spellman. This high level of staffing is the result of Title I funding and money from the Prince George's County District for being a Model Comprehensive School. Many of these staff members did not have their own classrooms because Spellman's hilly terrain could not accommodate portable buildings. Classroom teachers expressed frustration that they could not teach because students were constantly being pulled from class for special services provided by the additional staff. As Liebes explained, "What teachers said to me was, 'Every time I try to teach, somebody's at my door taking my kids.'"

These scheduling difficulties also seemed to reinforce a sense among teachers that academics were not a high priority. One teacher complained, "P.E. [physical education] and music set the schedule and we worked around that. Academics were not as important as frills."

CHANGING THE ORGANIZATION OF SCHOOLING

Innovative Scheduling

In response to the disruptions, Principal Liebes implemented a system of block scheduling, which she had used successfully to cope with similar issues at her previous school. Liebes had developed her interest in block scheduling through attending a presentation by Robert Lynn Canady (see Canady & Rettig, 1995). Spellman adapted this block-scheduling model (which the staff refer to as "Canady") to provide small group instruction in reading and language arts during a 90-minute block every morning. Each classroom teacher was paired with a specialist, who served as an instructional partner for a 10-day rotation. These two partners split the homeroom class in half; one delivered the main reading lesson for 45 minutes while the other reinforced the lesson through his or her specialty. During the second half of the period, students worked with the other instructor. The end result was that all students and instructors worked on reading and language arts in small groups for 90 minutes every school day.

Liebes was adamant that this time period would be free from interruptions. Expressing her commitment to the model she said, "It was sacred time. We did no announcements. We had no field trips. We had no assemblies. We didn't do anything, except Canady! On early dismissal days or late arrival days because of snow, everything else would be cut out, but you would have that hour and a half of reading and language arts instruction."

Teachers confirmed this sense of focus by explaining, "Liebes always used to say, 'time on task!' In her 4 years [at Spellman] reading was never, ever, ever disturbed. You did reading every day. From 9:20 to 11 a.m. this school shut down. You did reading."

Liebes made strategic decisions as she introduced the block-scheduling model. First, in an effort to cultivate faculty ownership for the proposal, she asked teachers to voluntarily attend a local presentation by Canady. But, Liebes said, "I made sure there were some kingpins on the staff that went with me to that first in-service." After interest had been generated among the wider staff, the initial team worked out a plan for pilot implementation. Dr Liebes described her strategy for introducing innovations; "I always call things like this a pilot, because in fact they are. Plus if you call it a pilot, people are more apt to respond and say, 'I'll try it.' It makes it sound like if it doesn't work it's okay. It's nobody's fault." This voluntary and gradual approach eased the change process. As Liebes said:

> I felt like we had the luxury to take that time, because at that point, test scores were an issue, achievement was an issue, but our school was not one of the reconstituted schools. So, we were able to take time. I felt like it was important to make it voluntary originally because I wanted people to own the process and feel like they had a part of it and were going to make it work.

Not only did this approach promote ownership, but also it gave "reluctant" teachers time to wait and see. Grade levels could elect to use the block schedule: in the first year (1995) Grades 2, 3, 4, and 5 used the new system, the next year kindergarten joined, and by the third year first and sixth grades had joined. As Liebes remembered, "The first grade had to sit back and watch it happen. Once they saw it work, then they clamored for it too."

However, Liebes was not hesitant to encourage those teachers who ultimately did not want to participate in her vision of reform to find employment elsewhere. Staff turnover was high during her tenure as she built a cohesive team around her notion of reform. As one teacher explained:

> She was nice, but stern. All she ever really said was "These are the expectations at Gladys Noon Spellman. This is what we do and this is how we teach. If this isn't something you're interested in doing, then let me know and I'll write you a wonderful evaluation and you can help yourself."

The new scheduling system provided a unified focus for the whole school. Liebes underscored this benefit by stating, "The beauty of it for me is that you have the whole school focused on the same thing at the same time. The kids know what is going on. They meet the same thing in the morning. Everybody is teaching the same objectives, the same goal."

Staff also described a variety of benefits of the scheduling model. First, teachers experienced support and validation in their role as educators with the new emphasis on academics. According to one teacher, "It gave us the opportunity to teach. After all, that's why we're all here." The small group instruction made it easier for teachers to do their job successfully especially given the overcrowded conditions at Spellman. Another teacher explained:

> The Canady situation makes things much better because, normally, you're dealing with a class of 30. With the Canady program you're teaching a class of half that size

during your reading instruction and you don't have the interruptions that distract both the teacher and the students during primary reading instruction.

Teachers attributed their improved collaboration to the experience of working as instructional partners on a daily basis. As one specialist explained:

> I think the Canady program fosters a lot of this [collaboration] because every single person in this school is responsible for instruction. Therefore, everybody's paired up with someone. Sometimes we change grade levels. So we have to interact with other people. It's almost forced. You have to talk to those people because you're working with them and you're working with everybody.

The pragmatics of shared responsibility has led to a strongly voiced ethos that all staff are responsible for the academic success of all children. A teacher affirmed this by saying, "Everybody's involved in language arts instruction, everybody is responsible for the increase in the scores because of what we do. It's not just the classroom teachers."

Changing Academic Instruction

During her first years at Spellman, Liebes sought to shift the mode of classroom instruction to the "performance-based" or "authentic-task" based instruction that characterizes Spellman classrooms today. Teachers defined authentic-task instruction as instruction that emphasized real-life problems in a manner that integrated multiple skills. As an example, an experienced teacher described a lesson she taught earlier that day:

> We've been studying forests. So I did a task on conserving paper. We had to do some math; they had to choose the appropriate operation to find out how much the paper cost in different years. We had to create a graph. Then we had to do writing, because they have to know how to restate and pull apart information from the graph and write the answers. After that we had to write a proposal as to how the school system could deal with the rising cost of paper. When they're writing that, they're going to go into some science, conservation, recycling. That's an example of authentic-task instruction.

Staff asserted that this method of teaching better prepared the students for the state assessment. A teacher explained:

> We began authentic-task instruction because that's how the state assessment is structured. On the test they are not going to say this page is math and that page is science. It's always going to be integrated. The task is going to draw from their knowledge of all

these different concepts. It's more like application. So we started teaching the way the test is structured.

Achieving this shift in teaching methods was neither quick nor simple. Indeed, Liebes recalled it as the greatest challenge that she encountered in the change process. As she said, "People bought into the Canady model pretty easily. But it was a little harder to change the instructional activities that happened once people were in that small group setting."

To support this reform, Liebes hired instructional specialists (also referred to as "performance-task" teachers by Spellman staff) who were able to model performance-based teaching (teaching that focused on helping students perform authentic tasks). Describing this strategy, which was the core of her approach to professional development, Liebes explained, "A very important part was the development of in-house master teachers, for lack of a better word. We had people in an instructional support role, in-house consultants. They support the instructional program, but live in the building, rather than provide out-of-building support."

Liebes used these instructional specialists both to introduce new methods and to provide intensive training and development when needed. She described a time when she used the specialists to train a relatively inexperienced teacher who was hired to fill a mid-year vacancy:

> I took the science teacher, the math specialist, and our reading specialist and said, "Get into that classroom and get that classroom going." Either through Canady assignments or in the afternoon through flexible scheduling, they were able to work intensively with that teacher, helping her plan, choose materials, and pace instruction. They did model lessons and then they would sit in the back of the room, watch her teach, and give her a critique.

Teachers and district officers gave credit to Liebes for selecting talented, effective instructional specialists. Their willingness to help was noted as a key part of their effectiveness. The current principal, Janet Lopez, who had spent many hours at Spellman in her previous district-level position, emphasized this point when speaking about one particularly valuable instructional specialist. "She had the kind of personality that made her easy to accept because she helped," Lopez said. "That is something very critical with all these performance-task teachers. They are perfectly willing to help the classroom teacher and offer their assistance."

Nonetheless, it took time for the instructional specialists to gain acceptance. For example, one encountered resistance as she began to model hands-on teaching in her science lab 5 years ago. Teachers had poor experiences with science lab in previous years and were skeptical about this new and relatively young teacher's ability to offer them anything of value. The principal provided concrete guidance and tacit support, which helped the new teacher weather criticism. She recalled, "Liebes told me, 'Please let me know if there is anybody who doesn't sign up.' I am sure she was going to speak with them."

The instructional specialists also reinforced the change process by doing additional work. As one of them recalled:

> In the beginning, at my principal's request, I did extra work. I gave the teachers the whole unit I was doing with their kids. I gave them two or three follow-up activities they could do each day to reinforce what we did in the lab. So I did a lot of extra things to show them that this really was a good program and they were really going to get something out of me. It wasn't just fluff and show.

Assessment Practice

At Spellman, there were regular and intensive assessment practices in preparation for the Maryland School Performance Assessment Program (Maryland State Department of Education, 2001). These practice sessions, conducted biweekly in Grades 3, 4, and 5, and monthly in Grade 2, are another central element of Spellman's instruction. Teachers and parents believed these practices contributed to the success and uniqueness of Spellman's program. Without hesitation a teacher described the school as "MSPAP driven." She went on to add:

> I'm comfortable with that because it is good teaching. If good teaching is going to serve two purposes, then it's a good situation. How can we lose? Not only that, I'm of the opinion that we are going to have MSPAP around for a long time and you might as well get on the bandwagon. You would be doing the students a disservice to not instruct that way if that's how they are going to be assessed.

A parent concurred:

> It surprises me that other schools don't do this. In middle school, the teacher told me that the kids from Spellman have skills that kids from other schools don't have. They have been prepared. They know these terms. They know how to write and how to read a map. They have skills you need for MSPAP and you need for life.

Every other week, beginning in October and continuing throughout the year, third-, fourth-, and fifth-grade teachers used the 90-minute morning period to present their students with practice tasks that were similar to those they faced on the assessment in the spring. The practice tasks were designed to incorporate and reinforce the curriculum. The administration and timing of test practice sessions reflected the conditions the students would experience in the actual testing situation. A teacher described a practice test that she just conducted with the fifth grade:

> I try to make [the practice tests] as real as possible.... I told the students there was an empty tank at the Baltimore aquarium and a deep sea fishing boat had gone out to find a new creature to put in the aquarium but they found two. So the students had to read these two short pieces, one about an archer fish that squirts water and another about a unicorn whale. They had to read them and highlight important information. Then they had to fill in a chart of basic information: how long they were, where they came from, and what they eat. Then they did a Venn diagram to compare and contrast the two creatures to help them decide which one might be easiest to keep. Finally, they wrote a letter to the aquarium staff making their recommendation.

An important feature of the practice task sessions is that students are provided the scoring tool (rubric) when they review the practice test results. Later in the school year, closer to test time, students construct their own scoring tools by breaking down the questions. A teacher who had assumed the role of testing co-ordinator explained: "We teach them how to break down the prompt and how to use that as a scoring tool. This is where some of the test-taking skills come in. For instance, they highlight all the verbs. I think some of these real easy test-taking skills have improved the test scores as well."

Teachers also emphasized the benefits of using scores from these practice tests to inform their instruction. After students took the practice tests, each teacher met with his or her instructional partner to score the tests. Through this process, the instructors gained a detailed picture of their students' strengths and weaknesses. Then, teachers held grade-level meetings in which they debriefed as a group, identifying the common areas in which their students still needed help. These insights were used to guide and refine instruction during the next weeks.

As was true of many other innovations at Spellman, the assessment practices were developed gradually. In this case, two instructional specialists came up with the idea of developing some of their tasks into a format that more closely resembled the state assessment tasks. They tried this out first with one grade and then through the years expanded the test practices to other grade levels. Again, success was achieved because the instructional specialists initially did extra work. One of the instructional specialists explained, "There were those of us who did the bulk of the planning or organizing. So, the teachers felt they could come to us. In the beginning we really handled everything and it was just a matter of them implementing it with their students." Today all classroom teachers work along with the specialists and the in-house testing coordinator to develop the practice tasks and scoring tools.

Inclusion

Teachers recounted a shift in their attitudes toward students; contrasting the predominant past belief that "only certain children were important," to the current feeling that "all children are important." The word *inclusion* peppers the speech of Spellman faculty. This orientation is demonstrated in Spellman policies and practices regarding students identified for special education and foreign language speakers. First, teachers and specialists emphasized their shared responsibility in teaching all students. The special education teacher said:

> This is the first school where I have had "performance task" people and that makes a lot of difference. In other schools once teachers know a child requires special education services, they just leave it to the special education teachers. Over here, everybody works with that child.

Another added, "From my perspective as a Spanish teacher, I know that special education students have various skill problems and I try to work with the special education teachers as well as the classroom teacher. I'm not unusual in this. Everybody does this."

During Liebes' tenure the time required to identify and refer students for special education services decreased from "years" to 4 or 5 months. Teachers attributed this improvement to Liebes' background in special education and her ability to "work the system." But here again, the benefits of small group teaching and team instruction were cited as critical factors in this change. A teacher reported:

> Dr. Liebes really encouraged people to look at their population and to start getting them into small groups. A lot of times, we did a lot with the special education teachers, or they would get to work during the Canady time with the children we had questions about. So when the children came up for evaluation, the special education teacher knew exactly what we were talking about. We didn't have to take 90 days playing games.

Teachers and parents described excellent outcomes with special education students. A new special education teacher recalled her impressions on arriving at the school 3 years ago. She stated, "I've seen the difference in how the students in special education perform compared to my other school. When I got here I saw some of the students' work. I thought, 'Why are you here? You're supposed to be in a regular classroom.'"

Staff also praised Liebes for her sound, research-based approach to students who were English language learners. Here again the principal was influenced by an approach to student grouping advocated by Robert Lynn Canady at a professional conference (see Canady & Riena, 1993). One teacher explained,

> She [Liebes] insisted that the ESOL children [children in the English for Speakers of Other Languages Program] work with high reading rather than low reading groups. This way they would get role models. Twenty percent of our population is ESOL. They're now taking the MSPAP and their scores keep going up.

A teacher explained how she worked with speakers of other languages in her classroom:

> We sit in what we call cooperative learning groups, so they are never by themselves, feeling like an oddball all day. As much as possible I try to group my students so those that have very limited English are in a group with someone of the same ethnicity, but who might be in his second or third year here at this school.

Building on Successes

A number of factors have helped Spellman sustain and build on its achievements. First, the school found that its students had made dramatic improvement in their state assessment results in 1995. This news came only 1 year after the school began many of the instructional reform strategies described previously. This news was motivating and validating for the administration and staff. Teachers began to see themselves as successful and unique in their approach to instruction. Janet Lopez, the current principal, explained, "Teachers felt they were doing something that was successful and that was different than other schools, and to me that was one of the keys in them getting better and better at what they're doing."

For Liebes, a main component of professional development was to encourage and support staff in making presentations at state and district conferences as well as to their colleagues within Spellman. Such experiences served to build staff capacity and fostered the establishment of a wide base of instructional leadership within the school. Indeed, Liebes asserted that her goal was to create a school where the success of the instructional program did not depend on any one individual or leader. As she said:

> We did have some key turnover of staff along the way. But things still continued to move along. That was my test. My test was that people could come and go, and even I could come and go, but that things would continue to improve and the school would remain strong. I wanted to create a process and a structure in an instructional program

that was people-proof in a way. You had good people, but if one cog left, it was okay. It would continue to roll along.

Now, with a change of principals this year and continued success at Spellman, there was even more evidence that Spellman had achieved its goal of building a broad base of leadership. In fact, when Lopez arrived at Spellman last summer she found a faculty that was remarkably self-sufficient and reflective. She underscored this by describing a letter that staff had written to her:

> On my desk was a letter that started, 'Dear Principal of Gladys Noon Spellman ...' On the last day of school the teachers knew Dr. Liebes wasn't coming back. They met and they made a list for whoever the principal would be. The list said these are the things we do very well, and these are the things that we need to work on. That is the nature of this staff. They consistently look for better ways to do things.

Lopez felt comfortable giving the staff the directive to "go ahead and keep on doing what you've been doing" because she had seen and recognized their ability to maintain and develop the instructional program. As a result, Lopez was able to devote extra attention to concerns about the school climate and community relations.

Changing the School Climate

Although student achievement has continued to improve each year since Liebes became principal at Spellman, there have been costs associated with what was perceived as her single-minded focus on academics. A parent shared this perspective, stating, "Liebes' whole agenda was to get test scores up. It was all she was about. And whatever it took to do that, she was going to get it done. And she did. Of course, many people were very unhappy about how that was accomplished."

Voices from many corners of the school community expressed the concern that high test scores were not enough; some important things had been lost or left out of the mix. Discipline, although slightly improved during Liebes's tenure, was still a problem and was cited by teachers as their primary concern at the end of the 1997–1998 school year. There was tension in the school. Faculty turnover was high. As one staff person explained, "We would have to look up daily to see how much the staff had changed." The once sizable and historically active group of school parents had dwindled significantly. For example, participation at PTA meetings had dropped to five members and no parents served on the School-Based Management Team last year.

In addition, some staff members noted that while gains had been made in the academic arena, more could be done to support students' emotional and character development. One staff member explained, "The 'please,' the 'thank you,' that's what we're missing. Our test scores are wonderful ... but if one can't deal with their own emotions about their day-to-day struggle, test scores don't mean a thing."

Principal Lopez came to Spellman in the fall of 1998 bringing a knowledge of Spellman's success and history due to her work in the school as a district-level community instructional specialist. On arriving at the school, she made it a priority to bring more calm and order to the campus and responded immediately to teachers' primary concern about discipline.

Lopez intentionally made herself visible in the halls and established a clear system for teacher duty stations during morning entry and afternoon dismissal. The school discipline plan, which had been developed several years ago, was re-established at the beginning of the school year and reinforced more consistently with a system of student tickets, fines, and incentives. Teachers, who were also involved in "reviving" the system, felt that the administrators supported them in enforcing the plan. In addition, all the students were reminded of their role in maintaining good behavior by a banner that flew at the end of all "fight-free" days. Just last year, in an effort to raise teacher morale, a new faculty member proposed a teachers' social committee. She and another veteran teacher took the lead in establishing this group, which hosts parties and breakfasts at teachers' homes.

During her 3 year tenure as vice principal, Regina Williams has taken the lead in developing programs that foster student citizenship. She has revamped the school safety patrol, initiated a student council, supported a teacher in establishing the SPARK program (Spellman Acts of Random Kindness), and created numerous other incentive-based student activities. Recently, responding to the students' need for after-school recreation, Williams announced try-outs for a coed basketball team. The response was overwhelming; more than 100 students filled the gym to compete for membership on the team.

Williams speaks proudly of the students' growing sense of responsibility. She relates this positive change to these opportunities and to the consistent modeling and guidance by staff. She shared a story of a sixth-grade student who had stopped to help a young child who was being chased by a dog. This student later told Williams, "I did that, because we are the leaders of the school and we have to help other people out."

Spellman staff recognize that these emotional supports and developmental opportunities enhance student performance. The school counselor provided students a measure of stability and a safe place to talk, He said, "I've been able to give kids that chance to say, 'I need to talk.'"

Changing the Relationships With Parents and Community

In her first 4 months as principal, Lopez made significant progress in restoring relationships with parents. They felt welcomed by her open-door policy. One parent shared her impressions:

> I came in August and introduced myself and my daughter to her [Lopez]. I didn't have a clue what she looked like. She came right out and introduced herself. Then she welcomed me into her office. In the past the door had always been closed, but this was very inviting. It was like you open your front door and say, 'Come into my living room and have a seat.' I was encouraged before school started that things were going to be more comfortable.

Parents have been reassured by the principal's presence in the hallways. Another parent explained: "Even being in the hallways there's a decided difference with Lopez. You see her in the hallways all the time. You see her in the hallways when the kids are coming to school. The kids know her. She knows them."

Parents have also noticed Lopez' commitment to improving school–parent communication. For instance she used Title I funds to have the school's automated phone service announce PTA meetings. Indeed, this simple act was quite effective in generating a remarkably large turnout. More than 70 parents attended the last PTA meeting.

CONCLUSIONS

During the past 5 years (1994 through 1998) administrators and faculty at Spellman have succeeded in raising student performance to levels that exceed their peers throughout the state. They have also managed to create a school environment in which all students are important, parents are welcome, and staff and faculty feel comfortable. These accomplishments have not always come easily. The Spellman staff has had to make, and weather, many significant changes in order to support the academic achievement of their students. These include, implementing an innovative block scheduling system to promote a school-wide focus on reading and language arts; shifting to a mode of authentic instruction that challenges students to solve real life problems using a range of interdisciplinary concepts and skills; regularly and systematically using data from student assessments to identify students' learning needs and to guide instruction; attending to the needs of all students, including speakers of languages other than English and students with disabilities; and working aggressively to ensure that parents feel welcome to visit and participate in their children's schooling.

Today the Spellman community awaits good news about their recent state assessment results. There is a sense of anticipation in the air, an awareness that years of hard work and difficult changes are coalescing to bring results. Academic achievement remains paramount at Spellman: it is a source of pride and motivation, and the predominant feature of the school culture. Nonetheless, the calmer halls, Lopez' open door, and the crowded gym all suggest that Spellman's definition of success has been expanding.

REFERENCES

Canady, R. L., & Rettig, M. D. (1995). The power of innovative scheduling. *Educational Leadership, 53,* 4–10.

Canady, R. L., & Riena, J. M. (1993). Parallel block scheduling: An alternative structure. *Principal, 72,* 26–29.

Maryland State Department of Education. (2001). School improvement in Maryland: Maryland school performance program. Internet. http//www.mdk12.rog/mspp/mspap/index.html. 3 January 2001.

III
Teacher Case Studies

12

Highly Accomplished Primary Grade Teachers in Effective Schools

Barbara M. Taylor
University of Minnesota/CIERA

INTRODUCTION

In the influential report, *Preventing Reading Failure in Young Children* (Snow, Burns, & Griffith, 1998) quality classroom instruction was singled out as the "single best weapon against reading failure." The National Reading Panel Report (2000) concluded that "appropriate teacher education does produce higher achievement in students." Much of the recent federal legislation pertaining to school reform and reading improvement such as the Comprehensive School Reform Act or the Reading Excellence Act stresses the importance of ongoing professional development for teachers to improve classroom reading instruction.

One way to enhance one's teaching skills is to learn from expert teachers (Morrow, Tracey, Woo, & Pressley, 1999; Pressley, Rankin, & Yokoi, 1996). To that end, two recent large scale studies have examined the characteristics of effective teachers of reading (Pressley et al., 2001; Taylor et al., 2000). Both studies found the following characteristics to be important: balanced reading

instruction, higher order thinking, small group instruction, and excellent classroom management.

In addition to the above characteristics, Pressley et al. found that in exemplary first-grade classrooms students were more engaged in reading and writing,
and teachers stressed the importance of reading for meaning and writing effectively. Additionally, teachers taught more literacy skills, often as applied to authentic reading and writing experiences, and encouraged students to use these
skills in a self-regulated manner.

In the Taylor et al. (chap. 1, this volume) study additional characteristics
that distinguished the most accomplished teachers from less accomplished
teachers included high pupil engagement and a teacher preference for coaching
children as they were attempting to perform or answer a question over engaging
students in recitation and telling them information. The teachers in the most
effective schools in this study were observed providing more literacy instruction
via small than whole groups and providing more time for independent reading
than teachers in the least effective schools.

Other recent research on effective teachers also has stressed the importance
of balanced instruction, higher order thinking, small group instruction, and effective classroom management (Designs for Change, 1998; Knapp, 1995; Morrow et al., 1999; Puma et al., 1997; Wharton-MacDonald, Pressley, &
Hampston, 1998.) However, with the current national emphasis on improving
classroom reading instruction, there is a need for additional work that goes beyond generalization and provides concrete examples of the teaching practices of
effective teachers of reading.

In addition to studying classroom practices through observations, expert
teachers can be interviewed to shed like on their perspectives and the conscious
decisions they make regarding their teaching (Wharton-MacDonald et al.,
(1998). Research on professional expertise has found that highly accomplished
professionals can articulate their understandings about what they do to be effective in their jobs. (Chi, Glaser, & Farr, 1988; Ericsson, & Smith, 1991).
Hence, the purpose of this chapter is to take a closer look at four of the most accomplished teachers in Grades 1 and 2 in the most effective schools from the
Taylor et al. study (chap. 1, this volume) to better understand the effective practices of these teachers. Across the four teachers, five components of effective
teaching emerged with a focus on (a) *how* these teachers organized their classroom for reading instruction and (b) their *beliefs* about effective reading instruction and how students learn to read. The five components included the
following: teaching with

- High expectations for student learning AND student behavior
- Teaching/coaching within instructional-level groups
- Enhancing literacy through authentic, engaging tasks
- Fostering independent learning (and learners)
- Establishing effective classroom management routines

THE TEACHERS

The four teachers included in this analysis shared two common characteristics: (a) they scored high on the scale of accomplishment used in the Taylor et al. (chap. 1, this volume) study, and (b) they taught in one of the most effective schools in that study. Lora Archer (all names are pseudonyms), a first-grade teacher, taught in a bilingual school in a small town in which 55 % of students received subsidized lunch. Cecelia Huxley, a first/second-grade teacher, and Heather Farmer, a second-grade teacher, taught in a suburban school in which 38% of the students received subsidized lunch. Matthew Thompson , a second-grade teacher, taught in an urban school in which 90% of the students received subsidized lunch. Each teacher was observed five times for 1 hour during their reading instruction period. Each teacher completed a 30-minute interview in the spring and two weekly logs of their instructional activities and grouping patterns during their literacy block.

The logs, observations, and interviews were analyzed for information on several aspects of their instruction: time spent in small and whole group instruction, time spent in independent reading, preferred interaction style, and student time on task. All four teachers revealed a preference for small group instruction in reading. In the examination of the interviews, several other similarities across the four teachers emerged pertaining to expectations for students' learning and behavior, the use of authentic and engaging tasks, the development of independent learners, and the use of effective classroom management routines.

Common Practices Across the Four Expert Teachers

Through the comments in their interviews and their actions in the classroom, the four teachers were especially cogent about the need to develop independent learners. To help children succeed, the teachers made sure they set up authentic, engaging tasks, especially for children who were working on their own, and had classroom routines that were student- as opposed to teacher-directed and that maximized instructional time. Trends across the five components of effective instruction (high expectations, small group instruction, authentic tasks, independent learns, and effective classroom management routines) are reported below.

Teaching With High Expectations for Student Learning and Student Behavior

Many people mention the importance of high expectations for students, but all four of these highly accomplished teachers were able to talk about their high expectations for their students in detail and with conviction. Comments addressed both student learning and student behavior.

When asked about her expectations for her students' learning, Lora said they were high. Perhaps more important, however, she helped her students create high expectations for themselves. "I expect that all of my students can and will learn. I expect them to become serious about their learning."

Cecelia said that she subscribed to the Pygmalion effect reporting, "You get what you expect." She also took seriously her role in helping children succeed in reading. She believed that all children could learn to read, but that it was her responsibility as a teacher to ensure that this happened. She also expected her students to have high expectations for themselves, to work hard, to stay on task, to do their best. Cecelia, however, did not just set up the ground rules and let whatever happened happen. The class had regular discussions about when these elements (e.g., high expectations, hard work, staying on task, doing one's best) were and were not present in their classroom.

When asked about her expectations, Heather acknowledged they were high, "perhaps too high." "I am always trying to stretch my students' thinking and explain to them why I do that." For example during one observation, she was circulating and individually reviewing her students' writing in response to a question about a story. She explained that in order to show her they had really been thinking, she wanted them to give good reasons to the question, "Why was first grade harder for Saruna (newly arrived from China) than other kids," or she had them rewrite.

Matthew, when asked about expectations, was sensitive to his students' need for success. "My expectations have to be just challenging enough. If they're too high, the children will feel defeated. They need to know they can reach it with a stretch."

Teaching/Coaching in Instructional-Level Groups

As reported earlier, all four teachers spent more time working with students in small than in whole group instruction for reading. The groups were at students' instructional level and were flexible, with students moving between groups based on need. Teachers talked about their ability to give more individualized attention in small groups. The observations revealed that they used this time to coach children in strategies to foster independence.

Lora, a master at both whole- and small-group instruction, used small-group time to coach students in word recognition and in use of strategies for independence. Across her observations, coaching was observed in 75% of the segments observed; as opposed to engaging in recitation (25% of the segments) or telling students information (17% of the segments). As a coach she paid attention to the wait time she gave children. Like Matthew, she also was sensitive to her students' feelings of success. "Children need to feel successful 90% of the time."

Cecelia believed that small, flexible, instructional-level groups were key to helping all students learn to read. "In the past I did more whole group instruction, but the research is clear. Children need to be coached at their instructional level." Cecelia was observed coaching in 74% of the segments (vs. engaging students in recitation in 26% of the segments observed and telling in 39% of the segments observed). She was frequently observed teaching word recognition through coaching during reading.

Both Cecelia and Lora regularly reviewed word-recognition strategies for figuring out words prior to reading and discussed specific strategies that were used to figure out words after reading. They praised students for using strategies, and when needed, provided general prompts (e.g., "What could you try?") or specific prompts (e.g., "What part do you see?" Yes, -ick , now add the "st") to help students succeed in decoding unknown words.

Heather provided 47 minutes a day of small group instruction as opposed to 33 minutes a day of whole group instruction. Her preferred interaction style was coaching (observed during 55% of the observation segments) versus recitation (18% of the segments) and telling children information (39% of the segments). Heather provided frequent coaching during story discussions by getting students to elaborate on and clarify their thinking. For example, when discussing the story about the new student from China, Heather asked, "What could you do to make a new student feel comfortable in our classroom?" One student said, "Be nice to her," and Heather prompted with, "How could you be nice? Give me one way."

Matthew spent much more time teaching in small groups (93 minutes per day) than in whole group (21 minutes per day). Matthew depended on both coaching (observed in 53% of the segments) and recitation (observed in 59% of the observation segments) in his interactions with his students. He was observed telling children information only 19% of the segments. Matthew also asked many follow-up questions to get children to elaborate on their thinking about the story they read together. When discussing a story about a boy who had fallen in the river, he asked how the boy must have felt. The children didn't answer. The teacher went to the text, "It says right here he was trembling. What does that mean?" The children didn't answer so the teacher asked, "How would you feel? Yes, scared. So how does the boy feel?"

Enhancing Literacy Through Authentic, Engaging Learning Activities

All four teachers had their students engaged in authentic, engaging literacy activities, with a heavy emphasis on reading books and on writing about what they read. This was true for teacher-directed instruction as well as independent seatwork activities.

The students in Lora's first-grade classroom averaged 38 minutes a day in independent reading and 8 minutes a day in writing in response to what they had read as opposed to 3 minutes a day in other independent activities. Lora provided her students with many audiences to read and write for themselves, volunteers, partners. She also tried to play off of children's interests. She wanted lots of "fun stuff" in her room to encourage kids to read for the love of reading. She wanted books to be of good literary quality so the children could relate to them. She also taught with an omnipresent sense of purpose related to the tasks she had her students engage in. She said she continually asked herself, "Is this authentic? Is it relevant? Will kids be able to use it?"

Cecelia reported that she stressed independent reading in her classroom, citing her belief that children become "better readers by reading." She had many leveled books in her room to entice her students to read, and read they did, averaging 32 minutes a day of independent reading. For other independent activities, children also wrote answers to comprehension questions or wrote about what they had read (16 minutes a day). During the classroom observations, students at their seats were always busy reading and writing, with her students coded as on task 95% of the time on average.

The students in Heather's class averaged 19 minutes a day in independent treading, 16 minutes a day in writing, 4 minutes a day in other seatwork activities. Although she did use a basal, Heather said she tried to go beyond it to appeal to things kids liked. She made a conscious effort to teach to their strengths and their interests. She tried to make her lessons relevant to them and talked to them about "these are areas in life that you'll need reading and writing." Heather's students did a lot of work in groups, which they found engaging, and did not do the same thing over and over, also something that helped to keep them engaged. Her students were on task 95% of the time on average.

Matthew's students spent an average of 30 minutes a day reading independently and 24 minutes a day of writing in response to what they had read. They also worked at independent work stations such as the computer or a math practice table. Although Matthew spent a lot of time with students in small instructional-level groups, his students, including those at their seats or at stations, were on task 94% of the time during our observations on average.

Fostering Independent Learners

All four teachers discussed the importance of developing independent learners. They did not want to do things for their students that their students could learn to do for themselves. And while they provided ample coaching, they also provided gradual release of responsibility to the students for their own learning.

To help her students become independent, Lora said that she was process-oriented. By focusing on *how* to do things, she felt her students learned how to depend on themselves rather than their teacher. To help students understand how to do various activities in the classroom, Lora did a lot of demonstrations or think-alouds about thinking and learning. She focused on metacognitive strategies. She also said that she taught her kids how to be teachers who helped one another. Lora and her students talked about how to use other resources when they got stuck.

Cecelia regularly reviewed strategies for independence with her students. In her room were charts that listed the steps to follow to perform a strategy such as "What to do if you get stuck on a word? Ask yourself: Does it look right? Sound right? Make sense?"

To foster independence, Heather talked about the technique of responding to students' queries with a question. "I try to phrase things they ask me about as a question so they become responsible for themselves and don't see me as always telling them the answer or what to do. Part of independence is problem-solving." For example, when a student comes up, unclear about an assignment, and says, "What should I do?" Heather would say, "Can you tell me what you think you should be doing?"

When asked about his vision for his classroom, Matthew said his goal "was to develop 20 independent workers who didn't need 'policing'." He carefully reviewed with students the different things they were to do at their seats while he was working with other groups, and what things they could do when they finished. For example during one observation he reviewed independent tasks,

"You should be reading your story, writing in your journal,, finishing Daily Oral Language. Then when you are done, you can work on math triangles or you can work at the computer, or you can read a book for fun." He also worked at helping his students learn to engage in self-evaluation. On the day of one observation he reported, "Today I asked each student to jot down what they were strongest in and what they needed to work on until the end of the year."

Establishing Classroom Management Routines

All four teachers discussed how they worked hard with the students to establish and stick to classroom routines. They mentioned the first 3 weeks or so of the school year as a crucial time for setting up these classroom routines.

1. Lora reported that she had two rules for her students to follow: "You can do what ever you want as long as it doesn't cause a problem for someone else" (including the teacher).
2. "I won't solve any problem you have a chance of solving for yourself."

She demonstrated and helped her students practice problem-solving methods so they could be self-directive.

Cecelia reported that her approach to classroom management was to be positive but with clear, firm expectations. She worked hard with her students in the fall with modeling, talking, and role playing—to help them learn how to work hard and show respect. They had discussions when things started to slip.

Heather explained that at the beginning of the year her class set up rights and responsibilities together. "I hold them to these and remind them. I am kind and gentle, but at the same time, I take a no nonsense approach to classroom behavior." Heather also sent a communication sheet home everyday. "If a student had a bad day, I let the parent know." But she also sent home positive comments on a regular basis. "It takes only 15 minutes to write 1 or 2 positive comments about all of my students."

During the first 3 weeks of school in the fall, Matthew and his students focused on the rules and routines of the classroom, reviewing them frequently. He also had a time in the afternoon where students shared compliments and concerns. He had set up this time so the children could solve their problems or grievances without his intervention. He started the session by complimenting them on things that happened during the day, and the students took turns complimenting each other. Then they discussed any complaints that came up that day.

Sharing Expertise

Today, there is a national emphasis on improving classroom instruction to increase students' reading achievement. With that goal in mind, this chapter has provided brief cases from four expert teachers about their approaches to establishing productive classroom environments for effective primary-grade reading instruction, and more important, about helping their students become independent learners within the classroom environments they have established.

In the final analysis, the reading of cases is probably not as helpful as learning first-hand from experts. In the CIERA School Change Project (Taylor & Pearson, 2001), which is a follow-up to our analyses of best practices, we are encouraging teachers to embrace the notion of sharing expertise in various aspects of reading instruction within their own buildings. Every building has one or more teachers who excel in one element of effective teaching or another. For example, one teacher may excel in classroom management, another in the use of coaching strategies, another in providing authentic, engaging tasks for independent work, and so on. To reach the goal of all students reading well in our elementary schools, teachers within buildings will need to learn together and share expertise to become the best teachers of reading they can be.

REFERENCES

Chi, M. T. H., Glaser, R., & Farr, M. J. (1988). *The nature of expertise.* Hillsdale, NJ: Lawrence Erlbaum Associates.

Designs for Change. (1998). *Practices of schools with substantially improved reading achievement.* (Chicago Public Schools) www. dfc1. org/summary/report. htm

Ericsson, K. A., & Smith, J. (Eds.). (1991). *Toward a general theory of expertise.* Cambridge, UK: Cambridge University Press.

Knapp, M. S. (1995). *Teaching for meaning in high-poverty classrooms.* New York: Teachers College.

Morrow, L. M., Tracey, D., Woo, D., & Pressley, M. (1999). Characteristics of exemplary first-grade literacy instruction. *The Reading Teacher, 52,* 462–476.

National Reading Panel. (2000). *Teaching children to read: An evidence-based assessment of the scientific research literature on reading and its implications for reading instruction.* Washington, DC: NICHD.

Pressley, M., Rankin, J., & Yokoi, L. (1996). A survey of the instructional practices of outstanding primary-level literacy teachers. *Elementary School Journal, 96,* 363–384.

Pressley, M., Wharton-McDonald, R., Allington, R., Block, C. C., Morrow, L., Tracey, D., Baker, K., Brooks, G., Cronin, J., Nelson, E., & Woo, D. (2001). A study of effective first-grade literacy instruction. *Scientific studies of reading, 5,* 35–58.

Puma, M. J., Karweit, N., Price, C., Ricciuiti, A., Thompson, W., & Vaden-Kiernan, M. (1997). *Prospects: Final report on student outcomes.* Washington, DC: U.S. Department of Education, Planning and Evaluation Services.

Snow, C., Burns, S., & Griffin, P. (1998). *Preventing reading difficulties in young children: Report of the Committee on the Prevention of Reading Difficulties in Young Children*. Washington, DC: National Academy.

Taylor, B. M., Pearson, P. D., Clark, K., & Walpole, S. (2000). Effective schools and accomplished teachers: Lessons about primary grade reading instruction in high-poverty schools. *The Elementary School Journal, 101*, 121–165.

Taylor, B. M., & Pearson, P. D. (2001). The CIERA School Change Project: Translating research on effective reading instruction and school reform into practice in high-poverty elementary schools. In C. M. Rolher (Ed.), *Learning to teach reading: Setting the research agenda*. Newark, DE: International Reading Association.

Wharton-McDonald, R., Pressley, M., & Hampston, J. (1998). Outstanding literacy instruction in first grade: Teacher practices and student achievement. *Elementary School Journal, 99*, 101–128.

13

A Case Study of Exemplary Practice in Fourth Grade

Lesley Mandel Morrow
with
Gregory Wamsley,
Kimberly Duhammel
Nancy Fittipaldi
Rutgers University

Investigations into exemplary practices in literacy development attempt to capture the many dimensions of expert performance to describe teaching excellence. With this type of research, investigators examine real-life situations in which many variables are successfully integrated. When observing and discussing literacy instruction, it seems that effective teachers are aware of the elements of their teaching because their teaching is a result of careful decisions about what works in their classrooms and what doesn't work (Chi, Glaser, & Farr, 1988; Ericsson & Smith, 1991; Hoffmann, 1992).

The results of the research on effective and exemplary teaching have many similarities (Morrow, Tracey, Woo, & Pressley, 1999; Pressley, Rankin, & Yokoi, 1996; Ruddell & Ruddell, 1995; and Taylor, Pearson, Clark, & Walpole, 1999). A list combining some findings about effective and exemplary teachers and their classroom practices includes the following characteristics:

1. Varied teaching strategies are used to motivate literacy learning.
2. Teachers create excitement about what is being taught.
3. High expectations for student accomplishment exist.
4. Instruction is adjusted to meet individual needs of students.
5. Guidance is provided in structured lessons for acquisition of skills such as phonics and strategy instruction in comprehension.
6. Positive feedback is provided for students.
7. Children are treated with respect.
8. Opportunities are provided for children to practice skills learned.
9. Classrooms are rich literacy environments with accessible materials.
10. Varied structures for instruction are utilized including whole-group, small-group, and one-on-one settings with the teacher.
11. Opportunities exist for children to work independent of the teacher either alone or in social-cooperative groups.
12. Emphasis is placed on careful organization and management of strategies and structures for optimal literacy development.

SELECTION OF EXEMPLARY TEACHERS FOR THIS CASE STUDY

We observed four exemplary fourth-grade teachers from three different school districts within one state. Supervisors and administrators in these districts were asked to choose exemplary teachers using criteria we set forth. We asked that supervisors select teachers who were successful in educating large proportions of their students to be readers and writers. We also asked them to check the achievement records, test performances, reading levels, and writing abilities of the students belonging to the nominated teachers over the last 5 years. We asked supervisors to identify teachers who could articulate a sound teaching philosophy that matched their practices in the classroom. Supervisors and administrators were asked to consider student enthusiasm and engagement regarding reading and writing in these classrooms. Finally, we asked that supervisors have first-hand observations of the nominated teachers and that they select individuals who were frequently referred to with positive comments from other teachers, administrators, parents, and students. Supervisors were asked to rate their own confidence in their evaluations of the teachers by indicating whether they were absolutely certain and highly confident in their opinion.

Data was gathered on the teachers through 25 hours of first-hand observation of the language-arts instruction and through ongoing dialogue with the teachers. During visits information was gathered about literacy instruction such as when language-arts activities occur in the school day, the nature of word study instruction, approaches to comprehension development, assessment strategies, the nature of social interactions during literacy instruction, effective teaching characteristics, student engagement, classroom management techniques, and the physical environment. Teachers were interviewed concerning their philosophies about teaching literacy and practices they chose to implement. At the beginning of the study, each of the observers coded his or her own data by classifying it into categories that emerged during the observed instruction. After every observer had been in each classroom three times, we compared classifications. Together we developed a set of categories that reflected a consensus of the observers about the characteristics of the classrooms. The categories continued to be refined as observations continued. Teacher interviews at the beginning and end of the study were used as data in the coding. The categories that emerged were types of reading and writing that occurred, content area connections, classroom environments, and classroom management.

In writing this case study I have chosen to create a synthesis of what was observed from all of the classrooms rather than reporting on each one. I speak of the teachers, however, as if they were one.

An Introduction to the Teacher

For the purposes of this case study I call the teacher Diana Roberts. Her school is considered middle-class in an urban/suburban setting and her students are ethnically diverse. She has been teaching in the same district for 7 years and has been a teacher for 13 years. Ms. Roberts had taught in the primary grades; only in the last five years has she taught in fourth grade. Her class for this academic year was an inclusion class; out of 21 students, 7 are classified. Ethnically, the students are representative of the community. There are 11 Caucasian children, 4 Asian, 4 Indian, 1 African American and 1 Hispanic child. There were 10 girls and 11 boys in the class. For approximately half the day there is a special education teacher in the room with Ms. Roberts. This teacher provides some direct instruction but acts more as a support teacher.

Teaching Philosophy

When asked to talk about her philosophy of literacy instruction Ms. Roberts said the following:

> "Our classroom encourages students to function as a community of learners. The atmosphere is one of acceptance and encourages children to be academic risk takers. Their ideas are shared and valued. Students are given and accept responsibility for their learning and contribute as members of a family. In our classroom all students are viewed as capable learners who progress at their own developmental level. As much as possible I use extended uninterrupted periods to devote to the language arts daily. Lit-

eracy instruction in my classroom involves the integration of the languages arts and into content area themes. Skills need to be taught within a meaningful context and in an explicit manner when necessary. Therefore I meet in small groups based on the specific needs of children. I know that all of this will work for my students only if there is a positive and supportive attitude in my classroom to motivate children to learn."

Classroom Environment

On entering Ms. Roberts's classroom, it becomes immediately apparent how much value she places on literacy. There is an area of the room labeled "Book Nook" with an easy chair set on a rectangle of carpet surrounded by numerous floor cushions and large bean bag chairs where students can settle in to read. Right next to the lounge chair is a book cart with a variety of books from which Ms. Roberts or the students can choose. The cart has many types of books, from light reading like *Squids Will Be Squids: Fresh Morals, Beastly Fabels* (Scieszka, 1998), to the more serious *When I Was Young in the Mountains* (Rylant, 1982). A "Word Wall" made of felt, containing different parts of speech, takes up a good portion of the wall in the "Book Nook." Posters of popular books such as *Harry Potter and the Chamber of Secrets* (Rowling, 1998) cover the remainder of the wall. Next to them are book reviews written by students for the class to read. There are posters that promote good reading hanging on the walls, file cabinets, and bookcases. Chart paper with publishing guidelines (prewriting, drafting, revising, editing and publishing) and definitions of literary terms, such as *onomatopoeia* and *alliteration* hang from a rope strung diagonally across the room. Around the periphery of the blackboard are varied smaller posters of other literary terms, the class rules, and the bell schedule. On the back wall of the room is another "Word Wall" that displays the most commonly misspelled words.

There are many bookcases filled with hundreds of books of all levels and genres. They are labeled according to type, such as *Reference, Fiction, Nonfiction,* and *Science.* In the nonfiction section there are books on fossils, dinosaurs, planets, and stars, to name a few. The reference section contains a set of encyclopedias, several dictionaries, and other resources. Prominently displayed on an open shelf is a book rack with "Personal Choice" books. Popular books by well-known authors of children's literature are part of the collection that includes *Nighty Nightmare* (Howe, 1987), *Tales of a Fourth Grade Nothing* (Blume, 1972), and *Runaway Ralph* (Cleary, 1970). They share space with trendy series books like the *Sweet Valley Kids* (Pascal, 1989–1998) books and R. L. Stine's *Goosebumps* series (1990–1999).

The remaining open shelves under the windows contain books grouped by specific type, current science topics being studied next to biographies of presidents used for social studies. The science topic being studied is natural disasters.

There are 20 books on the shelf about volcanoes, tidal waves, hurricanes, and earthquakes. Most titles are single copies but several have multiple copies such as *The Magic School Bus Inside a Hurricane* (Cole & Degen, 1995) and *Earthquakes* (Simon, 1991). On the wall near the shelf of science books is a corkboard with posters of the earth, weather patterns, earthquakes, hurricanes, and other similar topics.

Easels and bulletin boards are placed throughout the room with various topics. On one easel is a list with the titles "Said is Dead" on the top half and "Fun is Done" on the bottom half of the paper. Beneath the respective headings are synonyms students wrote on the chart that can be used in their written work instead of the overused "said" and "fun." Some of the alternative synonyms suggested by students for the word "said" are: replied, uttered, and bellowed. Synonyms for "fun" are: outstanding, excellent, and extraordinary.

The students' desks are grouped in clusters of four or five. In addition, there are several tables where individuals or groups can work. Ms. Roberts's desk is toward the back of the room. Near her desk are a computer and printer. Although there is only one computer in the classroom there is access to the Internet. Students use the Internet frequently for research and the computer is used a great deal for word processing.

Ms. Roberts encourages students to use this rich literacy environment she has created that accommodates the differences in reading ability in her classroom from first-grade to ninth-grade reading level. The first time I walked into the classroom it was apparent that every student was totally engaged in reading and using the environment during a "Sustained Silent Reading" (SSR) period. Students were reading sitting at their desks, others at tables, and some were found under the tables.

Classroom Management

Good management is evident in exemplary classrooms and Ms. Roberts sets an exceptional example. "I hammer home my expectations for the classroom routines in the first 2 weeks of school," says Ms. Roberts. "After that the class is able to function on its own." Occasionally she needs to remind the students to stay on task or to quiet down but it is just that, a reminder that has an immediate effect. On occasion Ms. Roberts redirects students simply by asking, "What are you supposed to be doing?" That question is indicative of her teaching style. She doesn't give the students the answers. They have to figure them out themselves with her support and encouragement. At one point Ms. Roberts stated that a 1-2-3 count to get the attention of the class is a lifesaver. She never had to count past two, however, during the observation period, before getting the attention of her students.

In the beginning of the school year, Ms. Roberts lays out four basic rules that she requires of the class:

1. Do things the FIRST time you are asked.
2. Respect the rights and property of others. Keep hands, feet, and other objects to yourself.
3. Have all appropriate materials at your desk and be ready to work when class begins.
4. Raise your hand and wait to be called on before you speak.

Without a lengthy list of "musts," the students seem to be able to focus in on the few key items that make the class run smoothly. Ms. Roberts has set up the classroom environment to facilitate good behavior and the daily activities.

Classroom materials are accessible throughout the room. Paper is kept by the chalkboard, as are boxes and cans of frequently used items, such as rulers and erasers. Desks are arranged in groups of four. The students at each cluster constitute a "team." This allows Ms. Roberts to work with small groups without constantly having to create them, greatly reducing time spent on getting organized. She dismisses students by teams, which speeds up the process. To encourage good behavior Ms. Roberts awards points to these teams. For example, after she has told the class to get ready for dismissal, Ms. Roberts never repeats herself. All she has to say is, "Ten points for this team, good job for getting ready so quickly." That gets the attention of the other students who scramble to be the next team ready. For the second team Ms. Roberts will award five points, then three. Points for good behavior result in rewards. Approximately once a month, Ms. Roberts changes the teams to allow the students to work with different classmates and try new roles within the new groups.

Planning is part of classroom management and, again, this is an area in which Ms. Roberts is always prepared with the materials, resources, and background information for daily lessons. She posts the schedule on the chalkboard so students know what is coming up and can be prepared for it. Consequently, students are usually ready for and productively engaged in interesting activities, which leaves little time to misbehave. If the class is working well, Ms. Roberts will stretch out the time for a given activity. Conversely, if something is not working, she will shift gears and move on to the next activity. A key to keeping students engaged is to make sure they know what to do when they finish with an assignment. Ms. Roberts has several projects that students can work on when they have free time. For example, they can write in their journals and they are always encouraged to read.

Types of Reading Experiences

Ms. Roberts provides for *Sustained, Silent Reading* (SSR) daily. During this time students can read whatever material they choose. During SSR, students are in various spots around the room, some alone, some with a partner, and some in a group. Students can also be found curled up on the rug reading in the "Book Nook." It is quiet during this period because students are quite absorbed. Occasionally a student will read something they want to share, in which case a whispered conversation might take place. *Scary Stories 3: More Tales to Chill Your Bones* (Schwartz, 1991), *I Was a Sixth Grade Alien* (Coville, 1989), *The Giving Tree* (Silverstein, 1964), and, quite frequently, one of the *Harry Potter* books (Rowling, 1999), are some examples of books that students choose to read during SSR.

Students read for a half hour and, when the time is up, they reluctantly return to their desks to begin the next activity. After SSR, Ms. Roberts has some students give a brief plug for the books they are reading. When one of the students said she was reading *P.S. Longer Letter Later* (Danzinger & Martin, 1998), Ms. Roberts bellowed, "LOVE THAT BOOK!!," while pounding her hand on a table to punctuate each word. She followed up with, "That is a MUST-READ!" There wasn't a student in the class, myself included, who didn't want to read that book next.

The atmosphere in her class is very much in keeping with her overall teaching philosophy—"My students have to read a lot and they learn to love to it. It's my job to give them the strategies to get inside the book. It's about the joy of having a book in your hands and pulling meaning from it." Every summer before school starts Ms. Roberts writes a letter to her new students in which she says: "If you don't love to read now, you will by the time you leave fourth grade."

A second type of reading is *guided reading groups*, which Ms. Roberts calls Book Clubs. The Book Clubs meet in different sections of the room. The students are grouped based on similar reading needs. Ms. Roberts sets up the Book Clubs based on what skills need to be taught for a particular group of students. Within the small guided reading group or Book Club, students are taught new skills and old ones are reinforced.

A third type of reading is *Literature Circles*. Here students select their own books for reading. These groups meet to engage in discussions about books. Ms. Roberts enjoys helping her students use this strategy. Students are well-trained by the teacher about the different roles to play as a member of the literature circle. In fact, for at least the first 2 months, the teacher models literature circle behaviors with the whole group, which includes aspects of good book discussions. After reading a book students make up questions and think of thoughtful comments that they write on post-its and place on the page that the questions and comments refer to. When they meet for discussion the post-its facilitate the discussion. Eventually students are able to make up their own discussion questions and carry out their literature circle discussions without the teacher.

The fourth type of reading that is common in this classroom is *partner reading*. Students are asked to pair up to read for pleasure to enhance content area reading. Pairs review books they have read and list the most important facts. To do this task, students must skim, analyze, and summarize the text together.

A fifth type of reading that occurs is *reading a book aloud*. In Books Clubs students often take turns reading books aloud that Ms. Roberts has already read to the class. Ms. Roberts rationale for her read-alouds is to expose students to as many incredible authors as possible.

Any reading activity that Ms. Roberts engages her students in is highly interactive. She is constantly questioning and encouraging students to dig deeper into the text. The following dialogue is from a whole class discussion of *The Big Wave* (Buck, 1947):

DR: Alright, let's find out what transpired in the reading.
Student: (Recaps the last chapter of the book.)
DR: Why does he want to be Jiya's father?
Student: Because Jiya doesn't have a family anymore.
DR: Why is Kino's father willing to give up Jiya? That's an incredible sacrifice, don't you think?
Student: It's like he's giving away his son.
DR: Yeah! Why do you think he would do that? What can Old Gentleman give Jiya that his father can't?

Ms. Roberts' questions don't allow students to merely retell the text. She asks "Why?" and "What do you think about that?" questions that force the students to reflect on what they are reading. The following dialogue occurred while Ms. Roberts was reading *Knights of the Kitchen Table* (Scieszka, 1991) aloud to the whole class.

DR: (After reading a few pages in the first chapter.) Crazy so far, huh? Now, does anyone have any questions about it?

Student: How did they get back in time?

DR: Excellent question. They never said what happened, did they? What else?

Student: How are they going to get out?

Student: Is the knight good or bad? (Students laugh.)

DR: That's actually a good question. Usually the black knight is the bad guy, but it hasn't really said, so we don't know yet. He could turn out to be good. Those are all good questions.

Even when she is reading aloud to the students, Ms. Roberts will stop and ask questions to get the students thinking. She often has the students assume the role of the teacher. They make predictions about the plot and ask questions that they would like answered from the text. The dialogue she encourages flows quickly and fluidly, always centered on the topic. If the focus starts to wander, Ms. Roberts will redirect the conversation to keep it on track and productive.

Types of Writing Experiences

In Ms. Roberts's class the types of writing in which the students engage are as diverse as the reading experiences. Often the day will start with the students writing a response in their Literature Response Log (LRL) to questions posted on the chalkboard, such as this one: "What surprising things happened in the last chapter we read in *The Big Wave* (Buck, 1947)? What do you think about it?"

After finishing the book *The Big Wave* (Buck, 1947), each student in a team had to choose a section of the story and write a synopsis that included the most pertinent events in the plot. Ms. Roberts had the students use a writing process approach that included brainstorming in their team, drafting, conferencing, editing, and revising.

Journals are used for students to write a response to assignments from Book Clubs or other readings. Generally the questions are highly thought provoking. Ms. Roberts reads the journals to check for comprehension of the text, as well as to assess the general thought patterns of the students. The following dialogue is an example of an assignment that was given during a Book Club meeting.

DR: What is aloneness? Why is Dewey feeling this?

Student: (Begins to answer.)

DR: No, listen, I want you to write in your journals. Wrap your head around this aloneness thing. Is Dewey alone?

Student: No, he's got his grandma there.

DR: So what does it mean he's alone? Why then, at that point in the
            story? He's not really alone. I know I've felt that before, though.
            Have you?

Students: (Several affirmatives.)

DR: It's interesting that you answered the way you did. Consider why
            you answered like that. Now get your thoughts on paper. This is
            pretty personal stuff, but later I'd like to ask if anyone is comfort-
            able sharing.

Ms. Roberts also encourages the students to keep a private journal to record
thoughts, emotions, and events. To show the students what a journal looks like,
Ms. Roberts keeps a copy of *Amelia's Notebook* (Moss, 1995). This is a mock
journal that provides a good base for students to start their own. One student
showed me hers and explained its use to me. She said, "It's a notebook and you
can put anything you want like private thoughts and pictures and stuff in there.
No one can look at it unless you let them."

Her journal was decorated with photographs and drawings, both on the
cover and inside. She showed me several photographs of her family and a postcard that a friend had sent to her from the Netherlands. Although the student
did not share any written sections, as she was flipping through the journal to
find the postcard, it was possible to see that there were numerous entries, some
brief and others quite lengthy.

Ms. Roberts has Writing Workshop in which students are given a brief writing
skill lesson and then time to write using the skill being taught. The minilessons are
based on the needs of individual students and the whole class. Lessons are varied
from learning about writing structural elements of a story to using new forms of
punctuation. The following minilesson was presented in preparation to write an
expository composition entitled "My Three Favorite Things."

DR: When you are getting ready to write your expository composition
            about your three favorite things, what will you write first?

Student: An opening.

DR: Right, we also call it the introduction and what comes at the end?

Student: The closing.

DR: Yes, and what about the middle?

Student: The paragraph on your favorite things.

DR: Good. Now are you going to have just one paragraph or what?

Student: You will have three paragraphs.

DR: Totally, because you have three things, right? You would probably
            do a whole paragraph on each thing. It's like a sandwich. There is

the bread on the top and bottom, that's the introduction and closing. The meat is in the middle, which are the middle paragraphs for
the piece. We would probably have to have meat, cheese, and let-
tuce because we have three paragraphs. Do you see how it looks
like a sandwich?

Ms. Roberts drew a sandwich on the whiteboard and labeled the top piece of
bread the *introduction*, the bottom, the *closing*, and the three layers of food in between, the *middle*. The class went on to discuss the content for each section.
The whole minilesson took less than 10 minutes.

Students are encouraged to "publish" written work for the bulletin board or
the classroom library. The class also publishes a student newsletter regularly.

Ms. Roberts engages her students in writing poetry often. Over the course of
several months, the students wrote different types of poems as they were introduced: haiku, cinquains, sonnets, and so on. The students kept the poems and,
when they had a collection, they typed them on the computer, published them,
and bound them in an anthology. Taking the project a step further, Ms. Roberts
turned the classroom into a coffeehouse for a day and had the students experience the beatnik scene complete with hot chocolate instead of cappuccino, jazz
music in the background, and poetry readings by students. Other types of writing in the classroom include summarizing texts, writing advertisements, and
writing scripts.

Cross-Curricular Content

Ms. Roberts ties every subject she teaches to literacy through thematic instruction and the use of the language arts.

Using themes allows me to incorporate meaning into the curriculum. In my
fourth-grade Social Studies curriculum we study Japan. I can make that really interesting and meaningful for my students by selecting a piece of literature to read such as *The
Big Wave* (Buck, 1947) which discusses a small Japanese fishing society that ties in so
well with our work in Social Studies.

Ms. Roberts incorporates writing into Math assignments. In one Math activity,
students were asked to conduct a survey by teams. Each team had to write out a
survey topic, administer the survey, and record the answers of their classmates.
After analyzing the results, the teams had to provide a written synopsis of what
they found and present it orally to the rest of the class. For another assignment,
Ms. Roberts required the students to write 10 math riddles. Each had to consist
of three statements and one question. The example she used was, "I have three
corners. I have three sides. I am a polygon. What am I?"

Social Studies incorporates a strong writing component. Whenever the class reads and discusses a text or Ms. Roberts teaches a lesson, the students take notes in a special Social Studies notebook. In one Social Studies activity, the students had to compare and contrast the lives of two different women they read about who lived in approximately the same time period but in different countries. They created graphic organizers and word webs with Ms. Roberts's guidance and filled the various categories with similarities and differences that they were able to draw from the two texts.

Teachable Moments

Ms. Roberts is always teaching and rarely lets a teachable moment slip by. During a discussion of famous people, for example, one student brought up Tiger Woods and his placement on the "money list." Realizing that the student did not have a clear understanding of what a "money list" was, Ms. Roberts pursued the topic.

DR: Mike, I was also reading about Tiger Woods and that he just won. The check he received for $297,000 put him at 40th on the "money list."

DR: That's interesting, he's a really great player. Do you know what a "money list" is?

Student: (Hesitates.)

DR: Can anyone help Mike with that?

Student: Isn't it the money that he won?

DR: That's part of it, but it's more than just what a person wins once. For a tournament, the first place winner might get $297,000, but doesn't the second place winner also get something?

Students: Yes.

DR: Does second place get as much money?

Student: No, they get less.

DR: How about third place?

Student: They also get something, but it's less.

DR: Right, so someone might win first place twice and second place three times and get money each time. Over the course of a year, the total amount of money that a person wins determines where he goes on the "money list." The number one on the money list has won the most money so far. Where can you find out who's on the "money list" and the rankings?

Students: In the newspaper.

DR: Where in the newspaper?
Student: The sports section.
DR: OK, Mike, your job tonight is to look through the newspaper and
           find the "money list" and bring it in and give us a report.

This example is typical of the way that Ms. Roberts handles such moments. The
general framework of such episodes is similar. Ms. Roberts notices a weakness
and probes to see the extent of the students' understanding. She asks questions,
explains when necessary, but nearly always makes the students do the work.
This takes just a few minutes out of the main discussion but allows her to add
new vocabulary and understanding about the issue. This sort of exchange is
common.

A Day in Fourth Grade

Figure 13.1 provides an outline of a fourth-grade day. The following discusses
the events in the day and highlights the language arts activities.
      Because departmentalization begins in most fourth-grade classrooms, the
language arts block is often spread throughout the day. A day is described that
illustrates how Ms. Roberts fits in important literacy instruction.
      When the students enter the room in the morning, there is a "Do Now" mes-
sage written on the chalkboard. This morning the teacher has asked the students to use important vocabulary words in sentences in their journals. She has
also written "Guten Morgen!" to expose the children to world languages. While
students are responding, some are also carrying out morning housekeeping
items described by several charts posted around the room.
      After about 15 minutes, students have completed the "Do Now." Ms. Rob-
erts reviews the sentences. One boy struggles with one of the sentences and the
teacher helps him complete the task. The class listens patiently as Ms. Roberts
provides clues and support to lead him to success. When he finally arrives at a
correct response, there is sincere praise from the teacher.
      Social Studies is the next subject Ms. Roberts teaches. The class is nearing
the end of a unit on the regions of the United States. Ms. Roberts finds ample
opportunities to gear her lesson toward literacy development. During the first
part, the teacher has the students listen to a new song called *Fifty Nifty United
States* and follow along on song sheets that have several spelling mistakes on
them. During the second part, she uses a popular picture book, *Brown Bear,
Brown Bear, What Do You See?* (Martin, 1983), as the source for the format for a
project. The students are asked to construct their own books using a particular
state as the topic. The teacher shows a finished product to the class. She reads

When Children Enter School
- Classroom Jobs
- Journal Writing (free-writing, skill practice)
- Buddy Reading

Social Studies (Students stay with their teacher)

Read Aloud and Snack
- Teacher leads prereading discussion
- During reading teacher models fluent reading

Math (Students go to another Teacher)

Lunch

Sustained Silent Reading
- Students choose any reading material
- They may read alone or with two or three children together
- They may go anywhere in the room

Language Arts Block
- Independent Activities Reviewed
  - a. Literature Circles
  - b. Journal Writing
  - c. Thematic Literacy Activities
  - d. Word Study Challenge Activities
- Guided Reading
  - e. Discuss a book that has been read with a skill such as understanding a character's point of view
  - f. Prepare for a new book with vocabulary development and background information about the story.
  - g. After previewing the book, have student read silently with a purpose presented by the teacher
  - h. Teacher keeps records of students' progress as he/she asks different children to read aloud privately

Writing Workshop
- Mini Lesson
- Independent Writing
- Conference with the Teacher

Meeting at the End of the Day
- Important activities of the day are reviewed
- Homework reminders
- Coming Attractions for Tomorrow

FIG. 13.1   A Day in the Fourth Grade.

from her book, "Ohio, Ohio, what do you see? I see Columbus shining at me." After going over the directions, with explicit information given regarding each aspect of the project, Ms. Roberts checks for understanding. Then the class goes off to work, either with partners or alone. At the conclusion of the time allotted for Social Studies, the work in progress is collected. The unfinished books are placed in a basket to read again at a later time.

Next on the agenda is a story to read aloud while students have a snack. Rebecca has brought a book from home to share with the class. It's title, *Calico the Wonder Horse: The Saga of Stewy Stinker* (Burton, 1996), is announced by the teacher. Before beginning to read, Ms. Roberts leads a brief discussion. She asks, "What's a saga? Why do you think it could be called 'Stewy Stinker'?"

They discuss the title and make predictions based on the cover illustration. As the story is read, they stop often to discuss issues prompted by the text. At the mention of the badlands as the setting for the story, the teacher asks the class if they know where they are. In this fashion, she ties the story to the content area of Social Studies, in which they have been learning about the regions of the United States. When the children are unable to provide the correct answer to the "badlands" question, instead of giving the answer to them, the teacher replies, "I'll leave it as a challenge. See if you can get it."

During the course of the story, Ms. Roberts encourages active engagement with the text. The questions she asks during the read-aloud provide a model for the questions she hopes children will ask themselves as they read independently. She asks them to predict, seek clarification of story elements, use context clues to understand vocabulary, and guides them to make connections between the text and their own prior knowledge. She reads with expression, and uses accents to portray the characters in the story. She makes the reading an interactive experience during which the modeling of effective comprehension strategies underscores the enjoyment one can derive from reading quality literature.

Next, the children collect their materials and proceed to their assigned math classes. In this school, the children are grouped according to ability for mathematics. After math, the children return to their regular classrooms and proceed to lunch and recess.

After lunch the remainder of the day is devoted to language arts instruction. When the students come back to their classrooms they begin the independent, self-selected reading activity of Sustained, Silent Reading (SSR). With the lights dim, a calm comes over the classroom. Children, with reading material in hand, make themselves comfortable. Some break off into pairs and threes, while others remain alone. Some choose to read in the hallway or outside the room's doorway, if weather permits.

Reading materials include various genres. Two girls take turns reading from a humorous book, *Wayside School is Falling Down* (Sachar, 1989). Another pair read a tall tale from the Newberry Medal winner, *Maniac Magee* (Spinelli, 1990). One boy reads from a Spanish language novel. A pair of boys share *The Complete Star Wars Trilogy Scrapbook: An Out of This World Guide to Star Wars, The Empire Strikes Back and Return of the Jedi* (Vaz, 1997). All around the room, students engage in reading various other works of children's literature, including *Mrs. Frisby and the Rats of NIHM* (O'Brien, 1974), *The Encyclopedia of the Dog* (Fogle, 1995), and *The BFG* (Dahl, 1982).

After 15 minutes Ms. Roberts switches on the lights and asks the children to put their books away. She then chooses a student volunteer to write and administer the dictation, a weekly assessment for the skills of spelling, capitalization, punctuation, and listening. Each sentence, often referring to subject matter from the Social Studies or Science curriculum, is read aloud three times. The sentences on this day are:

1. We're living in the United States, so we're Americans.
2. "Trenton is our state capitol," thought Sara.

When students finish writing, the class reviews the correct format of the sentences, which is recorded on the board.

The class moves into the "Reading" segment of the block. Ms. Roberts has guided reading groups or direct instruction of skills. The teacher forms the guided reading groups based on student needs and ability. While she works with these groups the rest of the children meet for Literature Circles.

The five Literature Circle groups consist of children who all chose the same book to read. They use post-its to question and comment about parts of the book they are having trouble with or want to discuss. The Literature Circle Groups move together with activities for independent work displayed in a pocket chart. The types of activities they participate in are: reading books independently, discussion of the books lead by a student, journal writing related to the book, or an art activity related to a book.

Ms. Roberts calls five students in the class for a guided reading lesson. They sit together at a round table. An easel is set up in front of them with a "Point of View" chart posted on it. First, they discuss this literary element in another book they have all read before. Then, they direct their attention to the novel they are currently reading, *Shiloh* (Naylor, 1992). This is a book for their guided reading selected by the teacher. Ms. Roberts models filling in the chart with one character but eventually withdraws to allow the group to work on its own.

After the reading groups meet, the teacher visits the Literature Circles' meetings. The first group she visits is reading *Mrs. Frisby and the Rats of NIHM* (O'Brien, 1974). Students are sharing their journal responses to the book. Afterward, they address discussion questions provided by the teacher about the book.

After about 45 minutes, the teacher asks the class to clean up their reading materials. She then begins her writing workshop. Ms. Roberts begins with a whole-class minilesson about the characteristics of nonfiction news articles. The students have been publishing this type of writing in a class newsletter. Together, they compile a chart entitled "Amazing Articles." The class is given the remaining time to work on their own newsletter articles

SUMMARY

Our goal was to describe characteristics identified as exemplary teaching of the language arts. This observational approach allowed us to answer the question, "What is the nature of exemplary literacy instruction?" The classrooms observed were happy and productive places for fourth graders. Teachers built a community for learning that included cooperation, respect, and strong expectations for work and achievement. These characteristics are found in the research on effective teaching.

The classrooms were rich with materials for children to have choices, challenges, social interaction, and success. There was exposure to literature and commercially prepared reading instructional materials. The classrooms had provisions for whole group, small group, and one-to-one instruction. The teachers provided varied experiences for skill development and to motivate reading and writing. Children had routines and rules to follow. They were taught to be independent, self-directed learners. Teaching was explicit, direct, and systematic. It included construction of meaning, problem solving, and taking advantage of spontaneous teachable moments.

Teachers were consistent in their management techniques, therefore children knew what was expected of them and consequently carried out work that needed to be done. The affective quality in the rooms was exemplary, teachers were warm and caring. Children were treated with respect and therefore respected the teacher and each other. The day flowed smoothly, from one activity to the next. The routines were consistent and therefore easy for the children to follow. The activities were varied to keep the children engaged. There was a lot to do, but it could be accomplished.

The children in these classrooms experienced literacy in many different forms. There was shared reading and writing, independent reading and writing, social-collaborative reading and writing with peers, and guided reading and writing for skill development. Children took part in oral and silent reading and writing and minilessons modeled by teachers. Content area themes were integrated into reading and writing experiences to bring meaning to skill development. Children had opportunities to perform or share reading and writing accomplishments.

The teachers created these excellent classrooms based on their experience and a philosophy about how children learn. The teachers were in schools that supported and expected outstanding performance from them. The atmosphere in their buildings was professional with frequent staff development sessions. Teachers had grade-level meetings often to share and plan and the principals played an important role in supporting curriculum development. Teachers took the initiative to expand their knowledge by obtaining Masters Degrees in education, attending professional conferences, and reading professional materials.

It became apparent that to be an excellent teacher you need to develop your own philosophy about the teaching of literacy and be able to create programs that illustrate your beliefs. What we observed occurred as a result of careful thought, planning, experience, and expertise. Exemplary teaching involves a great deal of knowledge and effort. The instruction in literacy involved skill development taught explicitly, in the context of authentic literature, as a part of writing, and with content connections. These exemplary teachers used both direct instruction and constructivism. Their explicit teaching of skills was a good start for constructivist activities and the constructivist activities permitted consolidation and elaboration of skills.

REFERENCES

Chi, M. T. H., Glaser, R., & Farr, M. J. (Eds.). (1988). *The nature of expertise.* Hillside, NJ: Lawrence Erlbaum Associates.

Ericsson, K. S., & Smith, J. (Eds.). (1991). *Toward a general theory of expertise.* Cambridge, England: Cambridge University Press.

Hoffman, R. R. (1992). *The psychology of expertise: Cognitive research and empirical.* New York: Springer-Verlag.

Morrow, L. M., Tracey, D., Woo, D., & Pressley, M. (1999). Characteristics of exemplary first grade instruction. *The Reading Teacher, 52,* 462–476.

Pressley, M., Rankin, J., & Yokoi, L. (1996). A survey of the instructional practices of outstanding primary-level literacy teachers. *Elementary School Journal, 96,* 363–384.

Ruddell, R., & Ruddell, M. R. (1995). *Teaching children to read and write: Becoming an influential teacher.* Boston, MA: Allyn & Bacon.

Taylor, B. M., Pearson, P. D., Clark, K. F., Walpole, S. (1999). *Beating the odds in teaching all children to read.* CIERA Report #2-006. University of Michigan, Ann Arbor: Center for the Improvement of Early Reading Achievement.

CHILDREN'S LITERATURE REFERENCES

Blume, J. (1972). *Tales of a 4th Grade Nothing.* New York: Dell Publishing Company.

Buck, P. S. (1947). *The Big Wave.* New York: Harper-Collins Publishers.

Burton, V. L. (1996). *Calico the Wonder Horse: The Saga of Stewy Stinker.* Boston, MA: Houghton Mifflin Company.

Cleary, B. (1970). *Runaway Ralph.* New York: Morrow Junior Books.

Cole, J., & Degen, B. (1995). *The Magic School Bus Inside a Hurricane.* New York: Scholastic Inc.

Coville, B. (1989). *I Was a Sixth Grade Alien.* New York: Pocket Books.

Dahl, R. (1982). *The BFG.* New York: Scholastic, Inc.

Danzinger, P., & Martin, A. M. (1998). *P.S. Longer Letter Later.* New York: Scholastic, Inc.

Fogle, B. (1995). *The Encyclopedia of the Dog.* Washington, DC: Dorling-Kindersley.

Howe, J. (1987). *Nighty Nightmare.* New York: Macmillian Publishing Company.

Martin, B. (1983). *Brown Bear, Brown Bear, What Do You See?* New York: Henry Holt & Company, Inc.

Moss, M. (1995). *Amelia's Notebook.* Berkeley, California: Tricycle Press.

Naylor, P. R. (1992). *Shiloh.* New York: Maxwell Macmillian International Publishing Group.

O'Brien, R. C. (1974). *Mrs. Frisby and the Rats of NIHM.* New York: Macmillian Publishers.

Pascal, F. (1989–1998). *Sweet Valley Kids* Series. New York: Bantam Dell Publishing..

Rowling, J. K. (1998). *Harry Potter and the Sorcerer's Stone.* New York: Scholastic Press.

Rowling, J. K. (1998). *Harry Potter and the Chamber of Secrets.* New York: Scholastic Press.

Rowling, J. K. (1999). *Harry Potter and the Prisoner of Azkaban.* New York: Scholastic Press.

Rylant, C. (1982). *When I Was Young in the Mountains.* New York: Penguin Putnam Inc.

Sachar, L. (1989). *Wayside School Is Falling Down.* New York: Avon Books, Inc.

Schwartz, A. (1991). *Scary Stories 3: More Tales To Chill Your Bones: Collected from Folklore.* New York: Harper-Collins Publishers.

Scieszka, J. (1998). *Squids Will Be Squids: Fresh Morals, Beastly Fables.* New York: Penguin Putnam Inc.

Scieszka, J. (1991). *The Knights of the Kitchen Table.* New York: Penguin Books.

Silverstein, S. (1964). *The Giving Tree.* USA: Harper-Collins Publishers.

Simon, S. (1991). *Earthquakes.* Morrow: New York.

Spinelli, J. (1990). *Maniac Magee.* New York: Scholastic Books, Inc.

Stine, R. L. (1990–1999). *Goosebumps* Series. New York: Scholastic Inc.

Vaz, M. C. (1997). *The Complete Star Wars Trilogy Scrapbook: An Out of This World Guide to Star Wars, The Empire Strikes Back, and Return of the Jedi.* New York: Scholastic Inc.

14

Scientific Literacy and Diverse Learners: Supporting the Acquisition of Disciplinary Ways of Knowing in Inclusion Classrooms[1]

Carol Sue Englert
Michigan State University

KaiLonnie Dunsmore
State University of New York at Albany

One of the challenges facing teachers is to teach children how to do, think, read, and write in scientific ways (Gaskins & Guthrie, 1994). This includes

[1]This research was part of a larger project "The Development and Evaluation of an Early Intervenion Program for Nonreaders and Nonwriters," funded by a grant from the Office of Special Education Programs (No. H023C50089) of the U.S. Department of Education. This research was also supported by the Center for the Improvement of Early Reading Achievement, funded by the Office of Educational Research and Improvement. The opinions expressed in this article do not necessarily reflect the position, policy, or endorsement of the U.S. Department of Education.

309

teaching the use of reading and writing as tools to learn, as well as searching for and recording information, using textbooks, tradebooks, illustrations, and taking notes (Gaskins & Guthrie, 1994). The complexity of meeting this challenge increases as the gap widens between the reading and writing abilities of their students, especially in the case of students with disabilities who are included for content area instruction.

The Literacy Environments for Accelerated Progress (LEAP) Project was designed to address the need for literacy curricula that would provide *access* to the general education curriculum and enhance the *participation* of students with disabilities. We recognized that children with disabilities may be overlooked or marginalized in general education classrooms, and, therefore, we intentionally designed activities to develop their social, literate, and cognitive abilities within the content areas of the general education curriculum. In contrast to a prevailing belief that facility in reading and writing is prerequisite to successful content area performance, we adopted the position that content area instruction is a fruitful medium for supporting literacy development, starting in the early grades when students might be considered emergent readers and writers.

The literacy activities of the LEAP Project were designed through a collaboration between university researchers and classroom teachers in elementary (Grades K through 5) classrooms in an urban school district. The LEAP curricular model reflected an effort to provide systematic instruction in strategies involving decoding and constructing meaning from print as well as in composing whole texts across a range of literary and expository genres. Additionally, a rich literacy environment was created where students engaged in reading and writing tasks for a variety of purposes and with many audiences in mind (students, teachers, other classrooms parents, community). The LEAP curriculum was intentionally based on an apprenticeship model of learning where knowledge and skills were modeled and made available through scaffolded participation for the appropriation and use of all students (Englert & Mariage, 1996). Quantitative data from the project suggested a statistically significant gain in reading and writing abilities of students in LEAP versus control classrooms (Gover & Englert, 2000). In this chapter, however, we focus not on the statistical evidence in support of the efficacy of the program, but rather on the ways in which teachers apprenticed children into scientific forms of reading and writing. We examine the case of two teachers, Mrs. Hart and Ms. Johnson, coteachers in a kindergarten through second-grade inclusion classroom. Their case illustrates the pedagogical process and the nature of inclusive teaching that allowed special education to participate fully and competently in the general education curriculum. Analyses of the discourse and practices during the two teachers' unit on fish ecology will be used to demonstrate the ways in which teachers in LEAP classrooms constructed classroom learning communities that facilitated the acquisition of scientific ways of knowing and doing literacy for *all* their students.

There were five principles associated with an apprenticeship approach that framed the design of the LEAP literacy activities. First and foremost, a cognitive apprenticeship was initiated by teachers as they intellectualized mental functions through modeling, thinking aloud, prompting, questioning, and coaching (Englert & Mariage, 1996). Second, the apprenticeship process was developed through the creation of participation structures that transferred increasing responsibility to students for performing these functions. Through their participation in these collaborative arrangements with teachers and students, students worked at the outer edges of their competence while receiving the social mediation and support that enhanced their mastery of the discourse and higher psychological processes associated with literacy. Third, the apprenticeship model required the full participation of students in the entire cognitive process in the situated context of its use (Vygotsky, 1978). Not being able to read and write in conventional ways was not constructed as a barrier or disability that precluded participation in literate practices (Baynham, 1995; Englert, Mariage, Garmon, & Tarrant, 1998), which meant that teachers had to find ways for all students to become active players and contributors in the curricular practices and processes of the discipline. Fourth, the apprenticeship model required that supports or scaffolds be used to bridge the gap between the child's actual developmental level and that required for independent performance. Teachers sought to scaffold reading and writing performance by modeling and providing access to semantic webs, diagrams, picture books, tradebooks, notes, mnemonic techniques, diagrams, and prompts (Wertsch, 1995). The fifth principle that framed the project emphasized students' participation in a community of practice, which is characterized by a set of shared practices, conventions, behaviors, values, beliefs and viewpoints (Roth, 1998). Wenger (1998) suggested that practice "exists because people are engaged in actions whose meanings they negotiate with one another. In this sense, practice does not reside in books or in tools, though it may involve all kinds of artifacts. Practice resides in a community of people and the relations of mutual engagement ..." (p. 73).

THEMATIC UNITS IN THE LEAP CURRICULUM

The expository texts of the content area curriculum often pose some of the greatest challenges to young readers and writers because it is presumed that reading and writing proficiency proceeds full participation in inquiry-based literacy activities. The LEAP thematic units, informed by the aforementioned principles, were designed to apprentice students in the genres and discourse of the academic discipline. Teachers provided an explicit explanation of what expository texts are for (social functions), how information is organized (text structure, taxonomies), and the way the text should be written to speak to the reader (lexico-grammatical features; Cope & Kalantzis, 1993; Kamberelis, 1999). Such a genre approach involved being explicit about the way language works to make meaning (Cope & Kalantzis, 1993, p. 1), including how experience is reconstituted into written language structures that entail particular kinds of structures, words, taxonomies, conventions, and practices (Halliday & Martin, 1993). In addition, four aspects of scientific discourse were incorporated within the grounded instructional framework to support the efforts of young readers and writers to read and construct expository texts, including: (1) the alignment of curriculum with everyday knowledge, (2) teacher modeling of specialized language and social practices, (3) the construction of representational systems that make visible the meaning and organization of ideas, and (4) the participation of teachers and students in a community of practice.

1. Aligning the Curriculum With Everyday Knowledge and Discourse

Knowledge in a discipline is rooted in everyday experience and discourse, which is transformed into scientific associations. Scientific understandings begin with child-centered language and experiences (Roth, 1998), which are used as resources to develop new abstractions and tools for observing, talking, investigating, and recording the world in ways that are reflective of the disciplinary structures that guide inquiry and sense making (Cope & Kalantzis, 1993; Daniels, 1996).

Everyday knowledge constituted a starting point for the LEAP curricular practices in Mrs. Hart and Ms. Johnson's K through 2 multiage inclusion classroom. Thematic units were launched by inviting class members to share what they knew about particular topics (i.e., fish ecology and biology). As students generated ideas (e.g., "fish breathe under water," "fish are slimy to protect their skin," "people eat fish"), the teachers recorded their ideas as notes on chart paper. The emphasis on children's oral language and experiences yielded a rich array of ideas and data that were unfettered by formal standards of correctness. Furthermore, all students could participate, and the frequent rereading of the notes as the teachers pointed to each word promoted sight word recognition, while communicating the complementary processes of reading and writing as cultural tools in a learning-to-learn process.

The conversations provided a fertile ground for introducing the nature of the inquiry and dialogic process. This occurred, for instance, when a student named Becky offered an idea ("fish are slimy and wet") that was questioned by another student ("Why are fish slimy and wet?"). Becky was positioned to defend her opinion, saying "I know that fish are slimy because they need to protect their skin." She attempted to further validate her opinion by explaining that she had fish at home. When the class displayed uncertainty about the meaning and accuracy of Becky's information, Ms. Hart used this occasion to draw attention to the ways in which the research process where "we observe things, read books, informational articles and talk to other people can be used to connect to, confirm, or contradict what we think we know from our experience." Mrs. Hart commented, "Right now we are just making a list of things we *think* we know. We can *verify* this when we do our research. When we watch videos or talk to experts and if we find out things are not true we can just cross it off our list. Here's the things we *think* we know about fish. What we are going to do over the next 3 to 4 weeks is to *verify* this is correct."

This example illustrated how teachers and students in LEAP used their everyday language as a cognitive resource and basis for asking questions (Christie, 1993; Lee & Smagorinsky, 2000). Children often have a difficult time asking questions about experience, explaining their opinions, or offering support, even in domains familiar to them (Herrenkohl, Palincsar, DeWater, & Kawasaki, 1999). School curricula, on the other hand, often ignore the informal or tacit knowledge that students bring and the kind that they will need to function expertly (Scardamalia & Bereiter, 1994). This is particularly problematic for students with learning disabilities, for whom knowledge transfer, questioning and self-monitoring is a pervasive difficulty (Deshler, Ellis, & Lenz, 1996; Wong, Wong, & Blenkisop, 1989; Wong, Wong, Perry, & Sawatsky, 1986). In LEAP classrooms, however, children were positioned to check each other's ideas, to challenge the claims put forth by others, and to initiate conversations about how one might think about specific phenomena. They were given opportunities "to cultivate a stance with respect to the world of experience that might be characterized as a disposition to engage in systematic inquiry about the questions or topics in which one is interested" (Wells, 2000, p. 63). Through their participation in these face-to-face interactions, students were given opportunities to align themselves with particular ideas and the content of the academic work, while being socialized into particular ways of speaking, questioning, doing, and thinking (Herrenkohl et al., 1999). Simultaneously, Mrs. Hart was able to use this occasion to introduce the language of inquiry by connecting their everyday discourse, experiences, and questions to the larger set of social practices and discourses associated with academic inquiry (e.g., the language and processes of gathering information and verification).

In this manner, the brainstorming session in Hart and Johnson's classroom emphasized the involvement of students in constructing and reconstructing prior knowledge in ways that might lead to personal engagement and ownership (Barnes, 1993), as well as in situating their knowledge within the discourse and practices characteristic of scientific communities (Lemke, 1982). Literacy development was promoted within the brainstorming and exploratory activity inasmuch as students were engaged in the frequent rereading of the class notes as Ms. Hart pointed to each word. The re-presentation of spoken ideas in the form of written notes also enabled Mrs. Hart, Ms Johnson and other LEAP teachers to model four aspects of written language in an inquiry process: (a) the complementarity between mental and written representations, (b) the role of notes in a process where mind extends beyond the skin to include written notations and questions, (c) the connections between the oral and printed alphabetic forms, and (d) the functions of reading and writing in a process of reciprocal activity involving the doing of inquiry activities (Halliday & Martin, 1993). For students with disabilities, the generation of written notes provided a critical record and artifact of classroom talk and actions that provided greater access to the language, discourse, words, and academic concepts of the units. Many students could read their own ideas represented on the class artifacts when other written texts proved too difficult to read, and students with disabilities often consulted the class notes to scaffold their own performance when they engaged in other thematically related reading and writing activities.

2. Modeling Specialized Language and Practices

A second aspect of scientific discourse arises from the ways in which scientific concepts and specialized vocabularies (ways-of-talking) and practices (ways-of-doing) are explicitly developed and employed during the research, synthesis, and writing aspects of the unit. Scientific concepts are those that are often learned through explicit instruction, and that are formed on the basis of systematic, organized, and hierarchical thinking (Artiles, Trent, Hoffman-Kipp, & Lopez-Torres, 2000; Daniels, 1996; Vygotsky, 1978). Inquiry in LEAP classrooms was used to further students' knowledge of thematic content through an exploration of the formal, scientific meanings and perspectives available to them through other formal sources, such as written documents, artifacts, experiments, or experts.

The juxtaposition of experiential and formal texts was designed to deepen students' conceptual knowledge while helping them discover the characteristic features, meanings, and functions of different informants in the inquiry process (Morgan, 1997). This entailed a process of "knowledge building," where their background knowledge was added to the information of others, either through participation in speech events, direct observations, or through the medium of print (Wells, 2000).

During the fish unit, for example, Mrs. Hart and Ms. Johnson's students visited a pet store that contained the largest aquarium in town and the widest selection of fish. Students were given an opportunity to interview the storeowner and employees who sold and cared for the fish. In preparation for the visit, the students generated a list of interview questions. One of the teachers recorded their questions onto slips of paper that were then cut apart. Each child chose or received questions from the overall list, and they practiced reading their questions to their teachers and peers in order to perform competently and confidently on the day of their field trip to the store. Ms. Hart gave the students clipboards to which she had attached a slip of paper with their interview questions. The two teachers expected all students to fully participate in the interview and to use the clipboard to take notes, as they apprenticed their students in an inquiry process encompassing the practices of generating questions, gathering information, taking notes, and sharing their knowledge with others.

As students conducted the interview, the answers provided by the owner and employees helped children make sense of the world in a tangible way through the concrete demonstrations and explanations that expanded the students' everyday knowledge. The teachers again expected each child to assume responsibility for mining the experience for information that could be transformed into personal representations and notes. Students later used these notes to communicate their findings and understandings to the rest of the class in community sharing time. Throughout the inquiry process, therefore, writing served as a cultural tool that mediated children's talk and actions, which they then used to mediate the talk and behavior of others (e.g., the storeowner and teacher; Minick, 1996). Students made decisions about what questions they asked, what information should be recorded in their own personal notes, how the notes were recorded (e.g., symbolic, pictoral), and later, what was shared and recorded in the class notes. The dialectical process associated with the generation of the written artifacts also allowed participants "to disambiguate the meanings of lexical terms" and experiences (Roth & McGinn, 1998, p. 43), facilitating the flow of cognitive resources (information, concepts) among the multiple actors (children, store owner, teacher) and serving as an interface between their multiple social worlds (Roth & McGinn, 1998). Each set of interactions was represented and transformed in symbolic forms that could be expressed, manipulated, and communicated to others.

Later, Mrs. Hart and Ms. Johnson engaged students in a discussion in which the practices associated with gathering and sharing cognitive resources were re-enacted, as well, on a more distant plane as they apprenticed the students into ways of interrogating the written rather than oral texts of experts and authorities. However, they laid the foundation for this subsequent inquiry in the context of face-to-face social interactions in genuine and meaningful contexts (i.e., the visit, the interviews, and oral discussions). Thus, students learned to engage in the language practices of inquiry in the context of conversational formats where they could make their meanings available to others, repair misconceptions, and develop theories of understanding in a social situation that afforded them ongoing feedback, interpretations, and explanation.

LEAP teachers, such as Mrs. Hart and Ms. Johnson, deepened students' participation in an ever-widening cycle of inquiry by involving students in observing the phenomenon themselves, as well as by reading and synthesizing what others had said or written about the phenomenon. During all of the inquiry activities, students learned to read, interpret, construct, and communicate expository ideas using a number of representational formats. To engage students in inquiry at the level of direct observation and data collection, the two teachers provided live goldfish in bowls that they placed in the middle of a table shared by four students. Students observed, took notes, drew pictures, and made diagrams of the live fish. These diagrams were shared in the small groups, and studied in relation to the diagrams produced by scientific authors. This helped students learn the distinction and relationship between real-world phenomena and the various ways of modeling or re-presenting them as mental images, written documents, spoken words, artifacts, and so on, a distinct kind of knowing and knowledge in scientific practice (Roth, 1998). In this manner, students were introduced to speaking, reading, and writing tools in the situated context of their practical use to accomplish social purposes related to the thematic unit. Simultaneously, this activity legitimated the multiple literacies that students possessed that contributed to proficient disciplinary performance (e.g., drawing, observing, recording, discussing, making illustrations, taking notes, comparing, using reference materials; Palincsar, Magnusson, Collins, & Cutter, 2001), furthering the participation of students with disabilities.

The evolving knowledge of students was linked to the intellectual work and resources of the broader scientific community. Students in the classroom watched videotapes, read informational books and articles, did Internet searches, and went on field trips. What especially distinguished the most effective teachers on the project was the extent to which they were successful in modeling and thinking aloud about the reading and writing strategies for culling information from texts, identifying important information, employing text features, notetaking, summarizing ideas and textual sources, taking notes, and so forth. Effective teachers made the curriculum artifacts, strategies, and practices transparent, that is, open to public inspection, comment, and understanding.

A good example of these teaching processes occurred in the fish unit as teachers prepared their students to take notes from reference texts about fish and ocean ecology. Although the teachers initially guided the notetaking process, they transferred increasing responsibility to students for generating their own notes and inscriptions using informational texts. This required that they model ways-of-thinking and practices with respect to both reading and writing informational texts. The transcript shown here demonstrates the nature of discourse that preceded the notetaking activity as the two teachers apprenticed their first- and second-grade students in the processes for reading and notetaking using informational books.

Ms. Johnson:	Here is a book about fish. Let's go through and pretend we don't know how to read. Let's just look at pictures. What could you tell me about this?
Shayla:	There's a fish.
Ms. Johnson:	Anything else?
Shayla:	It has a gill.
Ms. Johnson:	If I wanted to take some notes about the things I'm learning from this picture, and I had a piece of paper that said notes right on it, *what could I do to help me remember this picture?* What could I write? Remember when we took notes about butterflies, we wrote ideas we got from pictures? *Do you get any ideas from looking at this picture.*
Damon:	Fish have gills
Ms. Johnson:	What would I write?
Damon:	Fish have gills (dictating while teacher writes)
Ms. Johnson:	*What kind of fish is that? I might want to remember that.*
Ayla:	It's a goldfish.
Ms. Johnson:	[looks at the book] Oh! *Underneath this picture is a word.* So I can look right here and write the word. Is there space on the page for me to write this note? (Yes) What should I write?
Clement:	It's a goldfish

Ms. Johnson:	*How would I write goldfish?* [A looong Pause] /G/.... /O/ [produces sound]
Ayla:	D.... FSH
Ms. Johnson:	/I/
Ayla and others:	I
Ms. Johnson:	So I wrote goldfish and gills. Anything else about this picture I could take notes about?
Ms. Johnson:	Let's look at this next book and see the next picture. Oh! This book has lots of pictures. Nearly one every page and the title of this book is fish, so we know everything about this book is about fish.
Ms. Johnson:	*If I go back and reread my notes,* I have goldfish. Gills. Fins. What I'm going to let you do is you will take your own notes with the person sitting next to you. When you are both looking at your book, you will both have a piece of paper in front of you. But we only have one book to look at so you will have to share the book. Where would be a good spot to keep the book? Between us? So we can both look at the book. Can we talk about how to talk to each other before you take notes?
Ms. Johnson:	So, if I said, "Oh! I don't know what this is (points to an object in the picture). [Turns to Mrs. Hart]"
Mrs. Hart:	Hmmm.... It looks like a seahorse.
Ms. Johnson:	We could write sea horse. /S/ Seahorse starts with 's'. I noticed something, too. Do you think this is how you spell seahorse (points to word below the picture)? Lots of time when you come across pictures of books, they have the name right under this picture. So you can doublecheck. I see this starts with 's' I hear a 's' and there's the letter 's', and I hear an 's at the end. So I think this is the word seahorse. I can copy this.

In this example, Ms. Johnson modeled how to read captions and pictures, as well as made visible the qualities of the written genre. She modeled how to use invented spelling and how to spell by sounds. She modeled how to examine pictures for details, and how to confirm those details using the captions and the printed text. By presenting a variety of reading and notetaking strategies (captions, copying, spelling by sounds, pictures), she apprenticed her students in the language and tools of readers and writers, spanning the range of literacy abilities. She also deconstructed all the potential barriers (e.g., writing and reading conventionally) that might deny children access from participating in the activity, while simultaneously building their literacy skills in the situated context of the content area domain, including (a) phonemic awareness and word recognition skills, (b) a functional approach to teaching phonics and spelling-by-sounds; and (c) word recognition through repeated reading (combined with finger-pointing) of all class artifacts, including class maps, written drafts, and so on, to develop students' recognition and word consciousness abilities.

Recognizing that many of their students might be burdened by the reading and writing demands, the teachers added another layer of social scaffolding. They both modeled and provided occasions for talk and social interactions by allowing their students to work with a partner to take notes from the reference books. The notetaking session that followed was lively and filled with discussion, excitement, and conversations about discoveries. The partners prompted deeper conversations about the trade books and pictures, as each participant made different observations and brought their own enthusiasm to the inquiry process. Simultaneously, the two teachers wandered around the room to assist the partners and to harvest the cognitive strategies that might be valuable to the rest of the class. For example, when one special education student, Jeremiah, drew a diagram, the teachers held up the diagram and asked him to describe his notetaking strategy to the rest of the class. When a second special education student, Damon, used a picture to record information about his topic, the teachers again stopped the class to listen to his strategy for generating notes. When a third pair of students, Drew and Mahla, went back to the source material because they could not read their notes, Ms. Johnson shared with the class how they were verifying their information. In this manner, the teachers provided a form of apprenticeship by harvesting and disseminating the tools, practices, discourses and strategies of their students. These strategies were made public and accessible so that others in the community might borrow and appropriate the practices for their own use (Roth, 1998). Students found that their rich store of cognitive resources and their assumption of intellectual roles were encouraged, privileged and disseminated in the classroom.

By externalizing and verbalizing children's reasoning and strategies, teachers in LEAP classrooms distributed the cognitive resources for all students to borrow and use. Students, as well as teachers, were positioned as "givers" and "inventors" rather than "receivers" of information about tools, strategies, and ideas. Analysis of data from thematic units across LEAP classroom sites revealed that many students whose strategies were recognized were students with disabilities. Public recognition and dissemination of their literacy practices created new social positions and identities for students that were not solely linked to their conventional reading and writing abilities, but which were tied to their contributions and participation in the work of the community. As students employed, constructed and appropriated the valued resources and practices associated with competent performance (Wenger, 1998), competence became a dimension of their learning identity.

Modeling and interactive processes were used, similarly, by Mrs. Hart and Ms. Johnson when they introduced students to highlighting, identifying main ideas, and notetaking from academic texts, as shown in a lesson transcript in Fig. 14.1. In this example, the teachers again apprenticed their students in various literacy practices associated with reading and synthesizing academic texts, such as navigating the text (e.g., using a bookmark), predicting information ("so what are we going to be looking for?"), identifying main ideas (e.g., "Evan identified the main idea. He was able to figure out that the whole paragraph was about ____"), and highlighting details relevant to the research purposes. By reading the texts orally in small groups, no student was marginalized in the activity or precluded from the opportunity to acquire higher-order literacy practices by a lack of reading proficiency. Students interacted directly with the academic text as they highlighted individual copies of the text to construct their own personal artifacts associated with the joint notetaking activity.

Recursively, as in each phase of the inquiry process, LEAP teachers disseminated the knowledge of the participating members. The ideas and information that were highlighted and recorded by either partners or individuals were made available to the rest of the class during a public comment and sharing time that concluded each lesson. In the classwide sharing time, the teacher added the highlighted ideas, notes, and questions to the cumulative list of written information emanating from each phase of the research process. Socially, the public sharing allowed students to assume intellectual roles by sharing and distributing their expertise among the networked members (Wenger, 1998). Cognitively, the recording of ideas in a public space accomplished several goals: (a) allowing children to see the changes in the collective thinking over time; (b) reifying the group's knowledge by constructing a common artifact that might be a source of remembering, reflecting, communicating, and learning; (c) linking everyday and scientific language, as well as spoken and written language; (d) apprenticing and engaging students in reading and employing inscription-related practices to clarify, construct, and represent meanings (Roth, 1998; Wenger, 1998); (e) constructing meaning through the process of articulating ideas (Lee & Smagorinsky, 2000); and (f) reifying a spiral of knowing related to the transformation of one's knowledge through participation in a *progressive, situated, and shared* discourse about academic concepts (Wells, 2000). Simultaneously, it must be noted that these young students were engaged in acquiring and em-

Ms. Johnson:	So it's down on the very very bottom right hand corner. Lets go through and reread the whole paragraph and see what they are talking about.
Mrs. Hart:	You should really have a pointer finger ready to follow along with us, or a bookmark, or a highlighter.
Ms. Johnson:	*Swimming in style. To swim forward fish sweep their body from side to side ... some fish are faster than the sail fish. Speed demon from the see* Wow, lots of information there. I'm going to grab a bookmark. What is that paragraph talking about? Let me read it again. [she rereads it much quicker this time]. What are they talking about in this paragraph? Evan.
Elijah:	uhm, how fish can swim.
Ms. Johnson:	How fish can swim. So what are we going to be looking for then? What kinds of Important things are we going to be looking for?
Elijah:	uhm....
Ms. Johnson:	Things that tell us about ... [prompting]
Elijah:	How fish swim and how they move.
Ms. Johnson:	yeah, yeah.
Mrs. Hart:	So Elijah identified the main idea of that paragraph. After he heard it, he was able to figure out that the whole paragraph was about "How fish swim." That's called the *main idea.*
Ms. Johnson:	Is there anything that helped you with this?
Elijah:	[inaudible].
Ms. Johnson:	Let's go through line by line and see if we can underline or just highlight those words that we think are important words. Remember, yesterday, we talked about that not every word is going to be important—that we need to highlight but we want to get those big ideas? And if we decide that this paragraph is talking about *swimming* we want to get the *big ideas about swimming.*

FIG. 14.1.   Lesson Transcript of Highlighting Academic Text. *Introduction.* During this group activity, students sat in small groups of three to four students, each with his/her own copy of the article. It was repeatedly emphasized that only the important words were highlighted. After this process was completed with the entire paragraph, the highlighted information was turned into notes that were put on chart paper.

ploying a number of writing (e.g., using invented spelling, making diagrams and written representations, transforming ideas into written notes) and reading strategies (e.g., decoding, comprehending, summarizing, notetaking, highlighting, reading charts, identifying main ideas, questioning) related to successful content area performance.

3. Representation Systems and the Hierarchical Organization of Knowledge

A third aspect of scientific discourse is the manner in which experience within a discipline is *conceptually organized*, that is, abstract categories create hierarchical associations among events, ideas, and objects. Everyday experience is transformed into formal scientific associations, which are characterized by *hierarchical organizations* among ideas. Categories are not inherent to the structure of experience, but rather, imposed on it through the socially derived meanings that have come to collectively organize our interactions in the world. Thus, students must be *taught* to see the world in ways that reflect hierarchically organized and conceptually derived experiences in a scientific community of inquiry. According to Halliday and Martin (1993), this hierarchy is reflected in the ways in which systematic relationships between ideas are constructed similar to those that might be contained in a taxonomy. In other words, children must understand how knowledge can be represented as overarching or superordinate classes of information with subordinate details.

Consistent with the theoretical principles, the LEAP teachers chose mediational tools in the form of written artifacts, diagrams, and maps to make visible the abstract genres, taxonomies, and discourses underlying academic texts, as they sought to scaffold the performance of their students into the ways of reading and writing science. Mrs. Hart and Ms. Johnson initiated this process in their classroom by asking students to reflect on the collective list of researched ideas to find ideas "that could be put into groups or *categories*." As related details were identified, the teachers circled them with colored markers corresponding to a particular class of related ideas. For example, during the fish unit, the students came up with the concepts: *eat, live, do*. Generatively, when students discovered or generated new details (e.g., "has gills"), they were asked to construct new labels for the class, (e.g., "what a fish looks like" or "fish anatomy"). Although the learners were kindergarten, first, and second graders, teachers drew upon their natural oral language and cognitive abilities to see that their ideas could be grouped into classes representing particular classes or types of hierarchical relationships through a series of leading teacher questions ("Do you see any ideas that might go together?" "What can we call those ideas?"). What was helpful in the classification process was that teachers and students engaged in mode-switching between oral language and written classification schemes, thereby allowing ideas to be reciprocally developed as the talk moved back and forth from experiential knowledge to more specialized language forms. Because of this emphasis on mode-switching, all students could participate in the classification process, even students with disabilities. Thus, the process was inclusive of all children whether or not they could read and write in conventional ways.

Simultaneously, teachers introduced a lexicon for classifying. When Mrs. Hart asked students in week two of the fish unit: "What can we call these related ideas?," students were positioned to develop abstractions related to two types of knowledge. First, students were developing a lexicon related to the practices associated with taxonomizing or organizing ideas in hierarchical systems, which was represented more abstractly by words like *categories* and *details*. In these cases, the words represented a set of mental operations and practices that the students had just performed (e.g., finding details that go together, deciding what category label could be assigned to represent the meaning relationships). Teachers and children, thus, were developing a shared discourse about a set of practices associated with knowledge construction and representation in their classroom. These words then functioned as a metadiscourse that could be used to communicate or reference students' social practices associated with the learning process, or to convey the hierarchical relationships among a set of ideas.

Second, the students were acquiring abstractions pertaining to the classification of objects that might be brought to bear on the next unit of study. That is, students came to understand that many concepts were represented by specific abstractions such as "appearance, actions, habitat, family." Students were becoming conscious of the designations and distinctions that are often featured in taxonomies and in academic texts as part of an organized system of scientific knowledge (Daniels, 1996). Teachers then could transfer this knowledge to written texts as they guided their students to identify the categories and related details as part of a process of inferring the main ideas for a set of paragraph details, highlighting key ideas, generating summaries, or taking notes from academic texts (see example in Fig. 14.1).

The process of generating a taxonomy resulted in another artifact, namely a semantic web containing the color-coded details that had been classified by the students. The web was a repository of the collective information and decisions of the group. As an illustration, an example of a student web that evolved for the fish unit is shown in Fig. 14.2. The web was dialogically developed, and the resulting structure closely paralleled the structures in writing science, as described by

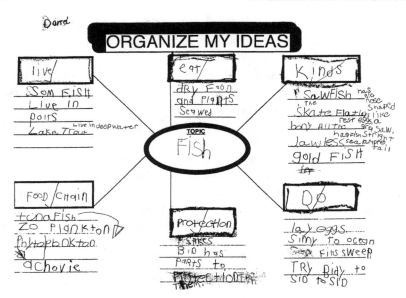

FIG 14.2. Darrell's Semantic Web for Fish Unit.

Halliday and Martin (1993). Each of the categories was individually listed in a circle that corresponded to a theme or class of information, and the details associated with each class were represented on lines emanating from each circle like the spokes in a wheel. In this way, the teacher made the infrastructure of the "writing science" genre visible to students. The knowledge, decisions and mental actions involved in categorizing were graphically represented and embodied in the notes and webs of the class, which correspondingly, became cultural tools and social practices for thinking, negotiating, communicating, and supporting the distributed work of the community (Roth, 1998).

Finally, the teachers apprenticed students in how the classes of information could be transformed into a written report that reflected the patterns of interactions, decisions and thought that typified its construction. Again, the oral interaction and webs served as the background against which participants made sense of each others' utterances and use of cultural practices. In week 3 of the fish unit, Mrs. Hart guided students by modeling how clauses could be arranged and constructed according to the hierarchy embodied in the web, with various clauses operating to coordinate, subordinate, and frame meaning. For instance, she modeled how authors stage an academic report through several topical devices, including an introductory paragraph, the use of questions or topic sentences, detail sentences, temporal (first, then, finally) or logical connectives (although, therefore), concluding sentences, and a concluding paragraph to help writers and readers look ahead and backward to communicate and locate meanings in the academic genre (Halliday & Martin, 1993; Kamberelis, 1999).

As Mrs. Hart led the class in rereading the ideas in the maps in the text construction process, she continually fingerpointed to each word to provide continual access to the identities of words. Each time a student suggested a detail from the web and transformed it into a sentence, either Mrs. Hart or Ms. Johnson modeled how to navigate the ideas in the web and text—modeling how to mark off the webbed ideas that were used, coaching students in how to transform ideas into sentences, and rereading the evolving draft to check the meaning and flow. Often the teachers engaged in role-playing exercises with each other, assuming the roles of student partners collaborating to produce a meaningful text by using the semantic web to guide the formation of sentences and paragraphs of related ideas. The teachers continually asked students to check the meaning by asking: "Does it make sense? Sound okay?" "How can we say that idea?" Thus, the teachers' implicit message was that written texts should make sense, and they modeled how to engage in reading and self-monitoring as part of the process of navigating the map to compose academic text.

Students then worked with partners to coparticipate in drafting a single expository text that reflected their joint ideas that was the culmination of the research process. Through students' joint engagement in the text construction process, teachers gradually shifted responsibility for text composition to students, with opportunities for social mediation and support from their collaborating partners. In these partnerships, expertise was distributed between the collaborating peers, with each member contributing their individual perspectives, notes, and cognitive tools. Even nonreaders and nonwriters were found to be active agents in this classroom who informed and influenced the composition and knowledge construction process (Englert, Berry, & Dunsmore, 2001). LEAP teachers routinely used such collaborations between partners as an acquisition space where students could develop their mastery of the discourse and practices associated with the construction of literacy artifacts in the content areas.

4. Community of Practice

Finally, scientific literacy is premised on the notion that knowledge is constructed within a *community of practice*. Knowledge is always subject to the validation, response, and acceptance of a larger group of scholars. The questions one asks, as well as one's research findings, are inextricably connected to the insights and practices of others engaged in scientific inquiry. As was already explained, when students in the LEAP classrooms engaged in research and notetaking either individually or in partners, findings and facts were always brought back to the whole group for expansion and validation as well as to contribute to the knowledge developed within the collective. Sharing information in a way that promoted group reflection on the ideas of the individual, and vice-versa, was central to the notion of a community of practice where literate knowing connected the actions of the individual with the socio-cultural practices of the group. In the LEAP classrooms, teachers came to realize the synergistic power of stretching the communication, cognition, tools, and processes associated with a particular discipline among the participants who worked and talked side-by-side (Gee & Green, 1998).

Becoming a member of a community of practice meant that students had to gain access to and mutually engage in the shared forms of life, practices, words, genres, discourses and tools of the academic discipline (Toulmin, 1999; Wenger, 1998). This was made possible through the teaching processes associated with modeling combined with mechanisms for ensuring the transfer of control of the literacy practices to students. Simultaneously, the participation of all individuals in the productive life of the classroom was promoted under four conditions: (a) students were given scaffolds and semiotic tools (e.g., language, scientific diagrams, webs) that supported cognition; (b) the multiple literacies of students were accepted and promoted, (c) social mediation supported individual performance, and (d) learning was seen as a developmental trajectory that was mediated by teachers based on the their assessment of the cognitive task and the cognitive resources that the students brought to it (Lee & Smagorinsky, 2000).

To illustrate the importance of these facets, we draw on the case of Darrell, a second-grade student with learning disabilities in Mrs. Hart and Ms. Johnson's multiage classroom. Our description above of the LEAP process for constructing thematic units focuses attention on to the ways in which the curricular process creates opportunities and participation practices that apprenticed students in the forms and functions of scientific writing. In this section, we provide microanalysis at the level of student activity to show how teachers' interactions with students individually provide scaffolded opportunities to both participate and develop literacy knowledge and expertise. At the beginning of the year, Darrell performed at a limited level. He read at a 0.3 reading level, reading primer passages with 67% accuracy, with a suggested instructional level at the preprimer level. Darrell had difficulty writing words, often using a random letter spelling strategy or initial consonants to compose texts. His September pretest story was as follows: "I like to tak kow (care) ovd (of) my cozn and my nes's and nau's (nephews)."

During the fish thematic unit in February, Darrell partnered himself with Rodney, a third grader with learning disabilities. The partners, constructing individual webs based on the collective class notes and experiences, generated the categories: "live, eat, kinds, food chain, protection, and do." These were enumerated with relevant details taken from the collective notes and experiences, as shown by Darrell's web in Fig. 14.2. Together, the boys jointly constructed a fish report, which is shown in Fig. 14.3. In comparison to Darrell's September story, the joint report exhibits the pairs' budding sense of the genre in terms of their beginning display of a linguistic architecture for organizing their ideas in text, and how those ideas are conveyed to the readers. Although primitive in its development, Darrell and Rodney began to use 1-word topical labels to introduce the categories (e.g., "Eat, Kinds, Protection Do," and to predict the details that follow). The ideas within each category were consistent with the hierarchical structure implied by these topics. When the partners wrote about kinds of fish, for example, they adhered to that topical structure by describing the sawfish, skate, and sea lamprey. They represented their own experimentation and inquiry within the unit when they wrote, "Goldfish are inexpensive, popular, and easy to study." Furthermore, the two boys demonstrate the emergence of voice as they write, "Watch out for those bad fish!"

The gap between the quality and quantity between Darrell's September story and the February fish story was attributable to the apprenticeship process, and the mediational tools and knowledge that were afforded the partners through their participation in the community of practice. The semantic web, as a mediational tool, served as a cognitive and social resource through which Darrell and Ronald began to organize, and exercise their own mental processes (John-Steiner & Meehan, 2000; Roth & McGinn, 1998). The web modified and enriched their cognitive activity (John-Steiner & Meehan, 2000) by helping the partners locate the key information and construct the relationship among the ideas, which in turn, guided the partners during the writing process by mediating their construction of paragraphs and details. Darrell and Rodney, operating with these mediational means, were able to increase the depth of their participation in the scientific discourse and practices (Roth, 1998; Wertsch, 1995). In fact, for many of the students in the classroom, the mediational tools and cognitive resources made available within the community obscured learning difficulties, while simultaneously allowing students to work at the outer edges of their competence (Scardamalia & Bereiter, 1994).

Through their involvement in the joint process associated with the construction of literacy artifacts, the partners assisted each other by questioning each other, and prompting themselves as they navigated the web and the

Fish

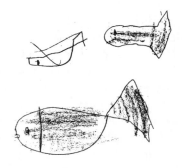

① Eat
Fish eat dry food and
seaweed.
    Kinds
Sawfish has a big nose
shaped like a saw. Skate is
flat. It has a gray tail.
Sea Lamprey is a jawless
fish. Goldfish are
inexpensive, popular and
easy to study.
    Protection
Watch out for those bad
fish! Porcupine fish have
sharp spikes. Fish bodies
have parts to protect them.
    Do
Fish lay eggs. Some fish
sweep their body from side
to side like a snake.

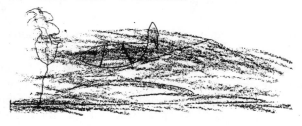

FIG 14.3.   February Fish Report.

coconstruction process. Their assumption of roles as writers, critics, composers, comprehenders, and teachers was recursive and dynamically changing. Each of their acts of meaning construction were not isolated activities, but represented extensions of prior events and social processes of which they had taken part (Rogoff, 1995). When the partners' shared expertise was insufficient to complete the task, Mrs. Hart and Ms. Johnson responsively scaffolded their performance during a writing conference. Mrs. Hart helped them, for example, transform some of their sketchy notes into well-formed detail sentences, and she modeled and supported the construction of topic sentences. When it is remembered that Darrell was reading at the preprimer level at the beginning of the school year, his participation and the artifacts that he produced during the fish unit are especially remarkable.

The deepening expertise of the two students within the community of practice was more fully ascertained by the report generated by the collaborating partners in May, as shown in Fig. 14.4. An examination of this second report showed a growing sophistication on their parts as they constructed an introductory paragraph that introduced their readers to the informational chunks contained within the report. Instead of single-word labels, the partners composed topic sentences that prepared their readers for the detailed information that followed. Furthermore, the topic sentences showed greater variation, including questions that might serve to engage their audience (e.g., "Did you know grasshoppers have 3 stages in their life cycle?"), as well as a declarative sentence that was highly predictive as to the number and type of information that follow (e.g., "Grasshoppers have three body parts."). Finally, there is the emergence of concluding sentences that wrap up the topical presentation of the authors (e.g., This is where grasshoppers live). Based on Halliday and Martin's (1993) classification scheme for scientific writing, the students exhibited an emerging sense of four of the five genre components: introductory paragraph, main idea–topic sentences that introduced each class of information, detail sentences, and concluding sentences for each class of information. What they had yet to acquire was the concluding paragraph that summarized and recapitulated the information in the text. Nevertheless, the measurement of students' performance over time showed increasing mastery of the genres and discourses related to academic writing. As Wells (2000) has suggested, when the knowledge of students was considered in light of their historical participation in the community, there was evidence of their appropriation and mastery of tools that had been afforded them through social interaction. Furthermore, the reading assessment conducted at the end of the year indicated that Darrell had also made gains of nearly 1.5 years. In May, Darrell could read a sight word list at the 2.2 grade

Grasshoppers

Did you know grasshoppers are interesting insects. I'm going to tell you what they eat and when they live. What they do and their life cycle. What they look like and their body parts.

Grasshoppers have 3 body parts. They have a head, a thorax, and a abdomen. They have 2 antenea attached to the head.

Did you know grasshoppers have 3 stages in their life cycle. First, the egg, then it's called a nymph, then the adult. This is how grasshoppers grow to the adult.

Did you know grasshoppers have brothers. Other insects look like grasshoppers. A Praying Mantis and a Walking Stick are because there the grasshoppers brothers. Other insects still look like grasshoppers.

Do you know where grasshoppers live? Grasshoppers live in holes in the ground and on a log and in the grass. This is wher grasshoppers live.

Do you know what grasshoppers eat? Grasshoppers eat leaves and sometimes they eat grass and sticks and wood off of sticks. This is what grasshoppers eat.

FIG. 14.4.   May Report on Grasshoppers.

level, and he was able to read a third-grade passage with 90% accuracy. Emphases on literacy learning across the curriculum seemed to have positively impacted both his writing and reading performance, transferring even to more standard measures of his ability to orally read narrative text structures. His participation in reading and writing across the curriculum in the scaffolded and mediated contexts supported by the LEAP curricular approach had advanced his literacy performance in synergistic ways.

SUMMARY

This chapter was intended to provide a description of the best practices of the LEAP project and what it afforded teachers and students in the disciplinary subjects. The following list summarizes the best practices that typified effective instruction by the LEAP teachers:

- *Models* and makes cognitive and literacy tools available in the *situated context* of their use, providing opportunities for the *authentic employment* of tools by students in problem solving and inquiry activities.
- Ensures the *full participation* of all students in the literacy practices by accepting the *multiple literacies* of student members, and encouraging *discursive interactions* that serve up the oral language and experiences of participants as cognitive resources for learning.
- Promotes literacy in the content area subjects, and ensures students' participation in the joint construction of artifacts that both reify their knowledge and support their implementation of the discourse and tools of the discipline.
- Teaches the academic genres by making visible the architecture of the content discipline, including the language, functions, taxonomies, practices, conventions, and text structures.
- Ensures that participation is supported and mediated by peers or teachers to help all students achieve a more competent level of performance than that they can achieve when working alone or in private contexts (Gindis, 1999).
- Disseminates the constructive use of literacy tools and strategies used by the members of the community to support knowledge construction and transformation, as well as identity construction and transformation.
- Provides opportunities for the coparticipation of all members of the community (including the teacher), who work, learn, and talk side-by-side; and by ensuring that communication, cognition and co-

> ordination is stretched and distributed among the participants through the joint construction of artifacts (Gee & Green, 1998).
> - Provides a variety of coparticipatory roles that are interdependent and dynamically changing (Rogoff, 1995 in Wertsch et al.), as well as design activities that allow for elements of problem solving, choice, self-monitoring, self-regulation, and self-determination.
> - Recognizes and teaches writing, reading, and oral language as tools within a process of learning and inquiry, and maintains an emphasis on process, ideas, and practices, rather than maintains a solitary focus on conventional spelling and reading to the exclusion of higher-order thinking.
> - Scaffolds knowledge through questions and processes that have the potential to lead, guide, and respond to students' participation in the community.

The teaching practices of teachers can ameliorate the disabilities of students. Effective teaching practices can make the inclusion of all students not only a reality, but a catalyst for the construction of a community of learners that enriches all participants. As McDermott and Varenne (1995) suggested, culture has the power to disable, as well as the power to enable. When classroom cultures are created that offer a wealth of cognitive resources, mediational tools, and social positions for students to inhabit, differences can be diminished (McDermott & Varenne, 1995). When literacy is something that individuals strive to collaboratively achieve together, then the participation and competence of members of the community can be enhanced in interdependent ways to maximize the learning of everyone, even in the in the face of mastering challenging academic content (Rueda, Gallego, & Moll, 2000).

REFERENCES

Artiles, A. J., Trent, S. C., Hoffman-Kipp, P., & Lopez-Torres, L. (2000). From individual acquisition to cultural-historical practices in multicultural teacher education. *Remedial and Special Education, 21*(2), 79–89, 120.

Barnes, D. (1993). *Supporting exploratory talk for learning.* Portsmouth, NH: Heinemann.

Baynham, M. (1995). *Literacy practices: Investigating literacy in social contexts.* New York: Longman.

Christie, F. (1993). Curriculum genres: Planning for effective teaching. In B. Cope, & Kalantzis, M. (Eds.), *The Powers of literacy: A genre approach to teaching writing* (pp. 154–179). Pittsburgh, PA: The Falmer Press.

Cope, B., & Kalantzis, M. (1993). Introduction: How a genre approach to literacy can transform the way writing is taught. In B. Cope & Kalantzis, M. (Eds.), *The Powers of literacy: A genre approach to teaching writing* (pp. 1–21). Pittsburgh, PA: The Falmer Press.

Daniels, H. (1996). Introduction: Psychology in a social world. In H. Daniels (Ed.), *An introduction to Vygotsky* (pp. 1–27). New York: Routledge.

Deshler, D. D., Ellis, E. S., & Lenz, B. K. (1996). *Teaching adolescents with learning disabilities: Strategies and methods.* Denver, CO: Love Pub Co.

Englert, C. S., Berry, R. W., & Dunsmore, K. L. (2001). Another Perspective on the Apprentice and the Scaffolding Metaphor. *Journal of Learning Disabilities, 34*(2) 152–171.

Englert, C. S., & Mariage, T. V. (1996). A sociocultural perspective: Teaching ways-of-thinking and ways-of-talking in a literacy community. *Learning Disabilities Research and Practice, 11*(3), 157–167.

Englert, C. S., Mariage, T. V., Garmon, M. A., & Tarrant, K. L. (1998). Accelerating reading progress in Early Literacy Project classrooms: Three exploratory studies. *Remedial and Special Education, 19*(3), 142–159.

Gaskins, I. W., & Guthrie, J. T. (1994). Integrating instruction of science, reading and writing: Goals, teacher development, and assessment. *Journal of Research in Science Teaching, 31*(9), 1039–1056.

Gee, J. P., & Green, J. L. (1998). Discourse analysis, learning and social practice: A methodological study. *Review of Research in Education, 23,* 119–169.

Gindis, B. (1999). Vygotsky's vision reshaping the practice of special education for the 21st Century. *Remedial and Special Education, 20,* 333–340.

Gover, M., & Englert, C. S. (1999, December). Quantitative results of the Learning Environments for Accelerated Progress (LEAP) Curriculum. Paper presented at the Annual Meeting of the National Reading Conference. Orlando, Florida.

Halliday, M. A. K., & Martin, J. R. (1993). *Writing Science: Literacy and Discursive Power.* Pittsburgh, PA: The Falmer Press.

Herrenkohl, L. R., Palincsar, A. S., DeWater, L., & Kawasaki, K. (1999). Developing scientific communities in classrooms: A sociocognitive approach. *Journal of the Learning Sciences, 8*(3, 4), 451–493.

John-Steiner, V. P., & Meehan, T. M. (2000). *Creativity and collaboration in knowledge construction.* New York: Cambridge University Press.

Kamberelis, G. (1999). Genre development and learning: Children writing stories, science reports, and poems. *Research in the Teaching of English, 33,* 403–460.

Lee, C. D., & Smagorinsky, P (2000). *Introduction: Constructing meaning through collaboration.* New York: Cambridge University Press.

Lemke, J. L. (1982). Talking physics. *Physics Education, 17,* 263–267.

McDermott, R., & Varenne, H. (1995). Culture *as* Disability. *Anthropology & Education Quarterly, 26*(3), 324–348.

Minick, N. (1996). The development of Vygotksy's thought: An introduction to Thinking and Speech. In H. Daniels (Eds.), *An introduction to Vygotsky* (pp. 28–53). New York: Routledge.

Morgan, W. (1997). *Critical literacy in the classroom.* New York: Routledge.

Palincsar, A. S., Magnusson, S. J., Collins, K. M., & Cutter, J. (2001). Making science accessible to all: Results of a design experiment in inclusive classrooms. *Learning Disability Quarterly, 21*(1), 15–32.

Rogoff, B. (1995). Observing sociocultural activity on three planes: Participatory appropriation, guided participation, and apprenticeship. In J. V. Wertsch, P. D. Rio, & A. Alvarez (Eds.), *Sociocultural Studies of the Mind* (pp. 139–164). New York: Cambridge University Press.

Roth, W. M. (1998). *Designing communities.* Boston: Kluwer Academic Publishers.

Roth, W. M., & McGinn, M. K. (1998). Inscriptions: Toward a theory of representing as social practice. *Review of Educational Research, 68*(1), 35–59.

Rueda, R., Gallego, M. A., & Moll, L. C. (2000). The least restrictive environment: A place or a context? *Remedial and Special Education, 21*(2), 70–78.

Scardamalia, M., & Bereiter, C. (1994). Computer support for knowledge-building communities. *Journal of the Learning Sciences, 3*(3), 265–283.

Toulmin, S. (1999). Knowledge as shared procedures. In Y. Engestrom, R. Miettinen, & R. Punamaki (Eds.), *Perspectives on Activity Theory* (pp. 53–64). New York: Cambridge University Press.

Vygotsky, L. S. (1978). *Mind in Society.* Cambridge, MA: Harvard Press.

Wells, G. (2000). *Dialogic inquiry in education: Building on the legacy of Vygotsky.* New York: Cambridge University Press.

Wenger, E. (1998). *Communities of practice: Learning, meaning and identity.* New York: Cambridge University Press.

Wertsch, J. V. (1995). The need for action in sociocultural research. In J. V. Wertsch, P. D. Rio, & A. Alvarez (Eds.), *Sociocultural Studies of the Mind* (pp. 56–74). New York: Cambridge University Press.

Wong, B. Y. L., Wong, R., & Blenkisop, J. (1989). Cognitive and metacognitive aspects of learning-disabled adolescents' composing problems. *Learning Disability Quarterly, 12,* 300–322.

Wong, B. Y. L., Wong, R., Perry, N., & Sawatsky, K. (1986). The efficacy of a self-questioning summarization strategy for use by underachievers and learning disabled adolescents in social studies. *Learning Disabilities Focus, 2*(1), 20–36.

15

Bilingual Teachers Speak About the Literacy Instruction of Bilingual Latino Students

Rosalinda B. Barrera
Robert T. Jiménez
University of Illinois at Urbana-Champaign

The voices of Latino teachers and researchers are curiously absent in the ongoing debate concerning early childhood reading instruction (Jiménez, Moll, Rodriguez-Brown, & Barrera, 1999; Reading Today, 2000; Snow, Burns, & Griffin, 1998). We believe that this marginalization is not unintentional and that it has significant ramifications for Latino students and the broader Latino community, particularly with respect to the formulation of state and national policies concerning language and literacy instruction. Nowhere was this connection made more explicit than in a recent editorial in a nationally circulated newspaper, in which the editorial writer argued that bilingual instruction be abandoned and replaced by all-English programs on the basis of a small increase in test scores for students in nonbilingual programs. The reported increase was 9 percentage points, and placed students at the 28th percentile, hardly cause for celebration or the formulation of national policy. Of concern, however, is that a mainstream, public discourse is growing that manipulates and distorts test-score results and appropriates the language of 'scientific research' to silence and marginalize the concerns of Latino students and the larger community. Keep in mind that the Latino community fought for decades to establish bilingual education as a more socially equitable and culturally congruent form of schooling (San Miguel & Valencia, 1998).

In this chapter, we present the results of a series of focus group interviews with teachers of Latino children in three urban centers with significant Latino representation: Chicago, El Paso, and Washington, D.C. Specifically, we sought these teachers' knowledge and understanding of school literacy practices that maximize success for this group of students. We recognize, however, that the continuing, prevailing context of hostility toward the use of non-English languages in public schools in the United States influences and affects the work conducted by bilingual teachers. This influence surfaces throughout the comments made by our participating teachers.

This hostility may reflect the mainstream reaction to recent growth in the Latino population. Latino youth currently constitute the largest group of racial/ethnic minority students in U.S. schools, calculated at 13.5% of the total (NCES, 1998a). Latino students also comprise three out of four of the approximately 10 million students from linguistically diverse backgrounds (Hispanic Dropout Project, 1996; NCES, 1997; NAEP, 2000). They continue, however, to demonstrate depressed levels of literacy development in comparison to students from mainstream backgrounds (NCES, 1998b).

Lemberger (1997) has pointed out that "bilingual teachers, as cultural liaisons, are in an important position to communicate across the family, school, community, and society contexts." In part, this point underscores the unique vantage that bilingual education teachers have that other educational parties such as school administrators, external researchers, or educational policymakers, do not have, and that can serve teachers in identifying literacy practices that work and make educational sense for Latino students. These teachers' perspectives and voices are grounded in the everyday, complex realities of schooling, and thus they have significant potential for informing us about how to make schools and literacy instruction better for Latino students.

Also of importance is that the majority of teachers working with Latino students are European American and/or novices who have not received training for working with children from diverse backgrounds (de la Rosa, Maw, & Yzaguirre, 1990; Zimpher, 1989; Zimpher & Yessayan, 1987). With this information in mind, and taking into consideration that teachers generally have the best interests of their students at heart, we believed that information with the potential to improve the literacy learning and instruction of Latino students would be appreciated, particularly by teachers from mainstream backgrounds.

Before presenting the results or our interview study, we offer a selective review of existing research on literacy instruction for Latino students in Grades K through 6, so that this information can help serve an interpretive backdrop for the present study. We then share the results of the study that elicited bilingual teachers' perspectives on four dimensions of their classroom practice: curriculum, instruction, assessment, and home–school connections. We conclude by providing a number of research questions that emerged from this analysis concerning literacy instruction for bilingual Latino students. It should be noted that this chapter is based on a longer report by the researchers that is available online at http://www.ncbe.gwu.edu/ncbepubs/reports/literacy/index.htm.

REVIEW OF RELATED RESEARCH

The extant research on school literacy instruction for Latino students in the United States comprises a relatively small, albeit heterogeneous, body of studies. In this section, we briefly review three strands from this body of inquiry: (a) studies on "effective practices" with bilingual Latino students, (b) studies on literacy instruction for bilingual Latino students, and (c) studies on literacy practices among bilingual Latino families. Salient findings from these past studies are related to results of the present study in a subsequent section.

Studies on "Effective Schooling" of Bilingual Latino Students

The research to date on effective bilingual schooling and teachers allows us to view practitioners in a variety of educational scenarios, serving Latino students from different ethnolinguistic backgrounds, geographic locations, and grade levels, within different types of bilingual education (and transition) program models, and utilizing different literacy instructional methodologies. Of interest is that, except for a study by Tikunoff (1985), all of the available research focuses on a limited number of teachers (Carter & Chatfield, 1986; García, 1988, 1992; Gersten, 1996; Gersten & Jiménez, 1994; Jiménez, Gersten, & Rivera, 1996; Jiménez & Gersten, 1999; Moll, 1988; Pease-Alvarez, García, & Espinosa, 1991; Reyes, Scribner, & Scribner (1999); Rutherford (1999).

However, an examination of this literature revealed that all of the teachers who were included as participants in this research sought to strike a balance between the role of meaning and skills in their instructional practice. They did this by either infusing meaning into skill-based instruction or skills into meaning-based teaching. These studies also revealed a common instructional mind-set among the teachers that included a belief in children's ability to learn and high expectations for their achievement. This mind-set extended to include positive perceptions of children's language, culture, families, and communities, which were viewed as potential resources, not problems. The research identified the alternation of native language and second language by the teachers and students as a recurrent attribute of effective practice. Finally, the theme of effective home–school connections with a particular emphasis on building and maintaining a strong relationship between the classroom teacher and the children's parents was pervasive within this literature.

Studies of Literacy Instruction for Bilingual Latino Students

Beyond the effective schooling research, studies of classroom literacy instruction for bilingual Latino students are relatively few in number and address a limited range of topics. The majority of the studies address Spanish reading and/or writing instruction in the primary grades (Delgado-Gaitan, 1990; Delgado-Gaitan, 1991b; Edelsky, 1986; Goldenberg, 1994; Goldenberg & Gallimore, 1991; Mulhern, 1997; Muñiz-Swicegood, 1994; Perez, 1994; Zecker, Pappas, & Cohen, 1998). Some of the studies also deal with English reading and/or writing instruction in the primary grades (Battle, 1993; Fitzgerald, 1999; Moll & Diaz, 1987; Padrón, 1992; Padrón, 1994; Reyes (1991a, 1991b). One study dealt with reading in both English and Spanish (Calderón, Tinajero, & Hertz-Lazarowitz, 1992). Studies of literacy instruction beyond the primary grades , either in Spanish or English, are less represented, however.

The primary-grade Spanish literacy studies reveal a strong code-emphasis in Spanish reading instruction in the focal classrooms and point to a tension between meaning and form in Spanish writing instruction, specifically in process writing (Zecker, Pappas, & Cohen, 1998). Effective practices for teaching emergent/beginning English literacy to bilingual Latino students are explored in several of the studies (Gomez, Parker, Lara-Alecio, & Gomez, 1996; Reyes, 1991a, 1991b). In the studies of literacy instruction in Grades 3 through 5, the research emphasis is on comprehension and strategy instruction, both in Spanish and English (Muñiz-Swicegood, 1994; Padrón, 1994). Some ongoing instructional issues that surface in the studies as a whole include code-switching, cross-linguistic transfer, and cultural relevance. There are a few examples of sustained inquiry of particular topics by the same or different researchers (e.g., of early Spanish reading instruction and of process writing).

Studies on Literacy Practices Among Bilingual Latino Families

Some researchers have challenged traditional stereotypical views concerning Latino parents (Delgado-Gaitan, 1991a, 1992; Delgado-Gaitan & Trueba, 1991; Goldenberg, 1987; Soto, 1988, 1997; Valdés, 1996; Vasquez, Pease-Alvarez, & Shannon, 1994). Three insights can be derived from their work. First, on the basis of considerable empirical evidence, these researchers have asserted that Latino parents do indeed hold positive values about the education and school achievement of their children. A second insight derived from their research is that Latino families of low socioeconomic backgrounds are able to draw from significant cultural and shared knowledge from their own families as well as their communities (Guerra, 1998; Moll, 1992). Knowledge of this information could be used to support Latino children's schooling if schools and educators would only tap this source. Finally, researchers have critiqued and dismissed the deficit view that the homes of Latino students are devoid of oral and written language (Delgado-Gaitan & Trueba, 1991; Pease-Alvarez & Vasquez, 1994; Vasquez, Pease-Alvarez, & Shannon, 1994). These conclusions have been qualified, however, by the understanding that there is considerable variability in how and how much Latino parents are able to support their children's school experience at home (Paratore, Melzi, & Krol-Sinclair, 1999).

Homework was shown to play an important role in terms of how school literacy enters the homes of Latino students (Paratore et al., 1995). Also, Latino parents have been found to rely on their own literacy learning experiences, which by and large were traditional and reductionistic, for making sense of their children's literacy instruction (Goldenberg, Reese, & Gallimore, 1992). In terms of reading, parents tend to focus on sound–letter relationships and on blending letters into syllables. For writing, they tend to emphasize correct letter formation (Goldenberg, 1987; Goldenberg, Reese, & Gallimore, 1992; Valdés, 1996).

Summing Up

Collectively, the three strands of inquiry reviewed above—effective practices, literacy instructional methods, and literacy practices among Latino families— offer varying insights into the literacy education of bilingual Latino students, including the four domains of curriculum, instruction, assessment, and home–school connections. However, the overall base of empirical evidence on bilingual Latino students' literacy development and learning represented here can best be described as modest, with many topics and issues within and beyond these four domains still needing to be explored. In effect, the available research does not yet provide an integrated tapestry of ideas or a propositional network that would lead us to an efficacious theory for teaching young Latino students. We contend that this state of the research increased the significance of the teacher interview study that was undertaken.

METHODS

Participants

We sought to interview teachers working in long-established and/or recognized bilingual education programs, preferably with assignments in kindergarten and first grade where initial literacy instruction typically occurs. In Chicago, we interviewed 11 teachers from one pre-K through eighth-grade campus, a school featured in an online series of successful bilingual schools produced by a federally-funded regional educational laboratory. In El Paso, we talked with nine teachers representing five Kindergarten through fifth-grade schools from one of the city's two urban school districts, a system with a long track record in bilingual education. In Washington, we met with 10 teachers representing three Pre-K through third-grade schools in the District of Columbia's public school system, among them an internationally acclaimed bilingual education site with an extensive history of innovation.

Teacher Background Characteristics

Among the Chicago teachers, prior teaching experience ranged from 1 to 12 years. One teacher had been trained in Mexico; most of the others in several colleges/universities in Illinois. One teacher had taught in Texas prior to moving to Illinois. A number of them had been teaching assistants prior to being certified. The majority had, or were pursuing, master's degrees. Two of the teachers were male; the rest female. All but one was of Latino background. This last teacher was a fluent Spanish speaker.

Prior teaching experience for the El Paso teachers ranged from 1 to 22 years. Most had done their professional studies at the local university, and some had been colleagues while pursuing their master's degrees in a special graduate program. A number of them were interested in pursuing doctoral studies. The third-grade teacher in the group was a former bilingual education teacher currently assigned to a monolingual English classroom. All the teachers were female; and with the exception of one, all Latinas. The non-Latino teacher was a fluent speaker of Spanish.

The Washington teachers reflected prior teaching experience that ranged from 5 to 28 years, with the most senior teacher having spent all her time at the acclaimed school. Two teachers had been trained outside the United States, one in Peru, the other in Puerto Rico. A number of them had taught in other states. Two of the pre-K teachers team taught at the highly lauded school, as did two of the first-grade teachers. All the teachers were female; all but three were Latinas. The Anglo teachers were fluent Spanish speakers.

Student and Program Characteristics

In Chicago, the pre-K and K teachers were in a fledgling two-way program while the rest of the teachers were part of the school's transitional bilingual education (TBE) program, which exited students at the end of third grade. The focal school has an enrollment of about 1200 students, of whom 92% are of Spanish speaking background, representing various ethnicities and countries of origin, but mostly of Mexican origin. Only about 40% of the students are enrolled in TBE.

In El Paso, participating teachers came from five of the focal district's 50 elementary (PK through 5) schools, whose percentage of limited-English-proficient learners ranged from 22% to 63%, most of them of Mexican American or Mexican immigrant background, while their proportion of minority students ranged from 82% to 97%. The focal district has about 12,000 students in its Bilingual Education Program, which encompasses both dual-language instruction and transitional bilingual education with exit at the end of fifth grade. The total district enrollment is more than 63,000 students, of which 84% are minority and 32% are LEP.

In Washington, our focal teachers were from three of the 104 elementary schools in the District of Columbia's public school system. One school had a transitional bilingual education program model in place, and another school, also TBE, was starting a two-way bilingual program in Kindergarten based on the model of the acclaimed school, but without two teachers in one classroom or the smaller class sizes found at the high-profile school. This third school's socioeconomically diverse enrollment is 60% Latino, 30% Anglo, and 10% African American. The focal system has more than 117 different languages represented. Latino students comprise more than 8% of the district's 71,000 enrollment and represent more than 21 Hispanic/Latino countries.

Interview Sessions

Procedures for focus group interviews by Vaughn, Schumm, and Sinagub (1996) served to guide our data collection. The interviews ran from 1½ to 2 hours, with a semi-structured format aimed at exploring four topics in the following order: curriculum, instruction, assessment and home–school connections. The basic stimulus questions were: What do you find effective for Latino students' literacy learning in terms of the curriculum? Instruction? Assessment? Home–school relations?

Analysis

Each taped interview was transcribed in its entirety by a doctoral student who was proficient in Spanish and English. Then the transcripts were read and checked for thoroughness and accuracy by one of the researchers. The final transcripts were read both individually and jointly by the researchers. Data reduction and analysis procedures adapted from Vaughn et al. (1996) and McCracken (1998) were applied in the following manner. During the readings, topics were highlighted on the transcripts, and after the readings, the identified topics were discussed in order to form higher-level propositions. Next, the propositions were reorganized into listings by interview site and topic. The listing for each site served as a guide for the construction of a summary of that particular interview session. After listings were established, they were then checked again by rereading the transcripts to verify their accuracy. Finally, the researchers reviewed the resultant listings and distilled and refined them for "goodness of fit" with the data. Then, the first author wrote an initial draft of the findings while at the same time she consulted with the second author.

RESULTS

Although the report on which this chapter is based contains interview data from the individual sites, in this chapter we provide only the results of a cross-case analysis of the interview data due to space limitations. Major similarities and differences in teachers' responses across the trio of sites are highlighted in the discussion.

Curriculum

Across all three sites, there were two aspects of curriculum that focal teachers consistently spoke about as helping to advance Latino children's literacy learning, not only at the emergent and beginning phases but into advanced levels as well: curricular integration and children's literature/trade books. Integration within the language arts and across the curriculum was being achieved primarily through thematic units. Such integration was explained as mutually beneficial for students and teachers. Within the language arts, linkages from reading to writing were mentioned most often, and writing was cited as a growing curricular emphasis. Integration with the content areas of science, social studies, and mathematics was mentioned in relation to reading and writing primarily, not the other language arts, that is, listening, speaking, and viewing. The fine arts—song, music, art, drama, dance, and poetry—were touted as a powerful means for motivating and supporting children's emergent and beginning literacy learning.

The teachers in Chicago, for example, described songs as the "next best thing" to teachers' read-alouds for helping young children grow in native-language literacy as well as second language oracy and literacy. At the lower grade levels this emphasis included a special program, referred to as basic reading through dance, for teaching young children "letters and sounds." One teacher explained that the program was "working wonders because [the children] are remembering the sounds better than any worksheets we could have been doing."

At each site, teachers consistently cited children's literature as an important curricular ingredient for enhancing the literacy learning of Latino students. Teachers talked about children's literature in two formats: within instructional materials (or the basal reading programs in use at each site) and in trade books. In relation to the former, there were repeated references to the basal anthologies and literature sets currently in use. Children's literature in trade book format was identified as a useful means for supplementing otherwise unsuitable curriculum materials, both in Spanish and English, whether in the content areas or in the basal anthology itself. Teachers in all three sites stressed the need for children's literature (both in Spanish and English) that reflects the experiences of the different Latino students served by them, namely, that provides meaningful, culturally relevant content, a requirement they stated goes unmet by Spanish translations of mainstream, English-language content.

In their overall endorsement of the use of children's literature for reading instruction, the El Paso teachers singled out one format—the picture book—as particularly helpful for their Latino students in L1 as well as L2 instruction. One fifth-grade teacher noted that she had begun to employ picture books for language-literacy instruction during that current academic year, and had observed that patterned-book language in these books expanded and improved her students' language while the illustrations helped them to construct story meanings. She commented: "Do you know, we have recent immigrants sometimes who depend on those illustrations to guide them through the story?"

Another teacher found picture books especially helpful in teaching language elements to be encountered by students on the state-mandated basic skills test; for example, she described the picture book as a "powerful tool" for teaching metaphors and similes, because the "children can visually see them." Additionally, she found that her students later utilized the language from picture books in their writing. Teachers emphasized the importance not only of having "good quality picture books" but also authentic literature in Spanish, not merely translated works. Authentic, culturally specific literature allowed their Latino students to identify with story characters and with "what is happening in the stories," one participant noted.

Instruction

Teachers' comments about instructional matters that make a difference in Latino children's literacy learning were far-ranging and diverse; however, two themes seemed to prevail: 1, writing as a motivational and instructional device, or teaching tool; and 2, the teacher's mediational role in both L1 and L2 instruction. There were repeated references to the power of writing, particularly "journaling," to stimulate children toward wanting to write initially and to write more. Although teachers did not explicitly link the concept of scaffolding to writing, they did point to the power of writing as a tool for learning language in general, for learning to make sense of print literacy, and for exploring content across the curriculum.

When the Washington, D.C. teachers were asked what helps children to become readers, one teacher spoke for many of her colleagues: "Reading and writing. They go hand in hand." In particular, teachers specified that "journal writing helps a lot" in the development of both native-language and second-language literacy. A kindergarten teacher described the motivating effects of journals in her classroom:

> Tienen un diario … todos los días escriben en ese diario y una de las cosas más interesantes que hemos encontrado es que empiezan con un libro que nosotros hacemos. Y entonces cuando se termina ese libro, la motivación es tener uno de estos cuadernos (shows tablet), y están locos por terminar ese libro para tener estó porque es ser grande. [They have a journal … every day they write in that journal and one of the most interesting this that we have found is that they begin with a book that we have made. And then when they finish that book, the motivation is to have one of these notebooks (shows tablet), and they go crazy to finish that book so that they can have this because it's a big thing.]

Some teachers stated they had Author's Chair on a daily basis for kids to share their journal writing:

> Everyday ... they can read and write in English or they can read and write in Spanish. The other thing that we do is the collaborative reading and writing ... The goal now is the reading, to get these children to read. And pre-k'rs, they think ... I don't know how to read. They don't know how to write ... That is where [on] day 1, the first day of school, the first thing to do when you walk in a room is to read or write. That is their choice. You get a paper and draw; you get a book and read it—everyday for 185 days in school.

The interview responses made it clear that a significant role played by bilingual education teachers is as mediator of texts and lessons used for L1 and L2 literacy instruction. Some of teachers' mediational behaviors are in response to more-or-less suitable L1 and L2 materials and lessons, whose content and language is comprehensible to young Latino learners. Such mediation in this case includes "generic" teaching strategies typically suggested for all learners, such as building on children's prior knowledge, encouraging children's predictions during reading, helping children make intertexual connections, and others.

Our focal group of teachers in Chicago were particularly adept at communicating their mediational efforts. For example, they identified cooperative grouping, hands-on activities, building on students' prior knowledge, and the use of writing as support, among others. One teacher noted she found that "a lot of repetition" worked for her students, with the same books being read first in one language and then the other:

> If I'm doing it in English, and the Spanish-speaking kids are really just trying to get the basic meaning, then I do it the next day in Spanish, and my Spanish-speaking kids are [now] making inferences. They're predicting outcomes, they're drawing conclusions, they're taking it to a deeper level.

Teachers also described instructional strategies for dealing with reading difficulties induced by inappropriate materials, particularly overly difficult English-language materials. These strategies included the use of exaggerated speech and gestures during read alouds, and translation of written text from English to Spanish. A fourth-grade teacher explained the latter: "All the books are in English, but when I see blank faces, I translate into Spanish. So for reinforcement, we use both languages. The written language is in English, and the reinforcement is in Spanish."

Assessment

There was virtual unanimity across the three sites that Latino students' literacy learning would be better served if multiple forms of assessment were employed across the grade levels, allowing students various ways of expressing their understandings and comprehension, both in Spanish and English. Teachers in the early grade levels, pre-K, K, and first, were particularly vocal about the need for flexibility and variety in assessing young learners, strongly advocating for informal, naturalistic, and ongoing means of assessment and decrying standardized high-stakes testing. Although during the interviews, none of the teachers used the terms *alternative, authentic,* or *performance-based* in relation to assessment, they made it clear that assessing children's learning ought to be done in creative, noncontrived, and dynamic ways. Teachers also called for assessments that are sensitive to the dual-language knowledge and abilities of bilingual learners, for example, citing the importance of allowing children to use their native language in second-language assessment and of monitoring their progress and achievement both in Spanish and English.

The teachers in El Paso spoke extensively about the need for multiple forms of assessment across L1 and L2 instruction, citing the importance of informal and formative assessments that eliminate "waiting until the end" of an instructional period to find out what children have learned. "Open-ended" assessment was defined as encompassing diverse, teacher-developed "activities that allow students to respond in many different ways." "It is not fill-in-the-blank," one teacher noted, but rather a broader, deeper undertaking to determine "what [children] learned, what they gained from the activity, and how [they] felt about it." The teachers acknowledged that developing "those types of [important] assessments for Latino children" requires a lot of planning, work, and research. They offered as an example the effort required to develop good questioning techniques that are central to informal, open-ended assessment. With well-crafted questioning, they concurred, the teacher is better able to guide children to higher levels of understanding.

Teachers at the pre-kindergarten and kindergarten levels overall delineated informal assessments used by them, including observational surveys, running records, checklists, observational notes, and anecdotal records. The consensus of the interviewees was that through these and other informal procedures, teachers are able to "see what strategies kids are using and what your focus needs to be." Then "you model the strategies he is not using," one participant added.

The El Paso teachers described the mutual benefits for Latino students and their teachers of using rubrics in assessment and evaluation, particularly in writing: "the children know from the start what the expectations are" and the teacher "can grade [children's writings] very efficiently." Another teacher pointed out that "it is more meaningful for them rather than A or B or C or D," especially if the rubric is jointly constructed by the students and teacher. Rubrics "set the standard for all" and students know what is acceptable work. With the aid of computers, rubrics can be quickly reproduced and stapled to writing assignments. "You are not giving them a grade; they are earning it," one teacher commented. The use of rubrics and of multiple forms of assessment as summarized previously, were viewed by the teachers as vehicles for strengthening their teaching.

Although the shadow of the state's mandated basic skills test, the Texas Assessment of Academic Skills (TAAS) looms over their district, El Paso teachers discussed it with a sense of self-assurance and perspective. "It takes care of itself." One experienced teacher stated, "I did not open a TAAS booklet this whole year until April, and the only reason I did that is because the students needed to be familiar with the format … [By] focusing on it in a different way … with less TAAS practice, the students are performing better." She recalled that this was not the way she had reacted to the test in her first year of teaching, spending undue time familiarizing her students with test format. Another teacher informed the group that at her school, bilingual students recently had "scored in some cases higher than the monolingual students," noting a 96% passing rate among fourth-grade bilingual students. She attributed this partly to that school's bilingual education model that ensures "that we do not exit students early." One teacher quipped that they were now teaching students "without TAAS-ing them." A colleague noted: "Without teaching to the test … in other words, teaching so that they are prepared not only for the test but for high school, for college and beyond."

Home–School Relations

Across the three sites, two common threads in the teachers' talk about aspects of home–school relations that serve to strengthen Latino children's literacy learning were systematic communication with parents and getting parents into classrooms to observe and undertake instructional activities. Teachers stressed establishing contact with parents early on in the school year and maintaining relations through multiple forms of communication, including phone calls, newsletters, conferences, journals, among others, all done bilingually. They also emphasized the ongoing need to involve more parents in school activities and to secure their cooperation in supporting school literacy at home, especially during children's emergent and beginning reading development.

All the focal teachers were of like mind about the importance of having parents in the classroom to better inform them about the nature of schoolwork in general and their children's instructional activities in particular. They recognized that Latino parents as a whole desire to support their children's school work but sometimes do not know how to do so, especially if they themselves are not schooled or do not know how to read and write. Teachers repeatedly mentioned the necessity and power of "modeling" or demonstrating actual teaching strategies for parents—in the classroom—so that these could later be emulated by them in volunteer tutorial work at school or at home with their children.

The need for teachers to know their students' parents was underscored by all the Washington, D.C., interviewees, and in particular by one first-grade teacher who stated, "You understand the child so much better when you understand the family." Various means for communicating with parents on a regular basis were identified, among them, "monthly newsletters explaining everything that is going on in the classroom," parent journals, messages via siblings, and other means. "Everything is done bilingually," said one teacher, even intercom messages by the principal. The benefit of communicating with families in both Spanish and English as emphasized by one teacher:

> Nos ayuda mucho la comunicación, el llamar por teléfono, el mandar notas, el utilizar a la mayor que está aquí o al que le sigue para hacer ese contacto con la familia. Este … esa madre que no sabe inglés … ella viene y se siente tan cómoda cuando tenemos la conferencia de los padres, se siente segura de que estamos hablando de su niño y nos estamos comunicando a través de su idioma, en parte. [Communication helps us a great deal, telephone calls, sending notes, making use of older and younger siblings to make contact with the family. That mother who doesn't know English … she comes and feels comfortable when we have parent–teacher conferences, she feels certain that we are talking about her child and that we are communicating through her language, in part.]

One teacher traced her affinity for a particular mathematics program in the school to its parental involvement component:

> Me gusta bastante [un programa de matemáticas] porque envuelve bastante a los padres de familia. Mandan unas bolsitas a las casas donde el padre tiene que trabajar con los niños en casa, después regresan al colegio y pueden trabajar con nosotros en el salón de clases … y nostros les damos todo el material … en español. [I like it a lot (a mathematics program) a lot because it involves parents. They send little bags to the homes where the father has to work with the children at home, later they come to the school and they can work with us in the classroom … and we give them all the material … in Spanish.]

In considering parental involvement across the different ethnic groups represented in their school population, two of the Washington, D.C., teachers pointed out that at their schools "actually the Latino parents are the ones who participate the most, like in the PTA."

The Washington teachers also talked about a long-standing, ongoing commitment to make parents aware of the important role played by their native language in their children's overall language development. As a group, they lamented the emphasis parents of very young Latino children often misplaced on speedy acquisition of English by their children. One teacher spoke about the negative consequences of this parental push toward English:

> [At our school] a lot of the Hispanic children are ... first generation Americans. And a lot of them are not as fluent in Spanish ... for many reasons. It is one of the fights we have with our parents. A lot of the time ... they want them not to have the hard times that they had when they came to this country, so they want their children to learn English right away. And, they speak to their children in English and don't speak to them in Spanish. And their English is not so good. So the child comes to school with neither language—they don't have the English, they don't have the Spanish. And, we have been working with that ... and explaining to the parents that it is really very important that they give them their culture and their language, that the English is going to come.

Teachers also bemoaned the change in some children's language preferences in the early grade levels although no explanations were offered for such occurrence. One teacher commented: "When they are 3 to 5 years old, they are so fluent in Spanish ...but then they go to first grade, and they don't want to speak Spanish anymore." Another teacher concluded: "So we need to validate their language, not just for a couple of years but we need to continue the growth of their language ... all the way through high school, if possible."

Uniqueness of Sites

A different mix of schooling factors at each interview site appeared to differentially influence the contexts for literacy teaching and learning reported by the teachers, giving each interview a "distinctive flavor." In Chicago, the dominant issue/concern appeared to be a push for reading achievement—and to a lesser degree, writing achievement—particularly in English, to satisfy the demands of an early exit transitional bilingual education model and high-stakes testing at the end of third grade. In El Paso, the dominant issue/concern seemed to be one of improving literacy instruction for all Latino students across monolingual and bilingual classrooms, with teachers noting that the high degree of homogeneity among the district's Mexicano-origin Latinos meant that similar student needs existed across all classrooms. In Washington, D.C., the dominant issue/concern appeared to be the need to elevate the status of Spanish among Spanish and English speakers, even in two-way bilingual immersion schools, such that English L2 literacy could be better supported by a solid base of native-language ability.

DISCUSSION

In this section, we discuss how the findings from the present study relate to insights gained from the existing research reviewed earlier in this chapter, that is, whether they confirm or disconfirm extant results. We also identify a number of research questions on instructional practice for bilingual students that emerged from the present study.

Most obvious is the high degree of concordance between the findings of this study and those of the effectiveness practices research of the past decade and a half, particularly in the areas of curriculum and instruction. The focal teachers repeatedly echoed the importance to bilingual Latino students of practices such as curricular integration, thematic teaching, use of culturally relevant curriculum materials, hands-on activities, and cooperative grouping. All such practices figure prominently in the effective schooling literature (e.g., Garcia, 1988; Pease-Alvarez et al., 1991; Reyes et al., 1999). The need for teachers to be caring but informed about bilingual Latino children's learning needs underlay much of their comments. Again, this is a consistent finding in the effective practices research conducted to date (Carter & Chatfield, 1986; Garcia, 1992; Tikunoff, 1985). Teachers repeatedly called attention to the affective dimension, both teachers' and children's attitudes, as influential to language and literacy learning and teaching.

While strongly supportive of bilingual education, the focal teachers nonetheless spoke candidly about the demanding work of bilingual teachers overall, much like the participants in Lemberger's studies (1996; 1997), specifically the work and resources required to create effective language and literacy instruction for bilingual Latino students. For example, they described the considerable mediation that is required in bilingual literacy instruction, both L1 and L2, and which they must carry out in order to be effective and responsive to children's learning needs. They echoed instructional strategies for mediating second-language reading tasks found in the existing research (e.g., Moll, 1988; Battle, 1993), noting the use of the native language as support for L2 reading. Unlike the existing research that has paid relatively little systematic attention to the texts used in instructing bilingual Latino students, the focal teachers gave considerable emphasis to the use of suitable children's literature as effective practice for bilingual Latino students. They noted the usefulness of culturally relevant trade books, especially picture books, as mediating, supportive resources for learners all along the developmental continuum.

Part of the challenging work in language and literacy teaching with bilingual Latino students, particularly in transitional bilingual education programs, was described by the focal teachers as ethical, political, and affective in nature, facets touched on mostly by Lemberger (1996, 1997) in the existing research. Teachers described ethical dilemmas in literacy teaching and assessment such as being required to move students into second language reading when they were not yet proficient enough in English, or having to prepare students for inappropriate testing. Teachers also reported political conflicts with their mono-lingual colleagues over the use of instruction, assessment, and interaction methods that reportedly fail to take into account the language and cultural background of bilingual Latino students. Teachers pointed to the affective de-mands of having to combat continuing resistance on the part of monolingual teachers as well as some parents toward native-language instruction.

Significantly, misunderstandings of parents and children with regard to lan-guage appeared to surface during all three interview sessions. Congruent with results from recent research in family literacy (e.g., Paratore et al., 1999; Krol-Sinclair, 1996) of limited bidirectional influence between schools and homes/communities, mainly school-centric views of parental involvement and families were revealed during the interviews. In general, parents apparently are respected and valued, but the full potential of their role in their children's lan-guage and literacy learning and development appears to be only partly under-stood. Vestiges of deficit views of family language and literacy became apparent at several points in the interviews.

From all three sessions, we gained renewed appreciation for the work that bi-lingual teachers must do to meet the needs of their students. As former bilingual education teachers, we agree with the veteran teacher who pointed out that much has changed for the better in the bilingual instructional arena in the quar-ter century of federally mandated bilingual education. However, we were dis-turbed to hear of a concomitant lack of change, attested to by the number of long-standing instructional woes that continue to plague the literacy education of bilingual Latino students, such as the lack of suitable curriculum materials for L1 and L2 reading and appropriate assessment measures for bilingual-biliterate learners. We found compelling two contradictions cited by the teachers as com-promising their current practice and professional integrity, apparently borne out of uninformed and/or misdirected policies. One is their pursuit of a rich and varied curriculum that encourages multiple ways of knowing and expressing knowledge but the widespread mandated imposition of a singular way to assess bilingual Latino children. The second contradiction centered around the teachers' dedication to better understand and respond to the language and lit-eracy needs of bilingual Latino children in contrast to the continuing tendency and push within the larger education community to treat these children as monolingual, monocultural individuals. In large part, such contradictions are an important reminder that much research and development still needs to oc-cur in the assessment of bilingualism and biliteracy of young learners. In the next section, we identify several research questions that emerged during the course of this study.

Emergent Research Questions

From the findings of the present study emerged a number of research questions pertinent to the design and improvement of classroom literacy instruction for bilingual Latino students. Educators and researchers would do well to consider such questions in this critical time of agenda setting and policy making relative to the literacy education of our nation's children. These questions are expressed further in broad and general terms.

Curriculum

The school-centric literacy curriculum traditionally has not been responsive to the learning needs of U.S. Latino students because it has excluded content that is familiar and meaningful to them. What does a culturally responsive, community-based literacy curriculum aligned with current reading/language arts standards look like?

Reading textbooks and trade books traditionally have not included content and images that reflect the life and heritage of U.S. Latino students. How do Latino children respond, cognitively and affectively, to culturally specific/authentic children's literature in Spanish and English?

Instruction

Vocabulary difficulties typically are associated with the English second-language reading of Latino students. How effectively and efficiently do Latino students process new vocabulary in second-language texts reflecting culturally familiar content versus texts with culturally unfamiliar content?

Although the term *lecto-escritura* implies a symbiotic relationship for literacy (reading and writing) in Spanish, the traditional approach to Spanish literacy instruction for U.S. Latino students has emphasized reading over writing. How effectively and efficiently would Latino students become literate in instruction that sought to codevelop reading and writing ability?

Spanish orthography has a more consistent phoneme-grapheme correspondence than does English. What influence does this orthographic feature have on U.S. Latino children's writing and spelling development? What role(s) should phonics play in beginning reading in Spanish? What role(s) should phonics play in beginning writing in Spanish? Just as important, how do these roles for phonics in Spanish differ from those applicable to reading and writing in English.

Assessment

U.S. bilingual Latino children have been expected to grow and develop in language and literacy much like monolinguals. What are key language and literacy developmental characteristics of children becoming bilingual and biliterate in early childhood?

Bilingual Latino children growing up bilingually and biliterate have usually been assessed according to monolingual standards for language and literacy development. What does an assessment approach sensitive to simultaneous development in two languages (Spanish and English) and two modes (oracy and literacy) look like?

Home–School Relations

Parental storybook reading during the preschool years has been identified as an important contributor to children's success in school literacy. How do Latino parents from different ethnolinguistic and socioeconomic groups support their children's emergent literacy (reading and writing in Spanish and English) during the preschool years?

Reading and writing homework reflects particular literacy theoretical orientations and seeks to develop particular literacy understandings. How do Latino parents from different ethnolinguistic and socioeconomic groups mediate instructional tasks, specifically homework, that require literacy beyond their own cultural and academic experience?

CLOSING REMARKS

We believe that this chapter makes a significant contribution to the field at an opportune time, offering a literature review that synthesizes the instructional research in bilingual literacy, both reading and writing in the elementary grades, and an empirically derived study of elementary bilingual teachers' perspectives on what makes for effective literacy instruction for bilingual Latino students. While we found the extant research base to be somewhat incomplete, the teacher data we collected through the focus interviews allowed us to contextualize our understanding of the major issues involved in teaching literacy to bilingual Latino children.

We remain convinced that teacher voices and perspectives must be considered in a thoughtful, respectful, and rigorously systematic fashion. These voices and perspectives are legitimate and valid sources of information not only for informing classroom practice but also for informing research and public policy. We hope that this chapter has accorded teachers their due role as the valuable professionals they are, particularly now as education becomes an issue of greater prominence at the national level as well as the state and local levels.

REFERENCES

Battle, J. (1993). Mexican American bilingual kindergarteners' collaborations in meaning making. In D. J. Leu & C. K. Kinzer (Eds.), *Examining central issues in literacy research, theory, and practice: Forty-second Yearbook of the National Reading Conference* (pp. 163–170). Chicago: National Reading Conference.

Calderón, M. E., Tinajero, J. V., & Hertz-Lazarowitz, R. (1992). *The Journal of Educational Issues of Language Minority Students, 10,* 79–106.

Carter, T. P., & Chatfield, M. L. (1986). Effective bilingual schools: Implications for policy and practice. *American Journal of Education, 95*(1), 200–232.

de la Rosa, D., Maw, C. E., & Yzaguirre, R. (1990). *Hispanic education: A statistical portrait 1990.* Washington, DC: Policy Analysis Center-Office of Research, Advocacy, and Legislation-National Council of La Raza.

Delgado-Gaitan, C. (1990). *Literacy for empowerment: The role of parents in children's education.* New York: The Falmer Press.

Delgado-Gaitan, C. (1991a). Involving parents in the schools: A process of empowerment. *American Journal of Education,* 20–46.

Delgado-Gaitan, C. (1991b). Relating experience and text: Socially constituted reading activity. In M. E. McGroarty & C. J. Faltis (Eds.), *Languages in school and society: Politics and pedagogy* (pp. 511–528). Berlin: Mouton de Gruyter.

Delgado-Gaitan, C. (1992). School matters in the Mexican–American home: Socializing children to education. *American Educational Research Journal, 29*(3), 495–513.

Delgado-Gaitan, C., & Trueba, H. (1991). *Crossing cultural borders: Education for immigrant families in America.* New York: The Falmer Press.

Edelsky, C. (1986). *Writing in a bilingual program: Había una vez.* Norwood, NJ: Ablex.

Fitzgerald, J. (1999). About hopes, aspirations, and uncertainty: First-grade English-language learners' emergent reading. *Journal of Literacy Research, 31*(2), 133–182.

García, E. (1988). Attributes of effective schools for language minority students. *Education and Urban Society, 20*(4), 387–400.

García, E. E. (1992). Effective instruction for language minority students: The teacher. *Journal of Education, 173*(2), 130–141.

Gersten, R. (1996). The double demands of teaching English language learners. *Educational Leadership, 53*(5), 18–22.

Gersten, R. M., & Jiménez, R. T. (1994). "A delicate balance: Enhancing literacy instruction for students of English as a second language." *The Reading Teacher, 47*(6), 438–449.

Goldenberg, C. (1987). Low-income Hispanic parents' contributions to their first-grade children's word-recognition skills. *Anthropology & Education Quarterly, 18*(3), 149–179.

Goldenberg, C. (1994). Promoting early literacy development among Spanish speaking children: Lessons from two studies. In E. H. Hiebert & B. M. Taylor (Eds.), *Getting reading right from the start: Effective early literacy interventions.* Boston: Allyn & Bacon.

Goldenberg, C., & Gallimore, R. (1991). Local knowledge, research knowledge, and educational change: A case study of early Spanish reading improvement. *Educational Researcher, 20*(8), 2–14.

Goldenberg, C., Reese, L., & Gallimore, R. (1992). Effects of literacy materials from school on Latino children's home experiences and early reading achievement. *American Journal of Education, 100,* 397–536.

Gomez, R., Parker, R., Lara-Alecio, R., & Gomez, L. (1996). Process versus product writing with limited English proficient students. *Bilingual Research Journal, 20*(2), 209–234.

Guerra, J. C. (1998). *Close to home: Oral and literate practices in a transnational Mexicano community.* New York: Teachers College Press.

Hispanic Dropout Project. (1996). *Data Book.* Washington, DC: U.S. Department of Education.

Jiménez, R. T., & Gersten, R. M. (1999). Lessons and dilemmas derived from the literacy instruction of two Latina/o teachers. *American Educational Research Journal, 36*(2) 265–301.

Jiménez, R. T., Gersten, R., & Rivera, A. (1996). Conversations with a Chicana teacher: Transition from native-to English-language instruction. *Elementary School Journal, 96*(3), 333–341.

Jiménez, R. T., Moll, L., Rodríguez-Brown, F., & Barrera, R. (1999). Latina and Latino researchers interact on issues related to literacy learning. *Reading Research Quarterly, 34*(2).

Krol-Sinclair, B. (1996). Connecting home and school literacies: Immigrant parents with limited formal education as classroom storybook readers. In D. J. Leu, C. K. Kinzer, & K. A. Hinchman (Eds.), *Literacies for the 21st Century: Research and Practice, Forty-fifth Yearbook of the National Reading Conference* (pp. 270–283). Chicago, IL: National Reading Conference.

Lemberger, N. (1996). Factors affecting language development from the perspectives of four bilingual teachers. *The Journal of Educational Issues of Language Minority Students, 18,* 17–31.

Lemberger, N. (1997). *Bilingual education: Teachers' narratives.* Mahwah, NJ: Lawrence Erlbaum Associates.

McCracken, G. D. (1998). *The long interview.* Newbury Park, CA: Sage.

Moll, L. C. (1988). Some key issues in teaching Latino students. *Language Arts, 65*(5), 465–472.

Moll, L. C. (1992). Literacy research in community and classrooms: A sociocultural approach. In R. Beach, J. Green, M. Kamil, & T. Shanahan (Eds.), *Multidisciplinary perspectives in literacy research* (pp. 211–244). Urbana, IL: National Conference on Research in English.

Moll, L. C., & Diaz, S. (1987). Change as the goal of educational research. *Anthropology & Education Quarterly, 18,* 300–311

Mulhern, M. M. (1997). Doing his own thing: A Mexican–American kindergartner becomes literate at home and school. *Language Arts, 74*(6), 468–476.

Muñiz-Swicegood, M. (1994). The effects of metacognitive reading strategy training on the reading performance and student reading analysis strategies of third grade bilingual students. *Bilingual Research Journal, 18,* 83–97.

NAEP. (2000). http://nces.ed.gov

National Center for Educational Statistics. (1997). *Dropout rates in the United States: 1995.* U.S. Department of Education.

National Center for Education Statistics. (1998a). *Report in brief. NAEP 1996 trends in academic progress.* U.S. Department of Education.

National Center for Education Statistics. (1998b). *Mini-digest of education statistics 1997.* U.S. Department of Education.

Padrón, Y. (1992). The effect of strategy instruction on bilingual students/ cognitive strategy use in reading. *Bilingual Research Journal, 18,* 49–66.

Padron, Y. (1994). Comparing reading instruction in Hispanic/limited-English-proficient schools and other inner city schools. *Bilingual Research Journal, 18,* 49–66.

Paratore, J. R., Homza, A., Krol-Sinclair, B., Lewis-Barrow, T., Melzi, G., Stergis, R., & Haynes, H. (1995). Shifting boundaries in home and school responsibilities: The construction of home-based literacy portfolios by immigrant parents and their children. *Research in the Teaching of English, 29*(4), 367–389.

Paratore, J. R., Melzi, G., & Krol-Sinclair, B. (1999). *What should we expect of family literacy? Experiences of Latino children whose parents participate in an intergenerational literacy project.* Newark, DE and Chicago, IL: International Reading Association and the National Reading Conference.

Pease-Alvarez, L., Garcia, E. E., & Espinosa, P. (1991). Effective instruction for language–minority students: An early childhood case study. *Early Childhood Research Quarterly, 6,* 347–361.

Pease-Alvarez, C., & Vasquez, O. (1994). Language socialization in ethnic minority communities. In F. Genesee (Ed.), *Educating second language children: The whole child, the whole curriculum, the whole community* (pp. 82–102). Cambridge, MA: Cambridge University Press.

Perez, B. (1994). Spanish literacy development: A descriptive study of four bilingual whole-language classrooms. *Journal of Reading Behavior, 26*(1), 75–94.

Reading Today. (2000, August/September). Moving beyond the debate: IRA endorses new NEA report. *Reading Today,* pp. 1, 9.

Reyes, M. L. (1991a). A process approach to literacy instruction for Spanish-speaking students: In search of a best fit. In E. H. Hiebert (Ed.), *Literacy for a diverse society: Perspectives, practices, and policies.* New York: Teachers College Press.

Reyes, M. L. (1991b). A process approach to literacy using dialogue journals and literature logs with second language learners. *Research in the Teaching of English, 25*(3), 291–313.

Reyes, P., Scribner, J. D., & Scribner, A. P. (1999). *Lessons from high-performing Hispanic schools.* New York: Teachers College Press.

Rutherford, W. (1999). Creating student-centered classroom environments: The case of reading. In P. Reyes, J. D. Scribner, & A. P. Scribner (Eds.), *Lessons from high-performing Hispanic schools* (pp. 131–168). New York: Teachers College Press.

San Miguel, G., & Valencia, R. R. (1998). From the Treat of Guadalupe Hidalgo to Hopwood: The educational plight and struggle of Mexican Americans in the southwest. *Harvard Educational Review, 68*(3), 353–400.

Snow, C., Burns, M. S., & Griffin, P. (1998). *Preventing reading difficulties.* Washington, DC: National Academy Press.

Soto, L. D. (1988). The home environment of higher and lower achieving Puerto Rican children. *Hispanic Journal of Behavioral Sciences, 10,* 161–168.

Soto, L. D. (1997). *Language, culture, and power: Bilingual families and the struggle for quality education.* New York: State University of New York Press.

Tikunoff, W. J. (1985). *Applying significant bilingual instructional features in the classroom.* Rosslyn, Virginia: National Clearinghouse for Bilingual Education.

Valdés, G. (1996). *Con respeto: Bridging the distances between culturally diverse families and schools.* New York: Teachers College Press.

Vasquez, O. A., Pease-Alvarez, L., & Shannon, S. M. (1994). *Pushing boundaries: Language and culture in a Mexicano community.* New York: Cambridge University Press.

Vaughn, S., Schumm, J. S., & Sinagub, J. (1996). *Focus group interviews in education and psychology.* Thousand Oaks: Sage Publications.

Zecker, L. B., Pappas, C. C., & Cohen, S. (1998). Finding the "right measure" of explanation for young Latina/o writers. *Language Arts, 76*(1), 49–56.

Zimpher, N. L. (1989). The RATE Project: A Profile of Teacher Education Students. *Journal of Teacher Education, 40*(6), 27–30.

Zimpher, N. L., & Yessayan, S. (1987). Recruitment and selection of minority populations into teaching. *Metropolitan Education, 5,* 57–71.

IV

Syntheses Across Cases

16

Research-Supported Characteristics of Teachers and Schools That Promote Reading Achievement[1]

Barbara M. Taylor
University of Minnesota/CIERA

Michael Pressley
Notre Dame University

P. David Pearson
Michigan Sate University/CIERA

[1]This research was conducted as part of CIERA, the Center for the Improvement of Early Reading Achievement and supported under the Educational Research and Development Centers program, PR/Award Number R305R70004, as administered by the Office of Educational Research and Improvement, U.S. Department of Education. However, the contents of the described report do not necessarily represent the positions or policies of the National Institute on Student Achievement, Curriculum and Assessment or the National Institute on Early Childhood development, or the U.S. Department of Education, and readers should not assume endorsement by the Federal government. This chapter appeared as a research report published by the National Education Association. Reprinted with permission.

INTRODUCTION

All educators want the best schools possible for children, schools that help them acquire the knowledge, skills, and dispositions they will need to pursue whatever dreams and paths they wish. Yet the reality is that many children are not reading well enough to keep up with the demands of school (Campbell, Donahue, Reese, & Phillip, 1996; Donahue, Voelkl, Campbell, & Mazzeo, 1999), let alone the demands of society or their personal dreams. In the recent national report, *Preventing Reading Difficulties in Young Children*, a National Academy of Science Committee concluded that "quality classroom instruction in kindergarten and the primary grades is the single best weapon against reading failure" (Snow, Burns, & Griffin, 1998). The committee recommended that the number one priority for educational research be to improve classroom reading instruction in kindergarten and the primary grades.

In addition to advocating improved classroom reading instruction, the Committee on the Prevention of Reading Difficulties in Young Children discussed the importance of systematic, schoolwide restructuring efforts in reading. The committee (Snow et al., 1998) recommended that low-performing schools consider reading reform efforts with a dual focus on improved classroom reading instruction *and* schoolwide organizational issues.

In an effort to share the good news about what can be done to increase learning and achievement for students in high-poverty schools, the research has been combed for this report to pinpoint those instructional and organizational factors that lead to student success. Specifically, the report represents an effort to explain how and why some schools across the country are attaining greater than expected reading achievement with populations of students who are at risk for failure by virtue of poverty. The terms *instructional* and *organizational* are emphasized because it is the conclusion of the authors, based on a thorough reading of the research, that only when both classroom level (instructional) and school level (organizational) facets of reform are attended to can aspirations to improve literacy for all students be met.

EFFECTIVE TEACHERS

A great deal is known about the teaching that occurs in elementary-level classrooms that are effective in promoting literacy development. This knowledge about effective teaching is the cumulative result of a number of research efforts in the latter part of the 20th century.

In the late 1960s and early 1970s, researchers began documenting the teaching processes that occurred in classrooms. The goal was to identify processes associated with an important educational product—high achievement, often reading achievement. Hence, this body of research came to be identified as process–product approach. Some of the now well-known researchers contributing to this tradition were Brophy (1973), Dunkin and Biddle (1974), Flanders (1970), Soar and Soar (1979), and Stallings and Kaskowitz (1974).

The process–product approach reflected the commitment in the middle part of the century of educational researchers to neobehaviorism and the concomitant belief that educational outcomes (i.e., products) could be understood as functions of educational inputs (i.e., processes). The unambiguous focus was on teaching behaviors and dimensions of teaching that could be measured by direct observation (e.g., Rosenshine, 1979). Several important practices were documented as part of this effort:

- More time spent engaged in academic activity produces better performance on objective tests of academic content. A high amount of time on task occurs in classrooms emphasizing an academic focus, with direct instruction by teachers especially effective in promoting elementary reading.
- Effective, direct instruction includes making learning goals clear, asking students questions as part of monitoring their understanding of what is being covered, and providing feedback to them about their academic progress.
- Effective classrooms, however, are convivial and warm, democratic and cooperative.
- Effective classrooms are places that respect individual differences between students, for example, with more teacher instruction provided to weaker students, who are also given more time to complete tasks.

Direct instruction evolved into an approach that emphasized the development of the component skills of reading. Its advocates (e.g., Carnine, Silbert, & Kameenui, 1997) were confident that mastery of such skills sums to a whole larger than its parts, with that whole being skilled reading. Direct instruction approaches to reading emphasize sound-, letter-, and word-level skills in beginning reading. Comprehension within the direct instruction model is less about constructing meaning in response to texts and more about learning vocabulary and specific comprehension skills, such as sequencing, sentence processing, summarizing, and making inferences (e.g., deciding whether the ideas in text make sense).

Gerald Duffy, Laura Roehler, and their associates (e.g., Roehler & Duffy, 1984; Duffy et al., 1987) conducted work in the 1980s that went beyond direct instruction, emphasizing the cognitive processes involved in excellent teaching. In fact, they emphasized teacher thinking much more than did the neobehaviorists. They also emphasized teaching as explanation, referring to their approach as direct explanation. What the good teacher explains are strategies that students can use for recognizing words and understanding texts. Yes, many of the strategies are remarkably similar if not identical to the skills emphasized by direct instructionists. The primary difference is that in the direct explanation model, the teacher does a lot more modeling of skill use, emphasizing to students his or her thinking as the skills are applied to new situations. For example, the teacher makes clear through modeling and explanation that word attack involves forming hypotheses based on knowing the sounds of the letters in words, blending those sounds, and reflecting on whether a word as sounded out makes sense in the sentence, paragraph, and passage context in which it appears. Similarly, the effective teacher overtly models and explains comprehension by making predictions about what might be in text that she or he reads to students. The teacher also tells students about images that occur to him or her as a reader, questions that occur during reading, and the big messages that seem to emerge from the text as reading proceeds. In short, the effective teacher mentally models the strategic activity that *is* skilled reading, demonstrating for students how good readers construct meaning and respond to text. The direct-explanation teacher encourages students to be active in the ways that skilled readers are active as they process texts (Pressley & Afflerbach, 1995).

Michael S. Knapp and Associates (1995) studied 140 classrooms in high poverty areas in California, Ohio, and Maryland, observing the teaching and measuring the student achievement. Their overarching conclusion was that effective instruction emphasized higher-order meaning making much more than lower-order skills. The more the teacher emphasized actual reading of text, rather than drilling of skills, the higher the student achievement.

Student achievement was also higher

- the more reading and writing were integrated,
- the more students discussed what they were reading,
- the more the teacher emphasized deep understanding rather than literal comprehension of text,
- the more that discrete skills were taught in the context of actual reading rather than out of context.

In short, the more the active cognitive processes and explanations that Duffy and Roehler favored occurred, the better reading seemed to be; the more that teachers emphasized using the skills taught as part of real reading and writing, the higher achievement seemed to be.

In recent years, much attention has been given to reading in the primary grades, with a great deal of debate about whether sound-, letter-, and word-level skills should be emphasized or whether focus on the reading and writing of real texts made more sense. In a CELA (Center on English Learning and Achievement) study, Pressley et al. (2001) and Wharton-McDonald, Pressley, and Hampston (1998) observed first-grade classrooms to find out how the teaching differed in classrooms where reading and writing went well, compared with classrooms where reading and writing achievement seemed less certain. They found that primary-level classrooms differed in the engagement of students in reading and writing, with the most engaged students becoming readers who read more complicated stories and books and wrote more coherent and complete texts. They found that teaching that stimulates high literacy achievement differs from teaching that does not. In the classrooms with high literacy achievement, there is more teaching of literacy skills, often in reaction to specific problems students encounter as they read and write real texts. Effective teachers expect and encourage their students to use the skills they learn in a self-regulated fashion, with teachers explaining to and modeling for students how to coordinate multiple strategies (e.g., attempt to recognize words by using phonics, word chunks, and semantic context clues such as accompanying pictures). Comprehension and writing strategies are taught as well, with the consistent message that understanding and effective communications—not just word recognition—are what literacy is about.

In the CIERA: (Center for the Improvement of Early Reading Achievement) Beating the Odds study of effective schools and accomplished primary-grade teachers, Taylor, Pearson, Clark, and Walpole (1999) compared the most accomplished teachers to the least accomplished teachers and the most effective schools to the least effective schools. The most accomplished teachers had higher student engagement, provided more small group instruction, had a preferred teaching style of coaching—as opposed to telling (the preferred style of the least accomplished teachers), provided more coaching during reading to help children improve in word recognition, and asked more higher-level comprehension questions. Teachers in the most effective schools provided more small group instruction, communicated more with parents, had children engage in more independent reading, provided more coaching during reading as a way to help children apply phonics knowledge, and asked more higher-level questions.

In short, excellent elementary literacy teachers seem to have taken a lesson from each period of research on effective teaching. This is consistent with the process–product framework to some extent, especially with regard to engagement, but goes beyond it in ways consistent with Roehler and Duffy's (1984) direct explanation approach and Knapp and Associates' (1995) emphasis on higher-order literacy instruction (i.e., instruction emphasizing comprehension and communication). Excellent elementary literacy teachers balance skills instruction with more holistic teaching (Pressley, 1998). In the best classrooms, students are engaged much of the time in reading and writing, with the teacher monitoring student progress and encouraging continuous improvement and growth, and providing "scaffolded" instruction, in which the teacher notices when students are having difficulty and provides sufficient support so that students are able to make progress. Furthermore, this skillful instruction is based on the exact strategies that students need to work on.

Numerous recent studies address the characteristics of effective teachers. Details about each study are listed in Table 16.1.

Common findings from three of the recent studies of effective teachers discussed above are summarized in Table 16.2. Also included are findings on classroom features from two recent studies of effective schools discussed in the next section.

EFFECTIVE SCHOOLS

Research on effective schools, much of which was conducted in the 1970s and early 1980s, was documented by Hoffman (1991) in a landmark paper, "Teacher and School Effects in Learning to Read," in the second volume of the *Handbook of Reading Research*. Hoffman uncovered eight recurring attributes of effective schools:

1. a clear school mission,
2. effective instructional leadership and practices,
3. high expectations,
4. a safe, orderly, and positive environment,
5. ongoing curriculum improvement,
6. maximum use of instructional time,
7. frequent monitoring of student progress,
8. positive home–school relationships.

Concerned specifically about high-poverty schools, Edmonds (1979) reasoned that research investigating high-achieving, high-poverty schools was needed.

TABLE 16.1

Recent Studies Addressing Characteristics of Effective Teachers

Name	Authors	Date Published	Focus
CELA	Pressley et al.	In press	Effective and more typical first-grade teachers in New York, New Jersey, Texas, and Wisconsin
CIERA: Beating the Odds	Taylor, Pearson, Clark, and Walpole	1999	4 high-performing schools compared to 10 lower performing schools
Teaching for Meaning in High Poverty Schools	Knapp	1995	A-2 year study of 140 classrooms
Chicago Schools with Substantially Improved Achievement	Designs for Change	1998	Report on 7 Profile Schools with large achievement gains in math and reading
Title I: Prospects	Puma et al.	1997	5 high-performing Title I schools selected from a pool of 400

TABLE 16.2

Characteristics of Effective Teachers: Trends Found in Recent Studies

	Study				
Feature Emphasized	CELA	CIERA: Beating the Odds	Knapp	Chicago Schools with Substantially Improved Achievement	Title I: Prospects
Excellent classroom management	X	X			
Balanced reading instruction	X	X	X	X	X
Small group instruction	X	X			X
Higher order thinking	X	X	X	X	X

Studies in the 1970s of high-poverty elementary schools with high reading achievement found several distinguishing characteristics: (a) a strong emphasis on reading, (b) strong leadership, (c) systematic evaluation of pupil progress, and (d) high expectations for students (Venezky & Winfield, 1979; Weber, 1971; Wilder, 1977).

For a host of reasons, research on effective schools was placed on a back burner in the late 1980s and early 1990s. In recent years, however, a revival of effective schools research has occurred, most likely due to widespread national concerns that the nation's schools are failing to meet the needs of the poorest children. Five large-scale studies on effective, moderate- to high-poverty elementary schools were published between 1997 and 1999. What is remarkable about them is that they report strikingly similar findings that both support and extend the earlier research. Details about each study are listed in Table 16.3.

Across these five studies, six factors emerged consistently. These six factors, along with their incidence across the five studies, are summarized in Table 16.4.

TABLE 16.3

Recent Large-Scale Studies on Effective Schools

Name	Authors	Date Published	Focus
Hope for Urban Education	Charles A. Dana Center	1999	9 high-performing, high-poverty schools around the country
CIERA: Beating the Odds	Taylor, Pearson, Clark, and Walpole	1999	4 high-performing schools compared with 10 lower performing schools
Title I: Prospects	Puma, Karweit, Price, Ricciuiti, Thompson, and Vaden-Kiernan	1997	5 high-performing Title I schools selected from a pool of 400
Successful Texas Schoolwide Programs	Lein, Johnson, and Ragland	1997	26 Texas Title I schools that surpassed 70% pass rate on Texas Assessment of Academic Skills (TAAS)
Chicago Schools with Substantially Improved Achievement	Designs for Change	1998	Report on 7 Profile Schools with large achievement gains in math and reading

TABLE 16.4

School Level Factors Responsible for High Achievement in High-Poverty Schools

Factor	Study				
	Hope for Urban Education	CIERA: Beating the Odds	Title I: Prospects	Successful Texas Schoolwide Programs	Chicago Schools with Substantially Improved Achievement
Focus on improved student learning	✔	✔		✔	✔
Strong school leadership	✔		✔		✔
Strong teacher collaboration	✔	✔		✔	✔
Consistent use of data on student performance	✔	✔		✔	✔
Focus on professional development and innovation	✔	✔		✔	✔
Strong links to parents	✔	✔	✔	✔	✔

Focus on Improved Student Learning

In four of these studies improved student learning was cited as the school's over-riding priority. This focus on improving student learning entailed a collective sense of responsibility for school improvement; teachers, parents, the principal, and the school staff worked together as a team to realize their common goal of substantially improved student learning.

Strong School Leadership

Three studies documented the importance of a strong building leadership, most often in the form of leadership from the principal. The *Hope for Urban Education* (*Hope*) report highlighted the role of school leadership—not necessarily limited to the principal—in terms of redirecting people's time and energy, creating a collective sense of responsibility for school improvement, getting staff the resources and training needed, creating opportunities for collaboration, creating additional time for instruction, and helping the school persist despite difficulties. The *Chicago Schools with Substantially Improved Achievement* (*Chicago*) report specified that the substantially improved schools had more effective principals who served as instructional leaders, closely supervised the change process, unified the school around the mission of improved student learning, and built a strong staff by hiring carefully and providing regular coaching to help teachers improve their instruction. The *Title I: Prospects* (*Prospects*) report found that the high-performing Title I schools had more experienced principals than other Title I schools.

Strong Teacher Collaboration

In addition to, or perhaps because of, strong leadership, strong staff collaboration was highlighted in four of the studies. In the *Hope* study, school leaders created opportunities for teachers to work, plan, and learn together—with a focus on instructional issues. In the *CIERA: Beating the Odds* (*CIERA*) study, teachers reported a strong sense of building communication and used a collaborative model in which classroom and resource teachers worked together to maximize time for small group instruction in the primary grades. In the *Chicago* study, the teachers worked more effectively as a team, especially in planning and in sharing information about students. In the *Successful Texas Schoolwide Programs* (*Texas*) study, cross-grade as well as within-grade collaboration among teachers was highlighted. Frequently, teachers were found to work with those who taught subsequent grade levels to better understand each other's curricula and expectations.

Consistent Use of Data on Student Performance

Four of the studies found that the effective schools systematically used student assessment data, usually on curriculum-embedded measures, to improve performance. In the *Hope* study, teachers carefully aligned instruction to standards and state or district assessments. In the *CIERA* study, the most effective schools engaged in regular, systematic evaluation of student progress and shared this data to make instructional decisions. In the *Texas* study, schools and/or districts aligned curriculum staff development efforts with the objectives of the Texas Assessment of Academic Skills (TAAS). Formative assessments were widely used by teachers to plan instruction. In the *Chicago* study, it was found that in the substantially improved schools, teachers carefully monitored students' reading progress through observations and tests. In many of the schools, assessment data were a part of the collaborative model: teachers got together to share data and reach consensus on instructional plans for particular students.

Focus on Professional Development and Innovation

In four of the studies, ongoing professional development and trying out new research-based practices was stressed. In the *Hope* study, school leaders made sure that teachers felt they had the materials and training they needed to help students achieve at high levels. In the *CIERA* study, the emphasis was on year-long professional development in which teachers learned together within a building. In the *Texas* study, teachers were encouraged to experiment with new ideas and to collaborate to help one another improve their instruction. Teachers at these effective schools were continually searching for new, effective ways of teaching and were described as a "community of learners." In the *Chicago* study, teachers were encouraged to try innovations, and principals provided workshops, coaching, and assistance to help teachers improve their instruction.

Strong Links to Parents

All five studies reported strong efforts within schools to reach out to parents. In the *Hope* study, the school staffs worked to win the confidence of parents and then build effective partnerships with them to support student achievement. In the *CIERA* study, the most effective schools made more of an effort to reach out to parents—by involving them in an active site council, by engaging them in phone or written surveys or focus groups, and by calling them just to stay in touch. In the *Prospects* study, the high-performing schools reported a better school climate, better relations with the community, and more parental support. In the *Texas* study, parents were regarded as part of the team effort to improve student achievement, and parents were treated as valued members of the school family. School staff made a concerted effort to accommodate parents who did not speak English. In the *Chicago* study, parents were treated with respect, participated in school events, including parent orientation sessions, and were encouraged to help children learn at home.

CONCLUSIONS

Recent research on effective teachers and schools is surprisingly convergent. Effective teachers have excellent classroom management skills and provide scaffolded, balanced literacy instruction, often in small groups, characterized by explicit instruction in skills and strategies, as well as frequent opportunities for students to read, write, and talk about text. Effective schools are typically characterized as collaborative learning communities in which staff assume a shared responsibility for all students' learning, monitor progress as a way of planning instruction for groups and individuals, help one another learn more about the art and science of teaching, and reach out to the families they serve.

It is interesting to note that schools in three of the studies (Hope for Urban Education, CIERA: Beating the Odds, Successful Texas) felt that packaged programs are not the magic ingredient in improving student achievement—in spite of all the pressure for schools to adopt off-the shelf reform programs. The success of these schools suggests that the common denominator for reading achievement is commitment and hard work that focuses on the classroom-level and school-level practices consistently identified in this research as important in helping students become proficient readers.

REFERENCES

Brophy, J. (1973). Stability of teacher effectiveness. *American Educational Research Journal*, 10, 245–252.

Campbell, J. R., Donahue, P. L., Reese, C. M., & Phillip, G. W. (1996). *NAEP 1994 reading report card for the nation and the states*. Washington, DC: Office of Educational Research and Improvement.

Carnine, D. W., Silbert, J., & Kameenui, E. J. (1997). *Direct instruction reading* (3rd ed.). Upper Saddle River, NJ: Merrill-Prentice Hall.

Charles A. Dana Center, University of Texas at Austin. (1999). *Hope for urban education: A study of nine high-performing, high-poverty urban elementary schools*. Washington, DC: U.S. Department of Education, Planning and Evaluation Service.

Designs for Change. (1998). *Practices of schools with substantially improved reading achievement*. Chicago Public Schools. www.dfc1.org/summary/report. htm

Donahue, P. L., Voelkl, K. E., Campbell, J. R., & Mazzeo, J. (1999). *NAEP 1998 reading report card for the nation*. Washington, DC: U.S. Department of Education.

Duffy, G. G., Roehler, L. R., Sivan, E., Rackliffe, G., Book, C., Meloth, M. S., Vavrus, L. G., Wesselman, R., Putnam, J., & Bassiri, D. (1987). Effects of explaining the reasoning associated with using reading strategies. *Reading Research Quarterly*, 20, 347–368.

Dunkin, M., & Biddle, B. (1974). *The study of teaching*. New York: Holt, Rinehart, & Winston.

Edmonds, R. (1979). Effective schools for the urban poor. *Educational Leadership*, 37, 15–27.

Flanders, N. (1970). *Analyzing teacher behavior*. Reading, MA: Addison-Wesley.

Hoffman, J. V. (1991). Teacher and school effects in learning to read. In R. Barr, M. L. Kamil, P. B. Mosenthal, & P. D. Pearson (Eds.), *Handbook of reading research* (Vol. II, pp. 911–950). New York: Longman.

Knapp, M. S., and Associates. (1995). *Teaching for meaning in high-poverty classrooms*. New York: Teachers College Press.

Lein, L., Johnson, J. F., & Ragland, M. (1997). *Successful Texas schoolwide programs: Research study results*. Austin, TX: Charles A. Dana Center, University of Texas at Austin.

Pressley, M. (1998). *Reading instruction that works: The case for balanced teaching*. New York: Guilford.

Pressley, M., & Afflerbach, P. (1995). *Verbal protocols of reading: The nature of constructively responsive reading*. Mahwah, NJ: Lawrence Erlbaum Associates.

Pressley, M., Wharton-McDonald, R., Allington, R., Block, C. C., Morrow, L., Tracey, D., Baker, K., Brooks, G., Cronin, J., Nelson, E., & Woo, D. (2001). A study of effective first-grade literacy instruction. *Scientific studies of reading, 5,* 35–58.

Puma, M. J., Karweit, N., Price, C., Ricciuiti, A., Thompson, W., & Vaden-Kiernan, M. (1997). *Prospects: Final report on student outcomes*. (Title I) Washington, DC: U.S. Department of Education, Planning and Evaluation Service.

Roehler, L. R., & Duffy, G. G. (1984). Direct explanation of comprehension processes. In G. G. Duffy, L. R. Roehler, & J. Mason (Eds.), *Comprehension instruction: Perspectives and suggestions,* (pp. 265–280). New York: Longman.

Rosenshine, B. V. (1979). Content, time, and direct instruction. In P. L. Peterson & H. J. Walberg (Eds.), *Research on teaching: Concepts, findings, and implications,* (pp. 28–56). Berkeley, CA.: McCutchan.

Snow, C. E., Burns, S., & Griffin, P. (Eds.). (1998). *Preventing reading difficulties in young children: Report of the Committee on the Prevention of Reading Difficulties in Young Children*. Washington, DC: National Academy Press.

Soar, R. S., & Soar, R. M. (1979). Emotional climate and management. In P. L. Peterson & H. J. Walberg (Eds.), *Research on teaching: Concepts, findings, and implications,* Berkeley, CA: McCutchan.

Stallings, J., & Kaskowitz, D. (1974). Follow through classroom observation evaluation 1972–73 (SRI Project URU-7370). Stanford, CA: Stanford Research Institute.

Taylor, B. M., Pearson, P. D., Clark, K., & Walpole, S. (1999). Beating the Odds in Teaching All Children to Read. (CIERA Report # 2-006) Ann Arbor, MI: Center for the Improvement of Early Reading Achievement, University of Michigan. This report is also being published as Effective Schools/Accomplished Teachers: Lessons about Primary Grade Reading Instruction in Low-Income Schools, *The Elementary School Journal, 101,* November, 2000, 121–165.

Venezky, R. L., & Winfield, L. (1979). *Schools that succeed beyond expectations in teaching reading* (Technical Report No. 1). Newark, DE: Department of Educational Studies, University of Delaware.

Weber, G. (1971). *Inner city children can be taught to read: Four successful schools* (CGE Occasional Papers No. 18). Washington, DC: Council for Basic Education. (ERIC Document Reproduction Service No. ed 057 125)

Wharton-McDonald, R., Pressley, M., & Hampston, J. (1998). Outstanding literacy instruction in first grade: Teacher practices and student achievement. *Elementary School Journal, 99,* 101–128.

Wilder, G. (1977). Five exemplary reading programs. In J. T. Guthrie (Ed.), *Cognition, curriculum, and comprehension,* (pp. 57–68). Newark, DE: International Reading Association.

17

Beating the Odds in Literacy Education: Not the "Betting on" but the "Bettering of" Schools and Teachers

Gerald G. Duffy
Michigan State University

James V. Hoffman
The University of Texas at Austin

This is a book about effective literacy teachers and effective literacy schools. It addresses a fundamental challenge in our society of making a quality education available to all students regardless of ethnic, racial, or economic background. It puts before us the reality that we have not in the past, and are not now, serving all the children in our nation's schools in a fair and equitable manner. The authors in this book argue that research can guide our efforts to make our schools and teaching better. They report studies that enlighten our efforts to serve students for whom the odds of success are low. We have been asked to speculate in this chapter on the book's contribution. To do so, we focus on what we view as the single most important finding from the last 25 years of the 20th century on effective literacy teaching—the multilayered complexity of the teaching task. This finding, in turn, leads us to argue that the essential message of this book is the need to invest in the bettering of teachers and schools, rather than betting on standards and accountability to do the job for us.

BACKGROUND

The historical antecedent for the research reported in this book is the early ob-servational research designed to identify correlates of effective instruction (see, for instance, Brophy & Good, 1986; Good & Brophy, 1986). In the early years of research on teaching, the expectation was that the data would result in a uni-versal template that would permanently guide all literacy learning in elemen-tary schools. With such a template in place, it was thought, policy makers and administrators could create effective literacy instruction simply by implement-ing each aspect of the template.

This view has great appeal in today's political climate of high-stakes testing and associated instructional mandates. It carries the aura of being "re-search-based," and success appears to be a simple matter of putting correlates in place.

However, we now know it is not that simple (see, for instance, Dole, Duffy, Roehler, & Pearson, 1991; Duffy & Hoffman, 1999; Hoffman, 1998). The effec-tiveness correlates identified in observational studies, although valid, are very broad and shallow. Classrooms and schools, in contrast, are multilayered and vary from context to context. One size does not fit all. So when we impose the seductively simple idea of implementing "research-based" correlates, we see only superficial improvements in teaching and only get gains only in low level literacy skills.

Creating substantive forms of instructional effectiveness and substantive forms of literacy achievement requires that we examine the deeper structures guiding teachers' and school leaders' *enactment* of teaching. This enacting is not a simple matter of technical compliance with observed correlates of effective-ness. Rather, the best teachers weave a variety of teaching activities together in an infinitely complex and dynamic response to the flow of classroom life, and the best school leaders weave school conditions together in an infinitely com-plex and dynamic response to life in schools. It is more like orchestration than straightforward implementation.

Hence, we frame our comments in the "orchestration" image. We highlight the complex and dynamic nature of effective literacy teaching in two parts.

First, we point out aspects of effective literacy teaching that earlier studies of effectiveness did not emphasize. Second, we suggest that observational data such as those reported in this book can mask essential keys of effectiveness. We conclude by arguing that these subtle and often masked aspects of instruction should be our focus as we continue to study literacy teaching.

ADDITIONAL COMPONENTS OF INSTRUCTIONAL EFFECTIVENESS

In their chapter summarizing trends in teacher and school effectiveness, Taylor, Pressley, and Pearson list major components associated with instructional effectiveness. We view these components as reasonable interpretations from their data. However, we believe that at least two additional components emerge from the studies reported here.

Component 1: Instructional Factors

As Taylor, Pressley, and Pearson note, the instructional factors traditionally associated with effective literacy teaching, and learning are good classroom management, balanced instruction, small group teaching, and emphasis on higher order thinking. The book's contents, however, suggest two other important instructional factors: early intervention and authentic instructional tasks.

Early instructional interventions.

"... students receive intensive instruction through the Right Start early intervention literacy program ..." (Colt & Mills, chap. 7, this volume).

"... kindergarten intervention occurred both inside and outside the classroom" (Walpole, chap. 8, this volume).

"... not many parents or teachers expect assessments to be given to kindergarten children but they can be very useful" (Paris, Paris, & Carpenter, chap. 5, this volume).

Chapter after chapter reports early identification of potential struggling readers and writers and intensive instructional interventions at the first sign of difficulty. Sometimes authors specify the details of the intervention. In other places, early intervention is more subtly noted, as in chapter 2 where Pressley, Wharton-McDonald, Raphael, Bogner, and Roehrig cite the impact of strategies associated with Reading Recovery. The reader must conclude from the evidence discussed in these chapters that direct and intensive interaction with varieties of text as early as possible is essential if we are to "beat the odds" with at-risk populations.

This has not been traditional practice, however. For decades, the tradition has been to place formal reading instruction in first grade and to reserve the kindergarten year for socialization skills. However, the stories reported in this book (as well as the success of early intervention programs such as Reading Recovery) lay that argument to rest. Instruction of traditionally at-risk school populations must include early identification and making all instructional resources available immediately.

Authentic Instructional Tasks.

"... the administrators and teachers facilitated 'real-world learning' via community-centered programs and local organizations that worked directly with classroom teachers and students" (Breaux, Danridge, & Pearson, chap. 9, this volume).

"... all four teachers had their students engaged in authentic, engaging literacy activities ... " (Taylor, chap. 12, this volume).

"... Ms. Roberts ties every subject she teaches to literacy through thematic instruction" (Morrow, chap. 13, this volume).

Although early intervention, as noted above, is crucial, instruction cannot be mindless drill and practice. Throughout the book, the case is made that literacy instruction is most effective when embedded in thematic units, play activity, simulations and other forms of engaging, worthwhile literacy activity. It matters not whether students are in regular classrooms, special education classrooms, or bilingual classrooms. All report the importance of authentic learning tasks.

Summary.   Both early intervention and authentic activity highlight the complexity of literacy teaching. Neither can be accomplished easily; both require creative and innovative restructuring of traditional instructional thinking. Hence, we are confronted once again with the need for orchestration rather than technical implementation.

Component 2: Change as a Correlate of Effectiveness

In one sense, this entire book is about change. Virtually every chapter reports how schools and teachers changed their instruction and became more effective. In that sense, change and how to accomplish it is a crucial component of effective literacy teaching. We noted five particularly important aspects of change.

Change is a Longitudinal Process.

"... the staff had a plan and a planning process ... it was a process they truly made their own" (Breaux, Danridge, & Pearson, chap. 9, this volume).

Change does not happen by accident. It is a process that happens because there is a plan. The various chapters of this book repeatedly emphasize the process of change, the plan that guided the process, the planning time that must be allocated to see the change through, the ownership that participants must have in order for the change to be effective, and the longitudinal nature of change.

Change is a Collaborative Process.

"... in this school, collaboration is valued as a means for exploring alternative ways of working together and generating solutions to problems" (Colt & Mills, chap. 7, this volume).

"... teachers attributed their improved collaboration to the experience of working as instructional partners on a daily basis" (Smith, Johnson, & Jones, chap. 11, this volume).

"... we found systematic collaboration among the staff members ..." (Walpole, chap. 8, this volume).

"... administration and teachers draw upon community 'funds of knowledge'" Breaux, Danridge, & Pearson, chap. 9, this volume).

The message about collaboration is clear. Teachers and administrators cannot make substantive instructional changes alone or in isolation. Instructional change, like cultural change, involves a community. The community enforces established practices. Changing practices, therefore, must be a community effort. Effective teaching and schools result only when the community as a whole commits to change. Hence, collaboration is essential.

Change Efforts Must Be Programmatic.

"... Sapphire does not appear to be 'out in front' of its district office ..." (Adler, chap. 10, this volume).

"... New teachers are informed in the interview process about Woodlawn's high expectations for students, the instructional practices used, and the staff development they will be required to take ..." (Taylor & Critchley, chap. 6, this volume).

For change to occur, all stakeholders must be committed to the expectations, goals, and mission. Teachers must be in alignment with each other and with the school administrator; the school must be in alignment with the district. From a curriculum perspective, there must be basic agreement on curricular emphases from grade to grade. From an instructional perspective, there must be basic agreement on instructional technique and materials from teacher to teacher. Effective literacy teaching cannot happen if various personnel are operating under different understandings.

Change Efforts Are Dynamic.

"... the instructional team at Stevenson was still working on many things ..." (Walpole, chap. 8, this volume).

"... hardly a year goes by when there is not a substantial change in one or more components of the program" (Adler, chap. 10, this volume).

"... though ... their reform efforts had been ongoing for several years under the leadership of their principal, they also admitted that the fruits of their efforts were not shown in achievement score gains until the last 2 years" (Johnson, chap. 3, this volume).

In the early days of research on teaching, instructional change was envisioned as a two-step process. First, identify the effective practices through observation of classrooms and schools; second, implement those practices. We naively expected to see immediate student results, and to not have to worry about it after that. The stories told in this book change that expectation. They demonstrate that change does not stop with the initial implementation of a new practice or technique. Instead, it is ongoing. A change made in 1 year interacts with other practices and generates new insights, which result in modifications and adjustments in subsequent years. Perhaps even more important, changes implemented in 1 year seldom pay off in immediate student results.

Hence, change is not quick. It is not a matter of making a change this year and then "returning to normal" next year. To the contrary, one change leads to more change. Ultimately, change itself becomes a culturally embedded practice, and instructional improvement becomes a permanent, ongoing characteristic of the school.

The Sheer Difficulty of Instructional Change.

"... these factors reflect the tremendous amount of energy and hard work that the administration, staff, students and parents have committed ..." (Breaux, Danridge, & Pearson, chap. 9, this volume).

"... There was tension in the school. Faculty turnover was high" (Smith, Johnson, & Jones, chap. 11, this volume).

"... perhaps a key difference between these schools and other less successful schools is that educators in these schools persisted" (Johnson, chap. 3, this volume).

The reader of this book is conscious throughout of the difficulty involved in making instructional changes. Although most chapters are triumphant and upbeat reports of "success stories," there is an undertone of huge difficulties being overcome. Therein lies a crucial lesson about becoming an effective teacher or an effective school. Becoming effective requires changes. And change does not happen easily. Change happens because professional educators make sacrifices, are persistent and maintain a level of commitment. Tenacity is essential. The various stories in this book make this very evident.

Summary. Teacher and school effectiveness has traditionally been treated as an uncomplicated matter of translating research findings into practice. In actuality, however, change is extremely difficult. It involves a long-term process and wrenching problems that can only be overcome by people of good will who sustain the effort. It requires creative orchestration, not technical implementation.

ISSUES WE NEED TO "TROUBLE" FURTHER

Observational research identifies external factors associated with instructional effectiveness. Such findings are important. However, external factors can mask the more subtle mechanism that actually control what is being observed. That is, the orchestration at the heart of instructional effectiveness can be obscured unless we persist in looking for the subtle deep structures underneath the external factors. To illustrate, we suggest five examples from our reading of the chapters that may mask important deep structure issues.

What Exactly is "Exemplary?"

"... not all schools believed to be exemplary in our study were, in fact, found to be so" (Taylor, Pearson, Clark, & Walpole, chap. 1, this volume).

The construct of "effectiveness" itself masks important issues. If the criterion for selecting effective teachers and schools is unexpected achievement gains, other qualitative aspects of achievement are masked. If the criterion is based on a teacher's or school's reputation, possible false positive identifications may mask better examples of effectiveness. Both are problematic in that the term *ef-*

fectiveness carries an aura of authoritative finality when, in actuality, important underlying questions about effectiveness are left unexamined.

Similarly, surface level explorations of effectiveness can mask deeper questions. For instance, Taylor, Pearson, Clark, and Walpole report time on task to be "... less amenable to building-level influence than other teaching practices ..." But how does this happen here and not in other areas? And in what specific ways is the system resistant to or supportive of effective practices? What is the controlling mechanism underneath these phenomena?

We should also "trouble" further the potential contradiction between effective schools characterized as having "strong leadership" on the one hand and effective teachers characterized as decision makers on the other hand. The two constructs may be antithetical. Is it possible that features associated with effective schools increase the teaching performance of poor and mediocre teachers but constrain the performance of excellent teachers? We doubt that all teachers are affected in the same way, but global concepts such as *strong leadership* and *teachers as decision makers* mask teacher–school interrelationships that almost certainly are essential to effective literacy teaching.

Similarly, this book links effective schools and effective teachers. The expectation is that one must go with the other. However, it might be productive to focus separately on effective teachers and effective schools. We suspect that the interconnections and mediating variables—that is, the orchestration element—would be more readily identified under such conditions.

Community and Culture.

"... the voices of Latino teachers and researchers are curiously absent in the on-going debate concerning early childhood reading instruction" (Barrera & Jiménez, chap. 15, this volume).

Many chapters in this book tie effectiveness to school–community and home–school relationships. This is good news. However, the discourse in most chapters is remarkably "culture" free. The absence of cultural voices stretches across ethnicities and races. Certainly there are subtle cultural differences from community to community that affect instruction. However, as Barrera and Jimenez argue, we know precious little about this.

Similarly, home–school relations are only superficially developed. Most examples are confined to calling home, or sending home a letter or newsletter, or sending home a traveling folder of students' work. We expect that a deeper, more fundamental home–school communication is present in effective schools, but we get little insight into the inner workings of this phenomenon here.

It is not enough to say that relations with community and home are associated with effective literacy instruction. We must delve into the nature of those relationships, how they are developed and how they are sustained. Only those data will inform our efforts to enhance literacy instruction.

Testing and Curriculum Alignment.

"... Liebes' whole agenda was to get test scores up. It was all she was about. And whatever it took to do that, she was going to get it done. And she did. Of course, many people were very unhappy about how that was accomplished" (Smith, Johnson, & Jones, chap. 11, this volume).

"... many teachers engaged in inappropriate or unethical testing procedures because of the pressure they were under ..." (Paris, Paris, & Carpenter, chap. 5, this volume).

We live in an era of high-stakes testing. The name of the game is achievement of low-level literacy skills. Thankfully, this book does not share this view, and describes testing as a means for focusing instruction, consistent with principles of instructional design. Paris, Paris, and Carpenter, for instance, describe assessment as important "... because instruction needs to be calibrated according to students' knowledge, skills, and interests."

Nonetheless, the shadow of high-stakes testing lurks in the corner of virtually all the stories told in this book. Chapter after chapter is influenced by the bottom-line concern for increased scores on measures of accountability.

We understand this concern and the tension it creates. But it masks more subtle questions that are crucial to understanding teacher and school effectiveness. For instance, if achievement scores increase, is it the result of increased performance of low-level and mediocre teachers? And, if so, what changes do these teachers make? And how are the best teachers in the building affected?

Similarly, what is the relationship between test literacy and the "higher order literacy" specified by Taylor, Pressley, and Pearson in chapter 14? To what degree does the drive for increased scores on standardized achievement tests, and the associated pressure on teachers to "teach to the test," result in diminished levels of "higher order literacy?" What is it that the best teachers do to be accountable for test literacy while also developing higher order literacy?

Test scores dominate literacy these days. But, as researchers, we need to "trouble" this area further by asking the questions underneath the prevalent question about how well our kids did on the test.

Balanced Reading Instruction.

"... our very best teachers expressed commitment to the principle that they would do whatever it took to meet a wide array of individual student needs encountered every day in their classrooms" (Taylor, Pearson, Clark, & Walpole, chap. 1, this volume).

"… the balance between skills instruction and more holistic reading and writing seemed most effective …" (Pressley, Wharton-McDonald, et al., chap. 2, this volume).

The terms *balanced instruction* and *eclectic teaching* appear throughout this book. We worry about these terms. What do they mean exactly? Do they mean an equal emphasis on two instructional approaches, as Pressley, Wharton-McDonald, et al. imply? Or does it mean a static formula in which a certain amount of time is allocated to this and another allocated to that?

We believe these terms mask crucially important deep structures that govern effective literacy teaching. We suspect that effective teachers do not measure out equal portions of skills-based and holistic instruction, nor do they allocate instructional time according to a static formula deemed to be "balanced." We suspect, instead, that they vary instruction depending on what their students' need. With some students, they are probably very skills focused; with other students they are probably very holistic. Some students spend lots of time in one set of activities and/or materials and other students spend lots of time in other sets of activities and/or materials. If we only look for balance in the distribution of activity structures then we may well miss what underlies the planning and decision-making of effective teachers: responsive and opportunistic instruction.

We do not doubt that effective teachers are eclectic. But we must dig deeper. How do teachers conceptualize this idea of *eclecticism*? How do they maintain a conceptual focus while employing various strategies and methods? How do they manage to sustain an eclectic approach in the face of multiple school, district and state forces that encourage conformity and standardization?

In summary, "balanced reading instruction" is too general and global. The only thing it eliminates is extremist positions, which recent research studies say is something most teachers don't do anyway (see, for instance, Baumann, Hoffman, Moon, & Duffy-Hester, 1998). We need instead rich description the deep structure thought processes that govern enactment of eclectic practices.

Usable Descriptions of "Instruction."

"… to help her students become independent, Lora said that she was process oriented. By focusing on HOW to do things, she felt her students learned how to depend on themselves …" (Taylor, chap. 12, this volume).

"… good thinkers are motivated to use appropriately the strategies they know, largely based on past successes … but also because of previous instruction and feedback …" (Pressley, Wharton-McDonald, et al., chap. 2, this volume).

"... all five classroom teachers frequently explain a process or strategy or coach their students ..." (Colt & Mills, chap. 7, this volume).

Similar to our concern about "balanced instruction," we are concerned about global descriptions of instructional practices. For instance, when we describe a teacher as "process oriented," or by reference to their use of techniques such as "coaching," we mask the thinking that drives "process-oriented" teachers or teachers who are good "coaches." What exactly does one do when one is "process oriented?" And how is a process orientation distinct from "explanation," or "coaching" or "feedback?" And how do teachers enact such aspects of instruction?

We have enough descriptive research on the various aspects of instruction to know that concepts such as *explanation* and *coaching* are richly layered and complex (see, for instance, Duffy, in press; Rodgers, 1999). They cannot be described as "new tricks" teachers can easily apply, as Pressley, Wharton-McDonald, et al. suggest. Such a perception puts us right back in the technical mode that we long ago learned was naïve and shallow. Instruction is a complex orchestration of techniques and materials that teachers creatively adapt from one instructional situation to another. Glossing over this complexity is misleading.

Summary

We must "trouble" further the subtle keys to effectiveness that exist under the external appearance of instruction. These keys govern the enactment of external correlates. Only when we examine the inner workings, variations, and complexities of these deeper structures will we understand literacy teaching well enough to improve learning for all students.

CONCLUSION

"... one ironic finding is that the most frequent and beneficial evidence ... may be the least visible ..." (Paris, Paris, & Carpenter, chap. 5, this volume).

This book carries at least three important messages. First, effective literacy instruction can be achieved. Second, achieving it is a complex and dynamic task requiring an understanding of more than just the observable external features of instruction. And, finally, effective literacy instruction requires a longitudinal investment of time, energy and resources.

These are particularly important messages in a time when politicians and policy makers are obsessed with the idea that effectiveness can be achieved by the imposition of accountability standards and punitive consequences. The choice is one of investing our resources on more tests and more accountability or investing in better teaching and better teacher education. The research reported in this book affirms the latter, not the former. It makes clear that it is indefensible to 'bet' on standard raising when the evidence points to bettering what we have: our schools, our teachers and our teacher education system. Two elements are essential.

First, we must move past easily observed features of teaching effectiveness to the complex orchestration that exists beneath the surface. We know from past experience with earlier observational research that external factors alone do not guarantee effectiveness. To have a true renaissance in literacy instruction, we must examine *internal* factors—the "inner workings" that allow teachers and administrators to enact effective teaching. This must be a priority.

Second, because the "inner workings" involve teacher and administrator judgment and decision making, teacher education must be a priority. Thoughtful, committed teachers and administrators do not just appear by magic; they are developed. And as chapter after chapter in this book illustrates, the development process itself is complex. It requires not only solid, substantive preservice education but also career-long continuing professional development and collegial collaboration. Consequently, resources and research must be devoted to this developmental process.

In summary, this book shouts out that "beating the odds" requires "bettering" of teachers and schools. In making this point, the various authors do us great service. They help us re-vision literacy instruction so that we focus on the subtleties at the core rather than on the external factors on the surface. As such, this book will guide continuing efforts to better literacy instruction for all children.

REFERENCES

Baumann, J., Hoffman, J., Moon, J., & Duffy-Hester, A. (1998). Where are teachers' voices in the phonics-whole language debate? Results from a survey of U.S. elementary teachers. *The Reading Teacher, 51*(8), 636–651.

Brophy, J., & Good, T. (1986). Teacher behavior and student achievement. In M. Wittrock (Ed.), *Handbook of Research on Teaching*, (3rd ed., pp. 328–375). New York: Macmillan.

Dole, J., Duffy, G., Roehler, L., & Pearson, P. D. (1991). Moving from the old to the new: Research on reading comprehension instruction. *Review of Educational Research, 61,* 239–264.

Duffy, G. (in press) The case for direct explanation of comprehension strategies. In M. Pressley & C. Block (Eds.), *Comprehension instruction*. New York: Guilford.

Duffy, G., & Hoffman, J. (1999). In pursuit of an illusion: The flawed search for a perfect method. *The Reading Teacher, 53*(1), 10–37.

Good, T., & Brophy, J. (1986). School effects. In M. Wittrock (Ed.) *Handbook for Research on Teaching* (3rd ed., pp. 570–603). New York: Macmillan.

Hoffman, J. (1998). When bad things happen to good ideas in literacy education: Professional dilemmas, personal decisions, and political gaps. *The Reading Teacher, 52*(2), 102–113.

Rodgers, E. (1999, December). *Language matters: When is a scaffold really a scaffold?* Paper presented at the annual conference of the National Reading Conference, Orlando, FL.

Author Index

M

Madaus, G. F., 143, *160*
Madden, M., 200, *214*
Madden, N. A., ix, x, 10, *71*, 96, *114*
Magnusson, S. J., 316, *333*
Mangubhai, F., 37, 63, *70*
Mariage, T. V., 310, 311, *333*
Marliave, R., 8, *71*
Martin, A. M., 295, *307*
Martin, B., 301, *307*
Martin, J. R., 312, 322, 324, 325, 329, *333*
Maruyama, G. M., 37, 63, *72*
Maw, C. E., 336, *354*
Mazzeo, J., 4, *70*, 362, *372*
McCarthey, S. J., ix, x
McCormick, C. B., 85, *87*
McCracken, G. D., 342, *355*
McDermott, R., 332, *333*
McGinn, M. K., 315, 316, 326, *333*
McIntyre, E., 62, *71*
McPartland, J., 218, *236*
Meehan, T. M., 326, *333*
Meeker, M. N., 240, 241, *259*
Meisels, S., 152, *160*
Mekkelsen, J., 117, 118, *139*
Meloth, M. S., 364, *372*
Melzi, G., 339, 351, *356*
Mills, R., 377, 379, 385
Millsap, M. A., 4, 9, *72*
Minick, N., 315, *333*
Moats, L., 199, *215*
Moll, L. C., 232, *236*, 332, 334, 335, 337, 338, 339, 350, *355*
Moon, J., 384, *386*
Morgan, W., 315, *333*
Morrow, L. M., 28, 62, *71*, 73, 79, 80, 81, 82, 87, 88, 279, 280, 287, 289, 306, 365, *373*, 378
Mosenthal, J. H., 117, 118, *139*
Moss, M., 298, *307*
Mulhern, M. M., 338, *355*
Muñiz-Swicegood, M., 338, *355*
Murphy, S., 144, *160*

N

Naylor, P. R., 304, *307*
Neff, D., 232, *236*
Nelson, E., 28, *71*, 79, 80, 81, 82, 88, 279, 287, 365, *373*

Newman, S. B., 62, *71*
Nieto, S., 230, 231, *236*
Nolen, S. B., 143, *159*, *160*
Novak, J. M., 230, *236*

O

Oakes, J., 60, *71*
Oberg, M., 230, 231, *236*
O'Brien, R. C., 304, 305, *307*

P

Padrón, Y., 338, *355*, *356*
Palincsar, A. S., 313, 316, *333*
Pappas, C. C., 338, *356*
Paratore, J. R., 339, 351, *356*
Paris, A. H., 143, 154, *160*, 377, 383, 385
Paris, S. G., 143, 152, 154, 155, *159*, *160*, 377, 383, 385
Parker, R., 338, *355*
Pascal, F., 292, *307*
Pearson, P. D., 12, 18, *72*, 117, *140*, 152, *160*, 163, 164, 171, *177*, 199, 200, *215*, 218, 221, 222, *236*, 259, *259*, 279, 280, 287, 288, 289, 306, 365, 367, 368, *373*, 376, 378, 379, 380, 381, 383, 386
Pease-Alvarez, L., 337, 339, 350, *356*
Perez, B., 338, *356*
Perry, N., 313, *334*
Peterson, P. L., ix, x
Phillip, G. W., 4, *70*, 362, *372*
Pikulski, J., 14, *71*
Pinnell, G. S., 10, *71*, 132, *139*, 175, *177*, 240, 241, *259*
Pressley, M., 8, 27, 28, 61, 62, 63, *71*, 73, 75, 76, 77, 78, 79, 80, 81, 82, 83, 84, 85, 86, 87, *87*, 88, 218, 233, *236*, 279, 280, 287, 289, 306, 364, 365, 366, 367, *372*, 373, 377, 383, 384
Price, C., 5, 6, 62, 69, *71*, 280, 287, 367, 368, *373*
Puma, M. J., 5, 6, 62, 69, *71*, 280, 287, 367, 368, *373*
Purkey, W. W., 230, *236*
Putnam, J., 364, *372*

Subject Index